THE
ORIGIN
OF THE
NATIONS

By

John Pilkey

Master Book Publishers
San Diego, California

THE ORIGIN OF THE NATIONS

Copyright © 1984
John D. Pilkey

MASTER BOOK PUBLISHERS, A Division of CLP
P. O. Box 15908
San Diego, California 92115

Library of Congress Catalog Card Number 84-60863
ISBN 0-89051-104-7

Cataloging in Publication Data

Pilkey, John D. 1942 -
   The origin of the nations.
   1. Bible—History of contemporary events, etc. 2. Bible—
History of Biblical events. I. Title.
                      220.9
ISBN 0-89051-104-7   84-60863

Printed in the United States of America

HIRSCHNATUR PANEL

GUNDESTRUP CALDRON
National Museum, Copenhagen

*What seest thou else
In the dark backward and abysm of time?
If thou rememb'rest aught ere thou cam'st here,
How thou cam'st here thou mayst.*

William Shakespeare
The Tempest

About The Author

John D. Pilkey is Associate Professor of English at Los Angeles Baptist College in Newhall, California. He obtained his B.A. degree in English at Tufts University in 1964; his M.A. in English at the University of Missouri at Kansas City in 1969; and his Ph.D. in the same subject at the University of Kansas in 1974. The following year he completed a Th.M. program with Dallas Theological Seminary. He now lives in Canyon Country, California, with his wife Marilyn and daughter Alice.

Since 1963, Dr. Pilkey has devoted much of his time to the study of the origin of the nations from Noah's family. His studies in Victorian literature have shown the interplay between the rise of Darwinism and the decline of the Christian euhemerist movement. For more than two decades, he has sought to reestablish the pre-Darwinian concept of Gentile origins.

Contents

Foreword

In this volume the author attempts to fill a void in human knowledge surrounding the development of Noah's family and the origin of human nations after the Flood. Based on years of study, the book is a synthetic reconstruction of the events and people of this largely forgotten period of history.

Dr. Pilkey has post-graduate degrees in both literature and theology. In addition, he has carried out deep studies into such fields as art, chronology, mythology, and philosophy so that he is uniquely qualified to advance a project that was begun by the Christian euhemerists of the 18th century but has been studiously neglected during the last one hundred years.

Readers will find that the book is based on young-earth creationism and that the author espouses a tightly woven chronology in which the Noachian deluge occurs at 2518 B.C. Pilkey realizes that "to dispute high chronology with a Darwinian is like blaspheming against the idea of eternity" because vast time periods have become for the Darwinists "a substitute for eternity."

He writes a compelling apologetic for what he calls "Noahic science," which he feels is "the atomic physics of world history.'' Pilkey believes that Noahic science when fully conceived will liberate us from Darwinism so that we will then be able to see the past for what it really was.

The author carefully and brilliantly exegetes such archaeological sources as the Gundestrup Caldron and Mesopotamian Seals. While paying attention to Scripture, Pilkey demonstrates that the myths and king lists of ancient societies support the Biblical pattern of monophylogenetic human origins.

Pilkey attempts to bring identity between such widely separated fields as human mythology, Biblical truth and the plight of modern man. Fascinating parallels are drawn, for example, between Peleg's struggle with Canaan and Elijah's later conflict with Jezebel, herself a Canaanite descendant.

To those who would argue that the Bible should be treated as a book of salvation alone, ignoring any of its historical, cultural, or related features, Pilkey answers as follows: ''The Bible functions as a book of salvation precisely because it is a book of science, literature, and philosophy. True science is salvation from ignorance; historical literature is salvation from pagan amnesia; and true philosophy is the Logos Jesus Christ, the Truth and Savior. One reason that secularism has spread in our day is that persons of religious background have become spiritually and, therefore, intellectually lazy, unimaginative, and apathetic toward key issues of faith.''

Specialists in history or mythology would do well to read the book consecutively. Interested general readers, however, might wisely begin with the last three chapters (7, 8, and 9) to achieve an overview of the principles involved before attempting to assimilate the array of details found in the earlier chapters.

Creationists and others desiring to understand Noah's family and its contribution to present-day national governments will find this volume indispensable. All students of ancient literature and mythology should consider their work deficient if they do not study this truly landmark endeavor.

— Dr. George Howe
Los Angeles Baptist College
1985

Chapter 1

The Challenge of Genesis 9 - 11

The Challenge

The text of Genesis 9-11 claims to narrate and outline the earliest origins of gentile mankind. Yet a comparison of the text with the known facts of antiquity leaves an immense gap of information and logic. Genesis 10:6, for example, names "Mizraim," the general Hebrew word for Egypt, a "son" of Ham. Yet there is not the slightest hint of the concrete steps by which this son or his offspring gave rise to the civilization of Egypt.

The brevity of Genesis 9-11 makes its information deeply mysterious. There is no hint of how the different racial types of mankind originated; or which languages resulted from the confusion of tongues at Babel; or where Noah's family journeyed after leaving the mountains of Ararat; or how his family first divided; or why Noah's curse fell on Canaan rather than Ham's other sons; or why the Hebrew people spoke the "language of Canaan," son of Ham, not Shem; or what the "language of Shem" would have been; or what the names and backgrounds of the wives of the ark were; or why there were only eight survivors of the Flood, just four couples and no children; or what the specific maternities of Shem, Ham, and Japheth were; or how and in what part of Noah's family pagan idolatry arose; or what specific religious doctrines and practices served as background for the Tower of Babel; or how the high longevities of Genesis 11 influenced the social and political life of the early postdiluvian world.

Christian scholars have generally ignored these questions for one reason. They have been intimidated by modern beliefs about world chronology; or, at least, they have not sought to challenge these beliefs by defending a recent, third millennium Flood. They have either rejected the chronology of Genesis 11, as a chronology, or have treated it as an apologetic liability.

The genealogy of Genesis 11:10-26 appears to contain a chronology for the interval between the Flood, named in 11:10, and the birth of Abram, named in 11:26. Shem's son Arphaxad is said to have been born two years after the Flood, as though to initiate a chronological process ending with Abram. Each of Arphaxad's descendants is said to have been begotten when his father reached a specified age. If these ages are summed without hypothetical gaps, only 220 years intervened between the births of Arphaxad and Abram's father Terah. In 11:26, the time of Abram's birth is established more vaguely as some time after Terah reached seventy. Even if Abram's birth date is hypothetically delayed, the interval between it and the Flood could not have exceeded three or four centuries; and, from other chronological notices in the Old Testament, the Flood could not have occurred much earlier than 2500 B.C.

The doctrine of a third millennium Flood has become an apologetic embarrassment because of strong scientific trends established in the nineteenth century when historians closed ranks with geologists in the perception that the earth was much older than formerly believed. Although the age of the earth is not strictly the same question as the date of the Flood, chronological revision upward became a mark of scientific sophistication. The third millennium Flood began to seem naive and implausible. An extrapolation of Manetho's Egyptian kinglist carried the accession of the first dynastic Pharaoh Menes back into the fourth millennium. Since 1900, the art of stratigraphy, development of refined chronological systems, and technique of carbon dating have all given the impression that progress in historical science depends on an evolutionary worldview at odds with any tightly structured, theologically coherent world chronology.

If, for example, we pick a Flood date at 2500, we run the risk of being suddenly embarrassed by purely scientific evidence that world population, at that time, was not eight but eighty million; or that some Middle Eastern city or network of cities was continuously inhabited between 2900 and 2000. A few historians may notice that 2500 often marks the boundary between the Stone Age and the

Bronze Age or the dawn of written records. But the general impression that recorded history begins about 2500 cannot shake the Egyptian chronology or the evolutionary philosophy which that chronology complements. The consensus is that empirical evidence alone has negated the third millennium Flood. But lurking beneath the surface of this scientific issue is a surprisingly intense ideological motive rooted in the soil of European Christendom. Noah's family has not been clearly conceptualized because there is something truly frightening about such a family to scholars of the modern democratic era. We all know that prodigious forms of central political power existed in ancient times and have recurred in modern times. Early Christians faced the worst of such power in the reign of Nero, one of many emperors who have claimed to be gods. Yet emperor worship is no casual freak of the pagan spirit. To realize its value is to reconstruct what Noah's family was; and, once we summon the imaginative power to realize such a thing, the chronological problem will tend to disappear, and the evolutionary philosophy along with it. The fear of falling victim to merciless despotism is the democratic soul of evolutionary thought, which refers the origin and maintenance of civilization to gradual or powerless processes rather than to charismatic power. A fourth millennium Pharaoh Menes is a harmless cipher; a third millenniium, postdiluvian Pharaoh Menes is part of a sublime and terrifying spectacle. The latter chronology implies that Noah's family were empowered to build world civilization overnight.

All Christians realize that the "powers that be are of God." They do not necessarily agree on how gentile political power subsists. Some may fail to recognize that this power, like that of the Christian faith, is spiritual in nature as sourced in a God who is the comprehensive "Father of spirits." We are liable to conceive of gentile political authority as static "office" in abstraction from any sort of concrete empowerment. We delight in observing the weakness of mere office holders and abhor those despots who suppose that they are anything more than office holders. As democrats, we reserve the right to paint emperors in our own image. We do this at the risk of fulfilling the prophecy of Jude who warned that some of us would deny the "monos despotes" Jesus Christ, through a popular distaste for despotism in general. Prior to the democratic revolutions of the latter eighteenth century, scholars found it easier to think clearly about

Noah than they do today, despite our advantage in positive evidence.

Euhemerism

Emperor worship is the practical analogue to the so-called euhemerist doctrine adopted by a school of historiographers who dealt seriously with Noah between 1650 and 1800. These writers included the French Samuel Bochart, Paul Pezron, and Antoine Banier, and the British Andrew Tooke, William Stukeley, and Jacob Bryant. Euhemerism is the belief that pagan gods such as Zeus or Osiris can be identified as ancient men. Bochart and Tooke, for example, believed that the Graeco-Roman Titan Cronus-Saturn was a version of Noah. The nineteenth-century euhemerist Alexander Hislop, in the school of Bryant, identified the Egyptian Seth as a rather vindictive version of Shem.

Classic Christian euhemerism was iconoclastic. As practiced by Lactantius and others, it sought to satirize pagan religion by reducing the gods to mortal men. Because the Neoclassical Age (1660-1800) was an age of satire, it is easy to assume that the euhemerism of the period was a vehicle of satire. Radical cultural changes around 1800 doomed euhemeristic thought to a premature scholarly death. Because the Romanticism of the next century glorified the human spirit, Romantics generally eschewed satire; and German Romantic thinkers such as F. W. J. Schelling and Jakob Grimm despised euhemerism as petty satirical malice, preferring to view the pagan gods as "creative powers."

Nevertheless, iconoclasm is just one side of the euhemerist idea. There is an undercurrent of heroic enthusiasm in the writings of Pezron or Stukeley entirely inconsistent with satire. The roots of the euhemerist movement lay in the age of Bochart's contemporary, John Milton, an epic poet devoted to grand and supernatural subjects and concepts. The true cultural model for Genesis 10 study is Milton's *Paradise Lost;* and, although that work contains a satirical dimension, at the expense of Satan, its dominant spirit is perfectly consistent with the Romantic ideal of "creative powers." Instead of having to choose between euhemerism and German idealism, we can reconcile both schools in the simple perception that Noah's family were "creative powers" of the highest order.

The mystery of euhemerism is established in principle in Exodus 7:1 where Moses, as charismatic leader of the infant nation of Israel, is described as a "god" in the eyes of Pharaoh: "And the Lord said unto Moses, 'See, I have made thee a god to Pharaoh; and Aaron, thy brother, shall be thy prophet.' " The verse means that Moses, a servant of God in "judging the gods of Egypt," shared in the same privileges as the family of Noah in the supernatural processes essential to founding nations. In effect, Moses was the last in a class of early postdiluvian "gods," although the emperors of Rome, Japan, Peru, and other nations have persisted in claiming the same Noahic privilege of human, political deity.

More particularly, Moses was a god in the eyes of Pharaoh because the Pharaonic institution arose in the early postdiluvian lifetime of Noah as a product of such privileges. The Exodus itself marked an important stage in the dispensational decline of the Noahic or gentile theocracy. Subsequent claims of imperial deity have, no doubt, been presumptuous and blasphemous. The Book of Acts records a definitive instance in which Herod Antipas is destroyed by special judgment after a claim of charismatic political deity: "And the people gave a shout, saying, 'It is the voice of a god, and not a man.' And immediately an angel of the Lord smote him because he gave not God the glory; and he was eaten of worms, and died" (Acts 12:22-23).

Yet the angelic agency in Herod's death reveals the extent to which despotic power on earth is shaped by and either sanctioned or judged according to the ethical framework of the angelic third heaven. In studying Noah's world—The Mesopotamian cylinder seals, the Sumerian Kinglist, or the Egyptian Geb-Nut Cosmogony—that angelic cosmos must not be forgotten. By viewing Noah as a mere survivor of the Flood rather than a builder of nations, we have not only neglected his 350-year postdiluvian lifetime, but have ignored those spiritual ideas which made the gentile world just that, a designed cosmos. When we term that cosmos satanic, we must recall that Satan is himself an angel and the member of an angelic order more ancient than the distinction between good and evil. Careful reflection on Exodus 7:1 will reveal what is meant by this logic. If the Pharaonic institution was nothing but an agency of Satan, how could God have made Moses a god in Pharaoh's eyes, an object of "strong delusion," without compromising Moses' image as an agent of holiness? The conflict between Moses and Pharaoh was played according to Noahic rules, which, like the Law of Moses, were given by the "disposition of angels."

The Gundestrup Caldron

Dispensational theologians have accurately recognized that Noah inaugurated a new dispensation of human government after the Flood. The Sumerian kinglist attests to the same fact, claiming that "kingship descended from heaven" after the Flood.[1] This descent of power was far more like the Christian Pentecost than we imagine. Its universal gentile symbol was the "Ka" sign, the pictographic image of a man with arms upraised at the elbows. The "Ka" was the spiritual entity by which the Pharaohs participated in deity and acquired their theocratic powers.[2] The "Ka" sign recurs among other nations. The Japanese "banzai" salute is a classic instance, among members of a Ural-Altaic linguistic stock which ranks high among the languages of Noah's theocracy.

The most striking example of the "Ka" posture is found as a sign of deity in the imagery of the Gundestrup Caldron, a Celtic artifact discovered in Denmark in the spring of 1891.[3] In the exterior panels of the Caldron, the "Ka" posture is duplicated in each depiction of the four male members of a set of four males and what are believed to have been four females.[4] It is impossible to imagine a more graphic portrayal of the idea of a cosmos arising from eight survivors of a universal Flood, four male and four female, as biblical tradition affirms (I Peter 3:20). Arranged in a circle, the exterior panels and their internal counterparts are the embodiment of a cosmos, as anthropologists have easily recognized. Unfortunately, most anthropologists are not known for their devotion to the Bible and, as a class, are not well equipped to perceive an analogy which is as obvious as anyone could wish.

The Celts of the Gundestrup Caldron were the ancient people of Bronze Age Europe. The term "Bronze Age" is empirical jargon for the early postdiluvian world of Noah. Although metalwork existed in the antediluvian period and "Stone Age man" persists into modern times, the true Stone Age is the impression made by the antediluvian world on students of mute archaeology; and "Bronze Age man" is the corollary mute version of postdiluvian man. The antediluvian period was necessarily rather primitive or barbaric because of its abstraction from the charismatic revolution just noted. If kingship "descended from heaven" in a revolutionary way after the Flood, it and its civilizing effects were largely unknown before the Flood. The primitive cultures of mankind are the antediluvian heritage as channeled through Noah's family to certain parts of the larger postdiluvian populace.

The Egyptian mythology of Osiris identifies this god as a civilizing agent; and the same could be said of all the "gods," including Moses. These were a race of charismatic geniuses, without whom high civilization would never have been realized. Although racists such as L. A. Waddell have clouded the issue of civilizing agency, the God of Noah created world civilization through a Pentecost of power just as surely as the Church is the concrete, historically defined product of the Apostolic Pentecost. For many nations, the use of bronze was a definitive mark of the Noahic heritage of nascent civilization. More impressive, however, is the Gundestrup statement, wrought in silver.

Any recognition of Noah's family, however, in the Gundestrup octad must face critical skepticism and the larger issue of historical verification. The Caldron speaks through mythological imagery and contains no script. No matter what principles of historical verification are adopted, the foundation of history remains written literature. The Caldron itself speaks more clearly than it otherwise could if the Roman Lucan had not written of the Gallic gods Teutates, Taranis, and Esus in plain Latin.[5]

In this respect, the challenge of Genesis 9:11 remains the brevity of the text and the paucity of coherently historical information from the nonbiblical third millennium. Sumerology is a godsend but is not without limits. Samuel Noah Kramer's standard *The Sumerians* is packed with invaluable insight; but it is no oversight that only a small fraction of the text is historical narrative. No one is prepared, today, to write a history of the third millennium replete with the sort of wealth of incident possible in histories of the Roman Empire, Crusades, or modern times.

The whole idea of historical verification loses some of its meaning in cases where certain events are knowable but too few in number to generate a sense of context. For example, Kramer can tell us just enough about the war between Erech and Aratta to make us sense that this was one of the chief events of the third millennium. But the sources are a set of Sumerian legends so imperfect in content and in state of preservation that we find no account of a climactic battle or of any specific hostilities: only a diplomatic war of words followed by an expeditionary invasion of undetermined consequence. We know a great deal more about the third millennium than did Bryant in 1774; but Bryant's methodology remains relevant to us because our limitations are logically comparable to his.

Jacob Bryant's Methodology

Bryant's technique was a process of comparing and identifying names, often through mere similarity of sound.[6] Despite its apparent naivete, this technique harmonizes with our general dependence on literature because all reading depends on the identification of words, a kind of names. In effect, Bryant proposed the formation of an international language of Noahic names. Such a concept can coexist with the perception that radically distinct languages divided the human race in the third millennium. Names tend to resist change in passing from one culture to another; and, even when radical change occurs, the universality of Noah's family enables us to translate the names correctly.

To confirm Bryant's method, it is essential to observe how universal the ancient names have been. In the southeastern corner of modern Latvia are a pair of towns, Dagda and Indra.[7]

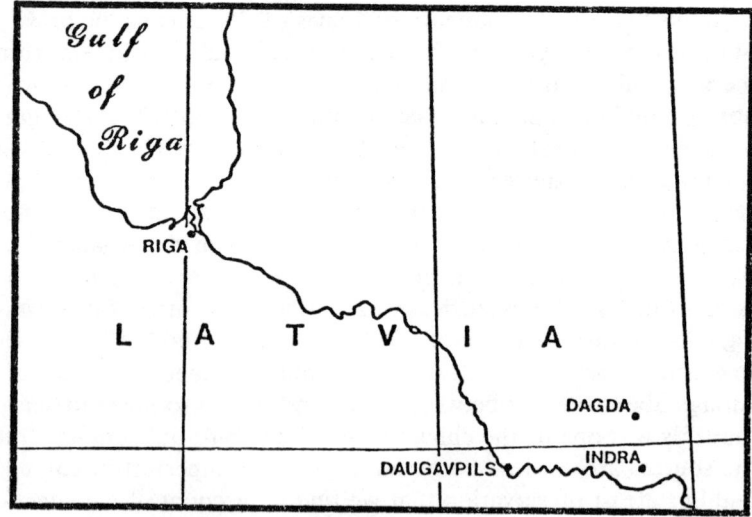

Letter for letter, these names match the standard orthography for two Indo-European deities, "Dagda of the Gaels" and the East Indian storm god Indra. The Gaels, as Celts, belong to the Centum division of the Indo-European stock; the East Indians are definitive members of the Satem division which extends southeastward from the Balto-Slavic speakers of Europe to Iran and India.[8] No one questions the comprehensive polarity of these two divisions. The two towns are arranged north and south as though to mark the spot where the two stocks divided in high antiquity. Because all Indo-Europeans are supposed to have originated at a point in White Russia not far from Latvia, the two names do not tell us a great deal that is not already known. Nevertheless, they do display a feeling for systematic design inconsistent with evolutionary concepts, yet consistent with the cosmos suggested by the Bible, the Gundestrup Caldron, and certain dimensions of Sumerology.

Because Indra and Dagda are separate deities, whom we do not seek to identify as one, the Latvian item has no direct bearing on the euhemeristic technique of identifying gods with patriarchs. Such observations only serve to strengthen the assumption that god names constitute an international language.

In the meanwhile, anthropologists have taught us to form qualified sorts of identifications between deities through common motifs, such as Celtic Cernunnus's pictorial resemblance to Dravidian Shiva Pashupati,[9] or through explicit tradition, such as the lunar cult common to Sumerian Nanna and Akkadian Suen.[10] Theoretically, these anthropological matches fall short of the kind sought by Bryant; but often they lead precisely in that direction. For example, we have found that the lunar cult of Mesopotamia was a species of worship first adopted by Shem's son Arphaxad I and that this prince should be identified, euhemeristically, both with Nanna and with other lunar deities, such as Yerikh of Ugarit, Khons of Egyptian Thebes, and Daksha I of East India. None of these names is cognate in origin or similar in sound; so our technique of euhemeristic identification owes at least as much to anthropological concepts as to Bryant's simpler logic of matching sounds. The goal of Genesis 10 study is not to advocate any one method of associating names but to use any and all means to remember the universal princes of Noah's family.

The Table of Nations

The prerequisite for all such study is a firm faith in the universality of the Flood and, thus, in the universal value of the names listed in Genesis 10. Since the days of Friedrich Schlegel, around 1800, Genesis 10 has been damned with faint praise through the Völkertafel or "Table of Nations" concept. Schlegel employed the word Völkertafel to reduce the meaning of the text from a Noahic record of the seminal nations of mankind to a Mosaic record of a few nations in proximity to Palestine.[11] His motive was to confirm J. G. von Herder's theory of the purely local origin and meaning of all nations: the view that Jewish tradition should be confined to Palestine and that radically distinct nations, such as the Teutons, must go their own way. Schlegel realized that Herder's view could be challenged if the Teutons could be traced from one or more of the princes or nations of Genesis 10. In earlier times, German Christians such as Martin Luther were content to trace themselves, with some delight, from a name such as Ashkenaz, son of Gomer, realizing that Ashkenaz was a universal personality, adequate to give the Germans whatever degree of antiquity and glory they might desire. But Herder's sense of glory lay elsewhere.

For Herder and Schlegel, it was a disgrace to be found in a Jewish book because, after all, "little Israel," could not compare in size or contemporary importance with the Teutonic linguistic stock of the eighteenth century. Accordingly, Schlegel sought to reduce Genesis 10 to a purely Semitic range of reference. He noticed, for example, that the largest block of sons assigned to any patriarch later than Shem, Ham, and Japheth is the Joktanites of 10:26-29. This, he felt, was proof positive of the narrow, pedestrian character of the chapter. The Joktanites, he believed, were nothing but the beni-Khitan of Arabia, perhaps a noble people, but hardly a major fraction of the earth's population. He ignored the possibility that the beni-Khitan might be a mere fraction of Joktan's progeny because he rested in the old belief that Genesis 10 refers to "races, not men." Thus the name Joktan, for him, meant little more than a part of Arabia.

Schlegel's logic persists wherever the phrase "Table of Nations" is used because the term precludes the idea that Genesis 10 is a "Table of Universal Progenitors." There is no question that Genesis 10 refs, in part, to nations. We have seen that the name Mizraim is Hebrew for "Egypt." Many of the names in the chapter are suffixed for plurality and ethnicity, for example, the "Anamim" of the Mizraim section and the "Hivite" of the Canaanite. Nevertheless Mizraim is called a "son" of Ham for a very good reason. If the entire human race could descend from Noah, the whole of Egypt could certainly descend from one of his grandsons, a son of Ham. The son in question passed under a variety of gentile names, three of them cognate: Egyptian Min, Celtic Mynogan, and Hellenic Oceanus. None of the names meant "Egypt." Yet the Hebrew name "Mizraim" is interpretive; and the interpretation hardly means that "Mizraim" had no personal existence, any more than the Duke of York had no existence because some called him "York" or because his name has found its way to an American city. The time has come to set aside facile skepticisms and to take stock of what Genesis 10 actually is: the record of a systematic feudal system formed by Noah's family for the purpose of generating "nations, tongues, and peoples."

Noahic Genetics

During twenty years of study, the central interpretive task in dealing with Genesis 10 has been to determine the concrete genetic history of Noah's family and thus to counterpoint the political structure outlined in the text. The names in Genesis 11 form a genealogy; those in Genesis 10 do not. Even in Genesis 11, mothers are never named. Maternity forms a missing dimension of genetic linkage. We have found that the female survivors of the Flood were quite powerful and that a certain fraction of the names in Genesis 10 refer to females on the personal level: Lehab, Naphtuh, Pathrus, and Caphtor in the Mizraim section; Sin, Arvad, Zemar, and Hamath in the Canaanite section; and Almodad, Jerah, Uzal, Sheba, Ophir, Havilah, and Jobab in the Joktanite section.

The maternal factor was supremely important because of Noah's task of preserving a plenitude of racial types from the antediluvian world. In Genesis 10, the names Cush and Havilah reproduce the names of two antediluvian regions grouped together in the system of the four rivers in Genesis 2. Curiously, the name Havilah appears twice in Genesis 10, once in the Cushite section and again in the Joktanite section. The reason for this is that the two persons named in these sections were genetic bearers of the racial type which had inhabited the antediluvian land of Havilah in 2:11.

In dealing with early Genesis, genetics must be treated as a metaphysical phenomenon. Adam and Eve were genetically unique for four reasons: (1) they had no human ancestry, (2) they possessed the genetic potential to generate all the racial types of mankind, (3) their offspring could bear children only through various degrees of incest, and (4) their offspring enjoyed high longevities unknown to modern man.

In their lack of human ancestry, Adam and Eve were apocalyptic, standing at the boundary between the natural and supernatural. A basic rule of apocalypse is the ritual symmetry of metaphysics, the visible disclosure of such things as the four elements and four humors. Such symmetries are the stock in trade of pagan tradition because of the diligence of Noah's family in preserving the Adamic heritage under the new empowerment of the dispensation of human government. The racial types, which evolutionists treat as the casual accumulation of individual variations, express a fourfold metaphysical potentiality within the gene pool of the first couple. Such a system appears in the meso-American tradition of the four Tez-catlipocas: red Chac, black Ed, white Zac, and yellow Kan.[12] These colors, assigned to the four ordinal directions, match the four basic racial types of mankind: the red Amerinds of the two Americas, the blacks of the Indian Ocean, whites of Europe, and yellow Mongoloids of the Far East.[13]

These races are a living document of Adamic genetic potential and Noahic eugenic control. A fundamental goal of Genesis 10 study is to discover which survivors embodied which races and how these strains were mixed and consolidated in the earliest postdiluvian offspring. The four males of the Ark could not be the key to race because three were the sons of the fourth, necessarily sharing his racial character. Instead, races were embodied in the four wives, who were selected, for this purpose, from the four racial stocks implied by the fourfold antediluvian cosmos of Genesis 2:10-14:

> Now a river went out of Eden to water the garden, and from it parted and became four riverheads. The name of the first is Pishon; it is the one which encompasses the whole land of Havilah, where there is gold. And the gold of that land is good. Bdellium and the onyx stone

are there. The name of the second river is Gihon; it is the one which encompasses the whole land of Cush. The name of the third is Hiddekel; it is the one which goes toward the east of Assyria. The fourth river is Euphrates. Henry M. Morris has noted the anachronistic effect of this passage, which blends together two worlds, the antediluvian and postdiluvian, as channeled through the minds of the original authors, in all probability Adam and Noah themselves.[14] Assigned to two of the four riverheads are the names of lands, Havilah and Cush. Both names reappear in Genesis 10, establishing traditional continuity between the two worlds.

Although the passage in Genesis 2 contains no reference to race, we are justified in giving its geographic system racial value because of the familiar value of the name Cush. Traditionally, this name represents a land on the Upper River Nile in black East Africa, south of Egypt. The lands of Cush and Egypt are regionally complementary in the same way that the names Cush and Mizraim head the list of Ham's sons in Genesis 10:6. If these two sons are embodied in the peoples of Ethiopia-Cush and Egypt, they were racially distinct because the ancient Egyptians were fairskinned in contrast with their Ethiopian neighbors. The implication is that Cush was Ham's son by a distinctly black woman, one of the four female survivors of the Flood. The duplication of the antediluvian name Cush in this woman's son implies that she was a representative of the antediluvian land of Cush and its race, the black quarter of Adam's progeny.

The corollary race of Havilah was the Amerind stock, traditionally conceived as "red" but distinguished by another racial characteristic: facial concavity, the familiar hook-nosed physiognomy. In Amerind folklore, the colors red and black are often grouped together. The Aztec god Tezcatlipoca is reckoned red and black;[15] and the same colors combine in masks of northwestern North America, where a ritual involving red and black arrows is also found.[16] A meso-American painting shows a warlike race, painted blood red, conquering black enemies.[17]

This coupling of reds and blacks echoes the antediluvian formula of Havilah and Cush. The two Havilahs of Genesis 10 are the Red Matriarch, appearing in the Joktanite section, and her antediluvian son Ham, who adopts the name Havilah as vassal to his own black son Cush in 10:7. The same two are pictured in the system of the exterior Gundestrup panels as chief subjects of the Braided Goddess and Dragon panels, where both display the same tendency toward facial concavity. The exterior panel of the Black Matriarch is missing; but she appears twice in the panel of the Braided Goddess as an attendant, symbolic of the distinct black races of Dravidian India and Cushite East Africa.

A limitation of the text of Genesis 2 is that the author does not bother to assign regional names to the antediluvian versions of the Tigris-Hiddekel and Euphrates, unless we take the anachronistic reference to Assyria as such. However, another antediluvian regional name, Nod, appears in the account of the curse of Cain in Genesis 4:16. The simplest explanation for the omitted regional names in Genesis 2 is that the author himself was familiar with the antediluvian lands of the Tigris and Euphrates because these were his own homeland. He names Havilah and Cush explicitly as remote from his experience.

The racial implication is that the author was neither Amerind nor black but belonged either to the Mongoloid or Caucasoid stock. Another evidence of the same limitation is his preoccupation with just two antediluvian stocks, Sethites and Cainites. These two stocks identify with the Mongoloids and Caucasoids respectively. The racist view that the blacks are Cainite is entirely untenable because of the clear distinction between the lands of Cush and Nod. The "sign" of Cain was the low pigmentation extreme of fair skin;[18] and the antediluvian Cainite civilization was a prototype of the high material civilization achieved by the whites of Europe. Noah, as Sethite, was chiefly Mongoloid; and his features, in the Gundestrup panel of the Boar-Holding Men, are distinctly brachycephalic (broad-skulled), a standard Mongoloid trait.

Noahic Marital Ethics

Any reader of the Old Testament realizes that marital irregularities existed on a large scale in ancient times. It would be rather strange if Noah, father of the gentiles, had practiced a higher standard of marital ethics than polygamous Abraham, ancestor of the Israelites, or polygamous David and Solomon, leading kings of Israel. More important, a certain degree of marital irregularity, by our standards, is built into the biblical scheme of origins. Adam and Eve could generate a world community only through sibling incest among their children.

To all appearances, Noah and his three sons were monogamous. Why else were the survivors of the Flood confined to eight persons? It is quite clear that each of the four females who survived the Flood was reckoned the political wife of one and only one of the four surviving males. The principle of monogamy was well established in some peculiar code of behavior. Yet we can be equally certain that that code also included various degrees of sibling incest and, along with it, a pattern of polygamous concubinage rooted in eugenic planning.

If each of the four Noahic couples had practiced strict monogamy, each would have duplicated the function of Adam and Eve in establishing its own separate version of the human race. Four racial stocks of mankind would have to be traced back to the four surviving males, as though Noah and his three sons were all racially diverse. Furthermore, we would expect to find a central type of each color group, a single "true" black race, red race, yellow race, and white race.

Such is not the case. The Dravidian blacks of India represent a distinct type from the blacks of Africa, just as "true" but radically different. The whites of Europe have been distinguished into Nordic, Alpine, and Mediterranean types; and the Amerindians display a characteristic "red" type in South and Central America and a more Mongoloid type in the north. To the biblical monogenist, these distinctions are far from haphazard.

The simplest and best explanation is that these radical diversities within each color group derived from a process of eugenic polygamy within Noah's immediate family. Because all four males were closely related, they could not have displayed enough variation to account for the distinctly colored groups by the close of the third millennium. But this limitation did not apply to the females, whose parentage is not specified and who could easily have been chosen to represent a plenitude of all the antediluvian racial types. They are the key to the early appearance of the four basic color groups; and their polygamous relationship to the sons of Noah accounts for the radical distinctions within each group, assuming that each male was enough like Adam, in genetic potential, to place his peculiar stamp on each group.

For example, we have found that African blacks descended from

Ham's black son Cush; Dravidian blacks from Noah's black son Riphath (a vassal to Gomer); Oceanic blacks, from Japheth's black son Seba (a vassal to Cush); and The Amerindian blacks (Olmecs) from Shem's black son Hul (a vassal to Aram). All four men were half brothers by the same mother, the universal Black Matriarch, a sole survivor of the antediluvian race of the land of Cush.

A truism of history is that feudalism results in the forced-match political marriage, adulterous courtly love, and other marital irregularities. Noah's family were the quintessence of feudalism. Their task was to divide the postdiluvian world into theocratic fiefs, bind one ruler to another through vassalage or political sonship, and reign through the archaic principle of tribal dynasty over peoples formed from their own progeny. Until the demands of this task are weighed and measured, we are in no position to judge their moral lives, marital or otherwise; and, until we seriously consider the implications of their high longevities, we have no idea what we are trying to judge.

The Noahic Aristocracy

Like the short chronology of Genesis 11, the high longevities have been treated either as an apologetic liability or as an ethical distinction, as though God were rewarding prodigious quantities of archaic sanctity with proportional quantities of years. This ethical explanation is unnecessary. The high longevities were another by-product of the metaphysical distinctiveness of Adam's gene pool. The best explanation for the declining scale of longevities in Genesis 11 is that the general cataclysm of the Flood included the break-up of an atmospheric canopy which had protected the antediluvian world from penetration by destructive cosmic radiation.[19] After the Flood, the new influx of such radiation resulted in chromosome damage reflected in reduced longevity and other defects.

A correlative of the protected genetic environment in earlier times was that incest could not have the damaging effects of later times. Incest is a necessary ingredient of any scheme of monogenetic origins and played a role in the families of both Adam and Noah. Sibling incest, for example, played a key role in creating the postdiluvian Caucasoid race of Europe because Noah's white sons, Shem and Japheth, were prohibited from mating with their mother, the White Matriarch, and had to await the maturity of white sisters to generate such a race.

The high longevities of Noah's immediate family combined with the gentile Pentecost of human government to make that family the most astounding aristocracy the world has known. Nothing in human experience can compare with it short of the Christian Apocalypse. According to Genesis 11:11, Shem lived for 502 years after the Flood: roughly the second half of the third millennium. During this period, all but one of the twenty-five dynasties of the Sumerian Kinglist and the first twelve dynasties of Egypt ran their course. Shem outlived most of them and shared in a number of them, appearing as Balih in the international dynasty of First Kish, as Dadasig of Second Kish, as Tata of Awan, as Sahlamu of the Amorites, and as Melchizedek of the late, Abrahamic period of Genesis 14.

If Moses was necessarily bilingual and bicultural, Shem gave prodigious meaning to the concept of international feudal aristocracy. He personally authored the entire Indo-European linguistic stock, inherited the Semitic stock as his personal possession, governed both stocks in his fief of Akkad, and reigned afterward as a Sumerian, a Ural-Altaic, an Amorite, and an Egyptian. Joseph was not the first Semite to know Egypt. Shem camped forty-two years on the Nile two centuries before the nation of Mizraim existed. In the euhemeristic pantheons of the nations, he was Sumerian Ishkur, Syrian Adad, Ugaritic Aliyan Bal, Egyptian Amon of Thebes, Hellenic Heracles, Celtic Teutates, Teutonic Thor, East Indian Brahma the Originator, and Aztec Tlaloc. These identifications have nothing to do with cultural diffusion. Shem had put his hand on all nations of high antiquity in their birth hour, preexisted them all by a full antediluvian century, and was personally and independently known to all.

These radical views follow logically from the chronological perspective of Genesis 11 but explain why conservatives have preferred to expand the chronology of that chapter. Some aspects of Christian orthodoxy are conservative; others, radical or apocalyptic. Noah's family was an apocalyptic phenomenon; and, like all such phenomena, this one requires a taste for "untying the knot," sudden, radical simplification. Mysteries are made to be solved; and this one solves itself through processes of comparison, identification, and arrangement. In fact, once we accept the premise that Genesis 11 fixes chronology, study of the third millennium is little more than an art of arrangement. The question is no longer whether the Hellenes remember Shem; it is merely which Hellenic name corresponds to Shem. In the Noahic context, neither Shem nor the Hellenes were hidden in a corner. To debate whether the Hellenes knew a traditional version of Shem is like asking whether Abraham Lincoln was familiar with Pennsylvania or had ever heard of Florida; and sectarian scruples about the great gulf fixed between Semite and Hellene are like denying Lincoln's awareness of Maryland because he was reared in Illinois.

Synthetic Historiography

Since 1860, the cause of Bryant, Faber, and Hislop has largely disappeared together with the general type of historiography which they represented. This type has been variously known as "prescientific," "speculative," "poetic," or "synthetic." To revive the monogenetic worldview (the Noahic cause) without reviving synthetic historiography is impossible for reasons contained within the subject itself. The principle of synthetic historiography can be defended by looking closely both at it and at its supposed opposite, the so-called "scientific" historiography of more recent times.

The word "science" is, of course, a synonym for "knowledge" with connotations from the power of experimentation to verify objectively. To claim command of a "scientific" historiography is to claim, in effect, that our knowledge of the past is subject to experimentation. In archaeology, for example, the social prestige of experimentation is achieved by registering sealed predictions that a given site will yield a certain kind of buried material and by testing such predictions against the event of digging in the predicted site.

Unfortunately, such "experiments" have no direct bearing on our knowledge of the past because they hold out no promise of physical interaction with past events. Because such events are physically non-functional, they are not subject to immediate experimentation. On the contrary, all knowledge of the past depends on the subjective mediation of "memory" or the power to convert documentation (objects of historical faith) into convincing images of past events. The memory remains a synthetic or "poetic" faculty; and, wherever the spirit of analysis gains complete mastery of the mind, all knowledge of the past disappears.

Nevertheless, scientifically-minded scholars have done their best to create a scientific historiography by imitating the cultural patterns established in the world of experimentation. The "scientific" historian is guided by an ethical commitment to "truth and fact" and strives to achieve an objectivity of viewpoint even though his particular science will not allow him the luxury of immediate experimentation. He cultivates attitudes of critical skepticism and of devotion to large quantities of data as though he were an experimenter prepared to prove and disprove in the manner of physical science.

The need for synthetic historiography does not become apparent until we pay heed to the New Testament ethics of memory as Bryant and Hislop must have done. It is not enough merely to avoid misconceiving of past events as scientific skeptics suggest. Some events must be remembered whether we run the risk of misconceiving them or not.

The New Testament Greek word for truth, *aletheia,* means "the unforgotten" or "that which must not be forgotten." The Apostle Peter brings this concept of truth to bear on the argument of II Peter 3 where a lawless indifference to the future Return of Christ is traced up from a sinful exercise in forgetting "what must not be forgotten." The argument of the chapter begins with the motive to "stir up your pure minds by way of remembrance" as though the power to remember were an ethical principle, a form of righteous behavior. The author then warns against the advent of a generation of scoffers who would reject the Return of Christ by cultivating a certain attitude toward past history, namely, that "all things continue as they were from the beginning of the creation." In other words, these skeptics refuse to believe in the reality of past dispensational revolutions such as the Flood. The author traces this mistaken interpretation of history from an intellectual behavioral problem: a "willing" or "wilful" disbelief in the biblical concept of origins.

According to the ethics of II Peter 3, the duty of historians is not just to select well-documented fields of history and neglect the rest but to see to it that certain branches of history are remembered whether they are heavily documented or not. This ethic is the reverse of the logical positivist or empirical school of thought, which suggests that our intellectual duty is to refrain from synthesis, assertion, and intepretation until masses of evidence move us of their own accord. The Christian historian cannot tolerate this policy. He must receive whatever evidence exists as a providential invitation to exercise one's memory as fully as the facts will allow. Faith moves us to try as hard as we can to remember the great revolution of the Flood and to treat this revolution as foundation for a general interpretation of history.

Bryant and Hislop understood perfectly well that the names listed in Genesis 10 constitute such an invitation: as profound and intense a scientific challenge as Christians have ever faced. A world of ancient names—tribe names, god names, kings' names—lie dormant at the feet of Noahic history, waiting to be synthesized through identification with the names listed here. The task can be done well or poorly; but it must be done.

According to biblical logic, Shem was once a quarter of the male population of mankind. He was destined to live throughout the second half of the third millennium, during which the civilizations of Mesopotamia, Syria, and Egypt grew from nothing to their full stature. A man of this importance cannot be confined to any one tradition. Although we have generally forgotten his relationship to the gentile nations, such relationships are a branch of truth, "that which must not be forgotten."

In the present study, Shem has served to synthesize a variety of remote ethnic traditions. Two of the most fascinating are supplied by physical artifacts from Gundestrup and from Lagash in the eastern part of ancient Sumer, the Noahic land of Lower Mesopotamia. The similarity between these two imageries is self-evident, but, in the context of the present study, has served to confirm rather than to inspire a new synthesis. If archaeologists can claim to have "proved" the validity of their historical concepts through prediction, the same claim of "proof" exists here. Our synthetic logic, at work on the Gundestrup Caldron, had associated Shem with a very peculiar set of images before a totally distinct logical process turned up the same combination of images at Lagash as the depiction of a totally distinct version of the same patriarch. In effect, a reading of the Gundestrup Caldron predicted the existence of an artifact at Lagash.

Of the four males of the Gundestrup exterior panels, the subject of the Hirschnatur panel (see frontispiece) was found to represent Shem. Rudolf Grosse's ethical interpretation of the panel matched the implications of Shem's identifications with Syrian Adad, Teutonic Thor, and Greek Heracles. Each of these identifications claimed its own argument; but unifying them all was a perception that the "Yahweh Elohim of Shem" named in Genesis 9:26 was known to the Noahic polytheists as a God of Storm, hence Shem's identity with the heroic storm gods Adad and Thor, together with the traditional identification of Thor with the hero Heracles. The Gundestrup tradition added that the Celtic brethren of the Teutons remembered a version of Shem between two stags in either hand.

A separate line of argument traced Shem's political and mythological image throughout the Sumero-Akkadian tradition of Mesopotamia. As Hislop and all Christian separatists recognize, the Mesopotamian world order became alienated from the God of Shem and, presumably, from Shem himself. We have found that the source of this alienation lay in the curse-blessing event of Genesis 9:26: a theocratic revolution favoring Shem and based on Noah's alienation from Ham.[20] The revolution split the Noahic world into two warring factions: and the opposition faction (headed by Canaan, Sidon, and Nimrod) gained the upper hand in shaping the traditions of Mesopotamia.

In a Sumerian tradition hostile to Shem, the revolution is termed a "theft of the Enlilship," that is, of the power to control the Semitic linguistic stock and, ultimately, to establish law codes in the manner of Ur Nammu, Hammurabi, and Moses. Shem obtained these privileges, legitimately, through Noah's blessing of the "Yahweh Elohim of Shem" and succeeded, historically, in imposing his name on the Semites and in precedenting the Law of Moses. But, in Sumerian mythology, he became the "thief of the Enlilship," the monstrous bird Zu, antagonist to Ninurta, pantheon version of Nimrod.[21] At Lagash, an early capital of Canaan's faction, the Zu appears as the Imdugud or Raincloud Bird,[22] subject of one of the most beautiful pagan artifacts ever discovered. Like the Gundestrup version of Shem, the Zu or Imdugud is pictured between two stags.

Whether the Imdugud image "predicts" the two-stag panel of the Gundestrup Caldron or the Celtic image "predicts" the two-stag Imdugud makes little difference. The point is that two entirely separate synthetic developments of Shem, at work on two remote cultures, ended in two very different portrayals of the peculiar symbolic idea that Shem stood between two stags. Further interpretation identified the stags as the two inchoate linguistic stocks obtained through Noah's blessing: the Semites of the Air God "Elohim" and the Indo-

Europeans of the Storm God "Yahweh." In a remote sense, the Imdugud and Hirschnatur images symbolize the two languages of the Bible, Semitic Hebrew and Indo-European Greek. At the foundation of both, stood the righteous and ubiquitous Shem, enemy of the spiritually corrupt Mesopotamian world order and forerunner of separatistic Israel.

Sample East Indian Pantheon

The ubiquitous dynamism of Noah's family is best expressed by the statuary art of East India, a nation which has maintained its original pagan heritage more firmly than most. If the Gundestrup Caldron gives us the pictorial code of Noah's world, East Indian art yields the truest ethical portrait of it. East India is the world's monument to the peculiar energy of the third millennium. Another challenge of Genesis 10 study is to determine just why this is. It would almost appear that the Satem Aryans who invaded Dravidian India were the last stock to have hosted the inner circle of Noah's family, giving to East India the same sort of traditional confidence that the deaths of the Apostles Peter and Paul, at Rome, yielded to Roman Catholicism. The Indian statues of Vishnu, Lakshmi, Shiva, Parvati, Rudra, and other gods exude an aura of confidence and pride tantamount to some grand millennial wedding feast. Some idea of the relationship between Indian tradition and Noah's family can be gained by profiling the Indian pantheon as it translates into the princes of Genesis 10.

The Indian pantheon is just one of three especially rich or catholic in their presentations of the Noahic cosmos. The others are the Sumerian and Hellenic. Because of the urban cult principle of Sumer, the Sumerian is the most systematic and authoritative. The Hellenic is highly synthetic, producing double and even triple versions of the same princes in different thematic contexts. Despite the vast number of Hindu and Sumerian deities, canons of major deities can be isolated; and significant thematic differences exist between the canons of these two pantheons.

The following profile of the Indian pantheon displays which sections of Genesis 10 are included and excluded, that is, emphasized and deemphasized. The identifications are merely displayed here:

Genesis 10	East Indian Pantheon
Noah	Indra of the Maruts
Shem	Brahma the Originator
Ham	Kama
Japheth	Brahma Prajapati
Gomer	Himavan
Magog	Rudra (Teutonic Kari)
Madai	Agni (Teutonic Logi)
Javan	Soma
Ashkenaz	Maka
Riphath	Bhat
Togarmah	Thammuz
Canaan	Marichi
Seba	Shiva the Destroyer
Sabtah	Ganesa
Nimrod	Varuna
Sidon	Kasyapa
Jebus	— (Hellenic Zeus)
Sin (Second Yellow Matriarch)	Lakshmi
Arvad (Second Black Matriarch)	Parvati
Zemar (Second Red Matriarch)	Ganga
Hamath (Second White Matriarch)	Sarasvati
Elam	Yama
Asshur	Manu
Arphaxad II (Salah)	Surya, Daksha II
Lud (Peleg)	Shiva Pashupati (Celtic Cernunnus)
Aram (Joktan)	Vishnu the Sustainer
Hadoram (Arphaxad I)	Daksha I (Sumerian Nanna)
Uzal	Diti (Sumerian Inanna)
Sheba (Yellow Matriarch)	Durga
Ophir (Black Matriarch)	Kali
Havilah (Red Matriarch)	Mahadevi
Jobab (White Matriarch)	Uma, Tattaka

The first noteworthy characteristic of this pantheon is its conservative preoccupation with the immediate family of Noah. All eight survivors of the flood are well defined except for the blurred distinction between Shem and Japheth as Brahma and Brahma Prajapati. The simple reason for this merger is that Shem originated the Indo-European stock; Japheth later assumed control of it. A similar tendency to blur distinctions is apparent in the Indian versions of the four females of the Ark, who appear as the Mahadevi complex.[23] In this case, the White, Black, and Yellow Matriarchs are treated as modes of the one Mahadevi or "Great Goddess," whose distinct identity is that of the Red Matriarch, Noah's royal wife (Tiamat in the Babylonian system of the Marduk Epic). This traditional elevation of the Red Matriarch explains why the Black Matriarch is pictured as her attendant in the Gundestrup panel of the Braided Goddess.

India also supplies definitive versions of Noah's chief postdiluvian children, who were eight in number: Gomer's vassals Ashkenaz, Riphath, and Togarmah in Genesis 10:3; Cush's vassal Sabtechah, in 10:7; and four daughters listed at the bottom of the Canaanite set in 10:17-18. The males of 10:3 appear in a local tradition of the Punjab, not far from where Noah's black son Riphath, father of the Dravidian race, obtained the first postdiluvian fief of the Indus Valley thirty-two years after the Flood. Noah's daughters are Lakshmi, wife of Vishnu; Parvati, royal wife of Shiva; Ganga, another wife of Shiva; and Sarasvati, beloved wife of Brahma in an important marriage duplicated in West Semitic tradition under the names Anath and Aliyan Bal.

Aside from Noah's immediate family, the strongest emphasis in the Indian pantheon falls on the consecutive Canaanite and Semite sections of Genesis 10:15-18 and 10:22. This emphasis means that the Satem Aryans retained a strong sense of the political importance of Shem, especially Shem's alliance with Canaan through the marriage of Arphaxad's daughter Diti (Inanna) to Canaan's son Sidon.[24] Thirty-seven years after the Flood, that marriage resulted in the birth of the next heir Salah, the most powerful of all Noahic princes, a virtual personification of gentile mankind. No other name is so essential to a definition of the gentile cosmos. He appears in the genealogy of Genesis 11 as Salah but in the Völkertafel system of Genesis 10 as the Arphaxad of 10:22, virtually Arphaxad II, in honor of his maternal grandfather, Arphaxad I son of Shem. In Indian tradition he was the sun god Surya, father of Yama and Manu, Indian versions of the Hebrew Elam and Asshur, who head the list of 10:22 as chief vassals of Shem. The Assyrians honored Asshur's father Salah as their great god Marduk, Babylonian protagonist of the Marduk Epic. Salah was also known as Asalluhe to the Sumerian pantheon; Lugalbanda, to the Sumerian legends of the Eanna regime; Bull El, to the West Semites; Mars, to the Romans; Tue, to the Teutons; and Dagda, to the Celts. Thus, the Latvian towns Indra and Dagda, in codifying the distinction between Satem and Centum Indo-Europeans also codify the overall structure of the Indian pantheon in its dual emphasis on Noah (Indra) and Salah (Surya-Dagda).

Noah died 350 years after the Flood[25] and could not have participated directly in the Aryan invasion of India. In fact, the Indian tradition assigns Indra to the Maruts or Amorites as though Noah spent his last years among the Semitic "Flood People," the Amorites of the Syrian Desert. Such a destiny would explain why Noah's antediluvian sons Shem and Ham reappear in the Amorite context of Palestine as Melchizedek and Bera of Genesis 14. But Noah's impact on the Satem culture was great enough to explain the peculiar charisma of East Indian statuary art.

In Genesis 9, Noah seems to convict himself, as well as Ham, of sexual misconduct; and there is no mistaking the connection between "the iniquity of the Amorites" and the sexual evils of Bera's notorious city of Sodom. Sexual anarchy was the tragic flaw of a people whose sexual privilege was to generate the entire human race. Perhaps it is fair to say that East Indian art is a sublimation of that privilege. The Bible nowhere teaches that sexual charisma is "animal instinct." On the contrary, the premise behind high biblical standards of sexual morality is that sex is itself the marital sacrament, sourced in the Garden of Eden, a physical ritual to be supplanted by the higher charismatic metaphysics of the resurrection body. To those Christians who reason firmly from the general resurrection, eroticism is a kind of cultural lost cause, an Adamic value given obsessive and criminal importance by the pagan spirit, the "corruption that is in the world through lust." But the charisma of East Indian statuary art is more than merely sexual. It memorializes the Noahic synthesis of values, a vital link in the dispensational history of man. The "iniquity of the Amorites" is a moral veil covering the face of a beauty rare and strange.

There is little question that the sexual factor has inspired the at-

titude of blind abhorrence in control of euhemeristic works such as
Alexander Hislop's *The Two Babylons* (1853). Hislop's book is not
just an anti-Roman Catholic work from the era of the Kingsley-
Newman debate. It is anti-catholic in a broad sense. It is Judaistic.
Hislop would have liked Shem to have been an Elijah. In some ways,
Shem was separatistic; but he was no Elijah. If Shem were the moral
equivalent of an Israelite, there would have been no need for the
call of Abraham or the sacred history of the Israelites. Judaistic
separatism is a vital link in the salvation history of mankind, a link
forged by Moses in the second millennium. The link forged by Shem
and Noah in the previous millennium was fundamentally different.
Ethically, the challenge of Genesis 9-11 depends on meeting the Christian challenge of Acts 10:28, the subordination of Judaistic
separatism to new principles: "Ye know that it is an unlawful thing
for a man that is a Jew to keep company, or come unto one of
another nation; but God hath shown me that I should not call any
man common or unclean." Dispensational theology, based on the
logic of such passages, has liberated the twentieth-century euhemerist
from the sort of negative obsession which rivets Hislop's attention
on Nimrod as an incarnation of evil. Great evils existed in the third
millennium; but the facile assumption that Nimrod was merely "common or unclean" destroys the subject by destroying any interest in
what righteous Noah contributed to the formation of Nimrod's
world.

Linguistic Specialization

Hislop's preoccupation with Nimrod was not an isolated problem.
Most of the euhemerists of Britain and France were too preoccupied
with monolithic villains or heroes to give balanced attention to
Genesis 10. More important, their scientific limitations compelled
them to seek for Noah through single, favored linguistic stocks.
Bochart was a Semitist preoccupied with the Phoenicians and
Assyrians. Pezron and Edward Davies favored the Celts. Bryant invented a race, the "Cuthites," and gave it villainous glamor. Sir
William Jones was a prototype of the conventional modern scholar
in his development of an empirical and linguistic expertise in the study
of the Satem Aryans of Persia and India.

Today, Sumerologists, Egyptologists, and others maintain the
nineteenth-century tradition that specialization in language is the one

thing needful in historical science. It is no coincidence, however, that such specialization usually serves the evolutionary philosophy. Specialization breeds the idea of polygenesis, the skeptical assumption that the various linguistic stocks are radically independent in origin. In writers such as L. A. Waddell, polygenetic bias took the form of virulent anti-Semitism; but basic polygenism is a calm and respectable assumption that a universal Noah is impossible because, after all, world civilization has evolved, at haphazard, from different physical environments in widely separate parts of the earth in widely separate centuries.

The present writer is no linguistic expert. Recognizing the high importance of linguistic study, he hopes to profit from the work of others. Linguistic expertise in a single field is not the one thing needful. In fact, linguistic specialists have shown little aptitude or inclination toward grasping the logical potential of fundamentalist Christianity or the great Noahic hypothesis. The one thing needful is the willingness to shift quickly from one linguistic context to another in order to solve universal problems.

A case in point concerns the name "Lelex" in the genealogy of Poseidon and Libya of Hellenic tradition.[26] This genealogy appears rather eclectic and international, to begin with, because one of its members, Belus, is evidently the Middle Eastern Bel Marduk; another, Phoenix, the "eponymous ancestor" of Phoenicia; and another, Cadmus, the alleged channel of the Phoenician alphabet into Greece. Conventionally, the genealogy is supposed to represent a Hellenic interpretation of certain foreign Asiatic motifs. We have found that it has much higher importance, furnishing some of the only insight into the genetic connection between the Javanites of Genesis 10:4 and Noah's family:

Helenic Pantheon	Genesis 10
Poseidon	Sidon (Canaanite list)
Lelex	Elishah (Javanite list)
Agenor	Amor (Canaanite list)
Belus	Salah (Semite section)
Phoenix	Tarshish (Javanite list)
Cadmus	Kitt (Javanite list)
Danaus	Rodan (Javanite list)

Eventually, a case must be made for each of these identifications. The special linguistic insight involves Lelex, "eponymous ancestor" of the Leleges, a people of western Asia Minor named in Homer's *Iliad.*[27]

The Leleges inhabited Caria, a region of southwestern Asia Minor whose nominal people, the Carians, belonged to the Asianic Semitic sphere of the Minoans of Crete. The Leleges are so obscure that we have not been able to identify their language; but the geographic context suggested that they might well have been Asianic Semites. The structure of the Javanite list suggests the same. The Gomerites and Javanites of Genesis 10:3-4 form a sevenfold unit analogous to the septad of 10:2. Theory demands that each such septad, with its feudal lord as eighth, formed interlocking relationships to all the other septads by distributing its members among the eight primary linguistic stocks of the cosmos. Each set of names in Genesis 10 includes a Ural-Altaic member, Hamitic member, Semitic member, and so forth. The apparent linguistic arrangement of Genesis 10:3-4 is as follows:

Ashkenaz	Ural-Altaic
Riphath	Dravidian
Togarmah	Sumerian
Elishah	Semitic
Tarshish	Indo-European
Kitt(im)	Amerindian
Rodan(im)	Hamitic

These archaic, personal associations are not to be viewed as exclusive. The Kittim of Cyprus were hardly Amerindian speakers; nor were the Danaans of Greece Hamitic. Lelex (Elishah) and Phoenix (Tarshish) form an interpretive crux because of the dual image of the Phoenicians: Semitic speakers in classic times but with an Indo-European undercurrent related to the Indo-European sojourn on the Syrian coast prior to their exile to the Baltic.

Special insight on this problem derives from a linguistic quarter radically diverse from either the Semitic or Indo-European. The name Lelex, whatever its supposed Hellenic value, resembles the Finno-Ugric word *lelek,* meaning "soul" and related to the word *lil,* "breath."[28] On the face of it, the existence of the word *lil* adds weight to Francisco Jos Badiny's theory that Finno-Ugric is virtually identical to Sumerian. The Sumerian word *lil* means "wind" and is incorporated as such into the familiar god name Enlil, "Lord Wind."[29]

This chain of coincidences adds technical weight to the theory that Lelex or Elishah was the designated Semitic member of the Javanite tetrad. Enlil was the Sumerian version of the universal wind or air god, appearing, for example, in the Egyptian pantheon as Shu. In our second chapter, it will be suggested that the wind god was the pagan counterpart to the Creator Elohim of early Genesis and that the cult of Elohim was the definitive essence of the Semitic linguistic stock as a whole. In other words, the original Semites were the people of Elohim, Enlil, or Shu. According to the Finno-Ugric suggestion, the name Lelex meant "Subject of the Enlilship" or simply "Semitic Vassal" of Javan. Just why the Hellenes depended on an alien Finno-Ugric word to designate such a relationship remains to be seen; but the existence of such a word, evidently cognate with a Sumerian word of high cultic importance, shows how powerfully study in all languages can illumine the Noahic cosmos.

Two Instances from Black Africa

Nevertheless, something is to be said for Bryant's method of matching names, through mere similarity of sound, in cases where linguistic insight plays no part. The method works, in some cases, because an international language of primitive names really exists. This is especially true of tribe names, according to the familiar Bible principle that tribes bear the names of actual, personal progenitors. In the nineteenth century, iconoclastic first-generation anthropologists scorned this principle, preferring to believe that Judah or Ephraim had no personal existence because names such as "Tupan and Guaran" could be interpreted as "eponymous ancestors," fictitious persons invented to give identity to tribes without scientific historical knowledge of origins. The concept of "eponymous ancestry" loses much of its logical force, however, in cases where coincidences of tribal names are observed at second hand and owe nothing to assertions by the tribes themselves

In the Ubangi-Chari region of central Africa are a wholesale series of matches between tribes of the Nilotic stock and a consecutive series of kings from the legendary solar line of East Indian Ayodhya. The matches are in two clusters based on kings 36-45 and 48-52. These matches of the solar line lie to the Nilotic west in the Central African Republic, Chad, and other lands. Kings of the parallel lunar line enter the picture five times, each time matching a tribe from the eastern Nilotic zone of Uganda, Kenya, and southern Sudan:

East Indian Kinglist	African Tribes
36. Bahuka	Bwaka (Nilotic Zaire)
37. Sagara	Nzakara (Nilotic CAR)
	Kara (Nilotic CAR)
	Sokoro (Nilotic Chad)
38. Asa-Manja	Manja (Nilotic CAR)
39. Karam-bha (lunar line)	Karamojong (Nilotic Uganda)
40. Dili-pa	Sila (Nilotic Chad)
41. Bhagi-ratha	Bagirmi (Nilotic Chad)
Shambhu (lunar line)	Samburu (Nilotic Kenya)
42. Suhotra (lunar line)	Suk (Nilotic Kenya)
43. Nabhaya	Baya (Nilotic CAR)
44. Ambarisha	Mbere (Nilotic CAR)
45. Madhu (lunar line)	Madi (Nilotic Uganda-Sudan)
48. Sarva-Kama	Sara (Nilotic Chad)
	Kum (Nilotic Chad)
49. Su-Dasa	Daza (Nilotic Niger)
50. Kal-masha-pada	Masa (Nilotic Chad)
51. Ashmaka	Maka (Sudanic Cameroon)
Kukura (lunar line)	Kuku (Nilotic Sudan)
52. Mulaka[30]	Laka (Nilotic Cameroon)[31]

The same name Sagara also appears in the Eastern Bantu Sagara of Tanzania, where it is flanked north and south by the Eastern Bantu Guru, a match for Upa-Guru, solar Videha king No. 49.

The crux names of the series are Sagara and Asa-Manja, whom Waddell identifies as East Indian versions of the Akkadian emperors Sargon and Manishtushu.[32] The key to this African mystery is a pair of Bantu tribes between Lake Victoria and Lake Tanganyika, the Haya and Tussi. These two names have the same sort of symbolic value for the African continent that Indra and Dagda have for the Indo-European world. Haia is the Sumerian pantheon name for Cush, general patriarch of black Africa. Because of the Sumero-

Akkadian cultural synthesis, the proximity of the Haya to the Tussi suggests that the latter name represents the Akkadian Manishtushu, in a variant of the Akkadian form as opposed to the Indian form of the Nilotic Manja. The Haya and Tussi have the Sumero-Akkadian code value of the biblical "Cush and Mizraim," inasmuch as Waddell builds a strong case for the identity of Manishtushu with the first Pharaoh Menes, builder of the Egyptian First Dynasty in Upper Egypt. On the eve of the Akkadian Empire both the Egyptian and black African stocks were camped near the Lower Tigris. Waddell shows evidence that Manishtushu used an imperial fleet of the Lower Sea to colonize Upper Egypt with Hamitic speakers (Egyptians). We need only add that the Akkadians treated the ancestors of black Africa in much the same way.

According to our reconstruction, the Akkadian Empire commenced 270 years after the Flood and just ninety years after the Sumerian epoch of First Kish, which was virtually the beginning of human political history. The East Indian kinglists commenced from the First Kish epoch as did other gentile traditions. The East Indian "Sagara," Akkadian Sargon, appears as thirty-seventh king of Ayodhya because the previous ninety years were taken up by just thirty-six "reigns" of two-and-a-half years each. For some reason, the ancestors of the Nilotes (unlike the Sudanic West Africans) disregarded most of the rulers of the ninety-year pre-Akkadian period but absorbed the East Indian names of the Akkadian emperors as well as those of kinglets who continued to function as local rulers somewhere within the empire.

If the Akkadian regime left a mark on Nilotic and Eastern Bantu tribe names, the Sumerian regimes of Lagash left an even deeper impression on a more compact set of tribes in and near Sudanic Nigeria. In this case, the text of Genesis 10 plays a major role, confirming the belief, held by some ethnologists, that the Palestinian Canaanites were connected with Africa. In the Sumerian record, the house of Canaan (Lagashite Gunidu) appears at Lagash.[33] The Sudanic tribes match a composite of the house of Canaan formed by Genesis 10:15-17, the Lagashite names, and, again, the East Indian kinglist as tied to Lagash by Waddell.[34] The only part of the Canaanite section of Genesis 10 lacking from the Nigerian system is the last four names, which have a radically distinct value. The matching names are as follows:

Hebrew	Sumerian	East Indian	African
(1) Ham	Gurmu	----------	Gurma (eastern Upper Volta)
(2) Canaan	Gunidu	----------	Gun (southwestern Nigeria) Kundu (western Cameroon)
(3) Sidon	Gudea	(Gadhi)	Gude (northeastern Nigeria—northern Cameroon)
(4) Heth (Chatti-Hittite)	----------	----------	Ekiti (southwestern Nigeria)
(5) Jebus	Ur-Nanshe son of Gunidu	(Haryashva)	Jibu (eastern Nigeria) Ijebu, Ibo, Ijaw (southern Nigeria)
(6) Amor (Hellenic Agenor)	----------	----------	Akyen (Ghana)
(7) Girgash	Akurgal son of Ur-Nanshe	Mogalla son of Haryashva	Igala, Iyala (south-eastern Nigeria)
(8) Hiv	Mugamimla son of Ur-Nanshe	Kampilya son of Haryashva	Mambila, Chamba (eastern Nigeria)
(9) Ark (Hellenic Arcas)	(Argandea of Erech)	(Markandeya of Indian tradition)	Arago (central Nigeria) Margi (northeastern Nigeria)[35]

All sixteen of the African tribes are contained within a rectangle bounded by Lake Volta and Lake Chad in the southwestern and northeastern corners. Some idea of the specific distribution of these tribes can be gained from the following plot based on the numbers supplied in our list:

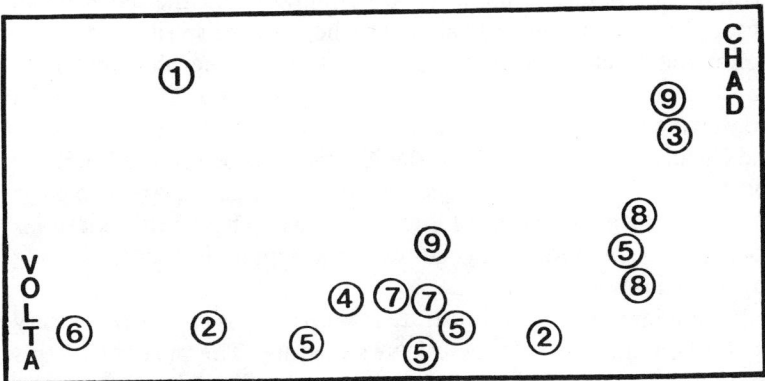

All of the tribes except the outlying Gurma of Upper Volta form a line running from Lake Volta to Lake Chad. To give some idea of the probability of chance coincidence in selecting such names from a larger field, we have omitted about eighteen Sudanic tribes shown by our source along the same line. Thus our sample represents about 40% of the tribes within the given field of ethnography as supplied by our source.

The Heroic Mode

In treating the African tribe names as evidence, we have used nothing but raw similarity of sound. In fact, the logic of the situation calls for little else. The African tribes, like all nations, share in the common charismatic endowment of the Noahic cosmos. The names of the kings were essential divisions of that endowment. The eastern Bantu Sagara and Nilotic Manja bear the names of the legendary kings Sagara and Asa-Manja, versions of the emperors Sargon and Manishtushu; and, by the power vested in those emperors, they exist as tribes and have done so for four thousand years. Did we suppose that those tribes have no share in the "powers that be"? Their powers are now limited by such nation states as the Central African Republic, Sudan, or Uganda. But such tribes are no whimsy of primitive evolution; they share in the very essence of political reality.

Bryant's effort to identify an international language of early postdiluvian names is no speculative fantasy, but the dawn of an absolute political science grounded in the world of spirit. Those who doubt that such a world exists or pertains to the phenomena of government have reason to be skeptical about the Mesopotamian origin of the Sagara, the Manja, the Mandara of King Mandaru, the Gurma of King Gurmu, or the Adamawa of King Adamu. They must reserve the right to confine Indian kings to India, Amorite kings to Tidnum, and Lagashite kings to Lagash. Their motives are indigenous to the human psyche, which interprets history according to its own laws.

It would be possible to illustrate from countless twentieth-century books how these psychological laws operate. The purpose of this study is not to criticize psychology or anthropology but to offer an alternative to the general tenor of antiquarian study in modern times. Our ethical goal is simple: to counter the elegiac pathos of the evolutionary worldview with a revival of the heroic mode. All Genesis 10 study is a sequel to the epic *Paradise Lost,* seeking to accomplish for the postdiluvian world what Milton accomplished for the antediluvian, with this difference: that Noah's postdiluvian world was the beginning of the same world which we inhabit today, opening the floodgate of positive historical evidence, rather than poetic tradition, to water the soil of the biblical account. Yet the distinction between epic poetry and scientific historiography—or historical research of any kind—is not absolute but relative. Poetry and historical science are two modes of the same activity, not just because the ancient narratives are poetic, but because both aim at the synthetic process of personal memory. The student of tenth-century Europe must remember that Henry the Fowler actually existed or all documentation pertinent to him will be neglected, forgotten, and eventually lost. The moral fact is that some men remember Noah as they read about him and others do not. Some readers sense the presence of a unifying force in the data of the third millennium and others do not.

The spiritual distinction between elegiac and heroic literature lies at the heart of our ability to conceptualize the past. Elegy is the weeping genre which laments lost causes, the wretchedness of the world, and the frailties of mortal human nature. Much modern "realism" in fiction and drama means little else. Because the elegiac spirit emphasizes defeat, the scientific correlative of elegy is an obsession with negative result. The objective scientist must be prepared to accept the limitations of human knowledge, the inadequacy of evidence to furnish answers, and the failure of theories. Defeat, however, is more than an objective experience. There exists an elegiac spirit, a predisposition to defeat or negative result. While questioning the value of the Gurmu-Gurma coincidence, we should also question why such coincidences are not better known. Plenty of them exist. The answer is that modern historical science is shackled to the elegiac mode. Such coincidences can seem irrelevant even before they are observed. Too much grandeur is implied by them to command modern respect. There is no argument against gloomy apathy. Historical conceptions based on gloomy ideas of man's bestial origins cannot be challenged from within the same culture which first generated such ideas. The elegiac spirit must run its course.

The only answer to Darwinism is stark ideological revolution. The lifeblood of Darwinism is high chronology. Evolution means nothing apart from vast periods of time. Such periods imply a world of mute prehistory, saharas of endless subhuman groping. What do such stretches of time imply about the image of humanity? They simply mean that the majority of human beings have always been hapless, featureless peasants lost in seas of negative result.

Darwinism is the end product of imaginative efforts to match the sea itself and the celestial sea of outer space with an appropriate reading of antiquity. Both the sea and outer space are natural realities which happen to feed the Baconian, scientific hunger for negative result: dimension without content. Charles Darwin went to sea, discovered the gross apathy of the Tierra del Fuegans, and drew a predictable conclusion. Percy Shelley had drawn the same sort of conclusion from his impression of the vast blankness of Mont Blanc. The time has come to question whether such impressions should continue to dictate our beliefs about early man.

In a more heroic age than Shelley's or Darwin's, Philip Sidney claimed that heroic literature clears away all "misty fearfulness and foggy desire." The given chronology of Genesis 11 has a unique capacity to accomplish just that. Short chronology puts the human spirit on war alert. The Darwinian sea of mute prehistory is the very projection of "misty fearfulness and foggy desire": a world without power, name, volition, design, or literature. It knows nothing of the cosmic grandeur of the two eyes of Horus Khenti-Irti. The alternative short chronology implies power and intrigue, confrontations of good and evil, immortal glory and immortal shame. Once the human spirit begins to move again and reclaim its heritage, the "misty fearfulness" of negative result and the "foggy desire" of natural selection will lose their appeal both ethically and intellectually. The chronology of Genesis 11 is the clarion call to a better worldview and to a nobler world.

NOTES

[1] Samuel Noah Kramer, *The Sumerians* (Chicago: University Press, 1963), p. 328. The Sumerian Kinglist also asserts that kingship had descended before the Flood to the various antediluvian dynasties; but we reject the premise that these earlier "dynasties" actually refer to the antediluvian period.

[2] Henri Frankfort, *Kingship and the Gods* (Chicago: University Press, 1948), pp. 61-78.

[3] Ole Klindt-Jensen, *Gundestrupkedelen* (Copenhagen: Nationalmuseet, 1961), p. 5. The various panels of the Caldron will be shown and analyzed in chs. 2-3.

[4] Only seven exterior panels are extant; but originally there were eight. Klindt-Jensen, "The Gundestrup Bowl: A Reassessment," *Antiquity,* 33 (1959), 161.

[5] Proinsias MacCana, *Celtic Mythology* (London: Hamlyn, 1970), p. 29.

[6] For example, he identifies Noah with the god Dagon on the basis of the latter's resemblance to Odakon of the Berosus kinglist. Jacob Bryant, *A New System or an Analysis of Antient Mythology,* 3rd ed. (London: J. Walker, 1807), IV, 140.

[7]See "Northern Europe," Map, *The National Geographic Magazine,* 106 (August, 1954).

[8]The designations "Centum" and "Satem" are from the words for "hundred" in these two divisions of the Indo-European system.

[9]MacCana, p. 38.

[10]Thorkild Jacobsen, *Toward the Image of Tammuz* (Cambridge, Mass.: Harvard University Press, 1970), p. 34.

[11]There was no mistaking Schlegel's motive to put an end to the reign of Genesis 10 as a basis of universal origins: "Die Mosaische Völkertafel zur Grundlage der allgemeinen Weltgeschichte zu dienen, wie man es fruherin so oft versucht hat, nie ohne grossen Zwang durchgefuhrt werden kann." The implied warning is not to attempt this species of Christian apologetics but to let nature take its course in revealing the limitations of the Bible. The frequent attempts Schlegel refers to were the school of Bochart, Pezron, and Bryant. Friedrich von Schlegel, *Philosophie der Geschichte,* in *Sämmtliche Werke* (Vienna: Ignaz Klang, 1846), XII, 186.

[12]Irene Nicholson, *Mexican and Central American Mythology* (London: Paul Hamlyn, 1967), p. 94.

[13]The ordinal directions of the four Tezcatlipocas fail to match the ethnography of existing races because they were based on antediluvian tradition.

[14]Henry M. Morris, *The Genesis Record* (San Diego: Creation-Life Publishers, 1976), pp. 89-90.

[15]Harley Burr Alexander, *Latin American,* in *The Mythology of All Races,* ed. Herbert Louis Gray, XI (New York: Cooper Square, 1964), 62.

[16]John Bierhorst, *Four Masterworks of the American Indian Literature* (New York: Farrar, Strauss, and Giraux, 1974), p. 70.

[17]Nicholson, p. 124.

[18]The so-called "mark" of Cain was a protective sign, a metaphysical blessing. All of the racial patterns have metaphysical sign value. Fair skin signifies the phlegmatic humor and a certain degree of physical helplessness (Genesis 4:14), hence the classic Caucasoid reliance on the arts of civilization for protection. Noah's white sons, Shem and Japheth, were a kind of redeemed remnant of the Cainite stock but, like Ham, Sethite in the male line.

[19]John C. Whitcomb, Jr. and Henry M. Morris, *The Genesis Flood* (Philadelphia: Presbyterian and Reformed, 1964), p. 399.

[20]Originally, Shem was the priest of Yahweh only; and Ham, the priest of Elohim. Noah's blessing of the "Yahweh Elohim of Shem" meant that he stripped Ham of the priesthood of Elohim and bestowed this privilege on Shem, giving the latter control of two linguistic stocks, Indo-Europeans and Semites. These events are summarized in ch. 4.

[21]James B. Pritchard, "The Myth of Zu," *Ancient Near Eastern Texts* (Princeton: University Press, 1955), pp. 111-13. The identification of Ninurta with Nimrod is a commonly held fundamentalist view, even where there is no euhemeristic policy. See Allen P. Ross, "The Table of the Nations in Genesis 10—Its Content," *Bibliotheca Sacra,* 138 (January-March 1981), 26.

[22]Jacobsen, p. 4.

[23]Veronica Ions, *Indian Mythology* (London: Paul Hamlyn, 1967), pp. 91-94.

[24]Noah allowed the political line of Shem to pass into the genetic line of Canaan in order to compensate the latter's faction for the political damage of the curse in Genesis 9:26. The female interval between Arphaxad and Salah explains the intervention of the Greek Septuagint's cipher name "Cainan" in the Messianic genealogy of Luke 3:36. Contrary to common belief, there was nothing holy in the genes of Shem or profane in the genes of Ham; but Shem's theocratic supremacy, after the fact, was quite real and was carried genetically from Salah to the Messiah. Any notion of "polluting the godly seed" could not apply to the immediate members of Noah's universal family. All eight survivors of the Flood were ritually holy.

[25]Genesis 9:28.

[26]The Poseidon-Libya genealogy is found in Apollodorus's *Bibliotheca.* See various members of the genealogy in J. E. Zimmerman, *Dictionary of Classical Mythology* (New York: Harper and Row, 1964), passim.

[27] Book X, 1. 429. Andrew Lang, trans., *The Iliad of Homer,* rev. ed. (London: Macmillan, 1900), p. 196.

[28]*Encyclopedia Britannica Micropaedia* (Chicago: William Benton, 1974), VI, 134.

[29]Jacobsen, p. 31.

[30]L. A. Waddell, *The Makers of Civilization in Race and History* (London: Luzac, 1929), p. 524.

[31]"The Peoples of Africa," Map, *The National Geographic Magazine,* 140 (December, 1971).

[32]Waddell, p. 201.

[33]Jacobsen, pp. 32-33.

[34]Waddell identifies Ur-Nanshe and his five sons with Haryashva, East Indian king No. 15, and his five sons. In Waddell's time, "Ur-Nanshe" was read "Ur-Nina"; and Waddell calls him "Uruash." *The Makers of Civilization,* p. 111.

[35]"The Peoples of Africa."

Chapter 2

The Noahic Cosmos

Plurality of Spirit

The eight survivors of the Flood were more than eight persons. They were an eightfold human system[1] analogous to the patriarchs of the twelve tribes of Israel or to the twelve Apostles of Christianity. Their purpose was to divide the world in three ways: genetic, linguistic, and political (or geographic). They created races, linguistic stocks, and nations. Contrary to conventional evolutionary ideas, they accomplished this task with their eyes open, that is, through rigorous utopian planning. The grandiose systematic despotism of the pyramid Pharaohs sprang immediately from these utopian impulses. In fact, the earliest pyramid Pharaohs were all members of the Genesis 10 community: Zoser and Huni, Ham and Canaan; Snefru, Tubal-Eber, son of Salah; Khufu, Gomer, son of Japheth; and Menkaura and Khafra, Javan and Meshech, grandsons of Japheth. The gigantic statuary art of Egypt expresses, for all to see, the sublime greatness of Noahic privilege and power.

The failure to connect this awesome privilege with Noah derives from a misunderstanding of the relationship between Christian orthodoxy and pagan polytheism. As Christians, we have neglected certain areas of apocalyptic truth essential to understanding the Noahic theocracy. Noah's utopian goals lay substantially outside the cultural range of pastoral Christianity, which seeks to minister to souls in need. Because of our fixation on the pastoral ethos of the Lamb of God, we have overlooked the implications of that Lamb's full presentation in Revelation 5:6:

> And I looked, and behold, in the midst of the throne
> and of the four living creatures and in the midst of the

elders, stood a Lamb as though it had been slain, having seven horns and seven eyes, which are seven Spirits of God sent out into all the earth.

The "seven Spirits of God" recur in Revelation 1:4, 4:5, and 5:6 and are a theological distinctive of the Apocalypse, without clear precedent in the Pauline theology of the earlier New Testament. They require an amplification of basic Trinitarian doctrine. Our God is one God, in three Persons, and in eight modes of work or of judging works. The Lamb, in itself, signifies the peculiar work of Christ's atonement and of various pastoral correlatives in the Church. The seven additional "eyes" signify seven radically distinct modes of work outside the compass of pastoral life and initiative. Together, the Lamb and His seven "eyes" constitute a spiritual octad essential to the formation of Noah's world or to any other conceivable cosmos. They are the universal ground of all ethical and cultural life and recur in all sorts of practical media. In literary history, for example, they explain the octad of standard genres: pastoral, heroic, elegiac, satiric, lyric, epigram (judgmental literature), comedy, and tragedy. In the New Testament, they account for the ascending series of virtues in II Peter 1:5-7, the pastoral premise of faith and seven more: heroic *arete* or "virtue," elegiac "knowledge," temperance, patience, godliness, brotherly kindness, and charity.

The seven "eyes" and their pastoral premise furnish a Christian explanation for the high pantheon of Sumero-Akkadian polytheism: the shepherd god Dumuzi, war god Ninurta, water god Enki (Akkadian Ea), moon god Nanna (Akkadian Suen), air god Enlil, storm god Ishkur, sun god Utu, and heaven god An (Akkadian Anu). If idolatry is degenerate polytheism, polytheism itself is a degenerate manifestation of the principle of divine plurality of spirit established in Revelation 5:6 and in the various names for God throughout the Hebrew Old Testament. Roughly eight such names occur and furnish analogies to the pagan high pantheon: Adonai Yahweh, to the shepherd god; El Gibbor, to the war god; El Olam, to the water god; El Shaddai, to the moon god; Elohim, to the air god; Yahweh proper to the storm god; Yahweh Sabaoth, to the sun god; and El Elyon, to the heaven god. Such names are scattered unsystematically throughout the Old Testament because the integrity of the Noahic theology had been broken by the time of Moses; but, wherever such a name occurs, it signifies a specific "eye of the Lamb" a distinct dimension of God as divine work and purpose.

Before judging pagan polytheism too harshly, we should notice how well the Egyptian concept of Horus Khenti-Irti, for example, conforms to the implications of Revelation 5:6. Moret explains that the Right Eye of Horus was reckoned the sun; and the Left Eye, the moon.[2] The metaphoric vehicle of divine "eyes" agrees with Revelation 5:6, and the tenor (or secondary vehicle) of Sun and Moon correlates these "eyes" with the imagery of the Mesopotamian high pantheon, including, as it does, the sun god Utu and moon god Nanna. In "presiding" over the two eyes, Horus takes the part of a priest of a dual name of God such as the "Yahweh Elohim of Shem."

Eight Theocractic Cults

Because Noah introduced the dispensation of human government, a logical place to seek for meaning in the personae of the Mesopotamian pantheon is in modes of political and, secondarily, economic power. The focus of each such power was a survivor of the Flood. Although Shem was destined to become Melchizedek, priest of El Elyon, he assumed this office only after the death of Noah, the original Anu or euhemeristic priest of the heaven god. Japheth was the original priest of the sun god; Ham, of the air god; and Shem, of the storm god. The Red Matriarch, Noah's royal wife, assumed the priesthood of the shepherd god from her ancestral land of Havilah and its stock, the race of Abel, first priest of lamb sacrifice. Shem's royal wife, the Yellow Matriarch, transferred the priesthood of the moon god, first to her son Arphaxad I, and, ultimately, to Arphaxad's heir Abraham, whose early life was spent at the lunar cult centers of Ur and Harran.[3] Japheth's royal wife, the Black Matriarch, transmitted the priesthood of the war god Ninurta to her Hamite descendant Nimrod; and the White Matriarch, Ham's royal wife, did likewise for the priesthood of the water god, bestowing it on her grandson Sidon, euhemeristic Enki, Ea, Koshar, and Ptah.

Falkenstein furnishes positive evidence of a Noahic theological octad in his analysis of eight generic classes of Sumerian gods: dingir-anna, "gods of heaven"; dingir-kia, "gods of earth"; dingir-ankia, "gods of heaven and earth"; dingir-kurkura, "gods of foreign lands"; dingir-hursagga, "gods of the mountains"; dingir-sharshara, "countless gods"; dingir-kilagash, "gods of the region of Lagash";

and dingir-galgal, "the great gods."⁴ These terms define eight cults as such, not eight deities, but eight generic spheres of deity. The dingir-anna define the sphere of the Heaven God El Elyon; the dingir-kia, the sphere of the Shepherd God, whose death motif correlates with the allied gods of earth and underworld; the dingir-ankia, the sphere of the intermediate Air God, who stands between earth and heaven; the dingir-kurkura, the sphere of the nationalistic and vindictive Storm God; the dingir-hursagga, the sphere of the lunar principle as reflected in the Yellow Matriarch's pantheon name Ninhursag (although this deity does not belong to the lunar family of Ur); the dingir-sharshara, the heavenly host of Yahweh Sabaoth, the solar principle; the dingir-kilagash, the sphere of the War God of Lagash; and the dingir-galgal, the sphere of the Water God and the White Matriarch, known to the pantheon both as the fish goddess Nanshe and as the "Great Goddess" Ningal.

Each of these eight cults possessed a definite political meaning. Noah's cult of the heaven god meant absolute despotism or the sovereign privilege of originating political power in others. In the antediluvian period, this privilege meant the authority to select the seven companions of the Ark, an authority tantamount to shaping the human cosmos. El Elyon is essentially the God of the third heaven, creator and ruler of angels, and ultimate source of the "Ka" or charisma of rulership in Psalm 82. In selecting the survivors of the Flood, Noah made each an eightfold division of the "powers that be," quasi-angelic agents of the new postdiluvian order. After the Flood, he retained this privilege long enough to bless Shem and curse Canaan in the episode of Genesis 9:20-26, altering the political destiny of mankind for all time to come.

If Anu was the god of absolute sovereignty, Utu, the sun god, stood for imperial executive authority. The solar image so dominated Egyptian thought that a study of the Pharaonic institution reveals the political meaning of solar worship. The leading idea which Frankfort assigns to the alliance between Pharaoh and the sun god Ra is regulation, the maintenance of a static, unchanging cosmos, including the power of restoration, "after a dangerous interruption of the harmony between society and nature."⁵

Such restorative power is tantamount to healing. Christians are familiar with the link between "healing" and the solar image in the final chapter of the Old Testament:

"But to you who fear My name
The Sun of Righteousness shall arise
With healing in His wings;
And you shall go out
And grow fat like stall-fed calves.
You shall trample the wicked,
For they shall be ashes under the soles of your feet
On the day that I do this,"
Says the Lord of hosts (Malachi 4:2-3).

The divine speaker is Yahweh Sabaoth, Hebrew counterpart to Utu and Ra: a "Lord of hosts," as the pagan divine Sun was believed to have guided the heavenly host of stars. Malachi's prophecy links the solar image and its ideal to the Messianic Second Advent of Christ, the ultimate restoration of order following the supreme anarchy of Antichrist. In the postdiluvian world of Noah, this ideal of restoration "after a dangerous interruption of harmony" applied to the contrast between nascent civilization and the barbaric antediluvian dispensation of conscience.

The cult of the air god Enlil corresponded to our ideas of "nature," natural law, and law in general. The correlative Hebrew Elohim was the author of nature, the Creator, in the first chapter of Genesis. In contrast with the restorative power of the sun god, the cult of the air god implied creation out of nothing, the power of innovation. In the works of the remarkable English poet Percy Shelley, we find both a preoccupation with images of air and space and the definitive statement that "poets are the unacknowledged legislators of mankind." Shelley was obsessed with the power of innovation, the will of the "West Wind" to alter the course of human affairs. In Noah's world, this power, the "Enlilship," meant legislative privilege as exercised by the authors of law codes, such as Sumerian Ur Nammu, Amorite Hammurabi, and Hebrew Moses. In Noah's family, a struggle over the possession of this privilege formed the central intrigue of his postdiluvian lifetime.

According to the metaphoric vehicle, the cult of the storm god must have differed little from the cult of the air god. In fact, the Sumero-Akkadian Enlil absorbed into himself the roles of both air god and storm god.[6] This Enlil was precisely equivalent to the dual "Yahweh Elohim of Shem." Nevertheless, "Yahweh Elohim" remained "two eyes" rather than one, a pair of distinguishable divine *erga,* labeled separately as Enlil and Ishkur in the original Sumerian pantheon. If Elohim stood for natural law and legislation, Yahweh stood for moral law and executive justice. The Hebrew *shophetim* or "judges" constituted the truest theocracy of Israel because they acted out the moral essence of Yahweh proper, the national God of Israel. In this respect, the Israelites were not mere Semites but Shemites, devotees of the personal ethos of Shem, whose original commitment to the storm god made him the human counterpart to Ishkur, Adad, Aliyan Bal, Thor, and Taru. Just how Shem undertook the ethical role of judge or agent of justice remains to be seen.

If the storm and air gods formed a complementary pair, the same was true of the moon and sun gods, who are coupled in many ways: the two "eyes" of Horus, the two male deities of the Gundestrup Trinity panel, the lunar and solar divisions of the East Indian kinglist, and even the geographic complement of Sumer and Akkad, one featuring the lunar cult center of Ur and the other, the solar cult center of Sippar. In the Sumerian pantheon, the moon god Nanna fathers the sun god Utu:[7] a curious arrangement reflected in their human counterparts Arphaxad I and his natural son Obal, the two princes featured on either side of the Yellow Matriarch in the Gundestrup Trinity panel. If we can discover why Arphaxad and Obal were theocratically aligned as they were, we can isolate the lunar principle as a variation of rulership distinct from solar or imperial restoration.

Arphaxad and Obal belonged to the first and second postdiluvian generations. Arphaxad I was born only two years after the Flood, at Harran in Syrian Mesopotamia, at the foot of the Caucasus Mountains where the Ark had come to rest. Bryant and Faber believed that the moon symbolized the Ark. Both the Mesopotamian and Egyptian traditions concur in picturing the moon as a boat.[8] Arphaxad gained his identification with the moon from the coincidence of his birth with the diluvian epoch. Noah's Ark represented both the practical idea of survival and of sectarian social identity, the "remnant" principle. The lunar cult was to the solar cult what sectarian nationalism is to catholic imperialism. Instead of restoring universal order, the lunar king enabled his peculiar people to survive. In the primitive year of Arphaxad's birth, Noah was accomplishing little else. Ideas of imperial restoration were reserved, symbolically, for the succeeding generation of Obal.

A corollary dimension of the lunar cult was the power of devastation as in the Flood or in militant nationalism. The Egyptian Seth, swallower of the moon, was a god of devastation. According to Franz Delitzsch, the name El Shaddai connotes God's devastating power: "The times of the patriarchs are the period of El Shaddai. Their characteristic is the violence done to the natural to make it subserve the purposes of salvation."[9] The chief Mesopotamian devotee of the lunar cult, Naram Sin, was the most warlike ruler of the third millennium. In the divine family of the lunar cult itself, Nanna's daughter Inanna raised up the Gutanu or Bull of Heaven to ravage Erech for insulting her.[10] The image of a bull, selected both for its destructiveness and its fertility, lay at the heart of the lunar cult. Both Nanna and his son Ninhar were pictured as bulls.[11] Inanna's mighty son Salah appeared in the Ugaritic pantheon as Tr Il, "Bull El." Naram Sin, Abram's grandfather Nahor I, took the Hebrew name "Nahor" from the image of a snorting bull and was pictured with bull horns both in the Naram Stele and in the Narmer palette.

The cults of the Black and White Matriarchs formed still another theocratic pair. A major link between the two was furnished by Gudea, patesi of Lagash, the Solomonic, phlegmatic Sidon, son of Canaan and incestuous offspring of the White Matriarch twice over. In euhemeristic terms, Sidon was originally the chief priest of the water god Enki. As such, he was the mysterious kingmaker of Canaan's faction, reigning mystic, and author of the cult of idolatry.[12] Nevertheless, in his late appearance as Gudea, he favored the war god Ninurta as Ningirsu, chief god of Lagash. Nimrod, the euhemeristic Ninurta, was Sidon's half-brother, a son of Canaan by a daughter of Cush and Noah's black daughter Arvad.

Nimrod became a "mighty hunter" because the cult of the war god gave him the power of military recruitment or impressment. This authority to form armies spearheaded the Akkadian Empire 270 years after the Flood and made that empire the "kingdom" of Nimrod in Genesis 10:10. At the heart of Nimrod's career was the military reconquest of the Enlilship, an act of vengeance against Shem and Noah for having humiliated his father Canaan in the curse of 9:26. This conquest gave to Ningirsu (Ninurta) a strange, composite image celebrated by Gudea in a mystical dream commanding him to build the god's Erinnu temple at Lagash:

In the dream, Gudea saw a man of tremendous stature

with a divine crown on his head, the wings of a lion-
headed bird, and a "flood wave" as the lower part of
his body; lions crouched to his right and left.[13]
The "wings of a lion-headed bird" are the Imdugud of Shem as Zu,
from whom Ninurta recovered the Enlilship. A crouching lion also
accompanies Ninurta in Mesopotamian Seal 685, which celebrates
the general victory of Canaan's faction over its enemies.[14] The "flood
wave" has been borrowed from Enki, the dominant figure of Seal
685, in order to symbolize the cohesion of the water god and war
god in achieving Canaan's idealogical and practical victory over the
Sumero-Akkadian world order.

All warlike regimes demand a "ministry of propaganda"; and such
was the cult of the water god, controlled by the master idealogue
Sidon. The language sacred to the water god was Gudea's own
Sumerian, the proper language of Enki. Thus, classic Sumerian
literature, as a whole, represented Sidon's "ministry of propaganda."
The Epic of Gilgamesh tells the story of Noah's Ark much as the
Bible does, but with fatal, strategic omissions. There is no Genesis
10 structure; no Shem, Ham, or Japheth; and no genealogy of
Genesis 11. Sidon has taught the polygenists of modern times how
to think by showing them what not to think. The Ark can be
remembered but in total abstraction from any program of building
nations. Sidon owed his existence to Noah but hated him eternally
for cursing his father Canaan. He expressed this hatred, in classically
phlegmatic fashion, by exercising a mendacious tact, the cool wrath
of wilful agnosticism.

Despite the strategic importance of Sumerian literature, the most
intense piece of Mesopotamian propaganda was composed in the
language of the air god, the Semitic. This work was the grand
baroque Marduk Epic, composed to celebrate the apocalyptic victory of Sidon's son Salah (Marduk) over the faction of Noah and
Shem in the Erech-Aratta War, some 216 years after the Flood. Salah
was a personification of the proto-gentile cause of Canaan's faction:
East Indian Surya, god of the Swastika. In the epic, his chief antagonists were Kingu, the arch-loyalist Peleg, and Tiamat, the Red
Matriarch, Noah's royal wife. As a descendant of Abel and formal
advocate of blood sacrifice, the Red Matriarch was the logical target
of a faction devoted to the Cainite principle of grain sacrifice,
featured at the apex of Seal 685. Judaeo-Christian orthodoxy tells

us what the Red Matriarch's cult meant. Sumero-Akkadian tradition suggests only that the enemies of Noah and Shem hated it and sought to suppress it by force. These conflicts not only stripped Noah of the power to complete the cosmos but have left us with an imperfect impression of the eight theocratic cults. Empirical data shows us only the scattered limbs of Noahic theology; and the same can be said for the text of Genesis 10, the divinely inspired record of Noah's feudal system in a partially ruined condition following the Erech-Aratta War. Nevertheless, enough remains to reconstruct both the theocracy and the matching feudal pyramid. The theocracy can be summed in eight terms coined from the Sumerian pantheon: Anship, despotic sovereignty; Utuship, the solar principle of imperial restoration; Enlilship, the innovative power of legislation; Ishkurship, the power to execute moral law; Dumuziship, the power of blood atonement; Nannaship, the power of sectarian national government; Ninurtaship, the power to raise armies and wage war; and Enkiship, the power of literature to shape popular ideology.

The Gundestrup Exterior Panels

The eight theocratic powers originated with the eight survivors of the Flood as pictured in the exterior panels of the Gundestrup Caldron. The purpose of each panel is fourfold: (1) to give a symbolic impression of the physical appearance of each survivor; (2) to characterize the authority claimed by each; (3) to represent certain events occurring at thirty-year intervals from the thirtieth to the 240th year after the Flood; and (4) to complement the function of the interior panels by designing ethnographic maps of various regions of the Middle East progressively explored by Noah's family.

The panel of the Black Matriarch is missing from the original eight. In chronological sequence, the eight were as follows:

Panel	Subject	Cult	Epoch
Boar-Holding Men	Noah	Anship	Year 30
Boxer and Dancer	Japheth	Utuship	Year 60
Two Dragons	Ham	Enlilship	Year 90
Hirschnatur[15]	Shem	Ishkurship	Year 120
Braided Goddess	Red Matriarch	Dumuziship	Year 150
Trinity	Yellow Matriarch	Nannaship	Year 180
----------	Black Matriarch	Ninurtaship	Year 210
Sphinx	White Matriarch	Enkiship	Year 240

The historical logic of the sequence will be developed in Chapters Four, Five, and Six.

An obvious trait of the seven extant panels is structural dualism in harmony with the dual structure of the human face. One subject holds two boars, another two dragons, another two stags, and so forth. This trait underscores Noah's motive to divide mankind into "nations, tongues, and peoples" as swiftly and decisively as possible. The Tower of Babel scheme to reunify the Noahic world was rebellious because it opposed this elemental motive to seek for a harmonious world order grounded in rigorous diversity. Noah's own peculiar power was the Anship to delegate authority; and that meant dividing authority. The dualism of each panel celebrates a new step in this process of "rightly dividing" the charisma of human government. Aside from the eightfold division implied by the eight panels, each panel subdivides its peculiar power through two subordinates each, expanding the range of power to twenty-four personae, analogous to the twenty-four elders of the Apocalypse.

PANEL OF THE BOAR-HOLDING MEN

The rugged brachycephalism of this depiction of Noah is intended partly to represent his Mongoloid racial distinction from his more

Caucasoid and Amerindian sons; but this cannot be the only explanation, because the Yellow Matriarch of the Trinity panel is neither crude nor much more brachycephalic than the White Matriarch. The principles at work in this version of Noah are the same as the ones displayed in the East Indian representation of Indra as a potbellied man with boar tusks sticking from his mouth.[16] On the one hand, these depictions remind us of Noah's greater relative age than the other males at the time of the Flood; on the other, they express his zeal for the "Eber," the symbolic function of the boar in dispersing the nations. Despite the striking difference in physiognomy between Noah and the others, the loops beneath his beard match those of the Hirschnatur subject Shem. All the other subjects wear the torc instead. This detail groups Noah with Shem in keeping with Genesis 9, the Babylonian tradition of Apsu and Mummu, and the Ugaritic tradition of Dagan and his son Aliyan Bal.

The two men in the grasp of the god represent Noah's sons, Shem and Japheth, full brothers by the White Matriarch. The same two are grouped with Noah in the upper horizontal row of the interior Taranis panel. In both cases, Ham is excluded, not necessarily through alienation, but through his independent association with the four antediluvian females in the separate system of the interior Medb panel. The boars upheld by the two men of Noah's panel are their two respective heirs, Arphaxad and Seba, aligned to represent the complementary lands of Sumer and Elam, on either side of the Lower Tigris.

Noah himself takes the relative position of the Lower Tigris for two reasons. His postdiluvian fief, established when his family first descended from the mountains of Ararat, was Subaria, equivalent to Assyria on the Upper Tigris. Second, the antediluvian land of the Hiddekel-Tigris was the source of the White Matriarch, whose two sons dominate the dual structure of the panel. Sumer and Elam were, in fact, the fiefs of the White and Black Matriarchs, respectively. The White Matriarch mothered both princes; and the Black Matriarch was the royal wife of Japheth and mother of Seba, the "boar" to the upper right. Noah's position on the Lower Tigris expresses his approval of a system of eight fiefs, created over the first thirty antediluvian years, ending with those of Elam and Sumer in that order.

Not to exclude the Yellow and Red Matriarchs from the celebrative process, two additional animals are added to the panel: a leaping dog in the Sumerian sector and a winged horse in the Elamite. The Sumerian deity of the dog image was Bau (Nininsina), goddess of Isin,[17] Noah's first post-diluvian daughter designated for the Yellow Matriarch. By grouping the dog with the figures of Shem and Arphaxad in Sumer, the design stresses the yellow-white affinity of both princes and, indeed, of the Sumerian race.

Logic suggests that the winged horse, in Elam, represents Noah's analogous daughter by the Red Matriarch, known to the Sumerian pantheon as Shenirda (Akkadian Aia), wife of the sun god Utu (Akkadian Shamash). In the East Indian pantheon, this daughter appears as Ganga, personification of the River Ganges, definitive of the eastern half of Aryan India. The Elamite grouping of Ganga with Japheth's black son Seba not only re-creates the red-black alliance of antediluvian "Havilah and Cush" but anticipates the marriage of Seba, East Indian Shiva, to Ganga, one of his many wives. As fief of the Black Matriarch, Elam was a regional stepping-stone to Dravidian India, as it was to greater Arabia, the land pictured in the Braided Goddess panel as the empire of Ereshkigal, East Indian Mahadevi, the Red Matriarch.

PANEL OF THE BOXER AND DANCER

The handsome, elegant features of this depiction of Japheth reflect
the man himself and the ethnic bias of the Celtic artist, inasmuch
as Japheth was the leading influence over Celtic origins. The
definitive word is "elegance" because this panel celebrates the ideal
of imperial civilization implied by the solar Utuship. This version
of Japheth is a kind of French knight, an embodiment of the Nordic supremacist L. A. Waddell's concept of "makers of civilization
in race and history." The Nordic supremacist devotion to the solar
cult was surprisingly explicit and meant little more than an affirma-
tion of the "civilization" principle isolated by Oswald Spengler as
a dominant cultural motive between 1850 and the rise of Nazism.
The solar principle simply exists, whether for good or for evil; and
the hideous injustice of Nazism should not obscure the intrinsic glory
of this principle. Discipline, order, and refinement are all splendid
ideals.

Japheth's panel celebrates the epoch, sixty years after the Flood,
when Noah's family had migrated westward to Canaan and Egypt
and were in process of establishing precedents for the forty-two
nomes of the River Nile. The geographic design of the panel is aligned
to a certain point on the Nile. The central subject represents the
dispersion point of the branches of the delta south of modern Cairo
and north of ancient Memphis. The Boxer and Dancer symbolize
the nomes of Letopolis and Heliopolis to the west and east of the
river. Heliopolis, "City of the Sun," embodies the solar ideal which
Japheth conferred on his creation, the so-called "Hamitic" linguistic
stock, the Egyptian people. The ethical contrast between the dancer
and boxer is precisely the Pharaonic contrast between solar civilization and the "dangerous" anarchy which precedes restoration. The
nome sign of Letopolis was a "piece of flesh,"[18] a barbaric image
symbolic of the struggle for survival featured in the shortarmed boxer
of the panel, which contrasts futile pugnacity with elegant celebration and order.

The nome god of Letopolis, Horus-Khenti-Irti or Horus the Elder,
was a pantheon version of Japheth himself, despite Japheth's appearance in the First Ennead as the earth god Geb, father of Osiris
(Seba). The solar-lunar synthesis of Horus' two "eyes" is a Hamitic
variation of the Mesopotamian synthesis of Akkadian Sippar and
Sumerian Ur. The Egyptians dramatized the ethos of solar restoration as the conflict between Horus and Seth, gods of light and

darkness. In the course of their battles, Seth gained power over the left eye, the moon, but never the right eye, the sun.[19] From this mythology, the pro-Semitic Hislop identified Seth with the heroic and righteously vindictive Shem; whereas the anti-Semitic Waddell, equating Semitism with the lunar cult, identified his Nordic supremacy with the imperial solar cult.

The myth of Horus and Seth dealt with some principle of conflict between the solar Utuship and lunar Nannaship, that is, between imperial rule and local kingship. The human Seth was Zud of the Mizraim clan, a red-haired son of Japheth: the historical Tudia, first of the Amorite kings who "dwelled in tents."[20] Most students of Egyptian tradition recognize the correlation between Seth and the hostile forces of Syrian Asia. The Egyptian-Syrian struggle, culminating in the Battle of Carchemish, arose from rival claims to Japheth's original postdiluvian fief, the land of Syria, west of the Upper Euphrates. Tudia represented a branch of Noah's family who adopted the Semitic tongue, claimed Syria for themselves, and reigned according to the rugged, anti-imperial principle of the lunar Nannaship, as local "kings dwelling in tents," the sort of petty kings featured in Genesis 14. Seth's mythological act of "swallowing" the left eye of Horus (the moon) meant the adoption of Nannaship by the Amorite kings, who commanded the general Syrian region where both Tudia and Arphaxad I were born within two years after the Flood.

The Boxer-Dancer panel includes a reading of the Seth-Horus conflict. In addition to the shortarmed boxer, the panel includes the image of an armless horseman below the figure of the dancer. Both the boxer and horseman express the concept of Seth's futile and endless war against Horus' solar glory. Because images of human arms figure so prominently in the Gundestrup portrayal of the "Ka," the shortarmed boxer and armless horseman are pictured as devoid of Pharaonic "Ka," as though pathetic antediluvians struggling to survive without the divine gift of the dispensation of human government.

The forces of Seth, in other words, were conceived as antediluvian and hapless: the futile strife of human nature apart from the power of despotic charisma. The whole point of the Flood was to lay to rest the savage futility of unaltered, uninspired human nature. This great theme of "culture and anarchy" was worked out in the nome sequence of the Nile and involved three personalities in addition to Japheth himself. The female dancer is identical to the one pictured twice in the Sphinx panel of Japheth's mother. Her structural correlation with Heliopolis implies a specifically solar cult identity. There is no sun goddess in the Mesopotamian high pantheon; but the logical choice is the mighty Inanna, Queen of Heaven, daughter of the White Matriarch and sister-wife to Japheth as the Egyptian Nut, sky goddess and wife to Japheth's earth form Geb. One of Inanna's versions in the East Indian pantheon is the female Surya, [21] counterpart to the male sun god Surya.

As for the boxer and horseman, these were precisely the Hellenic Dioscuri, Pollux and Castor, one a boxer and the other a horseman.[22] They were Japheth's vassals Tubal and Tiras, singled out as "twins" because of the structural significance of their birth years in Egypt. The two are pictured as antagonists to Inanna because of their role in the Erech-Aratta War. Tubal was born at the nome of Letopolis sixty-seven years after the Flood and thirty-seven years after Noah's family left Sumer to explore the West. His son Tiras was born at the nome of Denderah eighty-five years after the Flood and thirty-seven years after the beginning of the nome sequence. The recurrent pattern of the thirty-seventh year made the two "twins" as symbolic (and real) allies to Tubal's physical father Salah born thirty-seven years after the Flood.

In the panel, both of the "Dioscuri" accost the figure of Inanna because of their role in aiding Salah in the conquest of Inanna's birthplace Aratta. The boxer Tubal stands to the left to signify his role as Sumerian Meskiaggasher in founding the regime at Erech responsible for making war against Aratta. His son Tiras, in directing the attack on horseback, represents the entire Japhethite A clan, whose recruitment by the Erechite regime assured victory over Aratta. These actions belong to Japheth's panel because Tubal, as Meskiaggasher, founded Erech as "son of Utu," that is, vassal to Japheth in the name of Japheth's solar god of imperial restoration. The Gundestrup author, antagonistic toward the specific Erechite regime, pictures the cause as "armless," spiritually futile.

PANEL OF THE TWO DRAGONS

Rudolf Grosse recognizes that the Dragon panel expresses some eruption of the Id, an apocalypse of malign forces. Historically, it refers to the great catastrophe of Genesis 9:20-26, the sin of Ham and curse on Canaan: an event which split Noah's theocracy into two factions for all time to come. The subject of the panel is an appropriately gloomy Ham; and the geographic correlative is the scene of the disaster, the land of Yemen or South Arabia, opposite Upper Egypt. Because the panel of Ham's mother (the Braided Goddess) also refers to Arabia, that land was perceived as the postdiluvian counterpart to the antediluvian Havilah from which their distinctive race derived. This race, the universal source of the "Coriolanean nose," is the very definition of sublimity, both supernal and infernal: bloody secrets, intense passions, cults of blood sacrifice, daring innovations, gloomily terrifying elegiac realisms, Wagnerian heroic pathos, and Dantean visions of heaven and hell. Through various channels, the Aztecs and Mayas, hooknosed Scots and Hittites, Romans, Jews, and Arabs, all derive from this source. The greatest good and worst evil originate and end here. The race of

Havilah are the innermost soul of all mankind, the incarnation of religiosity, the gothic shudder of conscience, and the soaring eagle that dwells with God.

The panel, in its own way, celebrates the poetic principle of the Semitic Enlilship, the principle of ex nihilo innovation, evokings of what "eye hath not seen nor ear heard." The imagery is bizarre enough to have pleased Poe by inspiring a "willing suspension of disbelief." The two dragons are not mere dragons, but especially impossible dragons with the heads and forelegs of horses. The doubleheaded serpent along the base, with its dismembered pair of victims, belongs to the world of Hieronymus Bosch.

The dual feature of the Dragon panel records the sad fact of sectarian schism. The tetrad structure of the panel (two dragons and two victims) arises from the tetrad of Genesis 10:6, Ham's first four postdiluvian sons. By the ninetieth year, Noah's family had generated three linguistic stocks: Ural-Altaics, Hamites, and Semites. In the schism, the Ural-Altaics were divided to achieve a balance of stocks between the two factions; and these two Ural-Altaic divisions embody the two victims. The dragons represent the newer Hamitic and Semitic stocks under their traditional Hamite lords Mizraim and Canaan. The proto-Hellenic Phut (Iapetus) took possession of the western Ural-Altaics, defining them as Finno-Ugrians; and Cush took command of the eastern, Mongol division, who remembered him as Kara Khan, feudal lord of all four antediluvian males in the unique system of Genesis 10:7.

The Hamite regime of the Dragon panel implies that two of the four Hamites were expected to remain loyal to the faction of Noah and Shem. The loyalists were Cush and Phut, making both halves of the older Ural-Altaic stock loyalist counterweights to the Hamites and Semites, now defined as the very Egyptians and Canaanites who antagonized the Israelites in the Exodus of the next millennium. Although Noah's blessing of the "Yahweh Elohim of Shem" transferred the Semites to Shem, Canaan remained in control of them until the 120th year when they reverted to Shem in the land of Akkad.

Geographically, the four points of the Dragon panel represent four locations in South Arabia and Yemen. With practically no ethnographic value of their own, these points served to orient the sons of Ham to the four traditional lands of Ethiopia, Somalia, Egypt, and Palestine. The curving line of the doubleheaded serpent outlines the South Arabian coast between Aden and Hauta. At these positions, Cush and Phut established their traditional orientations to Ethiopia and Somalia, the ancient lands of Cush and Punt. Mizraim and Canaan took the correlative points inland toward Sabaea and Timnah, aligning themselves to the distant lands of Egypt and Palestine.

HIRSCHNATUR PANEL

Geographically, Shem's "Stag Nature" panel corresponds to his original fief of Akkad at the latitude where the two rivers of Mesopotamia draw closest together. The epoch of the panel is the 120th year when Shem had returned from Yemen to Mesopotamia to reign over the dual heritage of Noah's blessing, the Semites of the air god (Hebrew Elohim) and the newly formed Indo-Europeans of Shem's personal storm god (Hebrew Yahweh). The panel expresses the Ishkurship of executive justice in that the Semite stag has been captured from Canaan in accordance with Noah's curse-blessing of Genesis 9:26. The alignments of the two stags, Indo-Europeans on the Euphrates and Semites on the Tigris, resulted from a characteristically heroic initiative by Shem between the ninetieth and 120th years.

Evidence for this initiative is found in the Dragon panel where all four balanced structures are themselves dual. The two victims appear both as trunks and legs, and the two dragons as horses and dragons. This process of subdivision resulted from Shem's counterplot against Canaan's scheme to circumvent the political effects of Noah's curse. Realizing that the Semites would come under Shem's control in the 120th year, Canaan sought to return with them to Mesopotamia, as soon as possible, in order to reestablish Ham's fief in Martu, to the west of Akkad, as his (Canaan's) own eternal inheritance. He knew that the Semites were destined to inhabit Martu and believed that he could undo Shem's claim over them by planting them there in person. Noah's family had approached the West by sea; and their vessels were docked somewhere on the coast of South Arabia. Canaan's plan was to return with the Semites by sea; and he did so.

When Shem discovered the plan, he acted immediately by calling out recruits for a land trek through the heart of the Arabian peninsula directly toward the Martu camp west of the Euphrates. His goal was to capture the Martu fief and combine it with his Akkad fief according to the dual implications of the "Yahweh Elohim of Shem." He lacked the privilege to control the Semites until the 120th year; so he determined to create the Indo-European stock on the spot in South Arabia.

He drew recruits from all four segments of the Dragon panel. Those from the western dragon of Mizraim became Celts; those from the eastern dragon of Canaan (the Semitic stock) became Satem Indo-Europeans; those from the Mongol "victim" toward Aden became Teutons; and those from the Finno-Ugrian "victim" toward Hauta became Hellenes. Additional Indo-European stocks were formed later. But, in a strict sense, Celts are "Aryan Egyptians"; Teutons, "Aryan Huns"; Greeks, "Aryan Finns"; and Persians, Slavs, and East Indians, "Aryan Semites." Shem combined these four primitive stocks into a single force and managed to arrive in Martu before Canaan could approach with the main body of Semites from the Persian Gulf. He then kept the Semites from claiming Martu and pinned them on the Akkadian Tigris, under his own rulership, in the 120th year.

PANEL OF THE BRAIDED GODDESS

Historically, the Braided Goddess panel differs from all others because it has no direct reference to events of its designated period, the thirty years from the 150th to the 180th year. These were the years of the Tower of Babel scheme, when Noah's entire family were in Akkad. Yet the panel refers geographically to Greater Arabia and summarizes the southern and western explorations which had occurred between the thirtieth and 120th years. The purpose of this cryptic juxtaposition of eras was to connect the Tower of Babel scheme with its cultural antecedent: an exhausting tour of lands remote from the capital zone of Mesopotamia.

The theme of the panel can be labeled either the "Empire of Mahadevi," (the Red Matriarch as all-inclusive goddess of the East Indian pantheon) or the "Empire of Ereshkigal," the same Red Matriarch as Sumerian goddess of the underworld. The central subject is the Arabian peninsula as a whole. The attendant females to the upper right and lower left are the same Black Matriarch as mother of the Dravidian Indus and black Ethiopia. The human victim cradled under the goddess' left arm represents both the Hadramaut coast and one of its points, Noahic Camp No. 33, reserved for Noah's son Togarmah, the slain god Dumuzi the Shepherd.

Yet the victim itself, together with the fallen swine, is another representation of the disaster of Genesis 9:20-26. This time the disaster is conceived as a ruined tripartite structure analogous to the ones featured in Noah's own panel of the Boar-Holding Men. This duplication of the tripartite motif resulted from the Red Matriarch's status as Noah's royal wife. If the curse had not occurred, the panel would have pictured the goddess as upholding a male, representative of Ham, upholding, in turn, Canaan in the form of the "Eber." Instead, the figures of Ham and the boar Canaan are thrown on their backs. The political logic of this structure is that Noah had granted to his wife the absolute authority to do with Ham, in Greater Arabia, what he had done with Shem and Japheth in Sumer. As she consummated this goal in South Arabia, the sin of Ham occurred; and the structure was ruined.

An implication is that the ascending tripartite structure featured in Noah's panel was the ideological framework for the Tower of Babel itself. Because the Tower of Babel event occurred in the Red Matriarch's proper era, the panel interprets the divine overthrow of the Tower as a reenactment of Noah's curse on Canaan. Thus the viewpoint of the panel is intimately associated with the authorial viewpoint of Genesis 9-11, where the text implies that the evil of the Tower of Babel originated in the Sin of Ham.

TRINITY PANEL

The central subject of the Trinity Panel is the Yellow Matriarch, mother of Arphaxad I, who is pictured as the bearded god Taranis to the left of the panel. Because both flanking figures assume the "Ka" posture, the panel emphatically declares that the charisma of the dispensation of human government was poured out at the epoch of the Yellow Matriarch 180 years after the Flood. This circumstance would explain why a Mongoloid people, the Japanese, have recalled the image of the "Ka" so clearly as their "banzai." The panel informs us that the Noahic Pentecost occurred soon after the Tower of Babel judgment, affirming that the charismatic privileges of gentile rulership were not cancelled by that judgment. This timing of the Noahic Pentecost also explains why the Sumerian Kinglist mistakenly identifies the epoch of the Flood with that of First Kish, 180 years after the Flood itself. Because the full manifestation of the "Ka" was delayed for 180 years, the conceit of the kinglist is that all the postdiluvian events of the first 180 years were antediluvian, that is, spiritually limited to the pathetic, unempowered status quo of antediluvian man.

The smooth-shaven deity to the right of the panel is Arphaxad's son Obal, the classic sun god of antiquity: Sumerian Utu, Akkadian Shamash, Arabian Hobal, Egyptian Ra, and Hellenic Apollo. The Trinity panel is one of several Gundestrup illustrations of the solar-lunar polarity, in this case supplying the very house of Utu and Nanna. The design of the panel implies that the solar and lunar principle of imperium and kingship were to coexist, just as in the solar and lunar kinglists of the East Indian tradition. In fact, we have every reason to believe that the anachronistic Indian kinglists commenced, in reality, at pre-Sargonic Agade in the 180th year, along with the rulerships of the Sumerian Kinglist at Kish. Only ninety years, three Noahic eras, elapsed from the First Kish epoch to the rise of Sargon at Agade. As Sagara, he was the thirty-seventh king of the Ayodhya line. In ninety years, the previous thirty-six reigns consumed an average of precisely two and a half years or thirty months. Such fixed terms were the invariable rule throughout the second half of the third millennium. Iksh-vaku, founder of the Ayodhya line, began to reign at proto-Agade in the 180th year and reigned just thirty months, in the first of thirty-six such reigns previous to the rise of Sargon. Thus the Trinity panel celebrates the absolute inception of stable monarchy, in Akkad, at a moment identical with the inaugural dates of the First Kish and East Indian kinglists.

These chronological relationships define the Nannaship as a chronological principle. The month is, of course, a lunar unit based on the approximate period of thirty days in which the moon either passes through its phases or returns to a given point against the fixed stars. The year is a solar unit based on the analogous return of the sun to a given point against the stars. In some traditions, the year is rounded to 360 days, a multiple of thirty and the theocratic twelve. The thirty-year era, apparent throughout the structure of Genesis 11, implies a symbolic factoring of sun and moon, the lunar number thirty applied to the solar unit of the year.

Thus, the thirty-year era was a unit of imperium or solar rule; whereas the analogous lunar unit was the lesser order of thirty months. In the Sumerian Kinglist both Sargon and Naram Sin are said to have reigned fifty-six years, the sum of two Noahic eras, reduced from thirty to twenty-eight as in the legendary reign of Osiris. Unlike the earlier reigns of the kinglist, the chronological terms of the Akkadian emperors can be taken literally. These rulers did, in fact, reign for sixty-year periods. But these long reigns resulted from their assumption of full solar imperium, setting aside the lunar kingship principle of earlier times. Manishtushu became the first dynastic Pharaoh Menes because the imperium of his family was the solar Pharaonic institution reserved for full manifestation in the 270th year.

Between the 180th and 270th, the Nannaship held sway; and all reigns were confined to thirty months or some such limited term.[23] Despite the existence of a "solar line" from Iksh-vaku forward, none of the kings of "Ayodhya" enjoyed imperial reigns until the rise of "Sagara." The ninety years from the First Kish epoch to the rise of Sargon can be termed the "Sumerian age," not because the Sumerian language was universally in vogue, but because Noah's family confined themselves to a type of kingship characteristic of pre-Akkadian times when the urban dynasties of Sumerian tradition were first developed.

SPHINX PANEL

In the 240th year, the "Sumerian age" became the Sumerian era in a strict sense. This was the era reserved for the White Matriarch, whose fief was Sumer proper. Within this period occurred the reign of the self-styled Sumerian "emperor" Lugalannemundu. Before the 240th year, Sumerian history was not strictly Sumerian. Too many foreign stocks were dwelling in or near Mesopotamia. In the First Kish period, the entire human race was either between or near the two rivers. The Eanna epoch of the 210th year belonged to the War God of the Black Matriarch and witnessed the formative Erech-Aratta War between certain stocks of Mesopotamia and others which had migrated into central Iran. If the panel of the Black Matriarch were extant, it would have shown the geographic terms of this war. There is no question that the war made Mesopotamia safe for Sumerians. The Sphinx panel, accordingly, celebrates the postwar golden age of Sumer.

The panel is unmistakably Edenic. It complements the Boxer-Dancer panel. The dancing figures in the right of both panels are identical. The central subjects are mother and son, the White Matriarch and Japheth, as are the subjects of the Arabian panels of the two Havilahs, Ham and the Red Matriarch. If the Boxer-Dancer panel celebrates restoration of order in Egypt (together with its allusion to the Mesopotamian war against Iran), the Sphinx panel accomplishes much the same for Sumer, at the opposite end of the Fertile Crescent. The female on either side of the central subject is the same person, Uzal (Inanna), daughter of the White Matriarch and Arphaxad I; but the two versions of this figure are distinct enough to have entered the Sumerian pantheon as two distinct goddesses, Inanna to the left and Ninazimua to the right. The figure to the left embraces a wild animal and, thus, corresponds to the version of Inanna who is accused of mating with a series of animals in the Epic of Gilgamesh. Ninazimua is the wife of Ningishzida, Sumerian pantheon version of Japheth in the Southern Orchard group, where he appears with his father Noah (Ninazu) and son Madai (Damu) by Ninazimua.[24] The name Ninazimua means "Lady Productively Grown Branch" and, thus, explains the ground of leafy vegetation before the dancing figure to the right.

The panel possesses a geographic value for the Lower Euphrates of classic Sumer. In the interior Cernunnus panel representative of Mesopotamia in the earlier First Kish period, the Lower Euphrates appears as a serpent, equivalent to Ningishzida, the Sumerian version of Japheth as earth serpent. The Sphinx panel elaborates the same Lower Euphrates in the later Second Kish era. Because Inanna was a goddess of Erech, the figure embracing an animal orients Erech to the left. The Southern Orchard pantheon of Ninazimua lay down river from Erech, chiefly to the east, therefore to the right. The panel of the Boar-Holding Men pictures Sumer and Elam in more general terms, outlining both the Euphrates and Tigris, as does the Hirschnatur panel in the Akkadian latitude. The Sphinx panel focuses more narrowly on Sumer proper in the proper Sumerian era when regimes existed simultaneously at Sumerian Adab, Lagash, Erech, Ur, Umma, and Akshak, as well as the more distant Kish, Mari, and Awan.

Eight Linguistic Stocks

In the Victorian period, the German philologist Friedrich Max Müller popularized the view that language, rather than genetics, is the chief determiner of cultural identity. His philosophy survives in the generally held view that the Israelites owe more to their membership in the Semitic linguistic stock than to the personal histories of Abraham, Isaac, or Jacob. Although Müller's concept advanced the evolutionary philosophy by undermining the logical prestige of biblical genealogies, it possessed a certain validity. The spiritual power of language to define culture is almost limitless.

Genealogy is a vitally important but subordinate principle in Genesis 10. The dominant factor is feudal sonship, vassalage; and woven across every strand of feudal allegiance is a matching strand of linguistic affinity. Every clan or feudal brotherhood of Genesis 10 contains one and only one formal representative of each of eight languages disseminated over the formative period of the exterior panels. These languages were as follows:

Language of the Anship (Noah)	Ural-Altaic
Language of the Utuship (Japheth)	Hamitic
Language of the Enlilship (Ham)	Semitic
Language of the Ishkurship (Shem)	Indo-European
Language of the Dumuziship (Red Matriarch)	Amerindian
Language of the Nannaship (Yellow Matriarch)	Sino-Tebetan
Language of the Ninurtaship (Black Matriarch)	Austronesian
Language of the Enkiship (White Matriarch)	Sumerian

As a universal summation of languages, this list displays obvious difficulties. Linguists have only occasionally acknowledged the existence of an Amerindian linguistic stock; and whatever unity exists among the Amerindian languages cannot compare with the unity observed among the Semitic, Indo-European, or other groups. If Badiny is correct, there is little radical difference between Sumerian and Finno-Ugrian; and, if Finno-Ugrian is truly a branch of the Ural-Altaic, the distinction between the first and eighth languages is blurred. The Austronesian is a widespread stock extending from Malagasy to Polynesia and including such black peoples as the Papuans and Melanesians. But it fails to include the Dravidian of India or the languages of black Africa; so it remains an imperfect representation of the Black Matriarch's progeny. Finally, the world displays a variety of languages unclassifiable by this system such as the Basque and Etruscan of Europe or the so-called Japhetic of the Caucasus. Insufficient evidence exists for the linguistic identity of the crucial Gutians of Sumerian times; and the Elamite language has been studied but not clearly classified.

Nevertheless, the list represents the best approximation of a universal linguistic octad; and one modern linguist, Trombetti, has suggested that the languages of mankind can, in fact, be reduced to nine types.[26] Six of our eight are especially widespread, suggesting a universal origin, that is, a substantial fractional relationship to the whole of mankind. The two exceptions, Hamitic and Sumerian, remained confined because the bearers of these languages clung tenaciously to their choice homelands in the Fertile Crescent. The important point is that Noah sought for linguistic diversity and a plenitude of languages to capture the spiritual distinctives of the "seven eyes of the Lamb."

NOTES

[1]Despite its pejorative imagery, the clearest pagan version of this system is the Egyptian Ogdoad of Hermopolis. Another important

version, the set of primeval gods at the outset of the Babylonian Marduk Epic, includes all eight survivors of the Flood except for Shem's royal wife, the Yellow Matriarch, Amaunet of the Ogdoad. The Egyptian and Babylonian traditions are described and documented later.

²*The Nile and Egyptian Civilization* (New York: Barnes and Noble, 1972), p. 69.

³Abram's grandfather Nahor I was the Akkadian emperor Naram Sin, who favored the lunar cult at Abram's birthplace, Sumerian Ur. Abram's second city, Syrian Harran, became the chief lunar cult center of the north. Instead of perpetuating the pagan lunar cult, Abram received the Abrahamic covenant from El Shaddai, orthodox counterpart to the lunar "eye" or God as sustainer of individual nations.

⁴A. Falkenstein, "Die Anunna in Der Sumerischen Überlieferung," *Studies in Honor of Benno Landsberger* (Chicago: University Press, 1965), p. 127

⁵*Kingship and the Gods,* p. 150.

⁶Enlil, for example, is the outraged deity who takes the part of Shem's Yahweh in punishing Naram Sin for his transgressions. Kramer, *The Sumerians,* pp. 64-65.

⁷Jacobsen, *Toward the Image of Tammuz,* p. 26.

⁸For the Mesopotamian tradition of the lunar boat see Jacobsen, loc. cit. For the Egyptian, see Olcott's *Field Book of the Skies,* 4th ed. (New York: G. P. Putnam's Sons, 1954), p. 283.

⁹Franz Delitzsch, *A New Commentary on Genesis* (Edinburgh: T. & T. Clark, 1899), II, 32.

¹⁰"The Epic of Gilgamesh," *The Ancient Near East,* ed. James B. Pritchard (Princeton, NJ: University Press, 1958), p. 53.

¹¹Jacobsen, pp. 25-26.

¹²The chain of identities among Ea (Sumerian Enki), Koshar, and Ptah is established by William Foxwell Albright in *Yahweh and the Gods of Canaan* (Garden City, New York: Doubleday, 1969), pp. 136 and 222. In the Memphite Theology, Ptah is the creator of paganism generally, including the idolatrous principle of statuary gods. Frankfort, p. 30.

¹³Kramer, p. 138.

[14]The illustration number 685 is from James B. Pritchard, *The Ancient Near East in Pictures* (Princeton: University Press, 1954), p. 220.

[15]This term is adopted from the German of Rudolf Grosse, whose labels for the other exterior panels are translated here. *Der Silberkessel von Gundestrup* (Dornach, Switzerland: Philosophisch-Anthroposophischer Verlag am Goetheanum, 1963), passim. All photographs of the Gundestrup Caldron have been published by permission of the Danish National Museum.

[16]Ions, p. 14.

[17]Jacobsen, p. 33. The matriarch Sin was "designated for the Yellow Matriarch" but was evidently Noah's daughter by the White Matriarch, taking her Mongoloid character from Noah. The Egyptian depiction of the Yellow Matriarch as Mut is decidedly Mongoloid in appearance; whereas the East Indian version of Sin, Lakshmi, lacks this character except subliminally. The pagans evidently maintained traditions of the actual physical appearance of Noah's family, as well as yielding contemporary portraits from the ruling houses of Mesopotamia and Egypt.

[18]Letopolis was at the second nome of Lower Egypt. Moret, p. 57.

[19]Ibid., p. 70.

[20]The first ten of these Amorite kings are listed in William W. Hallo and William Kelly Simpson, *The Ancient Near East* (New York: Harcourt Brace Jovanovich, 1971), p. 67.

[21]Ions, p. 20.

[22]Zimmerman, p. 52.

[23]The Sumerian Lugalannemundu, who reigned at Adab within the generation preceding the rise of Sargon, claimed a reign of ninety years; but this period was merely the interval from First Kish to the rise of Sargon, claimed abstractly in accordance with the cosmic pretensions of Lugalannemundu's Enamzu temple.

[24]These members of the Sumerian Southern Orchard pantheon are defined by Jacobsen, p. 24.

[25]All of these reigns of the Sumerian Second Kish period are charted in Hallo and Simpson, pp. 52-53.

[26]The nine languages are Caucasian (so-called "Japhetic"), American Indian, Australo-Dravidian, Munda-Polynesian (now

known as "Austronesian"), Indo-Chinese, Hamito-Semitic, Bantu-Sudanese, Uralo-Altaic, and Indo-European. P. E. Cleator, *Lost Languages* (New York: John Day, 1961), p. 16.

Chapter 3

Outline of Identifications

The Political Logic of Genesis 10

The text of Genesis 10 records the political design of the Noahic cosmos at a particular point in time, after the Erech-Aratta War, about 216 years after the Flood. Except for the war, this design would have been even more balanced than it appears. In the war, the loyalist faction of Noah, Shem, and Peleg met defeat from the opposing faction of Canaan, Salah, and Joktan. The only portion of the design relatively unaltered by the outcome was the two perfect Japhethite septads of 10:2-4. These two reveal what the original system consisted of: a complete set of septads, ten in all, yielding seventy politically aligned princes.

Because Peleg (Babylonian Kingu) led the loyalist faction, the victorious Salah (Babylonian Marduk) dissolved his septad, leaving its youngest members visible only in the genealogy of Genesis 11 and distributing the other three among the clans of Cush and Joktan. Shem lost four vassals to Canaan and one to Joktan; and four more appear in Genesis 10:23 as secondary vassals of "Aram," Völkertafel name of Joktan. Yet the most striking result of the war settlement was that all four male survivors of the Flood appear in the Völkertafel as vassals of Ham's son Cush: Shem as "Raamah," Ham as "Havilah," Japheth as "Sheba," and Noah himself as "Dedan."

A rule of the Völkertafel is that its names are a self-contained code, excluding the genealogical names of Genesis 9 and 11. For this reason, members of Shem's genealogy who appear in the Völkertafel must do so under names distinct from the ones appearing in the narrative text. Aside from the antediluvian survivors just named, Shem's son Arphaxad appears in the Völkertafel as the Joktanite

Hadoram; Arphaxad's heir Salah, as the Shemite Arphaxad (Genesis 10:22); Salah's heir Eber, as the Japhethite Tubal; Eber's heir Peleg as the Shemite Lud; and Peleg's brother Joktan as the Shemite Aram. We see the effect of this duplicate naming process, for example, in the contrasting Phrygians and Lydians of Asia Minor. The first nation bears Peleg's genealogical name (Hellenic Phrixus and Teutonic Fricco) and the second bears his Völkertafel name "Lud." Teutonic tradition preserves the same distinction, assigning the Völkertafel name to Peleg, as brother to Joktan (Lodur to Odin), yet reserving Peleg's genealogical name for Frey-Fricco, head of a separate class of gods, the Vanir, distinct from Odin's Aesir race.

The following outline shows the system of Genesis 10 as it existed before the war, but also notes how the princes have been shifted to their extant places in the biblical text. Each entry includes the physical parentage of each prince, whenever this is known, as well as information on political, mythological, and ethnological identities.

Vassals of Japheth: First Seven

Genesis 10:2.

Gomer.

First Hamitic[1] Japhethite

Father:	Japheth
Mother:	Yellow Matriarch
Genetic Keys:	Himerus < Hellenic Lacedaemon
	Hler (Gymir) < Teutonic Fornjot
Portrait:	Memphite Khufu (Cheops)[2]
Kinglist:	Gumalum of Ebla
	Luh-ishan of Awan
	Khufu of Memphis
Pantheon:	Anhur (Egyptian)
	Himavan (East Indian)
	Himerus (Hellenic)
	Hler (Teutonic)
	Llyr (Celtic)
	Luk (Micronesian)
Ethnic:	Cimmerai (Asia Minor)
	Cymru (Britain)
	Egyptians of Memphis
	Chinese Hui
	Lurs (Iran)
	Shans (Burma)

Magog.   First Amerindian Japhethite
    Father: Japheth
    Mother: Red Matriarch
    Genetic Keys: Kari < Teutonic Fornjot
                    Rudra < East Indian Prajapati
    Portrait: East Indian Rudra[3]
    Kinglist: Kalibum of First Kish
                    Igrish-Halam of Ebla

    Pantheon: Hurricano (Amerindian)
                    Kari (Amerindian)
                    Kari (Teutonic)
                    Lei-kung (Chinese)
                    Rudra (East Indian)
                    Upuaut (Egyptian)

    Ethnic: Amazonian-Caribbean Indians
                    Gaels (Britain)
                    Hyrcanians (Iran)
                    Kung (Khoisan Namibia)

Madai.   First Indo-European Japhethite
    Father: Japheth
    Mother: Uzal (Inanna)
    Genetic Keys: Agni < East Indian Dyaus
                    Damu < Sumerian Ningishzida
                    Logi < Teutonic Fornjot
                    Mashda < Sumerian Atab
                    Svarogich < Slavic Svarog
    Portrait: East Indian Agni[4]
    Kinglist: Mashda of First Kish
                    Irkab-Damu of Ebla

    Pantheon: Agni (East Indian)
                    Ahura Mazda (Persian)
                    Damu (Sumerian)
                    Logi (Teutonic)
                    Svarogich (Balto-Slavic)

    Ethnic: Medes (Iran)

Javan.   First Sino-Tibetan Japhethite
    Father: Gomer
    Mother: Caphtor
    Genetic Key: Bran < Celtic Llyr and Don
    Portraits: Memphite Menkaura (Mycerinus)[5]
                    East Indian Soma[6]
    Kinglist: Emperor Yao of the Chinese

	Ar-Ennum of Ebla
	Menkaura of Memphis
	Ibranum of Gutium
Pantheon:	Babilos (Balto-Slavic)
	Bran (Celtic)
	Hyas (Hellenic)
	Hybla (Sicilian)
	Macar (Rhodian)
	Soma (East Indian)
Ethnic:	Iverni (Ireland)
	Cushitic Somali (Somalia)
	Yao (South China and Vietnam)
	Bantu Yao (Mozambique)

Tubal.

First Semitic Japhethite

Genealogical Name:	Eber
Father:	Arphaxad II (Salah)
Mother:	Red Matriarch
Birth Year:	2451 B.C.
Genetic Keys:	Atys < Phrygian Calaus
	Cepheus < Hellenic Belus
	Eber < Hebrew Salah
	Mider < Celtic Dagda
	Nabu < Babylonian Marduk
Portrait (caricature):	East Indian Kubera[7]
Kinglist:	Meskiaggesher of Erech
	Ebrium of Ebla
	Dasharatha of Ayodhya
	Snefru of Memphis
Pantheon:	Athamas (Hellenic)
	Atys (Phrygian)
	Bor (Teutonic)
	Cepheus (Hellenic)
	Cercaphus (Rhodian)
	Mider (Celtic)
	Mithras (Persian)
	Mitra (East Indian)
	Nabu (Babylonian)
	Pollux (Hellenic)
	Tamas (East Indian)
Ethnic:	Borusci (Prussia)
	Caucasian Japhetics
	(Georgian S.S.R.)
	Cephenes (Persia)

                    Hebrews of Palestine
                    Iberians (Spain)

Meshech.

First Ural-Altaic Japhethite	
Father:	Madai
Mother:	Swaha (Daughter of Arphaxad I)
Genetic Key:	Skanda < East Indian Agni and Swaha
Portraits:	East Indian Karttikeya (Skanda)[8]
	Memphite Khafra (Chephren)[9]
Kinglist:	Arurim of First Kish
	Mesgande of Erech
	Khafra of Memphis
	Irarum of the Guti
Pantheon:	Skanda (East Indian)
Ethnic:	Gutians of Iran
	Scythians of Central Asia

Tiras.

First Sumerian Japhethite	
Father:	Tubal (Eber)
Mother:	Caphtor
Birth Year:	2433 B.C.
Genetic Key:	Tyrsenus < Phrygian Atys and daughter of the river god Sangarius (Mizraim)
Kinglist:	Shura-Damu of Ebla
Pantheon:	Turms (Etruscan)
	Tyrsenus (Phrygian)
Ethnic:	Etruscans (Rasena) of Italy
	Sumerians of the Southern Orchard Region (as representative of the god Damu)
	Tyrsenoi (Asia Minor)

Vassals of Japheth: Second Seven

Vassals of Gomer. Genesis 10:3.

Ashkenaz.

Second Ural-Altaic Japhethite	
Father:	Noah
Mother:	Yellow Matriarch
Birth Year:	2513 B.C.
Genetic Keys:	Ashshirgi < Shulpae and Ninhursag

Political Key:	Maka < East Indian Salivahana
	Manawyddan < Llyr
Kinglist:	Alalgar of Eridu
	Ashmaka of Ayodhya
Pantheon:	Budantsar (Mongolian)
	Maka (East Indian)
	Manawyddan (Celtic)
Ethnic:	Budini (Sarmatia)
	Gedrosians (Iran)
	Arabian tribes: Macaei, Manitae
	Mannai (Caucasus)
	Mongols of Tataria

Riphath.

Austronesian (Dravidian) Japhethite

Father:	Noah
Mother:	Black Matriarch
Birth Year:	2512 B.C.
Genetic Key:	Bhat < East Indian Salivahana
Political Key:	Olifat < Micronesian Luk
Kinglist:	Enmenluanna of Badtibira
	Ibate of Gutium
Pantheon:	Bhat (East Indian)
	Sumerian Dumuzi-abzu (male version)
	Durumulun (Australian)
	Olifat (Micronesian)
Ethnic:	Dravidians of India

Togarmah.

Second Sumerian Japhethite

Father:	Noah
Mother:	White Matriarch
Birth Year:	2509 B.C.
Genetic Key:	Thammuz < East Indian Salivahana
Kinglist:	Dumuzi of Badtibira
Pantheon:	Dumuzi the Shepherd (Sumerian)
	Sokar (Egyptian)
	Tammuz (Semitic)
Ethnic:	Sumerians of the Central Herding Region
	Arabian tribes: Thamydeni, Thamyditae
	Tocharians (Central Asia)

Vassals of Javan. Genesis 10:4.

Elishah.

	Second Semitic Japhethite
Father:	Sidon
Mother:	Hamath
Genetic Keys:	Hela < Teutonic Loki
	Lelex < Hellenic Poseidon and
	Libya
Kinglist:	Elilin of Erech
Pantheon:	Chac (Amerindian)
	Hela (Teutonic)
	Lelex (Hellenic)
	Ochimus (Rhodian)
	Sha (Sumerian)
	Usmu (Akkadian)
Ethnic:	Nominal Amerindians:
	Arawak (Caribbean)
	Eyeish (Caddoan Louisiana)
	Nominal Africans:
	Arusi (Cushitic Ethiopia)
	Lele (Bantu Zaire)
	Leleges (Asia Minor)
	East Teutons (Gothic Europe)

Tarshish.

	Second Indo-European Japhethite
Father:	Amor son of Sidon
Mother:	Caphtor
Genetic Keys:	Dylan eil Ton < Celtic Don
	Fenris Wolf < Teutonic Loki
	Phoenix < Hellenic Agenor and
	Telephassa
Kinglist:	Lugal-Tarsi of Erech
	Ka-ap of Abydos
Pantheon:	Dylan eil Ton (Celtic)
	Ed (Amerindian)
	Fenris Wolf (Teutonic)
	Phoenix (Hellenic)
	Triopus (Rhodian)
Ethnic:	Nominal Africans:
	Buye (Bantu Zaire)
	Darasa (Cushitic Ethiopia)
	Boii (Gallic Europe)
	Nominal Amerindians:

Darazhazh-Pawnee (Caddoan
Nebraska)
Phoenicians (Phoenicia)
North Teutons (Scandinavia)

Kitt-im.   Second Amerindian Japhethite
                      Father: Amor son of Sidon
                      Mother: Caphtor
                      Genetic Keys: Amaethon < Celtic Don
                                               Midgard Serpent < Teutonic Loki
                                               Cadmus < Hellenic Agenor and
                                                 Telephassa
                      Kinglist: Lugal-Kitun of Erech
                                               Khetm of Abydos

                      Pantheon: Amaethon   (Celtic)
                                               Cadmus (Hellenic)
                                               Candalus (Rhodian)
                                               Macednus (Hellenic)
                                               Midgard Serpent (Teutonic)
                                               Zac (Amerindian)

                      Ethnic: Nominal Caddoans of North America:
                                                 Elishah. Eyeish (Louisiana)
                                                 Kitt. Caddo (Texas)
                                                 Tarshish. Pawnee (Nebraska)
                                               Cypriotes of Citium
                                               West Teutons (Saxony, Germany,
                                                 Holland, and England)
                                               Nominal Africans:
                                                 Ittu (Cushitic Ethiopia)
                                                 Kisi (Bantu Tanzania)
                                               Macedonians (Macedonia)
                                               Maedi (Thrace)

Rodan-im.   Second Hamitic Japhethite
                      Father: Arphaxad II (Salah) son of Sidon
                      Mother: Hamath
                      Genetic Keys: Angus < Celtic Dagda
                                               Danaus < Hellenic Belus < Posei-
                                                 don and Libya
                                               Sebek < Egyptian Neith
                      Political Key: Tenages < Hellenic Helius
                      Kinglist: Lugal-Kingineshdudu of Erech
                                               Ro of Abydos

                      Pantheon: Angus (Celtic)

	Ansa (East Indian)
	Danaus (Hellenic)
	Kan (Amerindian)
	Sebek (Egyptian)
	Tenages (Rhodian)
Ethnic:	Danaans (Greece)
	Nominal Africans:
	Anag (Nilotic Sudan)
	Angas (Cushitic Nigeria)
	Danakil (Cushitic Ethiopia)
	Gusii (Bantu Tanzania)
	Egyptians of Heliopolis
	Rhodians (Rhodes)

Vassals of Ham

Explicit Vassals of Ham. Genesis 10:6.

Cush.	Ural-Altaic Hamite	
	Father:	Ham
	Mother:	Black Matriarch
	Genetic Keys:	Hyperion < Hellenic Uranus and Gaea
		Kara Khan < Tatar Kudai Bai Ülgön
		Tane-mahuta < Polynesian Raki
		Xuthus < Hellenic Hellen
	Kinglist:	Magalgalla of Kish
		Ush of Umma
		Zoser II of Memphis
		Mandaru of the Amorites
	Pantheon:	Atum-Khepri (Egyptian)
		Chernobog (Balto-Slavic)
		Haia (Sumerians)
		Hyperion (Hellenic)
		Kara Khan (Tatar)
		Tane-mahuta (Polynesian)
		Vidar (Teutonic)
		Xuthus (Hellenic)
	Ethnic:	Cushitic Galla (Ethiopia)
		Bantu Haya (Tanzania)
		Nominal Ural-Altaics:
		Manchus (Manchuria)

Cushitic Mandara (Lake Chad)
Nilotic Mondari (Sudan)

Mizraim. Hamitic Hamite
Father: Ham
Mother: Yellow Matriarch
Genetic Keys: Oceanus < Hellenic Uranus
                     Pan < Hellenic Hermes
                     Pyrshak Khan < Tatar Kudai Bai
                     Ülgön
                     Tangaroa < Polynesian Raki
Kinglist: Enakalle of Umma
                     Sezes of Memphis

Pantheon: Amenominakanushi (Japanese)
                     Farbauti (Teutonic)
                     Min (Egyptian)
                     Mynogan (Celtic)
                     Oceanus (Hellenic)
                     Pan (Hellenic)
                     Pyrshak Khan (Tatar)
                     Sangarius (Phrygian)
                     Tangaroa (Polynesian)

Ethnic: Egyptians of Panopolis
                     Japanese (Japan)

Phut.   Indo-European Hamite
Father: Ham
Mother: White Matriarch
Genetic Keys: Aeolus < Hellenic Hellen
                     Iapetus < Hellenic Uranus
                     Suilap < Tatar Kudai Bai Ülgön
                     Tawhiri-matea < Polynesian Raki
Kinglist: Enlil-gi of Umma
                     Nebkara of Memphis

Pantheon: Aeolus (Hellenic)
                     Iapetus (Hellenic)
                     Stribog (Balto-Slavic)
                     Suilap (Tatar)
                     Tawhiri-matea (Polynesian)

Ethnic: Hellenes of Greece
                     Finno-Ugrians:
                         Hungarians (through Macareus)
                         Lapps
                         Votyaks

Ural-Altaics:
  Samoeds (through Salmoneus)
  Kalmuks (through Halmus)

Canaan.

Semitic Hamite
Father: Ham
Mother: White Matriarch
Genetic Keys: Cronus < Hellenic Uranus
  Dorus < Hellenic Hellen
  Enlil < Sumerian An
  Gunidu < Lagashite Gurmu
  Maricha < East Indian Tattaka
  Shulgi < Sumerian Ur Nammu
  Tös Khan < Tatar Kudai Bai Ülgön
  Tu-matauenga < Polynesian Raki

Kinglist: Aka of Kish
  Gunidu of Lagash
  Ukush of Umma
  Neferkara Huni of Memphis
  Shulgi of Ur

Pantheon: Byelobog (Balto-Slavic)
  Cronus (Hellenic)
  Dorus (Hellenic)
  Enlil (Sumerian)
  Eshmun (Phoenician)
  Hoenir (Teutonic)
  Maricha (East Indian)
  Ra-Harakhte (Egyptian)
  Resheph (West Semitic)
  Shulman (Assyrian)
  Tös Khan (Tatar)
  Tu-Matauenga (Polynesian)

Ethnic: Canaanites of Palestine
  Dorians (Greece)
  Nominal Sudanic tribes:
    Gun (Nigeria)
    Kundu (Cameroon)
  Teutonic Lygians (Poland)
  Nominal Nilotic tribes:
    Shilluks (Sudan)
    Turkana (Kenya)
  Turks (Huns) of Central Asia
  Nominal Bantu Turu (Tanzania)

Vassals transferred from Ham to Joktan as a result of the Erech-Aratta War. Genesis 10:29.

Ophir.   Austronesian Hamite
Antediluvian Black Matriarch
Parentage unknown. Antediluvian land of Cush
(Formal race of Adam)

Pantheon: Bast (Egyptian)
Callisto (Hellenic)
Dumuzi-abzu (Sumerian female
version)
Gaea (Hellenic)
Celtic Earth Mother, wife of Lugh
(Japheth)
Kali (East Indian)
Kauket (Egyptian version of Lahamu)
Babylonian Lahamu, wife of Lahmu
(Japheth)
Ninsun (Sumerian)
Prithivi (East Indian)

Ethnic: All black races of mankind
Austronesian linguistic stock

Havilah I.   Amerindian Hamite
Antediluvian Red Matriarch
Parentage unknown. Antediluvian land of Havilah
(Formal race of Abel)
Portrait: Gundestrup Braided Goddess

Pantheon: Adum (West Semitic)
Coatlicue (Aztec)
Kamrusepas (Hittite)
Mahadevi (East Indian)
Naunet (Egyptian version of Tiamet)
Babylonian Tiamat, wife of Apsu
(Noah)
Wazet-Buto (Egyptian)

Ethnic: All races exhibiting facial concavity
or aquiline noses
Amerindian linguistic stock

Jobab.   Sumerian Hamite
Antediluvian White Matriarch
Parentage unknown. Antediluvian land of Nod
(Formal race of Cain)
Portrait: Egyptian Selket[10]
Gundestrup Sphinx panel

Pantheon:	Hauhet (Egyptian version of Kishar)
	Ishara (Akkadian)
	Babylonian Kishar, wife of Anshar (Ham)
	Kanym (Tatar wife of Ham)
	Leto-Latona (Graeco-Roman mother of Obal)
	Nammu (Sumerian mother of Sidon)
	Nanshe (Sumerian mother of Hamath)
	Nina (Assyrian)
	Ningal (Sumerian mother of Uzal, Obal, and Diklah)
	Ningirda (Sumerian mother of Japheth)
	Selket (Egyptian)
	Tattaka (East Indian mother of Canaan)
	Tlazolteutl (Aztec)
	Uma (East Indian)
Ethnic:	All fairskinned races
	Sumerian linguistic stock

Vassals of Cush

Genesis 10:7. The Cushite clan did not exist before the Erech-Aratta War. Japheth's son Seba and grandson Sabtah belonged to Japheth's own Japhethite A clan in place of Tubal and Tiras, the alien members imported from Salah's family. The three antediluvian sons of Noah had joined his four postdiluvian sons to make up a separate Noahic clan. Tubal and Tiras belonged to the original family of "Poseidon and Libya" (the Javanite clan of 10:4) where Tubal appears under his Hellenic name of Cepheus. Salah (Hellenic Belus) belonged to the same Javanite clan together with his brothers Cepheus and Danaus, Tubal and Rodan. Salah's place in the Semite A clan had been taken by Noah, whose reciprocal vassalage to his son Shem anticipated the reciprocal vassalage of Ham and Cush in the extant clans of 10:6 and 10:7.

Seba.	Hamitic Cushite	
	Father:	Japheth
	Mother:	Black Matriarch

Birth Date:	2515 B.C.
Genetic Key:	Osiris < Egyptian Geb
Portraits:	East Indian Shiva at Elephanta[11]
	Egyptian Colossus of Osiris near
	Aswan[12]
Kinglist:	Ensipazianna of Larak
	Kikku-siwe-tempti of Awan
	Adamu of the Amorites
Pantheon:	Absyrtus (Colchian)
	Adapa (Sumerian)
	Dionysus (Hellenic)
	Fufluns (Etruscan)
	Osiris (Egyptian)
	Sabazius (Thracian)
	Shiva (East Indian)
Ethnic:	Sudanic Africa:
	Adamawa (Cameroon)
	Tiv (Nigeria)
	Negroid Colchians (Hellenic tradition
	of Heroditus)
	Bantu Africa:
	Kikuyu (Kenya)
	Cushitic Africa:
	Siwa (Egypt)
	(For Oceanic blacks see Sabtah below)

Havilah II.

Sumerian Cushite	
Genealogical Name:	Ham
Father:	Noah
Mother:	Red Matriarch
Genetic Keys:	Aranzah < Hittite Anu
	Ham < Hebrew Noah
	Hermes < Dardanian Zeus
Portraits:	Ur Nammu of Ur[13]
	Gundestrup Dragon panel
Kinglist:	Enmebaraggesi of Kish
	Gurmu of Lagash
	Zoser I of Memphis
	Bera of Sodom
	Ur-Nammu of Ur
Pantheon:	An (Sumerian)
	Anshar (Babylonian)
	Anu (Akkadian)
	Aranzah (Hittite)
	Hellen (Hellenic)

Hermes (Hellenic)
Huh (Egyptian version of Anshar)
Kama (East Indian)
Kudai Bai Ülgön (Tatar)
Raki (Polynesian)
Tezcatlipoca (Aztec)
Uranus (Hellenic)
Zehuti (Egyptian)

Ethnic: Africans through Cush:
                    Nilotic Anuak (Sudan)
                    Sudanic Gurma (Upper Volta)
            Hellenes through Phut (Iapetus)
            Polynesians and Japanese through
                    Mizraim (Tangaroa)
            Sumerians of Lagash through
                    Canaan's son Jebus (Ur Nanshe)
            Semitic linguistic stock (lost to Shem)

Sabtah.   Austronesian Cushite
Father: Seba
Mother: Arvad
Birth Year: 2501 B.C.
Genetic Key: Ganesa < East Indian Shiva and
                    Parvati
Kinglist: Yarlagan of Gutium

Pantheon: Ganesa (East Indian)
                    Saft el Hene (Egyptian)

Ethnic: Austronesian stock as reflected in
            members of the Cushite clan:
                    Seba. Andamese
                    Havilah. Polynesians
                    Sabtah. Melanesians
                    Raamah. Malays
                    Sabtechah. Papuans
                    Sheba. Formosans
                    Dedan. Indonesians
                    Nimrod. Micronesians

Raamah.   Indo-European Cushite
Genealogical Name: Shem
Father: Noah
Mother: White Matriarch
Birth Year: 2616 B.C.
Genetic Keys: Aliyan Bal < Ugaritic Dagan
                    Balih < Sumerian Etana

	Dardanus < Dardanian Zeus
	Shem < Hebrew Noah
	Teshub < Subarian Anu
Portraits:	Gundestrup Hirschnatur panel
	Theban Amon with Mut[14]
Kinglist:	Balih of First Kish
	Dadasig of Second Kish
	Tata of Awan
	Atoti I of Thinis-Abydos
	Sahlamu of the Amorites
	Melchizedek of Salem
Pantheon:	Aliyan Bal (Ugaritic)
	Adad (Syrian)
	Amon (Theban Egyptian)
	Amon (Egyptian version of Mummu)
	Brahma (East Indian)
	Dardanus (Trojan-Phrygian)
	Heracles (Hellenic)
	Ishkur (Sumerian)
	Mummu (Babylonian)
	Tar (Balto-Slavic)
	Taru (Hattian)
	Teshub (Subarian)
	Teutates (Celtic)
	Thor (Teutonic)
	Tlaloc (Aztec)
Ethnic:	Aramaeans (Akhlamu) of Syria
	(through Uz)
	Nominal African tribes:
	Cushitic Atta (Algeria)
	Sudanic Mum (Cameroon)
	Indo-European linguistic stock

Sabtechah.   Amerindian Cushite

Father:	Noah
Mother:	Red Matriarch
Birth Year:	2508 B.C.
Genetic Key:	Extrapolation of Noah's male
	colored tetrad. Sabtechah balances
	Seba, Arphaxad I, and Canaan as
	postdiluvian heir of a royal ante-
	diluvian couple.
Portrait:	Theban Mont[15]
Kinglist:	Alulim of Eridu
Pantheon:	Mont (Egyptian)

Tepeyollotl (Aztec)
Zababa (Akkadian)

Ethnic: Amerindians of Northwestern
America
Zapotec (Mexico)

Secondary Cushite vassals of Raamah (Shem). Genesis 10:7. In
this system, Japheth adopts the Yellow Matriarch's Völkertafel name
Sheba for two reasons: (1) to honor the Yellow Matriarch as antediluvian royal wife to the feudal lord Raamah-Shem, and (2) to honor
Gomer, his own son by the Yellow Matriarch, as leading vassal of
the first Japhethite septad. Note that among the "Hamitic" linguistic
stock created by Japheth, the Yellow Matriarch ranks high both as
Nekhebet and as Theban Mut, royal wife of Shem (Amon).

Sheba II.   Sino-Tibetan Cushite

Genealogical Name: Japheth
Father: Noah
Mother: White Matriarch
Genetic Keys: Japheth < Hebrew Noah
Lacedaemon < Dardanian Zeus
Tasmisu < Hittite Anu
Portrait: Gundestrup Boxer-Dancer panel
Kinglist: Atab of First Kish
Merbapen (Atab) of Thinis-Abydos
Zuabu of the Amorites

Pantheon: Dyaus (East Indian)
Fornjot (Teutonic)
Geb (Egyptian)
Horus Khenti-Irti (Egyptian)
Kuk (Egyptian version of Lahmu)
Lac (Vietnamese)
Lacedaemon (Hellenic)
Lahmu (Babylonian)
Lugh (Celtic)
Ningishzida (Sumerian)
Prajapati (East Indian)
Svarog (Balto-Slavic)
Tasmisu (Subarian)
Tonatiuh (Aztec)

Ethnic: Austroasiatics (people of Lac)
Celts listed under princes of
Genesis 10:2-4

Cushitic African tribes (through
   Seba):
   Gomer. Gimira (Ethiopia)
   Magog. Harari (Ethiopia)
   Javan. Somali (Somalia)
   Tubal. Boran (Kenya)
Additional East African tribes
   (through Seba):
   Madai. Nilotic Masai (Tanzania)
   Meshech. Bantu Ganda
     (Uganda)
   Tiras. Bantu Sena (Mozambique)
Kaoshans (Taiwan)
Lacedaemonians (Sparta)
Teutonic Swabians (Germany)
Hamitic linguistic stock (lost to Ham)

Dedan.

Semitic Cushite	
Genealogical Name:	Noah
Father:	Lamech
Mother:	Unknown
Birth Year:	3118 B.C.
Genetic Key:	Sethite genealogy of Genesis 5
Portraits:	Gundestrup panel of the Boar-Holding Men
	East Indian Indra (caricature)
Kinglist:	Etana of First Kish
	Didanu of the Amorites
Pantheon:	Abzu (Sumerian)
	Anu (Subarian version)
	Anu (Ural-Altaic version)
	Apsu (Babylonian)
	Dagan (Semitic)
	Indra of the Maruts (East Indian)
	Ninazu (Sumerian)
	Nun (Egyptian version of Apsu)
	Shulpae (Sumerian)
Ethnic:	All races of mankind
	Ural-Altaic linguistic stock

Vassals of Mizraim

Genesis 10:13-14

Zud-im.   Amerindian Vassal of Mizraim

Father:	Japheth
Mother:	Black Matriarch
Birth Year:	2517 B.C.
Genetic Key:	Seth < Egyptian Geb
Kinglist:	Tudia of the Amorites
Pantheon:	Seth (Egyptian)
	Tupan (Amazonian)
	Typhon (Hellenic)
	Vayu (East Indian)
	Zapana (Peruvian)
Ethnic:	Amazonian Indians

Seth had no Amerindian blood but served politically to divide the Amazonian stock between himself and his Amerindian half-brother Magog. The two appear together in Peruvian tradition as Zapana and Cari. Seth's adoption of the name of the antediluvian Mongoloid ancestor was analogous to his father Japheth's adoption of the name Sheba from the Yellow Matriarch. The transition in sound from "Seth" to "Zud" or "Tudia" is given by the Egyptian variants "Seth" and "Sutech."

Anam-im.	Sino-Tibetan Vassal of Mizraim
Father:	Zud
Mother:	Naphtuh
Genetic Keys:	Anubis < Egyptian Seth and
	Nephthys
	Hanuman < East Indian Vayu
Kinglist:	Anu-banini of the Lullubians
	Hanu of the Amorites
Pantheon:	Anubis (Egyptian)
	Hanuman (East Indian)
Ethnic:	Chinese Han

The Chinese, as distinct from the Ural-Altaic Mongoloids, owe their origin to Japheth, the Hui through his son Gomer and the Han through his grandson Anam. In the Austronesian system of the Cushite clan, Japheth fathered the Kaoshans of Taiwan, erstwhile province of China itself. Anam became a political vassal to Gomer's yellow half-brother Mizraim, proper patriarch of the Japanese.

Lehab-im.   Austronesian Vassal of Mizraim

Father:	Cush
Mother:	Arvad
Genetic Key:	Ninlil < Sumerian Haia and Nissaba
Pantheon:	Amenti (Egyptian) Ninlil (Sumerian)
Ethnic:	Bantu Lubi (Zaire) Lullubians of Iran Tehenus of Libya

Like the Gutians, the Iranian Lullubians are of unknown ethnic and linguistic polarity. It is conceivable that they were remnants of the Austronesian stock defeated in the Erech-Aratta War a century before Naram Sin re-conquered them. As wife to Sumerian Enlil (Canaan), Ninlil mothered Nimrod, Nigi of Aratta, capital of the Ural-Altaic and Austronesian alliance of Iran. The name Nimrod appears independently of biblical tradition in Libya of the Tehenus, where the Bantu stock originated. Although Egyptian tradition fails to picture Amenti as Negroid, the Tehenus themselves were clearly Negroid. Both of Lehab's parents were mulattoes.

Naphtuh-im.	Hamitic Vassal of Mizraim	
	Father:	Japheth
	Mother:	Uzal
	Birth Year:	2451 B.C.
	Genetic Key:	Nephthys < Egyptian Geb and Nut
	Portrait:	Nephthys with Menkaura of Memphis[16]
	Pantheon:	Nephthys, sister-wife of Seth, Lord of Upper Egypt
	Ethnic:	Egyptians of Diospolis Parva in Upper Egypt
Pathrus-im.	Indo-European Vassal of Mizraim	
	Father:	Japheth
	Mother:	Uzal
	Birth Year:	2449 B.C.
	Genetic Keys:	Isis < Egyptian Geb and Nut Ushas < East Indian Dyaus father of Agni
	Portrait:	East Indian Ushas[17]
	Pantheon:	Aurora (Hellenic)

		Isis (Egyptian)
		Nephele (Hellenic)
		Ushas (East Indian)
	Ethnic:	Phrygians (through Peleg, Horus son of Isis)

Masluh-im. Sumerian Vassal of Mizraim

Father:	Mizraim
Mother:	White Matriarch
Genetic Keys:	Inachus < Hellenic Oceanus
	Ur-Lumma < Enakalle of Umma
Kinglist:	Mesilim of Kish
	Ur-Lumma of Umma
Pantheon:	Bile (Celtic)
	Byleist (Teutonic)
	Inachus (Hellenic)
	Maslum (North American)
Ethnic:	Lycaonians (Asia Minor)
	Lukayo (Caribbean)
	Massylians (Algeria)
	Pelasgian Vlachs (Greece, Yugo-slavian Macedonia, and Rumania)
	Philistines (Palestine)
	Sumerians of Kish

The Hellenic genealogy of Inachus reads as follows: Oceanus, Inachus, Phoroneus, Pelasgus, and Lycaon.

Caphtor-im. Semitic Vassal of Mizraim

Father:	Mizraim
Mother:	White Matriarch
Genetic Key:	Don < Celtic Mynogan
Pantheon:	Don (Celtic)
	Mertseger (Egyptian)
	Minoan Serpent Goddess (Crete)
Ethnic:	Minoans of Crete

Vassals of Canaan

Genesis 10:15-17.

Sidon.   Sumerian Canaanite

Father:	Canaan
Mother:	White Matriarch
Birth Year:	2499 B.C.
Genetic Keys:	Enki < Sumerian Enlil and Nammu
	Poseidon < Hellenic Cronus
	Sidon < Hebrew Canaan
Portrait:	Gudea of Lagash[18]
Kinglist:	Iltasadum of First Kish
	Dumuzi the Fisherman of Erech
	Kalbum of Second Kish
	Gadhi of the East Indian lunar line
	Gudea of Lagash
Pantheon:	Enki (Sumerian)
	Kapula (Balto-Slavic)
	Karibu Ea (Babylonian)
	Kasyapa (East Indian)
	Loki (Teutonic)
	Poseidon (Hellenic)
	Ptah (Egyptian)
Ethnic:	Nominal Amerindians (through Khetm):
	Caddoans (Louisiana-Texas)
	Carib (Caribbean)
	Egyptians of Heliopolis (through grandson Rodan)
	Gauls (through grandson Tarshish)
	Nominal Africans (through half-brother Nimrod):
	Sudanic Gude (Nigeria)
	Nilotic Iteso (Uganda)
	Bantu Kuba (Zaire)
	Sumerians of Southeastern Marsh Region (people of Enki)
	East Teutonic Sidones (through son Elishah)
	West Teutons (through grandson Kitt)

Note that the four Javanites of Sidon's "Libyan" family form a continuous chain of nominal Bantu tribes from the position of the Kuba southeastward to Lake Nyasa: Lelex, the Lele on the upper Sankuru River, west of the Kuba; Tarshish-Boii, the Buye, west of Lake Tanganyika; Kitt-, the Kisi, on the north shore of Lake Nyasa; and Rodan, Sumerian Lugal-Kingineshdudu, the Kinga, southeast of the Kisi.

Heth.   Amerindian Canaanite
                    Father: Canaan (Resheph)
                    Mother: Red Matriarch (Adum)
                    Genetic Keys: Hades < Hellenic Cronus
                                         Heth < Hebrew Canaan
                    Kinglist: Iksh-vaku of Ayodhya
                                         Ukkutahesh of Awan
                                         Deva-kshattra of the East Indian
                                             lunar line

                    Pantheon: Hades (Hellenic)
                                         Tlaltecutli (Aztec)

                    Ethnic: Teutonic Chatti (Germany)
                                         Amerindian Dakota (North
                                             American)
                                         Nominal Africans:
                                             Sudanic Ekiti (Nigeria)
                                             Nilotic Ikasa (Congo)
                                             Bantu Kota (Congo)
                                             Bantu Kutshu (Zaire)
                                         Hatti (Anatolia)

Jebus-ite.   Indo-European Canaanite
                    Father: Canaan
                    Mother: Uzal
                    Genetic Keys: Amar Sin < Sumerian Shulgi
                                         Ur-Nanshe < Sumerian Gunidu
                                         Zeus < Hellenic Cronus and Rhea
                    Portrait: Ur-Nanshe Plaque of Lagash
                    Kinglist: Haryashva of Ayodhya
                                         Ur-Nanshe of Lagash
                                         Amar Sin of Ur

                    Pantheon: Horus of Edfu (Egyptian)
                                         Jupiter (Roman)
                                         Ullikummi (Subarian)
                                         Zeus (Hellenic)

                    Ethnic: Canaanites of Jebusi (Jerusalem)
                                         Nominal Africans:
                                             Sudanic Ijebu, Jibu, Ibo, and Ijaw
                                                 (Nigeria)
                                         Italic stock (Italy)
                                         Teutonic Marsi (Germany)

Amor-ite.   Semitic Canaanite
                    Father: Sidon

Mother:	Jerah
Genetic Keys:	Agenor < Hellenic Poseidon
	Nefertum < Egyptian Ptah and
	Hathor
Kinglist:	Akwaruwash of the Amorites
Pantheon:	Agenor (Hellenic)
	Nefertum (Egyptian)
Ethnic:	Amorites (Amurru) of Martu
	Nominal Africans:
	Sudanic Akyen (Nigeria)
	Nilotic Moru (Sudan)
	Teutonic Oqueni (Germany)

Girgash-ite.   Ural-Altaic Canaanite

Father:	Jebus
Mother:	Jerah
Genetic Keys:	Ahy < Egyptian Horus of Edfu
	and Hathor
	Akurgal < Sumerian Ur-Nanshe
	Ares < Hellenic Zeus and Hera
	Mogalla < East Indian Haryashva
Kinglist:	Mogalla of Ayodhya
	Akurgal of Lagash
Pantheon:	Ahy (Egyptian)
	Ares (Hellenic)
Ethnic:	Nominal Africans:
	Bantu Gogo (Tanzania)
	Cushitic Goroa (Tanzania)
	Sudanic Igala and Iyala (Nigeria)
	Khoisan Koroca (Angola)
	Albanian Ghegs
	Koreans (Korea)

Hiv-ite.   Hamitic Canaanite

Father:	Jebus
Mother:	Jerah
Genetic Keys:	Hephaestus < Hellenic Zeus and
	Hera
	Kampilya < East Indian Haryashva
	Mugamimla < Sumerian Ur-Nanshe
Kinglist:	Kampilya of Ayodhya
	Mugamimla of Lagash
Pantheon:	Hapi (Egyptian god of the Nile)
	Hephaestus (Hellenic)

Ethnic:	Egyptians of Edfu (as representative of Jebus)
	Hivites (Palestine)
	Hurrians (Subaria)
	Nominal Africans:
	Sudanic Chamba and Mambila (Nigeria)
	Khoisan Hukwe (Botswana)

Ark-ite. Austronesian Canaanite

Father:	Jebus
Mother:	Black Matriarch
Genetic Key:	Arcas < Hellenic Zeus and Callisto
Kinglist:	Argandea of Erech
Pantheon:	Arcas (Hellenic)
	Markandeya (East Indian)
Ethnic:	Sudanic Arago and Margi (Nigeria)
	Australian Aborigines (Aranda-Arunta)
	Nominal Arcadians (Greece)
	Khoisan Kindiga (Tanzania)
	Bantu Rundi (Burundi)

As sons of Jebus, Girgash, Hiv, and Ark form a genetic unit and are represented systematically among Khoisan tribes strung west to east from the Atlantic to the Indian Ocean: the Koroca on the coast of Angola, Hukwe in northern Botswana, and the Kindiga in northern Tanzania. Because Jebus was himself a son of Uzal (Inanna), the Elamite goddess Usan, a focal point for the Khoisan stock is the Nusan on the border of Botswana and Namibia.

Vassals of Shem: First Seven

Explicit Vassals of Shem. Genesis 10:22.

Elam. First Austronesian Shemite

Father:	Arphaxad II (Salah)
Mother:	Black Matriarch
Genetic Keys:	Gilgamesh < Sumerian Lugalbanda and Ninsun
	Ogma < Celtic Dagda
	Yama (Yima) < East Indian Surya

	Yamm < Ugaritic Tr Il
Kinglist:	Gilgamesh of Erech
Pantheon:	Gilgamesh (Sumerian)
	Ha (Egyptian)
	Ilus II (Dardanian)
	Jemshid (Persian)
	Lagomar (Elamite)
	Ogma (Celtic)
	Yama (East Indian)
	Yamm (Ugaritic)
Ethnic:	Elamites (Iran)
	Austronesians of Malagasy:
	Hova, Sakalava
	Bantus of Africa:
	Giryama (Kenya)
	Ha (Tanzania)
	Ila (Zambia)
	Ova Herero (Namibia)
	Additional African tribes:
	Khoisan Nama (Namibia)
	Nilotic Nyima (Sudan)
	Sudanic Tusyam (Upper Volta)

Shem's first vassal Elam was to the Elamites what Shem himself was to the Aramaeans. In the Austronesian system, the same dualism applies to the closely related Malays of Raamah (Shem) and the people of Malagasy.

Asshur.	First Semitic Shemite
Father:	Arphaxad II (Salah)
Mother:	Jerah
Genetic Keys:	Assaracus < Dardanian Tros-Ilus
	Athtar < Ugaritic Tr Il and
	Asherah
	Bodb Dearg < Celtic Dagda
	Manu < East Indian Surya
Kinglist:	Kaushika of East Indian lunar line
	Hishur of Awan
	Ishbi-Erra of Isin
	Ushpia of Assur
Pantheon:	Ashur (Assyrian)
	Assaracus (Dardanian)
	Athtar (Ugaritic)
	Bodb Dearg (Celtic)

Mannus (Teutonic)
Manu (East Indian)

Ethnic:

Assyrians
Rhenish Germans:
  Batavi
  Chauci
  Franks (through Pransu son
    of Manu)
  Frisians (through Prishadra
    son of Manu)
  Hermiones (through son of
    Mannus)
  Ingaevones (through son of
    Mannus)
  Istaevones (through son of
    Mannus)
  Usipetes
Nominal Africans:
  Bantu Aushi (Zambia)
  Sudanic Sia (Upper Volta)
  Nilotic Suri (Sudan)

Arphaxad.

First Indo-European Shemite

Genealogical Name: Salah
Father: Sidon
Mother: Uzal
Birth Year: 2481 B.C.
Genetic Keys: Belus < Hellenic Poseidon
Daksha II < < Daksha I
Marduk < Babylonian Ea
Surya < East Indian Kasyapa and
  Aditi
Political Key: Tros-Ilus < Dardanian Erichthonius
Portrait: East Indian Surya[19]
Kinglist: Barsalnunna of First Kish
Lugalbanda of Erech
Tuge of Second Kish

Pantheon: Actis (Rhodian)
Agdistis (Phrygian)
Asalluhe (Sumerian)
Belus (Hellenic)
Buri (Teutonic)
Calaus (Phrygian)
Dagda (Celtic)
Khnum (Egyptian)

Marduk (Babylonian)
Mars (Roman)
Surya (East Indian)
Tr Il (Ugaritic)
Tue (Teutonic)

Ethnic: Celtic Gauls (Gaul and Galatia)
                    Nominal African tribes:
                        Nilotic Banda (Central African
                            Republic)
                        Bantu Sele (Angola)

Lud.   First Amerindian Shemite
Genealogical Name: Peleg
Father: Tubal (Eber)
Mother: Pathrus
Birth Year: 2417 B.C.
Genetic Keys: Har-Iset < Egyptian Isis
                    Lakshmana < East Indian
                        Dasharatha
                    Lodur < Teutonic Bor
                    Lydus < Anatolian Atys
                    Peleg < Hebrew Eber
                    Phrixus < Hellenic Athamas and
                        Nephele
Portrait: Gundestrup Cernunnus panel
Kinglist: Puru-ravas of the East Indian
                        lunar line
                    Kullassina-ib'el of First Kish
                    Suhkeshdanna of Aratta
                    Peli of Awan
                    Ibbi-Sipish of Ebla

Pantheon: Bhrigu (East Indian)
                    Cernunnus (Celtic)
                    Frey (Teutonic)
                    Horon (West Semitic)
                    Horus son of Isis (Egyptian)
                    Kingu (Babylonian)
                    Lakshmana (East Indian)
                    Lodur Ve (Teutonic)
                    Lydus (Phrygian)
                    Nergal-Irra (Sumero-Akkadian)
                    Perkuna (Balto-Slavic)
                    Phrixus (Hellenic)
                    Prometheus (Hellenic)
                    Puluga (Andamese)
                    Xiuhtecutli (Aztec)

Ethnic: North Americans:
                    Algonquians (through son Reu)
                    Iroquoians
                    Muskogians (through grandson
                      Rimush)
                    Indo-Europeans:
                    Burgundians (Teutonic Vistula
                      and Burgundy)
                    Lydians (Lydia)
                    Phrygians (Phrygia)
                    Nominal Africans:
                    Iraqw (Cushitic Tanzania)

Aram.   First Sumerian Shemite
                 Genealogical Name: Joktan
                 Father: Tubal (Eber)
                 Mother: Uzal
                 Birth Year: 2423 B.C.
                 Genetic Keys: Car < Phrygian Atys
                                      Joktan < Eber
                                      Melicertes < Hellenic Athamas
                                        and Ino
                                      Odin < Teutonic Bor
                                      Ramachandra < East Indian
                                        Dasharatha
                                      Shara < Sumerian Inanna
                 Portraits: East Indian Vishnu with Lakshmi[20]
                                      East Indian Striding Vishnu[21]
                 Kinglist: Vishamsu of the East Indian
                                        lunar line
                                      Enmerkar of Erech
                                      Enetarzi of Lagash
                                      Ramachandra of the East Indian
                                        solar line
                                      Emsu of the Amorites

                 Pantheon: Car (Phrygian)
                                      Darya (Andamese)
                                      Esus (Celtic)
                                      Melicertes (Hellenic)
                                      Melqart (West Semitic)
                                      Odin (Teutonic)
                                      Ramachandra (East Indian)
                                      Shara (Sumerian)
                                      Vishnu (East Indian)
                                      Yarilo (Balto-Slavic)

Ethnic: Armenians (Armenia)
                         Carians (Asia Minor)
                         beni-Khitan (Arabia)
                         Khitans (Inner Mongolia)
                         Sumerians of the Farming Region

Vassal transferred from Shem to Joktan as a result of the Erech-
Aratta War. Genesis 10:28.

Sheba.   First Sino-Tibetan Shemite
              Antediluvian Yellow Matriarch
              Parentage unknown. Antediluvian land of the Sethites
                 (Formal race of Seth)
              Portrait: Theban Mut with Amon[22]

              Pantheon: Amaunet (Egyptian)
                                    Chalchiuhtlicue (Aztec)
                                    Durga (East Indian)
                                    Hannahannas (Hattian)
                                    Mut (Egyptian)
                                    Nekhebet (Egyptian)
                                    Ninhursag (Sumerian)

              Ethnic: Linguistic Sino-Tibetan stock.
                                    Reinforcement of Noah's genetic
                                      influence in determining all
                                      Mongoloid races and all other
                                      races displaying marked
                                      brachycephalism.

Vassal transferred from Shem to Canaan as a result of the Erech-
Aratta War. Genesis 10:18.

Hamath.   First Hamitic Shemite
              Father: Noah
              Mother: White Matriarch
              Birth Years: 2513 B.C.
              Genetic Keys: Anath < Ugaritic Dagan
                                    Ninmar < Sumerian Nanshe
              Portrait: East Indian Sarasvati[23]

              Pantheon: Anath (West Semitic)
                                    Hebat (Subarian)
                                    Libya (Hellenic)
                                    Neith Tehenut (Egyptian)
                                    Ninmar (Sumerian)
                                    Pallas Athena (Hellenic)

	Sarasvati (East Indian)
	Xochiquetzal (Aztec)
Ethnic:	Danaan Greeks (through son Rodan)
	Egyptians of Sais
	East Teutons (through son Elishah)

Vassals of Shem: Second Seven

Vassals transferred from Shem to Aram (Joktan) as a result of the Erech-Aratta War. Genesis 10:23.

Uz.

Second Semitic Shemite

Father:	Shem
Mother:	Red Matariarch
Genetic Keys:	Magni < Teutonic Thor
	Quetzalcoatl < Aztec Coatlicue and Ometeotl
Portrait:	Quetzalcoatl of Mexico[24]
Kinglist:	Lugalanda of Lagash
Pantheon:	Human (Elamite)
	Kukulcan (Mayan)
	Magni (Teutonic)
	Martu (West Semitic)
	Martu (Sumerian)
	Quetzalcoatl (Aztec)
	Umman (Assyrian)
Ethnic:	Aramaeans of Syria
	Cuman Uzes (Central Asia)
	Galindae (Sarmatia)
	Meso-Americans:
	Mayans, Uto-Aztecans
	Nilotic Lendu (Zaire)

Hul.

Second Austronesian Shemite

Father:	Shem
Mother:	Black Matriarch
Genetic Keys:	Wild Bull Dumuzi < Sumerian Ninsun
	Huitzilopochtli < Aztec Ometeotl
	Hullr < Teutonic Thor
	Hyllus < Hellenic Heracles
Kinglist:	Urukagina of Lagash
Pantheon:	Cagn (Khoisan African)

Wild Bull Dumuzi (Sumerian)
Huitzilopochtli (Aztec)
Hullr (Teutonic)
Hyllus (Hellenic)
Kemur (Egyptian)

Ethnic: Nilotic Acholi (Uganda)
                                 Khoisan linguistic stock of
                                     South Africa
                                 Bantu Nkole (Uganda)
                                 Olmecs (Mexico)

Gether.   Second Ural-Altaic Shemite
                   Father: Shem
                   Mother: Hamath
                   Genetic Keys: Agathyrsus < Hellenic Heracles
                                      Xipe Totec < Aztec Ometeotl
                   Kinglist: Gaur of First Kish
                                      Lugalure of Erech

                   Pantheon: Agathyrsus (Hellenic)
                                      Xipe Totec (Aztec)

                   Ethnic: Agathyrsians (Sarmatia)
                                      Nominal Nilotic Alur (Uganda)

Mash.   Second Indo-European Shemite
                   Father: Shem
                   Mother: Hamath
                   Genetic Keys: Camaxtli < Aztec Ometeotl
                                      Madhe < Teutonic Thor
                                      Math < Ugaritic Aliyan Bal
                                          and Anath
                                      Sarruma < Subarian Teshub
                                          and Hebat
                                      Scythes < Hellenic Heracles
                   Kinglist: Madhu of the East Indian lunar line

                   Pantheon: Camaxtli (Aztec)
                                      Khenti-Amentiu (Egyptian)
                                      Madhe (Teutonic)
                                      Math (West Semitic)
                                      Sarruma (Subarian)
                                      Scythes (Hellenic)

                   Ethnic: Nominal Nilotic Madi (Uganda)
                                      Sarmatians (Sarmatia)

Note that the Nilotes have distributed names of the four princes

of Genesis 10:23 in a brief compass along the northwestern and
northern borders of Uganda: Uz (Lugalanda), the Lendu, on the
western shore of Lake Albert; Hul, the Acholi, in northern Uganda;
Gether (Lugalure), the Alur, north of Lake Albert; and Mash
(Madhu), the Madi, on the Uganda-Sudan border, west of the Acholi
and north of the Alur.

Vassals transferred from Shem to Canaan as a result of the Erech-
Aratta War. Genesis 10:17-18.

Sin.

Second Sino-Tibetan Shemite
Father:	Noah
Mother:	White Matriarch
Birth Year:	2511 B.C.
Genetic Key:	Artemis < Leto
Portrait:	East Indian Lakshmi with Vishnu[25]
Kinglist:	Ku-Bau of Second Kish
Pantheon:	Artemis (Hellenic)
	Bau (Nininsina) of Isin (Sumerian)
	Diana (Roman)
	Lakshmi (East Indian)
Ethnic:	Sumerians of Isin
	Tibetans (Bautae)

Arvad.

Second Hamitic Shemite
Father:	Noah
Mother:	Black Matriarch
Birth Year:	2510 B.C.
Portrait:	East Indian Parvati[26]
Pantheon:	Nissaba (Sumerian)
	Parvati (East Indian)
	Seshat (Egyptian)
Ethnic:	Cushitic linguistic stock of Africa
	(through Seba)
	Nominal Cushitic tribe:
	Sab (Somalia)
	Egyptians of Hermopolis Magna

Zemar.

Second Amerindian Shemite
Father:	Noah
Mother:	Red Matriarch
Birth Year:	2512 B.C.

Portrait:	Egyptian Mayet[27]
Pantheon:	Aia (Akkadian)
	Ganga (East Indian)
	Mayet (Egyptian)
	Peruvian Moon Goddess (wife of Inti)
	Shenirda (Sumerian wife of Utu)
Ethnic:	Andean stock of South America
	Nominal Andean tribe:
	Aymara (Bolivia)

Vassals of Joktan

Genesis 10:26-28.

Sheleph.

Indo-European Joktanite	
Father:	Obal
Mother:	Almodad
Genetic Key:	Aesculapius < Hellenic Apollo and Coronis
Pantheon:	Aesculapius (Hellenic)
Ethnic:	Slavs (Eastern Europe)

Hazarmaveth.

Ural-Altaic Joktanite	
Father:	Arphaxad II (Salah)
Mother:	Jerah
Genetic Key:	Mot < Ugaritic Tr Il and Asherah
Kinglist:	Lugalannemundu of Adab
Pantheon:	Mot (West Semitic)
Ethnic:	Khazars (Central Asia)

Jerah.

Semitic Joktanite	
Father:	Obal
Mother:	Uzal
Genetic Keys:	Hathor < Egyptian Ra
	Hera < Hellenic Rhea
Pantheon:	Asherah (West Semitic)
	Hathor (Egyptian)
	Hera (Hellenic)
Ethnic:	Arabs of Hadramaut (through Hazarmaveth)

Hurrian-Subarians (through Hiv)
Koreans (through Girgash)
Semites of Ugarit

Hadoram. Sino-Tibetan Joktanite
Genealogical Name: Arphaxad
Father: Shem
Mother: Yellow Matriarch
Birth Year: 2516 B.C.
Genetic Keys: Arphaxad < Hebrew Shem
                   Erichthonius < Trojan Dardanus
                   Khons < Hellenic Amon and Mut
                   Telepinu < Hattian Taru
Portrait: Taranis of the Gundestrup Taranis
                   panel
Kinglist: Enmedaranna of Sippar
                   Enmenunna of First Kish
                   Menunna of Second Kish
                   Shushuntarana of Awan
                   Emperor Shun of the Chinese
                   Ur-Bau of Lagash

Pantheon: Adranus (Sicilian)
                   Daksha I (East Indian)
                   Erichthonius (Hellenic)
                   Khons (Egyptian)
                   Mesyevets (Balto-Slavic)
                   Nanna (Sumerian)
                   Saturnus (Roman)
                   Suen (Akkadian)
                   Taranis (Celtic)
                   Tecciztecatl (Aztec)
                   Telepinu (Hattian)
                   Yerikh (Ugaritic)

Ethnic: Adorsi (Prussia)
                   Latini (through the line of Saturnus
                   to Latinus)
                   Bantu Shona (Zimbabwe)
                   Tai (Thailand)

Uzal.   Sumerian Joktanite
Father: Hadoram (Arphaxad I)
Mother: White Matriarch
Birth Year: 2500 B.C.
Genetic Keys: Diti < East Indian Daksha I
                   Inanna < Sumerian Nanna and

	Ningal
Portrait:	Medb of the Gundestrup Medb panel
Symbolic Design:	Geb-Nut Cosmos[28]
Pantheon:	(A)diti (East Indian)
	Ashtart (West Semitic)
	Eshtar-Anunitum (Akkadian)
	Inanna (Sumerian)
	Ino (Hellenic)
	Medb (Celtic)
	Nanna (Teutonic)
	Nut (Egyptian)
	Rhea (Hellenic)
	Stone Mother of Ullikummi
	(Subarian)
	Surya (East Indian female version)
	Usan (Elamite)
Ethnic:	Oscan Italoi (Italy)
	Osyli (Sarmatia)
	Romans (through Jebus)
	Sumerians of the Herding Region
	(through Togarmah)

Diklah.

	Austronesian Joktanite
Father:	Hadoram (Arphaxad I)
Mother:	White Matriarch
Genetic Key:	Ninhar < Sumerian Nanna and
	Ningal
Pantheon:	Ninhar (Sumerian)
	Tukla (Balto-Slavic)
Ethnic:	Scoloti (Sarmatia)
	Siculi (Sicily)
	Austronesian Tagala (Philippines)

Obal.

	Hamitic Joktanite
Father:	Hadoram (Arphaxad I)
Mother:	White Matriarch
Genetic Key:	Utu < Sumerian Nanna and Ningal
Portrait:	Gundestrup Trinity panel (smooth-shaven male)
Kinglist:	Melam-Kish of First Kish
	Hatanish of Hamazi
Pantheon:	Apollo (Hellenic)
	Aten (Egyptian)

Baldur (Teutonic)
Dazhbog (Balto-Slavic)
Hobal (Arabian)
Inti (Peruvian)
Ra (Egyptian)
Shamash (Akkadian)
Utu (Sumerian)

Ethnic: Apulians (Italy)
                       Egyptians of Xois
                       Ophlones (Sarmatia)

Vassals of Peleg

Vassal transferred from Peleg to Cush as a result of the Erech-Aratta War. Genesis 10:8.

Nimrod.   Ural-Altaic Pelegite
                   Father: Canaan
                   Mother: Lehab
                   Genetic Keys: Ninurta < Sumerian Enlil
                                        and Ninlil
                                      Shu Sin < Sumerian Shulgi
                   Portrait: East Indian Varuna[29]
                   Kinglist: Nigi of Aratta
                                      Ilshu of Mari
                                      Lugalzagesi of Erech
                                      Iangi of the Amorites
                                      Shu Sin of Ur

                   Pantheon: Helius (Hellenic tradition of Rhodes)
                                      Illuyankas (Hattian)
                                      Ion (Hellenic tradition of
                                        Ionia-Caria)
                                      Ninigi (Japanese)
                                      Ninurta (Sumerian)
                                      Orion (Hellenic tradition of Chios)
                                      Shu (Egyptian)
                                      Varpulis (Balto-Slavic)
                                      Varuna (East Indian)

                   Ethnic: African tribes:
                                        Sudanic Anyang (Cameroon)
                                        Sudanic Anyi (Ivory Coast)
                                        Nilotic Yangere (Central African
                                          Republic)

Bantu Yeke (Zaire)

Vassals transferred from Peleg to Joktan as a result of the Erech-Aratta War. Genesis 10:26, 28.

Almodad.
Austronesian Pelegite
Father: Eber
Mother: Pathrus
Genetic Key: Sibling relationship of
                       Bilika to Puluga (Andamese)
                       Freya to Frey (Teutonic)
                       Helle to Phrixus (Hellenic)

Pantheon: Aphrodite (Hellenic)
                     Bilika (Andamese)
                     Coronis (Hellenic)
                     Helle (Hellenic)
                     Pele (Polynesian)

Ethnic: Polynesians

Abimael.
Indo-European Pelegite
Father: Javan (Soma)
Mother: Uzal (Surya)
Genetic Key: Caradoc < Celtic Bran

Pantheon: Caradoc (Celtic)

Ethnic: Kurds of Kurdistan

Vassals of Peleg dropped from the Völkertafel as a result of the Erech-Aratta War. Genesis 11:18-22.

Reu.
Amerindian Pelegite
Father: Peleg
Mother: Hellenic Chalciope, daughter of
                       Aeetes son of Nimrod (Helius)
Birth Year: 2387 B.C.
Genetic Keys: Argus < Hellenic Phrixus and
                       Chalciope
                     Reu < Hebrew Peleg
Kinglist: Sargon of Agade
                     Sagara of Ayodhya

Pantheon: Argus (Hellenic)

Ethnic: Algonquians of North America
                     Argives (Greece)

Nilotic Nzakara, Kara, and Sokoro
(Central African Republic
and Chad)
Bantu Sagara (Tanzania)

Serug.

Hamitic Pelegite	
Father:	Reu
Mother:	Tashlultum
Birth Year:	2355 B.C.
Genetic Keys:	Manishtushu < Akkadian Sargon and Tashlultum
	Schoeneus < Hellenic Argus
	Serug < Hebrew Reu
Kinglist:	Manishtushu of Agade
	Asa-Manja of Ayodhya
	Menes of Abydos
Pantheon:	Schoeneus (Hellenic)
Ethnic:	North Americans: Cherokee, Shawnee
	Egyptians of Thinis
	Nilotic Manja (Central African Republic)
	Bantu Tussi (Uganda)

Nahor.

Sumerian Pelegite	
Father:	Serug
Mother:	Unidentified
Birth Year:	2325 B.C.
Genetic Keys:	Naram Sin < Akkadian Manishtushu
	Nahor < Hebrew Serug
Portraits:	Narmer Palette
	Naram Stele[30]
Kinglist:	Naram Sin of Agade
	Karambha of the East Indian lunar line
	Narmer of Abydos
Ethnic:	Sumerians of the lunar cult at Ur

Terah.

Semitic Pelegite	
Father:	Nahor
Mother:	Tutashar-libbish
Birth Year:	2296 B.C.
Genetic Keys:	Sharkalisharri < Akkadian Naram Sin

	Terah < Hebrew Nahor
Kinglist:	Sharkalisharri of Agade
Ethnic:	Hebrews of Ur

NOTES

[1]The final adjective in each of these labels refers to language. The whole label, in this case, means "representative of the Hamitic tongue in the first clan of Japheth." The linguistic function of the princes of Genesis 10 was formative but never exclusive. As Gumalum of Ebla, Gomer presumably spoke Semitic, not Hamitic. Most of the nations listed in Gomer's ethnology section are not Hamitic speakers. The Lurs, for example, speak Indo-European in keeping with Gomer's high importance as Llyr of the Celts. Yet the Noahic council yielded Gomer a special relationship to the Hamitic stock, realized when he became Khufu, founder of the Pyramid Dynasty, and reflected in a fraction of the stock, listed in the ethnology section as "Egyptians of Memphis."

[2]I. E. S. Edwards, et al., *Ancient Egypt* (Washington, D.C.: National Geographic Society, 1968), p. 83. Gomer's Mongoloid origin in three quarters is quite apparent in this contemporary portrait.

[3]Ions, p. 36. Note that these statues have value in establishing posture, symbolic dress, and general ethical motif even when the features have little value as physical portraits. The wild, curly locks of this version of Rudra aptly characterize a prince known in another culture as Hurricano, "the Hurricane."

[4]Ibid., p. 79.

[5]Edwards, et al., p. 82. The distinctive puffy-cheeked features of Menkaura agree with the caricatured features of the matching East Indian Soma, suggesting the power of tradition to preserve some degree of personal imagery despite the lapse of centuries. We assume that the Menkaura portrait was contemporary and that the Soma portrait was not.

[6]Ions, p. 19.

[7]Ibid., p. 84. This portrait of Kubera yields an unflattering caricature of the so-called "Semitic" physiognomy, Eber's natural appearance, combining the stocky semi-Mongoloidism of his father Salah (see the East Indian Surya) with a renewed infusion of the hook-nosed Amerindian type of the Red Matriarch. If Salah was an incipient "Semite," Eber was the archetype. Eber's feudal vassalage as "Tubal" to Japheth owed nothing to his genetic make-up but had a profound effect on his historical importance inasmuch as the royal house of Ebla were the Japhethite clan of Genesis 10:2, in a Semitic-speaking context. Eber's genealogy from Noah was as follows:

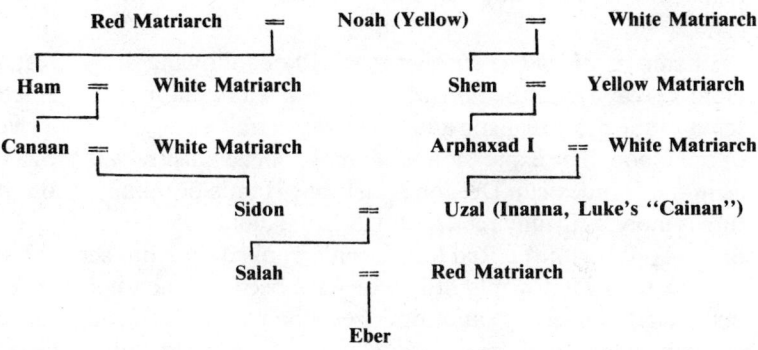

The White Matriarch entered the line four times, making the Hebrews substantially Caucasoid. The Yellow Matriarch entered once; and the Red Matriarch twice, the last time as Eber's mother, yielding the Hebrews their quasi-Amerindian or "Mediterranean" racial character. Noah's Mongoloidism reinforced the Yellow Matriarch's influence to produce the stockiness and brachycephalism observable in many Hebrews.

[8]Ibid., p. 85.

[9]I. E. S. Richards, et al., p. 83.

[10]Ibid., p. 27. Another, closer view appears in *Egyptian Mythology* (London: Paul Hamlyn, 1965), p. 97. Such is the Egyptian rendering of the mother of all the Caucasoids. The phlegmatic ethos of the race of Cain meant delicate, aloof beauty such as this.

[11]Ions, p. 27. Seba's Negroid maternity is apparent in this Indian version as in the Egyptian version of Osiris near Aswan. Unlike the Egyptians, the East Indian racists refused to admit that Seba was black and added, egregiously, that his wife Parvati, Noah's black daughter Arvad, was originally black but turned "golden" to please her husband (Ions, p. 91).

[12]*Egyptian Mythology*, p. 133. The version of Osiris at Luxor (p. 132) is a handsome mulatto type, precisely what we would expect from the royal union of the elegant Japheth with the Black Matriarch.

[13]Kramer, "Head of Ur Nammu," Plate following p. 64. Despite Ham's great age at the time of his reign as Ur Nammu, this statuette remains the most realistic and valuable portrait of any male survivor of the Flood. The expression of gloomy, poetic sensitivity is the same as in the Gundestrup Dragon panel; but Ham's peculiar racial mixture is more faithfully rendered. His Mongoloid paternity is apparent in the skull form; the Red Matriarch's hooked nose has served only to straighten what would otherwise have been a turned-up nose. But her facial concavity and dolichocephalism have produced the feminine delicacy of the mouth. Here is a face to remember: the face of a true Noahic aristocrat, eternally young, profoundly troubled, burdened with eternal duties and frustrated spiritual ambitions. This passionate and troubled man fathered a formal quarter of the human race. His Sumerian name meant "Champion of Nammu," his royal wife, the White Matriarch, as mother of Enki, his incestuous grandson Sidon.

[14]*Egyptian Mythology*, p. 94. This version of the Yellow Matriarch, with her royal husband Shem, pictures her as a compact and lovely Mongoloid type. The face of Shem, as Amon, confirms

our impression from the Hirschnatur panel, that Shem favored his Mongoloid father. The husband and wife have been stylized to look alike.

[15]Ibid., p. 88. As royal son of Noah and the Red Matriarch, Sabtechah was a postdiluvian full brother to Ham. This face shows the same v-shaped form, the same lips, and the same nose form as the Ur Nammu statuette, but with none of the unforgettable expression of gloom.

[16]I. E. S. Richards, p. 82. Nephthys is the figure to the right of the Pharaoh, her nephew through the common ancestry of Japheth, creator of the "Hamitic" linguistic stock.

[17]Ions, p. 21.

[18]Kramer, "Gudea, Ensi of Lagash," Plate following p. 64. The genealogy of Sidon is a subsection of the genealogy of Eber above. He was chiefly a Caucasoid type, both son and grandson of the White Matriarch. Noah's Mongoloid influence, however, is still apparent in the brachycephalism.

[19]Ions, p. 74. This stocky, richly ornamented figure is the great god of gentile mankind, prince of the Swastika, Marduk of the Babylonians, Bull El of Ugarit, and Mars of the Romans. His genealogy is another subsection of the genealogy of Eber above. The statue emphasizes his Mongoloid character as Arphaxad II, in the image of his maternal grandfather Arphaxad I, a three-quarter Mongoloid, son of Shem and the Yellow Matriarch. The face reflects the paternity of brachycephalic Sidon (Gudea) with strong Mongoloid reinforcement from Arphaxad's daughter Inanna. It is especially easy to envision how the heavy "Semitism" of Eber derived from this source in combination with the Red Matriarch.

[20]Ions, p. 90. This version of Joktan features the same thick, powerfully expressive lips as the father Eber (Kubera) and grandfather Salah (Surya). The vast physical pride of this rather erotic depiction speaks volumes about the Erechite faction of Salah (Lugalbanda) and Joktan (Enmerkar), the latter named Aram, the "High One," the all-conquering feudal lord of the final quarter of Genesis 10.

[21]Ions, p. 22. Although the Striding Vishnu seems a more emblematic, less realistic portrait of Joktan than the version with

Lakshmi, the face stresses Joktan's Mongoloid polarity as reinforced by his mother "Ino," another version of the same Inanna who had entered his line previously as mother of his grandfather Salah.

[22]*Egyptian Mythology*, p. 94. Again, this version of the Yellow Matriarch shows her as an ideally compact, sweetly youthful Mongoloid woman.

[23]Ions, p. 89. The great lyrical beauty of this statuette belongs to the same Edenic milieu as the Gundestrup Sphinx panel, linking Hamath to her mother the White Matriarch. The same two appear together, in the Sumerian Southeastern Marsh pantheon, as the mother Nanshe and daughter Ninmar.

[24]Nicholson, p. 109. The facial features combine the facial concavity of the Red Matriarch with the rugged aspect of Shem as pictured in the Hirschnatur panel.

[25]Ions, p. 90. Lakshmi (Sin) and Sarasvati (Hamath) were full sisters; but their appearance is quite different both ethically and physically. Their parentage was the same as Shem's and Japheth's; and they displayed the same sort of polarity, Lakshmi favoring the Mongoloid father and Sarasvati the Caucasoid mother. The present version of Lakshmi is stylized to blend with her "Semitic" husband Joktan; but it is clear that the "Semitic" tendency toward weight arose from Shem and Lakshmi themselves, as Mongoloid-Caucasoid blends favoring the stockiness and brachycephalism of Noah.

[26]Ions, p. 92.

[27]*Egyptian Mythology*, p. 115. Despite the stylized identity of eye form, this version of the second Red Matriarch differs radically from the Egyptian Selket, the White Matriarch. Even the painted flesh tone is adapted to express the yellow-red blend of Noah and the Red Matriarch. The aquiline nose is a universal symbol of power.

[28]Ibid., pp. 52-53. Another version is given in James B. Pritchard, *The Ancient Near East* (Princeton: University Press, 1965), Illustration 158.

[29]Ions, p. 14.

[30]Pritchard, Illustrations 84-86.

Chapter 4

The Nomadic Age

Eight Postdiluvian Fiefs

Noah's family spent the first century and a half after the Flood in a constant state of migration from one annual camp to another. Their purpose was to form the geographic matrix of civilization. The earliest cities of literate history, in Syria, Mesopotamia, Iran, and Egypt, document their activity. Because all of postdiluvian mankind derived from this family, every city was the product of such activity. For the first century and a half, world population remained too small to populate cities; so Noah's purpose was to divide the earth in the abstract, through feudal fiefs based on pre-urban camps.

In Sumerian tradition, this nomadic period did not exist. The propagandists of Sumer, wedded to the existing urban cults, refused to acknowledge the reality of a peculiar early postdiluvian age. Instead, the Sumerian Kinglist claims that kingship descended to the city of Kish immediately after the Flood. In reality, this epoch of First Kish occurred 180 years after the Flood at the scene of the Tower of Babel episode described in Genesis 11. By this time, the period of Nomadic exploration had ended; and a fairly populous world community was concentrated in Mesopotamia. The ancestors of these "Mesopotamians" had spent the previous 180 years in Syrian Mesopotamia, the Syrian Desert, Iran, the Persian Gulf, India, the Red Sea, Palestine, Egypt, and Arabia.

They regarded Mesopotamia as their heartland and treated Akkad as a "capital zone" from the beginning. The land of Akkad was one of eight fiefs established within the first thirty years of the Flood. These initial fiefs entered Sumerian tradition and became the standard political geography of the Sumerian world, appearing as an octad in an inscription of the Sumerian ruler Lugalannemundu of Adab. A ruler of the Second Kish (pre-Akkadian) period of Sumerian history, Lugalannemundu claimed tribute from an empire of eight lands: Cedar Mountain land, Elam, Marhashi, Gutium, Subir, Martu, Sutium, and Eanna.[1]

Scholars have located six of these lands. Elam lay to the east of the Lower Tigris; Gutium, in the Zagros Mountains north of Elam; Subir, on the Upper Tigris in a region roughly equivalent to Assyria; Martu, in the Syrian Desert region west of Akkad; Sutium, between the two rivers as equivalent to Akkad; and Eanna, further south as equivalent to Sumer. An interpretive problem concerns Cedar Mountain land and Marhashi.

Our theory demands that these two lands lay at either end of the Sumerian world in Syria, to the northwest and Persia proper, to the east of Elam. It makes little difference which name labels which land. Kramer assumes that both lands lay to the east of Sumer, at least that Cedar Mountain was in the east.[2] The older view was that Cedar Mountain itself was the Amanus Range north of Syria. At the same time, Waddell identifies Marhashi (or Parashi) with Persia proper.[3] Apart from Kramer's challenge, Cedar Mountain land would identify the Syrian fief; and Marhashi, the Persian fief. Two such fiefs had to exist for the Noahic octad to be complete.

The eight fiefs began with Subir as Noah's family approached the Upper Tigris from the east after descending from the Caucasus Mountains. As the first fief, Subaria belonged to Noah personally. The ancient city of Gasur, equivalent to Nuzi, in the heart of this land, matched the name of the second Ural-Altaic Shemite Gether (Sumerian Gaur). Gether's race, the Agathyrsians, belonged to the Finno-Ugric stock. When this race was supplanted by the Semitic Assyrians, the East Indians transferred the tradition of Noah's Flood to a version of Asshur (Manu),[4] realizing that the land of Assyria originally belonged to Noah as personal fief.

Japheth claimed the second fief of Syria as Noah's family reached the pre-urban camp of Carchemish on the west bank of the Upper Euphrates. Japheth's people of the Utuship, the Egyptians, tried to reclaim this primitive fief in the Battle of Carchemish, penetrating no further to the east. So strong was the archaic link between Syria and Egypt that Japheth's clan of Genesis 10:2 filled out the Pyramid dynasty of Memphis only after reigning as kings of Syrian Ebla.

Gomer, the Eblaite Gumalum, became Memphite Khufu; his son Javan, the Eblaite Ar-Ennum, Memphite Menkaura; and Tubal-Eber, the Eblaite Ebrium, Memphite Snefru. "Egyptian" history had begun abstractly at the camp of Carchemish just three years after the Flood. When Noah's family turned south from Jebel el Bishri eight years after the Flood, Ham claimed Martu as the third fief. His people of the Enlilship, the Semites, made Martu the center of their power throughout history, moving in all directions from that common center to become the Akkadians and Babylonians to the east; Assyrians, to the northeast; Aramaean Syrians, to the northwest; Canaanites to the west; and Arabians to the south. The control of Martu became the central intrigue of Noahic history in the years following Noah's curse on Canaan some ninety years after the Flood. Martu had become an irrevocable fief of the Semitic Enlilship eighty years earlier.

When Noah's family recrossed the Euphrates twelve years after the Flood, they made Shem's personal fief the "capital zone" of Akkad. Except for the upheavals of the Erech-Aratta War, this region would have been permanently inhabited by Shem's original stock, the Indo-Europeans. By the 120th year, the newly formed Indo-European stock had camped along the Euphrates. After the 180th year, they remained in or near Akkad long enough to establish the East Indian concept of the dynastic line of "Ayodhya," as anachronistic Lagash. After the 210th year, however, they served as part of the Erechite army which invaded Iran under Salah and Joktan. Instead of returning to Sumer, they migrated to the Syrian coast and eventually colonized the Baltic.

The Babylonians of Akkad preserved a tradition of the first four postdiluvian fiefs in the opening lines of the Marduk Epic. This introductory portion of the epic presents a series of primeval gods in husband-wife pairs: Apsu and Tiamat, Lahmu and Lahamu, and Anshar and Kishar.[5] The last couple give birth to the vertical genealogy of Anu, Nudimmud (Ea), and Marduk. Another name "Mummu" refers to Apsu's vizier.

The myth describes the royal antediluvian couples of the first three fiefs: Noah and the Red Matriarch (Apsu and Tiamat) in the Subarian fief, Japheth and the Black Matriarch (Lahmu and Lahamu) in the Syrian fief, and Ham and the White Matriarch (Anshar and Kishar) in the fief of Martu. Mummu stands without a wife as Shem of the Akkadian fief. The effect of these mythological genealogies was to aggrandize the line of Ham and humiliate the line of Shem, in keeping with the Inanna succession; but the sequence of the first three fiefs remained intact.

After recrossing the Tigris, Noah's family entered the Iranian zone of the Medb panel, a special region dominated by the antediluvian females in abstraction from their husbands. In the Marduk Epic, Iran becomes the realm of Tiamat, the Mahadevi or "Great Goddess" at the head of this antediluvian female sect.[6] Tiamat or Mahadevi herself, the Red Matriarch, claimed the first Iranian fief: Gutium of the Zagros. This fief complemented the Subarian fief of "Apsu," yielding to Noah and his royal wife the only contiguous pair of fiefs in the marital system, unless we extend Martu southward to the Sumerian Euphrates linking the fiefs of "Anshar and Kishar," Ham and the White Matriarch.

Excluding Sumer of the White Matriarch, the Iranian "Empire of Tiamat" included three fiefs and three races, all destined for humiliation and expulsion in the Erech-Aratta War: the Amerindians of the Red Matriarch, in the fief of Gutium; Sino-Tibetans of the Yellow Matriarch, in the fief of Marhashi; and Negroes of the Black Matriarch, in the fief of Elam. The three races entered these regions, for brief sojourns, only after the 180th year. In forming the geographic matrix of these Iranian fiefs, Noah's family had spent six years there in as many camps between the seventeenth and twenty-second years after the Flood.

Noah completed the system of the eight fiefs by leading his family across the Tigris for the third time, this time westward from Elam into Sumer. In the twenty-fourth year, he camped at the pre-urban site of Nippur, toward Akkad, making this camp the seat of Enlil. In the following year, he descended to the Southern Orchard region of the Lower Euphrates, making the twenty-fifth camp the focus of the White Matriarch's Sumerian fief. In that context, the Sumerians knew her as Ningirda,[7] mother of Ningishzida, their version of her favored antediluvian son Japheth, the classic Caucasoid of the Boxer-Dancer panel. When these proto-Sumerian camps were established, the Sumerian race did not yet exist, unless we refer that race to the genetic potential of the Sethite and Cainite stocks of antediluvian times. In the twenty-fifth year after the Flood, all races were in Sumer; yet none were.

The concluding nomadic sequence of Iran, Nippur, and the Sumerian fief of Ningishzida inspired the tripartite Geb-Nut Cosmogony of Egyptian tradition. The Egyptian and Sumerian myths of origin united at the focal point of proto-historical Nippur. As air god, the Egyptian counterpart to the creator Enlil of Nippur was Shu, the figure who forms the central vertical shaft of the Cosmogony. Both Shu and Enlil were the pagan counterparts to Hebrew Elohim, the creator of nature in the first chapter of Genesis. Shu stands below Nut, the goddess of heaven, to signify the priority of the angelic creation of the third heaven to the creation of nature.

The Sumerian heaven goddess Inanna, equivalent to Egyptian Nut, doubled as a goddess of Iranian Aratta because her euhemeristic counterpart, Uzal, was born at the camp of Aratta eighteen years after the Flood. The lapse of six years from Noah's settlement at Aratta to his settlement at Nippur explains the formal transition from Nut to Shu. The prone figures of Geb, beneath Shu, corresponds to the Sumerian twenth-fifth camp because Ningishzida (Japheth as earth serpent) was precisely equivalent to Geb, the Egyptian earth god, Japheth as foundational patriarch of the First Ennead.[8] Thus the sequence of Nut, Shu, and Geb summarized the sequence of Camps 18, 24, and 25 through which Noah completed the eight fiefs, a foundational manifestation of the apocalyptic octad required by his cosmos.

The Gundestrup Interior Panels

The panels of the Gundestrup interior are five in number in addition to the design of a bull on the floor panel. Three of the interior panels refer, in part, to the historical process just stated. These three panels, however, together with the other interior panels, accumulate in their designs a set of later events, enacted within the geographic matrix formed by the primitive camps. The unifying theme of the interior panels is Mithraic, based on the root motif of the ancient Persian mystery religion of Mithras the Bull-Slayer.[9] One of the five panels displays the ritual slaughter of three bulls. The floor panel shows a warrior, equivalent to Mithras, attacking a giant bull.

The Mithraic cult was to the loyalist faction of Noah and Shem what the cult of the Marduk Epic was to the opposing Mesopotamian faction of Canaan, Sidon, and Salah. The Marduk Epic celebrated a Mesopotamian victory over Iranian forces in the Erech-Aratta War some 216 years after the Flood. The Iranian Mithraic cult celebrated the Gutian (Iranian) victory over Mesopotamian Agade 125 years later. This latter victory meant so much to the Indo-European stock and to the loyalist faction, that they wove it into their mythological portrayal of the earliest Noahic beginnings. It was as though Noah survived the Flood for the sole purpose of enabling the Gutians to sack Naram Sin's Agade.

The giant bull of the floor panel represents the Akkadian Empire of Naram Sin. Grosse has drawn attention to a tripartite cosmic design, analogous to the Geb-Nut Cosmogony, marked on the bull's forehead and nose and showing a sunburst in the central position with a lunar crescent beneath.[10] This version of sun and moon represents the solar and lunar cult centers of Sippar and Ur and, therefore, the two lands of Naram Sin's empire, Akkad and Sumer. The warrior attacking the bull represents the Gutians to the northwest of Mesopotamia; and the dog on the opposite side, the Amorites who harassed Mesopotamia from the southwest.[11]

The overall coordination of the interior panels can best be understood by focusing on the Messianic or imperial line of Genesis 11:10-22:

Genesis 11	Gentile Equivalent	Interior Panel
Shem (11:10)	Teutates	Teutates Panel
Arphaxad (11:10)	Taranis	Taranis Panel
"Cainan" (Luke 3:36)	Medb (Inanna)	Medb Panel
Salah (11:12)	Dagda (Tr Il)	Floor Panel
Eber (11:14)	Mider (Mithras)	Floor Panel
Peleg (11:16)	Cernunnus	Cernunnus Panel
Reu (11:18)	Sargon of Agade	Triple Bull Panel
Serug (11:20)	Manishtushu of Agade	Triple Bull Panel
Nahor (11:22)	Naram Sin of Agade	Triple Bull Panel

The climactic events of the Mithraic cult belonged to the Imperial Age and, thus, to the following chapters. Our present purpose is to abstract these events from the other dimensions of historical meaning in the Gundestrup interior, especially the primitive events of the first thirty years after the Flood. The Triple Bull Panel can be dismissed here because it refers to the three Akkadian emperors as such and contains no geographic meaning. The same is true of the Teutates Panel, which describes the Gutian attack on Agade, and of the Floor Panel, which symbolizes the same event in Mithraic form.

The Taranis, Cernunnus, and Medb panels remain. These take their spatial structure from the primitive camps of the eight fiefs, combining this geography with political events later enacted there. The geographic value of these three panels can best be represented by a single comprehensive map of the Near East:[12]

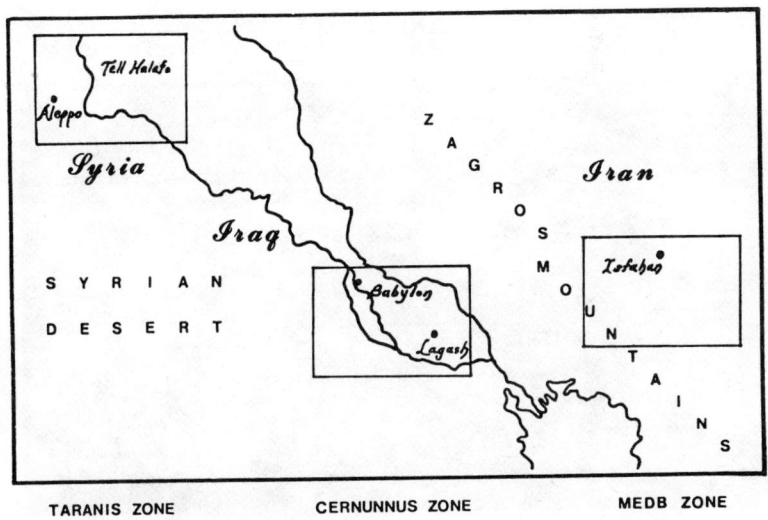

TARANIS ZONE   CERNUNNUS ZONE   MEDB ZONE

The Taranis and Medb panels and their respective zones are strongly analogous. Both panels are constructed in two horizontal rows of figures one above another:

TARANIS PANEL

MEDB PANEL

The dominant faces of the two panels refer to father and daughter, born in quick succession in the second and eighteenth years after the Flood: Taranis and Medb, Nanna and Inanna, Arphaxad I and Uzal. Each face marks the relative position of each birthplace, Arphaxad's at Syrian Harran and Inanna's at Iranian Isfahan (Aratta).[13] The two lands of Syria and Iran are complementary as uplands relative to the basin of Mesopotamia. The two panels are complementary in other ways as well.

Mesopotamia itself is outlined by the panel of Cernunnus, Celtic version of Peleg the Divider:

CERNUNNUS PANEL

The serpent in Cernunnus' left hand describes the course of the Lower Euphrates from the Akkadian latitude to the Persian Gulf. The figures to the left of the serpent mark three camps in Martu, to the west of the Euphrates. The lion at the top center stands at Akkad: the dog, at Nippur in the north of Sumer. The two lion-rams to the lower right mark two points in the southeastern marsh region of Sumer, Lagash to the west and a point at or near the Lower Tigris to the east. The fish and rider mark a pair of camps on either bank of the Akkadian Tigris near Al Kut; and the bull of the upper right corner marks a point in the Zagros foothills at the approach to the Medb zone.

The various animals that populate the three panels belong to the same symbolic milieu as in Jacob's blessing of the twelve tribes of Israel in Genesis 49. Each animal represents a Noahic tribe inhabiting each camp a century and a half and more after Noah's family first founded the camps. The tribes of the Cernunnus zone of Mesopotamia are the First Kish order 180 years after the Flood; tribes of the Medb zone, converging forces of the Erech-Aratta War, 216 years after the Flood; and tribes of the Taranis zone include the Hurrian and Gutian invaders of the Akkadian empire some 340 years after the Flood.

Absolute Chronology

Much of early postdiluvian history can be sketched through relative chronology. Basic to this relative system is the thirty-year generation stressed throughout the genealogy of Genesis 11, together with the concept of annual nomadic camps. Nevertheless, a strict adherence to the chronology of Genesis 11 will eventually result in an absolute chronology.

An estimate of the Flood date can be established, at once, from our conviction that Sargon's Akkadian Empire commenced nine Noahic generations or 270 years after the Flood.[14] Published works differ in their estimates of the accession date of Sargon. Students of mute archaeology sometimes favor high chronology. We find Sargon's accession date as 2371 B.C. in the archaeological milieu of *Chronologies in Old World Archaeology*.[15] Paolo Matthiae dates the same event 2350 and the fall of Ebla to Naram Sin a century later in 2250.[16] Works inclined more toward historical narrative such as Kramer's *The Sumerians* and Hallo and Simpson's *The Ancient Near East* favor later dates because of their sense of coherent relationship between Akkadian age and subsequent Sumerian history.

Kramer gives no explicit dates for Sargon but estimates the accession of Ur-Nanshe of Lagash at about 2450.[17] He notes that the Sumerian golden age introduced by Ur-Nanshe lasted down to about 2300, a de facto accession date for Sargon who terminated this Sumerian age in the overthrow of Lugalzagesi. Hallo and Simpson concur in dating the rise of Sargon about 2300.[18] This date would place the Flood at 2570, about a half-century too early to harmonize with biblical data.

However, P. Van Der Meer, a specialist in chronology, dates the accession of Sargon at 2242 through a backward extrapolation of dates from the early second and late third millennium.[19] This accession date would place the Flood at 2512, just six years later than Niessen's estimate of 2518 based on strict adherence to Genesis 11 and the generally accepted date of 2166 for the birth of Abram.[20] Niessen posits an interval of 352 years between the Flood and

Abram's birth, assuming that Terah was 130 years old at that time on the authority of Acts 7:4. The even sixty-year discrepancy between Acts 7:4 and Genesis 10:26 suggests that Terah begat new heirs at each thiry years and that Abram was the last of the three named in 10:26.

Niessen's Flood date would place the accession of Sargon at 2248, six years earlier than Van Der Meer's 2242 and, thus, six years closer to the rough estimate of 2300 suggested by Kramer and Hallo and Simpson. The Flood date of 2518 has much to recommend it; and we can add to it one additional, very specialized argument.

We have noted previously that the specious Flood epoch of the Sumerian Kinglist actually refers to the epoch of the First Kish order 180 years after the actual Flood. The propagandistic motive for confusing the two epochs was to bury in oblivion the shame of the Tower of Babel incident and to suppress any knowledge of the Nomadic Age and of Noah's role in regenerating the world's population. We would expect this propagandistic mythology to have infiltrated the traditions of other nations in addition to the Sumerians.

The legendary proto-history of the Chinese *Shu Ching* claims a cataclysmic flood of the Yellow River between the years 2357 and 2355.[21] In those years, the ancestors of the Chinese were located, not in China, but in Mesopotamia together with all other nations. The dates are too late to agree with the actual Flood but fall just nineteen to seventeen years previous to the First Kish epoch which, according to Niessen's Flood date, occurred at 2338. The discrepancy of nineteen to seventeen years is not a liability but an asset because it makes perfect sense to assume that the ancestors of the Chinese remembered, not the First Kish epoch, but its cataclysmic prelude, the divine judgment on the Tower of Babel itself. Because the First Kish design of the Cernunnus panel implies an orderly process of migration among the various stocks in Mesopotamia, a period of time must have elapsed from the hour of judgment down to the First Kish epoch. A period of seventeen years means that the Tower of Babel was completed and judged after the first decade of the thirty years allotted for it.

This logic becomes very precise if we can show cultural evidence that the one-third point of a Noahic generation was the logical time to have celebrated an accomplishment such as the Tower of Babel. To restate the argument: Niessen's Flood date of 2518, combined with the implication of the mythological Chinese river flood, results in a dead reckoning for the completion of the Tower of Babel in the eleventh or twelfth year of the ritual thirty-year generation reserved for it.

According to the Flood date of 2518, a basic chronology of early postdiluvian history runs as follows:

Eight Fiefs:

Subarian Fief: Tell Halaf	2517
Syrian Fief: Carchemish	2515
Fief of Martu: Camp 11	2507
Akkadian Fief: Camp 12	2506
Gutian Fief: Camp 17	2501
Persian Fief: Camp 20	2498
Elamite Fief: Camp 22	2496
Sumerian Fief: Camp 25	2493

Birth of Salah: Camp 37 (Tyre)	2481
Nomes of the Nile: Camps 48-90	2470-28
Curse on Canaan: Camp 91	2427
Birth of Peleg: Camp 101 (Martu)	2417
Tower of Babel Commenced	2368-66
Tower of Babel Judged	2357-55
First Kish Epoch	2338
Eanna Epoch: Erech-Aratta War	2308-02
Second Kish Epoch: Era of Ur-Nanshe and Lugalannemundu	2278
Accession of Sargon	2248
Gutian Attack on Agade: Deaths of Peleg and Nahor	2178-77
Death of Noah: Birth of Abram	2168-66
Guti Dynasty	2128-2031
Birth of Isaac	2066
Late Reign of Ham as Ur Nammu	2050-32
Death of Shem	2016
Death of Abraham	1991

In this chronology lie three major problems, two concerning overall chronological dimension and a third concerning detail: (1) the brevity of the Ur-Nanshe era, (2) the late date for the beginning of dynastic Egypt, and (3) the chronology of Naram Sin and the death date of Nahor. A fourth problem similar to the third is that Noah's death date furnishes an early terminus ad quem for the reign of the Amorite King Didanu. In dating the accession of Ur-Nanshe at 2450, Kramer posits an interval of 150 years between that event and the rise of Sargon. Our chronology reduces that interval to a single Noahic generation of thirty years, a fifth of Kramer's interval. The period in question is the one charted in eight generations of contemporary reigns in Hallo and Simpson's "Rulers of the Early Dynastic II Period."[22] Further-more, Dadasig of Second Kish appears in the seventh of eight "generations" of the previous "Legendary and historical rulers of the Early Dynasty II Period." In effect, Hallo and Simpson's charts extend our thirty-year Second Kish era to ten generations of con-ventional reigns.

We challenge this chronology through the concept of tribal dynasty in which rulership is shared by family members contemporaneous-ly. Internal harmony in the East Indian legendary kinglist suggests that the standard reigning term for this period in human history was thirty months or two and a half years.[23] According to that term, the ten "generations" in question were a mere twenty-five years from the reign of Dadasig to the reign of Sargon.

A strong clue to the true state of affairs is the legendary claim that Lugalannemundu reigned ninety years.[24] Because he claimed a universal imperium over the Noahic cosmos, Lugalannemundu laid claim to all three Noahic generations which intervened from the out-pouring of the "Ka" at First Kish to the rise of Sargon ninety years later. Although the Second Kish setting of Lugalannemundu's reign was only the latter third of this period, devotees of the emperor could verify his claim in a number of ways. First, he was an early postdilu-vian born long before the First Kish epoch and lived throughout the full span of ninety years. After the judgment on the Tower of Babel, he was fully capable of making Sumerian Adab his seat at any time. To claim a retroactive empire at Adab several decades after the chaotic Erech-Aratta War followed logically from the ideal of im-perial restoration and from the pacific ideal of the Sumerian golden age of Second Kish.

The problem of Egyptian chronology is essentially the same issue applied to a question of a full millennium rather than two centuries. In the case of the Second Kish era, we condense Sumerian history by a factor of eight from two centuries to twenty-five years. The same factor applied to Egyptian chronology would contract the 1400 years from Menes to the year 2000 to a period of 175 years. In fact, our chronology requires 228 years from the rise of Menes to the year 2000. In both cases, conventional historians have interpreted reigns of two and a half years as reigns of roughly eight times that length or about twenty years.

In our view, the sober-looking terms given the early Egyptian reigns by Manetho are often little better than the impossibly grandiose terms given the early reigns in the Sumerian Kinglist. On the other hand, the Akkadian emperors who launched the dynastic history of Egypt claimed actual imperia of sixty years and began to alter the lengths of reigns from the primitive Noahic pattern to the conventional pattern in which a ruler spent his entire adult lifetime in a single reign of twenty years or more. Kramer and Hallo and Simpson realize that, in dealing with the kings of early Sumer, they are operating in the shadowland between legend and history. Scholars have failed to grasp what that shadowland meant in terms of the kinds of men who actually reigned between 2500 and 2250 and the kinds of reigns they enjoyed. The chronology of Genesis 11 alters the political logic of the third millennium.

The problems posed by the deaths of Naram Sin and Didanu, Nahor and Noah, are matters of detail, not chronological perspective. According to Genesis 11:25, Nahor died 119 years after begetting Terah, according to our chronology 2177, a date fifty years too early to coincide with Van Der Meer's belief that the Guti rose to power at Naram Sin's death in 2123 (+ 6 = 2129).

Van Der Meer's useful estimate of 2242 for the rise of Sargon derives from his backward extrapolation of four Akkadian reigns from 2123 for the rise of the Guti. If the date of 2242 has value (and it does), the extrapolative process must have value. The total span from 2242 to 2123 is 119 years, one year short of Four Noahic generations or two sixty-year periods. Van Der Meer is correct in his estimate of the total span of time from the rise of Sargon to the Gutian regime; but he has followed a misleading tradition concerning how that period was divided by the various members of Reu's family. In considering those two periods we notice that the Sumerian Kinglist claims reigns of fifty-six years each for both Sargon and Naram Sin as though the entire Akkadian imperium were designed for such a 120-year period.

Because there were just four Akkadian rulers in this period, it would appear that the abstract Akkadian imperium called for four successive reigns of the Noahic thirty years each. If all had gone as planned, Sargon would have reigned from 2248 to 2218; Rimush, from 2218 to 2188; Manishtushu, from 2188 to 2158; and Naram Sin, from 2158 to 2128. Instead, the Akkadian emperors innovated against Noahic precedent; and the Gutian leaders responded by tearing the imperium apart and executing Naram Sin in 2177 after his premature and violent reign. Nevertheless, their respect for Noahic precedent was such that they allowed the full period of 120 years to elapse before taking control of Mesopotamia. The terms used by Van Der Meer represent an orderly subdivision[25] of the 120 years abstractly assigned to the imperium and venerated, as such, in Mesopotamian tradition, as expressed by the two fifty-six-year reigns of Sargon and Naram Sin.

The Amorite Kinglist which includes Noah as Didanu has no explicit place in time except for a contemporaneity or two, such as Tudia's contemporaneity with Ebrium of Ebla in the earlier part of the Akkadian age. If Noah and Didanu are the same, the first ten Amorite kings reigned at some time between 2250 and 2150, with Didanu's reign falling previous to 2168. Noah was the East Indian Indra of the Maruts, a leader of the Amorites, allied with the Gutians in a common cause against the Akkadian Empire. It is conceivable that, as Amorite leader, he fell in battle against the Akkadians, although this is somewhat doubtful when we consider that the death of Naram Sin occurred nine years previous to his own.

Camps of the Taranis Sector: Syrian Mesopotamia

The Nomadic Age lasted a century and a half from 2518 to 2368. This period included the first five Noahic eras and the revolutions of the first five exterior panels: Noah's Boar-Holding Men, Japheth's Boxer-Dancer, Ham's Dragon, Shem's Hirschnatur, and the Red Matriarch's Braided Goddess. Because the last of these panels shows a large fraction of the entire nomadic geography, its function was to summarize the Nomadic Age as newly completed. The same 150 years can be subdivided according to distinct geographic stages in

Noah's plan of exploration:

Source Design	Region	Period
Taranis panel	Syrian Mesopotamia	2518-10
Cernunnus panel	Martu, Mesopotamia, and Elam	2510-02; 2496-93
Medb panel	Iran	2502-2496
"Antediluvian" Kinglist	Sumer	2488-81
Braided Goddess panel	Transitional Arabia	2488-81
Canaanite cities	Greater Canaan	2481-70
Nomes of the Nile	Egypt	2470-28
Constellation of Scorpius	Arabia and Mesopotamia	2428-13
Cult centers of Ninazu and Dagan	Subaria and Syria	2413-2398
Cult centers of the Sumerian pantheon	Mesopotamia	2398-68

In the first year after the Flood, Noah's family approached the zone of the Taranis panel from the northeast. They pursued the four points of the top row from east to west and the four points of the lower row, from west to east, spending the eighth year at a point on the Euphrates northeast of the Jebel el Bishri. The eight points of the Taranis panel were as follows:

Figure	Camp		Designated Prince
Eastern Leopard	1. Tell Halaf.	2517	Noah
Taranis	2. Harran.	2516	Arphaxad I
Lugh	3. Carchemish.	2515	Japheth
Western Leopard	4. Sinabit.[26]	2514	Shem
Western Griffin	5. Halab.	2513	Hamath
Serpent	6. Emar.	2512	Zemar
Middle Griffin	7. Tuttul.[27]	2411	Sin
Eastern Griffin	8. Jebel el Bishri.	2510	Arvad

The serpent of the panel, like the one in the Cernunnus panel, describes a segment of the Euphrates, in this case the stretch flowing eastward from Emar toward Tuttul. The animals face in the opposite directions from Noah's route because of an historical overlay. The two leopards, for example, represent interim versions of the Gutain and Hurrian stocks in their descent from Asia Minor to attack the Akkadian Empire. These two races temporarily held the posts first established by Noah and Shem, core of the anti-Akkadian cause, at Tell Halaf and Sinabit.

The two leopards, like the similar tiger of the Medb panel, represent antediluvian males. The cognate mythological tradition is the four fathers of the Mayan *Popul Vuh:* Balam Acab, Balam Quitze, Iqui Balam, and Mahucutah.[28] The Mayan word "balam" meant "tiger" or "jaguar." These four fathers journeyed to the Mayan version of the known world after discovering that the sun would not rise, a reference to the deferred Utuship of primitive early postdiluvian Syria. The name Mahucutah evidently represents the one non-tiger of the antediluvian four: Japheth as the anthropomorphic Lugh pictured in the panel.

The princes of each camp were designated in one of two ways. Adults ruled their respective camps; but other princes were designated as infants born at a given camp. In the case of these birth camps, the chief was the last adult to have reigned previously. Noah, for example, ruled his own camp at Tell Halaf and Arphaxad's birth camp at Harran. Japheth, as adult, ruled the camp at Carchemish. Because no adults intervened between Camps 4 and 17, Shem ruled both his own camp at Sinabit and all the subsequent Camps 5-16, covering the rest of Syria, Martu, and Akkad.

This procedure obviously aggrandized Shem, gave Japheth a limited importance, and slighted Ham, whose camp designation was delayed until the twenty-first year at a point in Iran south of Isfahan. The Marduk Epic answered in kind by exalting Ham as the head of Marduk's line, giving Japheth limited importance as Lahmu husband of Lahamu, and slighting Shem as Mummu, without royal wife and, thus, without a place in the scheme of eight fiefs.

Noah assigned the last four Syrian camps to his infant daughters, destined to join the Canaanite clan and to give their names to such Syrian cities as Arvad, Emar, and Hamath. This procedure served to polarize the complementary Taranis and Medb zones, one featuring postdiluvian females and the other, the antediluvian females of the Mahadevi complex. Each zone claimed its share of antediluvians: three males in Syria and one male and four females in Iran. This pattern should tell us something about Noah's conception of world geography.

Because all four antediluvian males were Sethite in the male line, the predominance of such males in the Taranis sector served to identify Syrian Mesopotamia or the Caucasus as a kind of Sethite homeland. All eight princes of the Taranis sector were notably Sethite, the four females as daughters of Sethite Noah, the two antediluvian sons likewise, and Arphaxad-Taranis, visible head of the panel, as a three-quarter Sethite son of Shem and the Yellow Matriarch. Because the Caucasus is the watershed of Mesopotamia, the symbolic purpose of the Taranis arrangement was to interpret Noah's Sethite race as the fountainhead of all other postdiluvian races in the male line. The Mongoloids of the Far East are the patriarchal monogenetic stock of all mankind.

Camps of the Cernunnus Sector: Mesopotamia

In the Cernunnus panel, historical overlay is especially important. The figures of the panel represent eleven comprehensive divisions of the human race, under Peleg the Divider, at the First Kish epoch. The system is so orderly that Peleg must have consulted primitive Noahic tradition in assigning a given stock to a given location. Nevertheless, the First Kish order was an innovation because it included, within the compass of Mesopotamia, nations originally intended for the larger scope of the eight fiefs.

Despite consulting early precedent, Peleg could not resist the tide of political changes triggered by the curse on Canaan. Only five of the eleven figures lie at what might be considered conservative positions: the bull to the upper right, Ural-Altaics at an approach to Subaria; the fish and rider, Sino-Tibetans at the twin camps of yellow Gomer and yellow Mizraim on the Akkadian Tigris; and the two lion-rams, two divisions of the black race to the southeast. All the figures to the north and west lie in surprising if not unprecedented positions: Cernunnus himself, the Indo-European stock at a contested Camp 11 in Martu; his stag, the Amerindian stock at Camp 10 in Martu; the bull to the upper left, the Finno-Ugric (and Sumerian) fraction of the Ural-Altaic stock at the northernmost

Camp 9 in Martu; the leaping lion, Hamites at the scene of the Tower of Babel in Akkad; and Cernunnus' dog, the Semites at Nippur in northern Sumer.

Originally, these eleven points were eleven camps of the primitive nomadic itinerary, eight settled previous to Noah's journey into the Iranian mountains and three settled afterward. These eleven camps were as follows:

Figure	Camp		Designated Prince
Western Bull	9. Martu A.	2509	Togarmah son of Noah
Stag	10. Martu B.	2508	Sabtechah royal son of Noah
Cernunnus	11. Martu C.	2507	Canaan royal son of Ham
Lion	12. Akkad.	2506	Seba royal son of Japheth
Western Lion-Ram	13. Lagash.	2505	Cush son of Ham
Fish	14. Southbank Akkadian Tigris.	2504	Mizraim son of Ham
Rider	15. Northbank Akkadian Tigris.	2503	Gomer son of Japheth
Eastern Bull	16. Northern Elam.	2502	Ashkenaz son of Noah

★　★　★　★　★　★

Figure	Camp		Designated Prince
Eastern Lion-Ram	23. Lower Tigris.	2495	Riphath son of Noah
Dog	24. Nippur.	2494	Magog son of Japheth
Serpent	25. Lower Euphrates.	2493	Madai (Damu) son of Japheth (Ningishzida)

At Camp 10 in Martu, Shem began a process of assigning camps to royal sons, that is, sons of the royal couples outlined at the opening of the Marduk Epic. Noah had already assigned Shem's royal son Arphaxad to Camp 2, a possible explanation of why Shem appears in the Marduk Epic as the vizier Mummu without a wife. The Marduk Epic belonged to the Babylonians, a branch of the Amorite people who originated in Martu and settled at Babylon in Akkad. It is conceivable that they designed their epic according to their conception of Camps 9-12, extending from Martu into Akkad.

To Camp 10, Shem assigned the Stag prince Sabtechah, royal son of "Apsu and Tiamat," Noah and the Red Matriarch. As a yellow-red patriarch, Sabtechah defined the Athapascan race; and his camp hosted the entire Amerindian stock as the stag of the Cernunnus panel. An infant at Camp 10, Sabtechah was a young prince at Camp 26, capable of ruling there as Alulim, "Stag," of "antediluvian" Eridu. In receiving two camps, 10 and 26, Sabtechah demonstrated his early importance as royal postdiluvian son of Noah.

Canaan appears in the Marduk Epic as Anu son of Anshar and Kishar, Ham and his royal wife, the White Matriarch. In receiving Camp 11 somewhere near the Akkadian Euphrates in Martu, Canaan focused Ham's Martu fief and embodied the Semitic-speaking stock of the Babylonians to the east and Canaanites to the west. In the Cernunnus panel, Canaan is supplanted by the figure of Peleg (Cernunnus) as a result of Noah's curse on Canaan. For this reason, the Mesopotamian pantheon interpreted Peleg as Nergal "Enemy of Babylon"; and the Marduk Epic treats him as Kingu, Marduk's chief male adversary.

For some reason, Shem embodied his own Akkadian fief in Japheth's royal heir, the mulatto Seba, Egyptian Osiris. This circumstance offers still another explanation of why the Marduk Epic treats Shem as it does. Evidence for the selection of Seba at Camp 12 is the Egyptian lion in the Cernunnus version of Akkad, together with the Talmudic tradition that the Tower of Babel was chiefly an Egyptian initiative. The Egyptian custom of erecting the Sed pole, spine of Osiris, has a strong bearing on the logic of the Tower of Babel and of Akkad as capital zone of the earth.

Camp 13, at Lagash, was assigned to Seba's black half-brother Cush. As a consequence, Cush's special heir Nimrod became the chief god of Lagash, Ningirsu-Ninurta. The interplay between Camps 12 and 13, the earliest two camps of Mesopotamia proper, lay at the heart of the Zu-Ninurta struggle between Shem and Nimrod over the "Enlilship" of Nippur between the two camps. In Ninurta's victory over Zu, Nimrod gained control of the inner core of Mesopotamia, which is styled "the land of Nimrod" in Micah 5:6.

Camps 14 and 15 were a twin camp on either bank of the Tigris near Al Kut. In returning to the Tigris, Noah and Shem reverted to the logic of the Taranis panel in stressing Mongoloids, making camp princes of Arphaxad's Mongoloid half-brothers, Mizraim by

Ham and Gomer by Japheth. The two camps programmed, in effect, the two most powerful races of the Far East, the Chinese and Japanese. Gomer fathered the Chinese Hui; and the patriarch of the Chinese Han, Gomer's Japhethite nephew Anam, appears in Genesis 10 as a vassal of Mizraim. Gomer's son Javan fathered the Sino-Tibetan Yao and appeared in Chinese tradition as the legendary Emperor Yao. Mizraim, as Amenominakanushi, also fathered the Japanese, exotic Ural-Altaic speakers. The Gundestrup fish and rider, symbolizing both camps, is a familiar feature of Chinese art.

Mongoloid continuity was established at Camp 16 by Noah's Yellow son Ashkenaz, the first vassal of Gomer in Genesis 10:3. Lying somewhere to the east of the Akkadian Tigris, Camp 16 helped to define Subaria as a Ural-Altaic sphere, Ashkenaz embodying an eastern Ural-Altaic stock whose pronounced Mongoloid character, among Mongols and Koreans, reflected the Mongoloid purity of a son of Noah and the Yellow Matriarch. The biblical name Ashkenaz is supposed to be Persian; and Ashkenaz appeared twice on the periphery of Iran, first at Camp 16 and later at Camp 31 on the Makran coast where he gave his name Maka to the Persian province of Maka-Gedrosia.

After Noah's family returned from the Medb zone, Gomer's next vassal Riphath took Camp 23 somewhere to the east of Lagash. Because Riphath was Noah's son by the Black Matriarch, Camp 23 complemented the Black Matriarch's own Camp 22, focus of the Elamite fief. The Sumerian pantheon identified both Riphath and the Black matriarch by the same name, "Dumuzi-abzu," sometimes male and sometimes female, like Puluga and Bilika of the Andamese.

As previously noted, Camp 24 was Nippur seat of the God Enlil, Sumerian version of the Creator Elohim, definitive God of the Semitic linguistic stock. Like Anu, Enlil's euhemeristic identity underwent constant change, stabilizing among the Sumerians as Canaan. In the primitive context of Camp 24, the chosen representative was Japheth's red son Magog, known to many cultures as a wind god equivalent to "Lord Wind" of Nippur. As for the Semitic tongue, Magog joined the other members of the septad of Genesis 10:2 to become Igrish-Halam of Semitic Ebla. At Nippur, Magog complemented Seba of Camp 12, bringing the red-black polarity of "Havilah and Cush" to the heart of Mesopotamia.

Camp 25, Girsu on the Euphrates, terminated the process of the

Cernunnus panel with the Sumerian fief of the White Matriarch, mother of Japheth (the local serpent god Ningishzida) and twice grandmother of Ningishzida's son Damu. This son Madai was the delayed white son of Japheth, reappearing with his father in the First Kish dynasty as Mashda son of Atab.

Japheth's sons Gomer, Magog, and Madai appeared together in Teutonic tradition as the allegorically designated sons of Fornjot: Hler of the Sea, Kari of the Wind, and Logi of Fire.[29] Whatever this allegorical system represented, the primitive camps of these three sons formed a continuous chain from the Fish Rider through the Dog to the Serpent, that is, from Al Kut through Nippur to Girsu on the Euphrates. With his black son Seba claiming Camp 12 in Akkad, Japheth dominated all of the primitive Mesopotamian camps except for the southeastern camps of the two lion-rams claimed by black sons of Ham and Noah. Nevertheless, Japheth's personal fief lay entirely outside Mesopotamia, in Syria, between the Upper Euphrates and the Mediterranean.

Camps of the Medb Sector: Iran

The Iranian camps offer a special interpretive challenge because of the obscurity of Iranian locales in Sumerian tradition. Three Iranian city states appear in Sumerian tradition: Aratta, Awan, and Hamazi. None of these has been located through excavation. One source places Awan on the River Karkheh at a latitude intermediate between Nippur and Kish;[30] and another suggests the identity of Aratta with Isfahan (ancient Aspadana)[31] in central Iran south of Tehran. The Isfahan-Aratta identification is plausible and serves to orient the Medb zone as the birthplace of Medb-Inanna, analogous to Harran in the Taranis zone.

A noteworthy detail of the Sumerian legends of the Erech-Aratta War is that Inanna appears as local goddess of both cities.[32] In fact, the war becomes a contest over the right to represent this goddess, matriarch of the Messianic or imperial line. Both Medb and Eshtar-Anunitum, Akkadian version of Inanna,[33] are war goddesses; and there is little question that the war-chariot motif of the Medb panel represents the disposition of forces in the Erech-Aratta War, drawn up at the primitive positions of Camps 17-22. The biblical book of Esther—with its Persian setting, heroine named for Eshtar, and bloody outcome—seems to echo the political logic of the Medb panel.

With only one fixed point at Isfahan, the Medb zone cannot be defined without making assumptions about geographic dimensions. Camp 17 defined the Gutian fief of the Zagros Mountains; but these mountains fill most of the interval between Akkad and Isfahan. If we identify Elamite Camp 22 with Awan on the Karun, Camp 17 would fall near the upper River Dez toward the chief peak of the Zagros, the Oshtoran Kuh, in the region designated "Anshan" by Beek. The distant points at the eastern end of the zone can only be characterized by regional names such as Aria and Persia; and the identification of Ham's Camp 21 with historical Hamazi[34] is a judicious guess:

Figure	Camp		Designated Prince
Western Elephant	17. Anshan.	2501	Red Matriarch (Havilah)
Medb	18. Aratta.	2500	Inanna (Uzal)
Eastern Elephant	19. "Aria."	2499	White Matriarch (Jobab)
Eastern Griffin	20. "Persia."	2498	Yellow Matriarch (Sheba)
Tiger	20. Hamazi.	2497	Ham (Havilah)
Western Griffin	22. Awan.	2496	Black Matriarch (Ophir)

In terms of the Marduk Epic, this set of six camps is the empire of Tiamat, Iranian counterpart to the Arabian empire of the Mahadevi featured in the Braided Goddess panel. The Red Matriarch functioned in the Medb system precisely as Noah functioned in the Taranis system. The strong analogy between the two systems can be further plotted as follows:

Taranis Structure	Medb Structure
1. Noah	17. Red Matriarch
2. Arphaxad	18. Uzal
3. Japheth	19. White Matriarch
4. Shem	20. Yellow Matriarch
8. Arvad	22. Black Matriarch

Each system began with a member of the Apsu-Tiamat couple, followed by a member of the lunar Nanna-Inanna pair, then added a member of the Ningishzida-Ningirda pair (Japheth and his closely allied mother), proceeded to a member of the Amon-Mut couple (Shem and the Yellow Matriarch), and concluded with the Second Black Matriarch and her black mother.

Ham's function as the lone male member of the Medb system is a mystery. A partial explanation is that he became Havilah II, unique antediluvian son of the dominant Red Matriarch. The idea apparent in the Medb system is that the race of Havilah was reckoned an equal and opposite counterweight to Taranis' race of Seth. To complete this logic, the intervening Mesopotamia was reckoned the land of Adam and Cain, blacks and whites, combining the black Camps 12 and 13 with the Sumerian fief of the White Matriarch.

The last five camps of the first thirty years after the Flood belonged to the land of Sumer and to explicit Sumerian tradition as the five "antediluvian" cities of the Sumerian Kinglist:[35]

Camp		Designated Prince
26. Eridu.	2492	Sabtechah (Alulim)
27. Badtibira.	2491	Togarmah (Dumuzi the Shepherd)
28. Larak.	2490	Seba (Ensipazianna)
29. Sippar.	2489	Arphaxad I (Enmeduranna)
30. Shuruppak.	2488	Noah (Ziusudra)

These five camps entered Sumerian tradition through the sequencing of Camps 24-26. Camp 24, Nippur, was the seat of the Sumerian creator god Enlil and, therefore, the chronological counterpart to a new creation realized in the Sumerian fief of Camp 25. According to this logic, Camp 26 at Eridu was the first step of Sumerian history, the earliest of five "antediluvian dynasties."

The princes who were selected for the five "antediluvian" camps recapitulated much of the logic of Camps 1-12, transferring the principalities of the north to the Sumerian south. Noah, Arphaxad, Togarmah, Sabtechah, and Seba had been designated for Camps 1, 2, 9, 10, and 12. The ruler of Badtibira, Dumuzi the Shepherd, was Sabtechah's half-brother Togarmah, son of Noah and the White Matriarch and thus a yellow-white cornerstone of the Sumerian race. The political process of drawing the northern principalities southward helps to explain why Noah led his family as far north as Sippar, in Akkad, just two years before launching a new stage of exploration by taking to the sea in the thirty-first year. However, the strange retrograde northward from Eridu to Sippar also suggests a practical motive. Noah's family took to sea so readily in the thirty-first year that they had to have prepared one or more vessels for that purpose in the concluding years of the "antediluvian" period. Several converging factors suggest either the re-use of the Ark or a ship-building enterprise analogous to building the Ark. The ruler of northern Sippar was Arphaxad I (Enmeduranna), head of the lunar pantheon with its central image of the lunar boat, equivalent to Noah's Ark. Noah's concluding reign at Shuruppak served the Sumerians as context for their fictionalized version of the story of Noah's Ark. Clearly, the Sumerians conceived of the maritime explorations which followed the thirtieth year as a mythological counterpart to or ritual reenactment of Noah's diluvian voyage.

Camps of Arabia and Greater Canaan

This divisional title is somewhat misleading because only one or two of the next set of camps was settled within Arabia proper. Nevertheless, the Arabian Peninsula served to outline the maritime sphere covered within the first seven years after Noah's reign at Shuruppak. The camps of these seven years laid the groundwork for the Arabian design of the Braided Goddess panel:

Figure	Camp		Designated Prince
Eastern Thunderbird	31. Makran.	2487	Ashkenaz (Maka)
Eastern Attendant	32. Indus.	2486	Riphath (Bhat)
Victim	33. Hadramaut.	2485	Togarmah (Thammuz)
Western Attendant	34. Site in Ethiopia.	2484	Cush
Leaping Lion	35. Site in Egypt.	2483	Seba (Osiris)
Palm Bird	36. Site in Sinai.	2482	Uz son of Shem
Western Thunderbird	37. Tyre.	2481	Salah (Tr Il)

Sumerian, Semitic, and Egyptian tradition united in picturing this stage of Noahic experience as a death and prelude to resurrection. The deity of the Arabian panel was known to the Sumerians as

Ereshkigal, goddess of the underworld into which Dumuzi the Shepherd (Togarmah of Camp 33) was forced to descend.[36] Dumuzi was pursued into the underworld by Inanna, the dominant goddess of the Iranian sect whose Hebrew names (Uzal, two Havilahs, Ophir, Sheba, and Jobab) were destined to take root in Arabia, as though Inanna's regime were cast from Iran into the "underworld" of Arabia. The land of Camp 33, Hadramaut, took its name from the Hebrew Hazarmaveth, "Tower of Death," an allusion to the ruined "tower" of the boar-holding structure featured in the panel. Seba-Osiris' part in this traditional sequence of camps contributed to his Egyptian image as a dying god.

In this largely maritime stage of the nomadic itinerary, Noah covered much greater distances than during the previous thirty years. These distances, combined with the act of taking to sea and leaving the "capital" land of Mesopotamia far behind, were perceived as a corporate death, as well as a recapitulation of the diluvian voyage. The legend of Osiris pictures the slain god as floating in a chest,[37] another evidence of the equation of death with going to sea.

The seven-year transitional period concluded with the birth of the mighty Salah thirty-seven years after the Flood (Genesis 11:10-12). The native pronunciation of the port of Tyre is Sur, equivalent to Salah's East Indian name Surya. One of Salah's chief cults, as Tr Il, lay further up the coast at Ugarit. Tyre itself lay just south of the port of Sidon named for Salah's physical father, the firstborn of Canaan (Genesis 10:15). Tyre was an imperial birth camp closely analogous to the camps of Harran and Aratta, birthplaces of Salah's Messianic grandfather Arphaxad I and mother Inanna.

In its position up the coast from Tyre, the port of Sidon inaugurated another stage in the primitive itinerary, based on the elevenfold structure incorporated into the Canaanite clan of Genesis 10:15-18. This clan stands apart from the other systems in Genesis 10 because of its emphasis on cities. In the previous chapter, we explained the Canaanite eleven as a combination of Canaan's own septad with Noah's four daughters lost to Shem through the Erech-Aratta War. Because the urban system was elevenfold from early times, the full set of eleven was originally supposed to have been jointly ruled by Canaan and Shem, in celebration of the family alliance established by the marriage of Sidon and Inanna. This celebration began, in effect, with the birth of Salah; so the system of eleven Canaanite cities took shape immediately as eleven camps settled over the next eleven years.

The sequence of the eleven Canaanite camps is problematic in that Hamath, last of the eleven, lies far to the north in the Syrian interior, remote from the Nile Delta where the next sequence of camps began. Nevertheless, the remoteness of Hamath from the Delta is small objection in view of the great distances covered during the seven years of transition. If we follow the given sequence of Genesis 10:15-18, we perceive that Noah worked his way unevenly northward toward the Syrian zone of the Taranis panel, satisfied himself that he had closed the gap between West and North, and returned immediately to the Nile:

Camp		Designated Prince
38. Sidon.	2480	Sidon son of Canaan
39. Hebron.	2479	Heth son of Canaan
40. Jebusi.	2478	Jebus son of Canaan
41. Heshbon.	2477	Amor son of Sidon
42. Sea of Galilee (east bank).	2476	Girgash son of Jebus
43. Mount Seir.	2475	Hiv son of Jebus
44. Arca.	2474	Ark son of Jebus
45. Sin.	2473	Sin daughter of Noah
46. Arvad.	2472	Arvad daughter of Noah
47. Sumra.	2471	Zemar daughter of Noah
48. Hamath.	2470	Hamath daughter of Noah

Noah spent the first six of these years in the Palestinian south penetrating as far south as the Hurrian (Hivite) focal point of Mount Seir before returning to the Phoenician coast to complete this stage of his work by reassigning his daughters to a chain of camps approaching their original camps along the lower row of the Taranis system. The Syrian city of Hamath (modern Hama) lies roughly a hundred miles south of Hamath's first camp at Halab (Aleppo). Noah completed the circle of his geographic cosmos along the road from Hama to Aleppo forty-eight years after the Flood, before concentrating on the Nile.

Forty-two Nomes of the Nile

The forty-two "nomes" or districts of the Nile are known to have been extremely ancient, preexisting the dynasty of Pharaoh Menes.[38] They are also known to have been feudal units, designated by heraldric banners or totem signs such as the "Beast of Seth."[39] In short, the forty-two nomes furnish a rare glimpse at Noah's primitive camp system *in situ* as distinct from the cities later built over such sites.

The total of forty-two is an integral product of seven and implies that Noah, on the Nile, continued the process of building the Genesis 10 clans begun in Greater Canaan. If we omit the septads of Joktan and Peleg (yet to be born) and the two represented in the Canaanite eleven, just six remain: two for Japheth, three for Ham, and one for Shem. It is reasonable to assume that Noah assigned the forty-two camps of the Nile to the forty-two members of these six septads.

The identities of the forty-two nomes can be approached inductively because many are named for specific deities as in Bubastis, "House of Bast," the Black Matriarch, or Buto, "House of Wazet," the Red Matriarch. This method, however, remains imperfect because of duplications and other irregularities in a system which was worked over by incoherent, politicized traditions for many centuries. The role of induction, in this case, is to furnish hints of the original design underlying these traditions.

The structural key to the nome system is a fascinating interplay between the nomes of Heliopolis and Pithom in Lower Egypt. At one stage in their development, both nomes claimed as their deity Atum,[40] Egyptian version of Cush. We have seen that, in the East, Cush claimed Noahic Camp 13, Lagash, handing it down to his vassal Nimrod, the euhemeristic Ninurta-Ningirsu. Remarkably, the two nomes of Atum read as thirteenth of Lower Egypt both from top and bottom, Pithom from the north and Heliopolis from the south.[41]

Noah's family created the nome system from the north but realized that it would be read from the south, in harmony with the Braided Goddess' Egyptian lion, which leaps straight upward toward the Delta. In Hellenic tradition, Cush and Nimrod appear together as the sun Titan Hyperion and the personified sun Helius. In the earliest version of the nome system, Heliopolis belonged to Helius-Nimrod (as Ionu, the "pillar") and Pithom, "House of Atum," to Cush as Atum. Noah's family was so devoted to the structural precedent of

Lagash that they numbered Pithom the thirteenth nome from the Delta and anticipated the formation of a sequence running northward from Memphis and making Heliopolis the traditional thirteenth nome of Lower Egypt. Similar principles must have governed the formation of the twenty-two nomes of Upper Egypt further south.

In the same way, they matched Seba's Camp 12 with the nome of Per-Osiris neb-Zed (Busiris), twelfth from the north. The alignments of Per-Osiris and Pithom meant that Noah conceptualized the nome sequence as a new beginning of the camp sequence, matching the first thirteen camps of Greater Mesopotamia with the first thirteen nomes from the north. Nevertheless, the Egyptian and Mesopotamian sequences remained quite different. The Mesopotamian system had begun with antediluvian males and delayed the antediluvian females until the Medb sector. The locations of Buto and Bubastis, houses of the Red and Black Matriarchs in the Delta, make it plain that the antediluvian females played a different structural role in Egypt, the "land of Ham," unless, in fact, we read the nome sequence from south to north, making Buto and Bubastis concluding nomes.

The forty-two camps of the Nile were as follows:

Camp		Designated Prince
49. Arabian nome.	2469	Uz (Horus Seped) son of the Red Matriarch
50. Buto.	2468	Red Matriarch (Wazet)
51. Bubastis.	2467	Black Matriarch (Bast)
52. House of the Island of Amon.	2466	Gether son of Shem (Amon)
53. Mendes.	2465	Salah (Khnum)
54. House of Zehuti.	2464	Ham (Zehuti)
55. House of Horus.	2463	Madai (Horus Lord of Mesent)
56. Heliopolis.	2462	Nimrod (Helius-Ionu)
57. Sebennytos.	2461	Gomer (Anhur)
58. Pharbaethos.	2460	Japheth (Horus with the Two Eyes)
59. Athribis.	2459	Hul (Kem-ur)
60. Busiris.	2458	Seba (Osiris)
61. Pithom.	2457	Cush (Atum)
62. Metelis.	2456	Elam (Ha)

Camp		Designated Prince
63. Xois.	2455	Arphaxad I (Bull of the Desert)
64. Sais.	2454	White Matriarch mother of Hamath (Neith)
65. Prosopis.	2453	Uzal sister of Hamath (Neith)
66. Libyan nome.	2452	Lehab (Amenti)
67. Letopolis.	2451	Tubal (Eber's birth camp of the 67th year)
68. Memphis.	2450	Elishah brother of Amor (Nefertum)
69. Northern Aphroditopolis.	2449	Pathrus (Isis)
70. Crocodilopolis.	2448	Rodan (Sebek)
71. Heracleopolis Magna.	2447	Shem (Herishef)
72. Oxyrrhynchos.	2446	Javan (Iru-shepes)
73. Het-benu.	2445	Tarshish (Phoenix)
74. Cynopolis.	2444	Anam (Anubis)
75. Hibis.	2443	Meshech (Horus Vanquisher of the Oryx)
76. Hermapolis Magna.	2442	Phut (Un) son of Ham (Zehuti)
77. Cusae.	2441	Asshur son of Jerah (Hathor)
78. Lycopolis.	2440	Magog (Upuaut)
79. House of Horus Nubti.	2439	Kitt (Horus Vanquisher of Seth)
80. Hypselis.	2438	Zud (Seth)
81. Aphroditopolis.	2437	Caphtor daughter of Mizraim
82. Panopolis.	2436	Mizraim (Min)
83. Thinis-Abydos.	2435	Mash (Khenti-Amentiu) son of Shem (Amon)
84. Diospolis Parva.	2434	Naphtuh (Nephthys)
85. Denderah.	2433	Tiras (birth camp in 37th year of the nome sequence)
86. Coptos.	2432	Masluh son of Mizraim (Min)
87. Hermonthis.	2431	Sabtechah (Mont)
88. Nekhen.	2430	Yellow Matriarch (Nekhebet)
89. Edfu.	2429	Canaan (Harakhte)
90. Elephantine.	2428	Sabtah (Indian elephant Ganesa)

As Harakhte of Edfu, Canaan appeared toward the close of the nome sequence much as he later appeared as Aka of Kish at the close of the First Kish dynasty. In both cases, he was to dominate the logic of subsequent events: the curse against himself after the ninetieth year and the Erech-Aratta War after the 210th.

The Curse on Canaan

The Egyptians claimed that the mythological war of Horus and Seth began in the 336th year of the reign of the sun king Ra-Harakhte,[42] a version of Canaan of Edfu. The war in question was the same one featured in mythological form in the Marduk Epic: the conflict between Mesopotamia and Iran in the reign of Enmerkar of Erech. Because that war occurred 216 years after the Flood, the Egyptian tradition meant that Ra-Harakhte had begun to reign 120 years before the flood, precisely the point specified for the end of all flesh in Genesis 6:3, as prelude to Noah's ark-building enterprise. Canaan, obviously, did not exist 120 years before the Flood. The claim made for Ra-Harakhte originated from the antediluvian worldview of the White Matriarch, a daughter of the Cainite stock and royal mother of Canaan. By tracing the reign of Ra-Harakhte back to the beginning of Noah's ark-building career, the faction of the White Matriarch, Canaan, and Sidon were establishing a case against Noah's theocratic authority.

Noah belonged to the Sethite stock, the Mongoloid race. The narratives of Genesis 4-5 imply that Seth was much younger than Cain and Abel, born to Adam when he was 130 years old (Genesis 5:3). The races of Cain and Abel were the Caucasoid and Amerind, white and red, the colors chosen to represent the two Egypts.[43] The same two races were embodied in the royal couple "Anshar and Kishar," Ham and the White Matriarch, as reflected in their white son Canaan. The Egyptians treated the name "Seth" as a symbol of innovative evil, the creation of chaos as prelude to solar restoration. In picturing Canaan as Ra-Harakhte, Canaan's faction based their claim to power on the priority of Cain and Abel to Seth. In their eyes, Noah was an upstart and rebel against an ancient order of solar unity existing in the elder stocks of Cain and Abel.

The Canaanite faction proposed Canaan as a theocratic substitute for Noah. Such is the implication of Bochart and Tooke's view that the Hellenic Cronus absorbed characteristics of the biblical Noah.[44] At the same time, the grotesque Hellenic myth of the castration of Cronus refers to the splitting of Noah's Ural-Altaic stock as the two

victims with severed legs in the Gundestrup Dragon panel. In
genealogical terms, Cronus is strictly Canaan, father of the Olym-
pians Poseidon (Sidon), Hades (Heth), and Zeus (Jebus). Thus the
parallels between Cronus and Noah imply that Canaan absorbed
Noah's identity. The same thing occurs in the Marduk Epic where
the genealogically aligned Canaan—Anu son of Anshar and Kishar—
has supplanted Noah as An, priest of the Ural-Altaic Anship, the
cult of El Elyon.

The Marduk Epic credits Canaan's son Sidon (Nudimmud) with
overthrowing Noah (Apsu). The text tells us little more than that
Nudimmud employed a magic circle in accomplishing this goal.[45]
Whatever the device, the Canaanite faction believed that they had
successfully thrown Noah's curse back on his head. The Mesopotamian world order of Marduk the Great was based on this ideological
foundation.

Before losing his power of Anship, Noah invoked it to curse
Canaan to servitude. As the expression of political sovereignty, this
curse can only be understood as a detail of a politico-economic caste
system. The East Indian caste system is a tetrad based partly on racial
distinctions: the Brahmin priest caste, warrior Kshatras, merchant
Vaisyas, and black Sudras, the slave caste.[46] If modern blacks are
offended at this system, let them realize that it is merely the East
Indian variation of a racial tetrad which takes a totally different form
in Genesis 9:26-27.

Ham's royal heir Canaan was specifically white, the Slavic "White
God" Byelobog, a prototype of the Mediterranean variety of the
Caucasoid race and the formal representatve of his mother's
Caucasoid stock. In the curse of Genesis 9, Noah reverted to the
antediluvian conflict between Sethites and Cainites by punishing the
white Cainites, despite exempting his white sons Shem and Japheth
from the curse. The purpose of the curse was to realign the prestige
of the four royal couples of the cosmos by realigning the four royal
heirs: white Canaan, yellow Arphaxad I, red Sabtechah, and black
Seba.

We have seen from the Geb-Nut Cosmogony that Noah's primitive
fief sequence had hierarchic value, with its "heaven" term at Camp
18, "air" term at Camp 24, and "earth" term at Camp 25. This
version of the "great chain of being" furnished the logical foundation for a caste system such as the one reflected in Genesis 9. Because

Camp 25 defined the White Matriarch's Sumerian fief, the ultimate target of Noah's hierarchic curse was Canaan's mother, the White Matriarch, who had broken the law against mother-son incest by bearing Sidon to Canaan. The Aztec mythology, determined by Noah's loyalist wife, pictures the White Matriarch as Tlazolteutl, goddess of filth and immorality; and the Egyptian system concurs, indirectly, by identifying the White Matriarch, Selket, with the scorpion image of the Akkadian White Matriarch, Ishara, goddess of sexuality.

In early Genesis, a prototype of the curse on Canaan is the curse on the serpent (Genesis 3:14). The serpent image winds in and out of the intrigue involving Noah, Ham, Canaan, and the White Matriarch. In Aztec iconography, Tlazolteutl grasps a serpent[47] just as Peleg-Cernunnus, at Canaan's erstwhile Camp 11, grasps a serpent representative of the White Matriarch's Lower Euphrates. Although the rebel faction succeeded in equating the serpent image with the White Matriarch's antediluvian son Japheth (Ningishzida), there is little question that Noah intended to impose the image on her postdiluvian son Canaan. The loyalist logic of the Cernunnus panel implies that Peleg has not only taken over Canaan's Camp 11 but has taken control of the serpent Canaan and his rebel faction for the thirty years of the First Kish period.

The punishment for Ham's misbehavior fell on his royal wife as though she had instigated Ham's actions. Her motive was to supplant the Red Matriarch as Noah's royal wife and "Mahadevi," empress of Greater Arabia (including India and Egypt).[48] Ham witnessed his father's nakedness as a ritual step toward breaking the law against filial incest by claiming his mother, the Red Matriarch, as his own royal wife.[49] In doing so, he claimed Noah's Anship for himself. The Sumerian, Greek, and Polynesian traditions unite in treating him as the heaven god or heaven Titan. One of the purposes of the Abrahamic war narrative of Genesis 14 is to reject Ham's claim by showing that Melchizedek (Shem), rather than Bera (Ham), claimed the legitimate Anship after Noah's death.

According to the scheme devised by Ham and the White Matriarch, the Anship reverted to Ham as husband of the Red Matriarch; and Noah claimed the Enlilship as husband of the White Matriarch. So potent was this strategy that Noah himself honored it in wielding the Enlilship as his own, conferring Elohim on the dual "Yahweh

Elohim of Shem." As further corollary, Japheth claimed the Yellow
Matriarch as royal wife, taking her name "Sheba" in the system in
Genesis 10:7. Shem now claimed the Black Matriarch, redefining
his cult heir as the black son Hul, whose name in Sumerian,
"Rigorous,"[50] indicates his identity with the judgmental cult of
Shem's Yahweh.

Camps of the Scorpion

The Egyptians identified the White Matriarch as Selket, goddess
of the scorpion image. The constellation of Scorpius lies on the eclip-
tic south of Ophiochus, the Serpent-Bearer, and of Hercules, the
Hellenic (and Roman) version of Shem as hero.[51] In the previous
chapter, we noted Shem's heroic act of distilling a new Indo-
European stock from the four stocks of the Dragon panel and
withdrawing these from South Arabia to Mesopotamia. Because of
its design and alignment with Ophiochus and Hercules, Scorpius
served as frame of reference for the next fifteen Noahic camps extending over that geographic interval.

The figure of Ophiochus matches the Celtic version of Peleg, Cernunnus, as serpent-bearing ruler of the First Kish order of
Mesopotamia. The figure of Hercules does the same for the heroic
image of Shem in the Hirschnatur panel. Given these associations,
we are justified in interpreting the ascending design of Scorpius as
the geographic and chronological ascent of Shem and Noah to the
heartland of Mesopotamia. The Scorpion goddess (White Matriarch)
now functioned as royal wife of Noah and royal mother of Shem,
despite her alienation from both. According to the chronology of
Genesis 11:16, Peleg was born 101 years after the Flood, in the
eleventh year of the era of the curse on Canaan. From this circumstance, we discover a structural coincidence. In the Cernunnus
panel, Peleg holds the position of Noahic Camp 11. As in the Nile
Delta, Noah determined to inaugurate a new series of camps as variations of the original series, making the eleventh camp after the
ninetieth year coincide with the eleventh camp after the Flood. Peleg
was born as Noah and Shem reached Camp 11-101, making him the
loyalist counterpart to Canaan and the bitterest enemy of Canaan's
faction.

The tail-design of Scorpius loops momentarily southward before
beginning the northward ascent toward Ophiochus. The southern-

most stars of the main design, Sargas and Eta Scorpii, lie fifth and sixth of the main design, counting from the tail at Lesuth.[52] If we align Sargas and Eta Scorpii to the two victims of the Dragon panel, at Aden and Hauta, the first four stars lay further north and west in Yemen, from a first point toward the source of the Wady Maur to a fourth point toward Zabid on the Red Sea coast. Noah's family crossed the Red Sea in the ninety-first year from Upper Egypt to Yemen, landed near the mouth of Wady Maur, and penetrated inland to the first camp at the point of Lesuth.

According to this logic, Noah's family spent four years in Yemen, two in South Arabia, and one in Hadramaut before ascending through the heart of the peninsula to Martu and Mesopotamia. After a foreshortened ascent through four more stars, the point of the climactic Camp 11-101 coincides with the alpha star Antares, "Rival of Mars," symbolic of Peleg as Kingu, rival of Marduk. The constellation then concludes with four more stars, three in the "claw" section, symbolic of camps to the east of Mesopotamia, ending with Eshnunna on the River Diyala, point of departure for further migrations in the north.

In ancient times, the cult of astrology was known as the "Sabaean heresy," as though it originated in Sabaea-Yemen. Noah's family evidently began to use the globe of the fixed stars for geographic reference during their four years in Yemen. Because of the traditional association between Arabia and Joktan, the princes of the fifteen Scorpion camps were the ones destined for inclusion in the clans of Joktan and Peleg. These were simply the thirteen members of the given Joktanite clan in addition to Joktan and Peleg themselves. Like the Delta nomes of Buto and Bubastis, the Arabian system began with the antediluvian females who gave such traditional names as Sheba and Ophir to the south of Arabia:

Star of Scorpius	Camp		Designated Prince
Lesuth	91. Wady Maur.	2427	Jobab (White Matriarch)
Shaula	92. Wady Maur.	2426	Havilah (Red Matriarch)
Kappa Scorpii	93. Hadeida.	2425	Ophir (Black Matriarch)
Iota Scorpii	94. Zabid.	2424	Sheba (Yellow Matriarch)
Sargas	95. Aden.	2423	Joktan
Eta Scorpii	96. Hauta.	2422	Sheleph

Star of Scorpius	Camp		Designated Prince
Zeta Scorpii	97. Hadramaut.	2421	Hazarmaveth
Mu Scorpii	98. Saudi Arabia.	2420	Jerah
Epsilon Scorpii	99. Saudi Arabia.	2419	Hadoram (Nanna)
Tau Scorpii	100. Martu.	2418	Uzal (Inanna)
Antares	101. Martu.	2417	Peleg
Al Niyat	102. Sippar.	2416	Obal (Utu)
Pi Scorpii	103. Camp 14-15.	2415	Diklah (Ninhar)
Dschubba	104. Camp 16.	2414	Abimael
Graffias	105. Eshnunna.	2413	Almodad

Encapsulating the Mesopotamian end of the Scorpion system, Peleg and his sister Almodad gave a loyalist capstone to the entire system. The two appeared in Andamese tradition as Puluga and Bilika. According to the Andamese, Puluga divided the earth by moving to the northeast, leaving Darya in the southwest.[53] Clearly, Darya represents Joktan at the distant southwestern point of Aden; and the axis of Puluga and Darya is the Andamese memorial of the system. Because the Gulf of Aden opens into the Indian Ocean, it is appropriate that a people of the Indian Ocean should remember this aspect of the Noahic heritage.

Joktan intruded into the Joktanite sequence at the point of Sargas because Aden was his birth camp ninety-five years after the Flood when his father Eber was twenty-eight. He was thus Peleg's elder by six years. Despite his seniority and lofty maternity from Inanna, he was passed over as Messianic heir. This fate explains, in part, why he became the enemy of Noah and Shem as Enmerkar of Erech. The grand proportions of the extant Joktanite clan indicate how much the Erechite campaign against Aratta sought to compensate him for his loss of Eber's birthright.

Camps of Ninazu of Eshnunna

When Noah's family reached Eshnunna on the River Diyala, a full forty-five years remained before the imperial epoch of the Tower of Babel. In these forty-five years, Noah completed the program of the Nomadic Age, despite the discord created by his curse on Canaan. His first step was to return to the northern land of the Taranis panel, including his own Subarian fief. His goal was to leave his personal stamp on a large enough chain of camps to counteract the scheme to undermine his authority throughout the swelling postdiluvian populace. His strategy was twofold: (1) to reestablish his presence in the north and (2) to establish colonies, loyal to himself, throughout Mesopotamia.

The first of these two goals was met within the next fifteen years, prior to the epoch of the Hirschnatur panel. Colonization in Mesopotamia would unfold during the thirty years of the Hirschnatur panel. The whole aim of the Tower of Babel scheme, in the succeeding era, was to undermine Noah's colonization program. His enemies felt that they could win their ideological war with him if they could reduce world population to a single people speaking a single language. They understood that Noah had sought for a balanced diversification of his people from the year of the Flood forward. In the final forty-five years of the Nomadic Age, Noah and Shem sought to enforce this process of diversification as strenuously as they could.

To the Sumerian pantheon, Noah was known as Ninazu, the "Water Knower," father of Ningishzida, pantheon version of Japheth. A key detail of the pantheon is that Ninazu claimed a secondary, northern cult center at Eshnunna[54] as well as the domestic cult center of Enegir on the Lower Euphrates. Eshnunna lay toward the heart of Subaria, so that its cult of Ninazu implanted a euhemeristic version of Noah in the legitimate region of Noah's fief. The religious dread of shrines or cult centers was so strong that Noah's enemies never succeeded in erasing his cult names from Eshnunna or from the various northern centers of his Semitic cult name of Dagan.

The northern itinerary of the fifteen years between 2413 and 2398 can be pieced together by filling the intervals between Noah's centers at Eshnunna, Tell Halaf, Ebla, and Tuttul. Tell Halaf was Noah's original postdiluvian camp; Ebla, the setting of a Semitic pantheon featuring Dagan; and Tuttul, the chief cult center of Dagan. The itinerary of these years formed a loop, working first northwestward from Eshnunna to Assyria, westward across the original upper row of the Taranis panel, further west to the coast at Ullisu, eastward to Ebla, Tuttul, and Mari, and southeastward down the Euphrates to Mesopotamia. The practical effect of the itinerary was to lay the groundwork for the northern empire of Ebla in Syria and proto-Assyria in the time of Ebrium and Tudia.

The princes of these new or renewed camps complemented those of the Scorpion system, deriving from the original two septads of Noah's heir Shem, including the four daughters of Noah later transferred to Canaan. The northern itinerary not only passed through Assyria but brought Asshur to his homeland, as a concrete vassal of Shem for the first time. Because Genesis 10 presents the Joktanite thirteen as an extension of the vassals of Shem, the northern camps simply continued the process begun in Yemen, defining the greater Semitic world from South Arabia to Assyria and the Syrian coast:

Camp		Designated Prince
106. Gasur (Nuzi).	2412	Gether son of Shem
107. Assur.	2411	Asshur son of Salah
108. Calah.	2410	Salah (Calaus) heir of Shem
109. Ninevah.	2409	Hamath daughter of the White Matriarch (Nina)
110. Harran.	2408	Sin daughter of the Yellow Matriarch
111. Carchemish.	2407	Elam son of Salah
112. Halab.	2406	Aram (Joktan) son of Eber
113. Ebla.	2405	Lud (Peleg) son of Eber
114. Ullisu.	2404	Hul son of Shem
115. Emar.	2403	Zemar daughter of the Red Matriarch
116. Tuttul.	2402	Noah (Dagan)
117. Hamath.	2401	Mash son of Shem and Hamath
118. Damascus.	2400	Uz son of Shem and the Red Matriarch
119. Mari.	2399	Arvad daughter of the Black Matriarch
120. Ana.	2398	Sheba (Yellow Matriarch)

The epoch of the 120th year stood out as equivalent to the completion of the Ark 120 years after the "end of all flesh." The new epoch marked the end of the strictly nomadic stage of Noah's initiative as he began to colonize the cult centers of Mesopotamia. The remarkable fact about those cult centers is their systematic design. In general, every Sumerian city claimed a single cult deity; and the high pantheon was distributed, with minor duplications, throughout Sumerian Mesopotamia. Sumerian civilization was a theocracy and owed its origin, as such, to the theocratic ideals of Noah himself.

To appreciate the colonization program of the Hirschnatur period, it is essential to analyze the political and geographic disposition of the four linguistic stocks in 2398. The Hirschnatur panel pictures just two of these, Indo-Europeans on the Euphrates and Semites on the Tigris. The Semites had returned to Mesopotamia via the Persian Gulf under the rebel leadership of Canaan. The Hamites, under Mizraim, were poised somewhere to the east, prepared to play the role attributed to the builders of the Tower of Babel in approaching Mesopotamia from the east. As Enakalle, ensi of Umma, Mizraim later named a son Ur-Lumma, "Champion of the Land Elam,"[55] as though the Hamites regarded part of Elam as their homeland. A logical point of settlement was Ham's Camp 21, Hamazi, south of Aratta.

The divided Ural-Altaic stock appears in the Cernunnus panel at Camps 9 and 16, on either side of Mesopotamia in northern Martu and northern Elam. It is uncertain whether these Ural-Altaic positions in the First Kish order define the locations of these stocks sixty years earlier in 2398. It is clear, however, that the Finno-Ugrians of Camp 9 returned to the vicinity of Mesopotamia by the loyalist Scorpion route; whereas the Mongol group of Camp 16 returned, under rebel leadership, from the east. The design of the Hirschnatur panel suggests that Shem kept all non-Semites and non-Indo-Europeans out of Mesopotamia between 2398 and 2368. It is reasonable to assume that the Finno-Ugrians were in Martu, the Mongol group in northern Elam, and the Hamites at Hamazi.

This analysis means that the human race was in five divisions in the period dominated by Shem. A significant coincidence is that Genesis 10:22 enumerates the primary vassals of Shem as five. The implication is that these five served as local governors, subordinate to Shem, in the Hirschnatur period. These five governorships were as follows:

Governor	Stock	Location
Elam	Hamites	Hamazi
Asshur	Ural-Altaics	Subaria

Governor	Stock	Location
Arphaxad II (Salah)	Semites	Akkadian Tigris
Lud (Peleg)	Indo-Europeans	Akkadian Euphrates
Aram (Joktan)	Finno-Ugrians (and Sumerians)	Martu

From this primitive system, constructed previous to the Tower of Babel, Elam derived his nominal association with the land Elam; Asshur, his claim over Subaria-Assyria; Salah, his supreme Semitic importance as Marduk; Peleg, his embodiment of the Indo-European stock as the ethnographic Cernunnus figure of the First Kish order; and Joktan-Aram, his nominal identification with the land Aram (Syria).

The populace who followed Noah and Shem from Eshnunna to Ana were a combination of Indo-Europeans and Finno-Ugrians (proto-Sumerians). It is logical to assume that Noah anticipated his new colonization program by leaving the Finno-Ugrians at Camp 9 about the time of his progress from Damascus to Mari in 2400. Elam, Asshur, and their father Salah had all participated in the northern itinerary, were present at Mari and Tuttul, and were available to effect rendezvous with the three eastern stocks and take command of them at the transition of power in 2398. Salah's commission was to take command of the Semites from his grandfather Canaan and lead them across the Tigris into Mesopotamia.

The task of the Indo-Europeans and Semites of the Hirschnatur panel was to colonize thirty cities in Mesopotamia between 2397 and 2368 and thus to establish the political interests of Shem and Noah in the capital zone of the earth forever. The cities of Sumer were founded, not by Sumerians, but by the Indo-Europeans and Semites. They were occupied by Sumerians at the time of the Erech-Aratta War when the other two stocks became the Erechite army, evacuating Mesopotamia in order to invade Iran.

In designating the cults of the thirty cities, Noah duplicated the princes of the original thirty camps, with nine exceptions caused by political changes. The exceptions were as follows: at Colony 129, Arphaxad's son Diklah, for his full brother Gether of Camp 9; at Colony 131, Peleg, for Canaan of Camp 11; at Colony 132, Hul, for Seba of Camp 12; at Colony 134, Lehab, for Mizraim of Camp

14; at Colony 135, Javan, for Gomer of Camp 15; at Colony 137, Salah, for the Red Matriarch of Camp 17; at Colony 141, Joktan, for Ham of Camp 21; at Colony 144, Canaan for Magog of Camp 24; and at Colony 150, Eber, for Noah of Camp 30.

Of the thirty colonies, ten were colonized by Indo-Europeans and twenty by Semites. The ten Indo-European colonies maintained their corporate identities and can be equated with ten Indo-European stocks, five from the Satem division and five from the Centum. The system began at Noah-Ninazu's Sumerian cult center of Enegir and ended at the scene of the Tower of Babel. The Indo-European colonies were confined to the Southern Orchard and Farming regions:

Colony		Designated Prince
121. Enegir.	2397	Noah (Ninazu): Balts[56]
122. Ur.	2396	Arphaxad (Nanna)
123. Gishbanda.	2395	Japheth (Ningishzida-Svarog): Slavs
124. Bitkarkara.	2394	Shem (Ishkur)
125. Guabba.	2393	Hamath (Ninmar)
126. Zararim (Larsa).	2392	Zemar (Shenirda) wife of Obal (Utu)
127. Isin.	2391	Sin (Bau-Diana) sister of Arphaxad (Saturnus): Italics
128. Eresh.	2390	Arvad (Nissaba-Parvati): East Indians
129. Kiabrig.	2389	Diklah (Ninhar)
130. Kish.	2388	Sabtechah (Zababa)
131. Cuthah.	2387	Peleg (Nergal-Fricco): Phrygians
132. Kullab.	2386	Hul (Wild Bull Dumuzi) son of Black Matriarch (Ninsun)
133. Girsu (Lagash).	2385	Nimrod (Ningirsu-Orion): Hellenes
134. Tummal.	2384	Lehab (Ninlil): Celts[57]
135. Agade.	2383	Javan (Aba)
136. Kesh.	2382	Ashkenaz (Ashshirgi) son of Yellow Matriarch (Ninhursaga): Teutons
137. Ku-ar.	2381	Salah (Asalluhe)
138. Erech.	2380	Uzal (Inanna)
139. Nina.	2379	White Matriarch (Nanshe)
140. Adab.	2378	Yellow Matriarch (Ninhursaga): Tocharians[58]

Colony		Designated Prince
141. Umma.	2377	Joktan (Shara)
142. Kinirsha.	2376	Black Matriarch (female Dumuzi-abzu)
143. Vicinity of Eridu.	2375	Riphath (male Dumuzi-abzu)
144. Nippur.	2374	Canaan (Enlil): Hittites (Anatolians)
145. Girsu on the Euphrates.	2373	Madai (Damu): Iranians
146. Eridu.	2372	Sidon (Enki)
147. Badtibira.	2371	Togarmah (Dumuzi the Shepherd)
148. Larak.	2370	Seba (Ensipazianna)
149. Sippar.	2369	Obal (Utu)
150. Babylon.	2368	Eber (Nabu)

Such was the shortlived empire of the Hirschnatur panel, combining the two stocks of the "Yahweh Elohim of Shem," under the imperial rulership of Shem. World population was still too small to justify the term "empire"; but the process of colonization foreshadowed things to come. If the regime built by Shem had lasted, there would have been no irreversible gentile apostasy and no need to form Israel as a counter-world. But Shem's regime was shortlived. Semites and Indo-Europeans remained in Mesopotamia until the Erech-Aratta War; and the Semites of Agade later took control of Mesopotamia under Sargon. But Shem's version of the Mesopotamian world order began to collapse thirty years after its origin as Canaan's faction came to power, reorganized the Noahic stocks within Mesopotamia, and constructed the Tower of Babel.

NOTES

[1]Kramer, *The Sumerians,* p. 51.

[2]Ibid., p. 281.

[3]*Makers of Civilization,* p. 306.

[4]Ions, p. 29.

[5]These three couples appear within the first twelve lines of the epic. Alexander Heidel, *The Babylonian Genesis* (Chicago: University Press, 1963), p. 18.

[6]Medb, given mistress of the Iranian sector, is entirely distinct from the Mahadevi. Medb was Inanna of Aratta (Camp 18); Mahadevi, the Red Matriarch of Camp 17 in the Zagros Mountains, somewhere to the west of Aratta. Rulership of the Iranian region was redefined at various points of time.

[7]Jacobsen, *Toward the Image of Tammuz,* p. 24. Ningirda's derivation from Enki means that she derived from the depths of the antediluvian past. In reality, the euhemeristic Enki was her grandson Sidon through her royal son Canaan. According to the same specious logic, the Egyptians identified Canaan as Ra-Harakhte, who was supposed to have begun his reign 120 years before the Flood.

[8]The First Ennead or first set of nine gods in the Egyptian pantheon, is analyzed in Chapter Five. It included Inanna as Nut, Japheth as Geb, and Japheth's sons Seba and Zud as Osiris and Seth.

[9]For a definition of this religion, see M. J. Vermaseren, *Mithras, the Secret God* (New York: Barnes and Noble, 1963), passim.

[10]Grosse, *Der Silberkessel von Gundestrup,* p. 83.

[11]Hallo and Simpson, *The Ancient Near East,* p. 64.

[12]See "People of the Middle East," Map, *National Geographic Magazine* 142 (July 1972), 1A.

[13]For the equation of Aratta with Isfahan see Hartmut Schmökel, "Mesopotamian Texts," *Near Eastern Religious Texts Relating to the Old Testament,* ed. Walter Beyerlin (Philadelphia: Westminster Press, 1978), p. 86.

[14]The eight epochs of the exterior Gundestrup panels extended down to the 240th year, making that date the last of its postdiluvian kind. Sargon's imperial power derived from a new imperial status

quo established for the next epoch of the 270th year.

[15]Robert W. Ehrich, ed., *Chronologies in Old World Archaeology* (Chicago: University Press, 1954), p. 178.

[16]"Ebla in the Late Early Syrian Period: the Royal Palace and the State Archives," *Biblical Archaeologist* 39 (September, 1976), 97-99.

[17]*The Sumerians,* p. 53.

[18]*The Ancient Near East,* p. 54.

[19]P. Van Der Meer, *The Chronology of Ancient Western Asia and Egypt,* 2nd ed. (Leiden: E. J. Brill, 1963), p. 48.

[20]"A Biblical Approach to Dating the Earth: A Case for the Use of Genesis 5 and 11 as an Exact Chronology," Richard Niessen, *Creation Research Society Quarterly* 19 (June, 1982), 62.

[21]The great flood occurred during the reign of Yao. Kenneth Scott Latourette, *The Chinese Their History and Culture* (New York: Macmillan, 1964), p. 27. Yao's reign is dated 2357-55 in *Sources of Chinese Tradition,* ed. William Theodore de Bary (New York: Columbia University Press, 1960), I, xix.

[22]Hallo and Simpson, pp. 52-53.

[23]The first thirty-six "Ayodhya" reigns previous to the reign of Sagara-Sargon divided the ninety years from the First Kish epoch to the Akkadian epoch.

[24]Kramer, p. 51.

[25]Van Der Meer explicitly names a total of 119 years for the accumulated reigns of four Akkadian emperors, namely, Sargon, Rimush, Manishtushu, and Naram Sin. The total misses just one year of the abstract imperium of 120 years. The important figure is this 120-year period, beginning in the middle of the twenty-third century as Van Der Meer suggests. The individual terms are less authoritative and less significant. For example, Van Der Meer gives Sargon the fifty-six years specified in the Kinglist but gives Naram Sin only thirty-six, twenty less than the same fifty-six specified for him. It is assumed that whatever sources yielded these specific terms were exercising liberty in dividing the imperium of 120 years. Van Der Meer, loc. cit.

[26]Astour shows this second millennium village at the appropriate distance west of Carchemish. It serves merely to symbolize Camp

4. Michael Astour, "Hittite Syria Ca. 1275 B.C." (Map), ed. Gordon D. Young, *Ugarit in Retrospect* (Winona Lake, Indiana: Eisenbrauns, 1981), p. 8 (facing plate).

[27]Because Tuttul existed in the third millennium, the location given by Astour suggests an actual camp site, near the confluence of the Euphrates and Balikh Rivers south of Harran. Tuttul was a leading cult center of the god Dagan, standard Semitic cult version of Noah. Astour's suggested location differs from those given by other authorities but supplies a striking definition for Camp 7. Ibid.

[28]Cyrus Gordon names the four, then notes the analogy between them and the diluvian octad: "It may be a mere coincidence, but it is curious that P. V. traces the human race to four men and four women, even as the Bible derives all surviving humanity from Noah and his three sons and four women: one wife for each of the four men saved in the Ark." *Before Columbus* (New York: Crown, 1971), 155, 164. The mythic detail of the unrising sun appears in Alexander, *Latin American Mythology,* p. 166.

[29]John Arnott MacCulloch, *Eddic Mythology, Mythology of All Races* (New York: Cooper Square, 1964), II, 281.

[30]Martin A. Beek, *Atlas of Mesopotamia,* trans. D. R. Welsh (London: Thomas Nelson, 1962), p. 63.

[21]Schmökel, loc. cit.

[32] Kramer, p. 270.

[33]Jacobsen, p. 34.

[34]Because of its political association with northwestern Ebla, Pettinato locates Hamazi in northwestern Iran between the Caspian and Lake Urmia. This position lies intermediate between our Taranis and Medb zones rather than in the south of the Medb zone as we suggest. Pettinato's three-sphere analysis of Ebla, Kish, and Hamazi resembles our three-sphere analysis of the Taranis, Cernunnus, and Medb zones. Giovanni Pettinato, *The Archives of Ebla* (Garden City, NY: Doubleday, 1981), p. 108.

[35]Kramer, p. 328.

[36]Ibid., p. 153.

[37]Moret, p. 88.

[38]Ibid., p. 40.

[39]Ibid., p. 45.

[40]Ibid., p. 58.

[41]Ibid.

[42]Ibid., p. 107.

[43]Wazet wore the red crown of Lower Egypt; and Neith, the white crown of Upper Egypt. Ibid., pp. 111-12.

[44]Andrew Tooke, *The Pantheon,* rev. ed. (London: C. Elliot, 1784), pp. 144 ff.

[45]Heidel, p. 20.

[46]*The Epic of Rama,* trans. Romesh Dutt, in *The Wisdom of China and India,* ed. Lin Yutang (New York: Modern Library, 1942), p. 142.

[47]Nicholson, p. 113.

[48]One evidence of this supplanting role is that one of the White Matriarch's most important Sumerian versions bears the name Ningal, "Great Lady," analogous to Mahadevi, "Great Goddess." Jacobsen. p. 26.

[49]Leviticus 18:8 furnishes a loose analogy except that the sexual polarity of the verse reverses the situation in Genesis 9, equating the mother's nakedness with the father's. If this logic is inverted, Ham's act of witnessing his father's nakedness meant claiming his mother's nakedness as his own.

[50]Gordon defines the Sumerian *hul* as "harmfulness, unpleasantness, rigour." This definition aptly characterizes the cult of Yahweh from the perjorative angle of Sumerian culture. Edmund I. Gordon, *Sumerian Proverbs* (New York: Greenwood Press, 1968), p. 365.

[51]The Hellenic system of constellations derived from Babylonian precedents and was almost entirely independent of the Egyptian system. The constellation systems, like all forms of mythology, are valued here for their logical productiveness.

[52]William Tyler Olcott, *Field Book of the Skies,* eds. R. Newton Mayall and Margaret W. Mayall, 4th ed. (New York: G. P. Putnam's Sons, 1954), p. 171.

[53]Radcliffe-Brown, A. R., *The Andaman Islanders* (Glencoe, IL: Free Press, 1948), passim.

[54]Jacobsen, p. 24.

[55]The name appears in Hallo and Simpson, p. 53. The meaning

of Sumerian *ur,* "champion," is given by Gordon, p. 428.

[56]Noah, the Latvian "Indra," found representation on opposite shores of the Baltic in the Finns and Balts. The Finns or Sitones took their name from Siton, a variant of Noah's standard identity as Dagan father of Aliyan Bal.

[57]The Celts knew Lehab's black grandmother as their Earth Mother, wife of Lugh (Japheth). They derived from the original Hamitic stock of Egypt and are believed to have reached Europe from North Africa, the general region of Libya named for Lehab.

[58]The Centum Tocharians settled in the same region of Central Asia where the Khazars of Hazarmaveth originated. Hazarmaveth is the Hebrew name of Lugalannemundu of Adab in the Sumerian farming region.

Chapter 5

The Imperial Age I: Mesopotamian Consolidation

The Tower of Babel

Talmudic tradition accurately interprets the Tower of Babel as an Egyptian phenomenon, not because the Hamitic stock was solely responsible for the Tower scheme, but because the Hamitic tongue of the Utuship was supposed to have been the universal imperial language of mankind. The divine judgment on the Tower of Babel did not generate but confused languages. Noah's adversaries, coming to formal power a century and a half after the Flood, succeeded in a scheme to impose the Hamitic tongue on all mankind in celebration of a new Imperial Age. They completed the Tower a decade later and experienced the confusion of tongues a year later in 2357 B.C.

Although the logic of the Geb-Nut Cosmogony originated with the primitive "creation" sequence of Camps 18-25, its chief purpose was to celebrate the ethnography of the Tower of Babel era. In the previous era of the Hirschnatur panel, mankind was divided into four linguistic and five regional stocks: Ural-Altaics in northern Elam and northern Martu, Hamites in the Medb zone of Iran, and Semites and Indo-Europeans in various cult centers of Mesopotamia. According to the Geb-Nut alternative, the same Noahic race was divided into three regional stocks and only one linguistic stock. The two halves of the Ural-Altaic stock of the Anship were reunited in the inverted triangle of Nut along the Akkadian Tigris and Euphrates; the Semites of Enlil-Shu formed a vertical axis running southward from the site of Babel (Camp 12) to Enlil's cult center of Nippur;

and the Indo-Europeans took the prone position of Geb (Japheth-Ningishzida), extending east and west from the Sumerian Euphrates to the Tigris. The Hamites were an implicit presence in all these lands, having undertaken the missionary endeavor of teaching their imperial language to all three of the other stocks.

If Noah's will had prevailed, the Red Matriarch would have celebrated the epoch of the 150th year by introducing a language peculiar to herself, creating a fifth linguistic stock out of her progeny, the Amerindians. Instead, the chaotic revolution of the curse of Canaan had transformed the Red Matriarch into the royal "wife" of her son Ham, who now acted through her to shape the world into a pan-Hamitic form. The Hamitic stock now merited its name, serving Ham rather than its author Japheth. At the opening of the era, Ham and his mother descended from the Medb zone in grand style, at the head of the imperial Hamitic stock, traveling westward into Akkad (Genesis 11:2). Because the Medb zone belonged to the heaven goddess Inanna (Nut), their pretense was to bring the cult of heaven with them into the heart of the capital zone, creating what would have been the Mesopotamian cult center of the god Anu, whose lack of such a center eventually testified to the impact of the Tower of Babel judgment.

Some versions of the Geb-Nut design are decidedly triangular, offering a two-dimensional image of the pyramid design. There is little question that the Tower of Babel was a prototype of the Mesopotamian ziggurat and Egyptian pyramid, a numinous form symbolic of the cosmos of the third heaven.[1] Ham reverted to much the same form in his beautifully designed lunar temple at Ur. In addition to symbolizing heaven, this form represented the human cosmos of monogenetic genealogy, expanding downward and outward from the apex of a single patriarch. Noah was just such a patriarch and had obtained the Anship of heaven, before yielding it to Ham and later to Shem as Melchizedek, priest of El Elyon. To make good his new claim to the Anship, Ham determined to build the archetypal temple of heaven, in his own name, at what would have been the sacred focal point of El Elyon on earth. The Polynesian version of Ham, the heaven god Raki, was supposed to have declared, "All of you carry me above, that I may be elevated."[2]

Ham's political goal was to break Shem's monopoly over Mesopotamia. This could only be done through subterfuge. The linguistic missionaries were a standard feature of the Noahic cosmos; and Ham's emissaries were supposed to have taught the new Amerindian tongue to a fraction of each colony. Once the program began, it was a fairly simple matter to substitute Hamitic for the new tongue and to spread it throughout every colony. The sequence of events in Genesis 11:1-2 implies that the linguistic missionary work preceded the advent of the main body of Hamites in Mesopotamia.

The British Protestant school of euhemerists believed that the ringleader of the Tower of Babel scheme was Nimrod. A close inspection of the Egyptian First Ennead reveals the extent of Nimrod's importance at this time. The nine deities of the First Ennead were the political structure proper to the Tower of Babel era. The unmarried sun god Ra generated the first couple Shu and Tefnut, parents of Geb and Nut, who generated two couples, Osiris and Isis and Seth and Nephthys.[3] At the core of the system was the Egyptian Atlas figure Shu, upholder of heaven in the central vertical shaft position of the Cosmogony. As air god, Shu was the Egyptian counterpart to Enlil, holding the value of Enlil in the Tower of Babel regime. Although the Sumerian Enlil was Canaan, the Egyptian Shu was his son Nimrod, Sumerian Ninurta.

Ninurta's motif of recovering the Enlilship took rise from the transition of power in the 150th year. Canaan selected his son Nimrod to supplant Shem as "upholder" of the Mesopotamian world order. Thus Shu upholds Nut in the same way that Shem of the Hirschnatur panel upholds the two stags. We have seen how Nimrod, as Ninurta, absorbed Shem's double-stag image into the Imdugud of his own cult at Lagash. The British euhemerists were correct to the extent that Nimrod was the imperial core of the Noahic cosmos in the era of the Tower of Babel; and this insight brings to bear on the Tower of Babel scheme the logic of Genesis 10:10, the beginning of Nimrod's "kingdom" at Babel, Erech, Accad, and Calneh (Nippur).

As a tetrad, the four locations of Genesis 10:10 suggest capitals of local governorships under the four couples of the Ennead. Although Erech was not formally established until the 210th year, the name Erech implies the station of Geb-Japheth (Ningishzida) in the southland of Sumer. When Meskiaggasher later founded Erech, he did so as son of Utu,[4] indicating the theocratic tie between his regime and the earlier regime of the sun god Ra in the Tower era. As Shu-Enlil, Nimrod logically reigned from Enlil's cult center of

Nippur, primitive Camp 24. As Osiris, Seba recovered his Camp 12 in Akkad, making it the scene of the Tower of Babel; and his brother Seth-Tudia governed the prototype of Agade, foreshadowing the rise of Agade in the pan-Semitic age of Sargon and Ebrium.

To complete the system, the sun god Ra-Utu (Obal) reigned independently of Nimrod's "kingdom" at his traditional cult center of Sippar. The geographic cosmos of the Tower era had a decidedly Akkadian polarity. Babel, Agade, and Sippar all lay in Akkad; Nippur, in northern Sumer; and Erech, not far from Nippur. Because the Hirschnatur cosmos had divided mankind into five divisions, we are safe in assuming that the five males of the Ennead drew these five stocks to the locations indicated.

Regime of the First Ennead: 2368-2357 B.C.

Prince	Stock	Location
Obal (Ra)	Finno-Ugrians (Sumerians)	Sippar
Nimrod (Shu)	Semites	Nippur
Japheth (Geb)	Indo-Europeans	Erech
Seba (Osiris)	Hamites	Babel
Zud (Seth)	Ural-Altaics	Agade

This scheme was the rebel variation of what would have been a far-flung colonization program outside Mesopotamia. The builders of the Tower of Babel were motivated by a fear of being "scattered abroad over the face of the whole earth" (Genesis 11:4). We have seen that the design of the Braided Goddess panel refers both to the geography of the primitive maritime transition from Sumer to Egypt and to some application of the same geography to the Tower of Babel era. That geography contains eight points, the seven transitional camps in addition to the point of the fallen boar in Yemen. It is quite apparent that eight of the First Ennead were supposed to have colonized these eight points leaving a ninth colony within Mesopotamia. Such was the loyalist plan thwarted by the Tower of Babel scheme.

This loyalist alternative scheme called for dividing the five regional stocks of the Hirschnatur era into nine regional stocks by subdividing the three undivided stocks (Hamites, Semites, and Indo-Europeans) in the same fashion as the Ural-Altaics and by adding a new Amerindian stock created by the Red Matriarch. The nine personae of the First Ennead would then have governed these stocks in the colonies of the Braided Goddess panel as well as Mesopotamia:

Location	Stock	Prince
Mesopotamia	Sumerians	Obal (Utu)
Makran	Ural-Altaics	Uzal (Inanna)
Indus	Indo-Europeans I	Japheth (Prajapati)
Hadramaut	Semites I	Nimrod (Ninib)
Yemen	Semites II	Sin (Gula)
Ethiopia	Hamites I	Seba (Osiris)
Egypt	Hamites II	Naphtuh (Nephthys)
Sinai	Amerindians	Zud (Tupan-Zapana)
Greater Canaan	Indo-Europeans II	Pathrus (Nephele)

Much of this alternative scheme was realized in later times through the persistence of the loyalist faction in enforcing Noah's ideas. The Sumerians obviously settled in Mesopotamia. On the eve of the Erech-Aratta War, the Ural-Altaics settled at Aratta, if not in the land of Maka-Gedrosia intended for them. The Semites eventually claimed Arabia; and the Hamites, East Africa. Nevertheless, the Tower of Babel scheme delayed all of this colonial activity and damaged much of its integrity and purpose.

Driven by their fear of colonial dispersion, the builders of the Tower of Babel sought to "make a name" for themselves. The Geb-Nut design shows what sort of "name" they sought. The rebel faction attempted to counter the divine dual name "Yahweh Elohim" with a triple divine name of their own. Both Hellenic and East Indian tradition include "three-eyed" deities, Zeus Triophthalmus and Shiva Tryambaka. These multiple eyes clearly refer to "eyes of the Lamb," the divine names. In Sumerian terms, the dual name of Shem's God would have read "Ishkur Enlil." The analogous formation of the Geb-Nut triad would have read, "An Enlil Ningishzida," that is, "Nut Shu Geb." One of these names, Geb, does not belong to the theocratic octad but represents Japheth in abstraction from the Utuship of Ra. If we insert the pan-Hamitic Utuship into the Geb-Nut triad, the composite name actually reads

"An Utu Enlil of Japheth," analogous to the "Ishkur Enlil of Shem."

Another evidence of the triad formation of the Tower of Babel ideology is the Lagashite Imdugud variation of the two lions.[5] At the heart of the Lagashite pantheon stood Ninurta, Nimrod-Shu, heart of the Tower of Babel order. If the Imdugud bird of the two stags represents Shem in control of two stocks in the Hirschnatur era, the analogous Imdugud bird of the two lions represents Nimrod in the analogous position of Shu in the Tower of Babel era. The lion's head of the Imdugud bird makes all three figures of the Imdugud-lion design leonine. The lion symbolized the Hamitic linguistic stock, both in the Cernunnus and Braided Goddess panels. The Imdugud bird of the two lions proclaims that Nimrod succeeded in transforming the three regional stocks of the Tower of Babel order into Hamitic speakers. Yet the Imdugud of the two lions also suggests that Nimrod maintained this status quo by violence. The bird is pictured as clutching the lions' hindquarters as they twist upward to bite its outspread wings. Thus Nimrod was the first tyrant in the full sense, forcing the Ural-Altaic and Indo-European stocks to submit to him against their wills.[6]

The regime of the First Ennead lasted only eleven years until the Tower of Babel judgment. Everyone understood from the judgment that an authoritative supernatural power opposed the pan-Hamitic idea and that the different linguistic stocks would have to be maintained as such. The judgment might have been expected to discredit Canaan's rebel faction and to inspire an immediate restoration of Shem and Noah; but such was not the case. Nineteen years remained to the era allotted to Canaan's faction; and Shem and Noah were too devoted to political due process to interrupt the era with a new regime of their own.

Instead, a minor revolution occurred within Canaan's faction. The First Ennead had been a compromise coalition, featuring Japheth-Geb as original author of the Hamitic stock. In it, Nimrod-Shu had stood alone as a member of Canaan's immediate family. In 2357, instead of handing power over to the loyalists, Canaan made the inner core of his family a new and less compromising rebel imperium, the system of Seal 685.[7]

Canaan's firstborn Sidon now entered center stage of Noahic history as Enki of the Seal and Egyptian Ptah, "heart and tongue of the Ennead."⁸ East Indian tradition interprets its version of Sidon, Kasyapa, as an Atlas figure, upholding the world, because he had replaced the previous two Atlas figures, Shem and Nimrod, as heart of the Noahic cosmos. The other anthropomorphic members of the Seal were his son Elishah (Sha-Usmu), son Salah (rising sun god), wife Uzal (Inanna as grain goddess), and brother Nimrod (Ninurta as bowman).

The symbolic function of the Seal is to describe how Sidon's new rebel coalition took command of the nine linguistic stocks originally designed by the loyalists and newly sanctioned by the judgment at Babel. The design of the Seal is fourfold, showing Sha to the right, Enki to the right of center, the sun god and grain goddess to the left of center, and Ninurta to the left. Each of these accounted for a pair of linguistic half-stocks except for Enki, who controlled the new Amerindian stock in addition to two half-stocks. The nine stocks of Seal 685 were disposed as follows:

Stock	Figure	Prince
Semites A-B	Double-faced Sha	Elishah
Sumerians	Enki	Sidon
Ural-Altaics	Kneeling Bull of Enki	Javan
Amerindians	Palm Bird of Enki	Uz
Indo-Europeans A (Satem)	Rising Sun God	Salah (Surya)
Indo-Europeans B (Centum)	Grain Goddess	Inanna (Medb)
Hamites A (Lower Egyptians)	Hunter	Nimrod (Shu)
Hamites B (Upper Egyptians)	Roaring Lion	Canaan (Harakhte of Edfu)

An important detail of Seal 685 is the representation of Japheth's grandson Javan as a bull kneeling beneath Enki's feet. Half-buried in the base of the seal, this bull matches the prone figure of Geb-Japheth in the Geb-Nut Cosmogony, establishing mythological continuity before and after 2357. Javan replaced Japheth for the same reason that we find recorded in Genesis 10:4, namely, that Javan became the feudal lord of Sidon-Enki's "Libyan" family, including Elishah-Sha, pictured to the right of the seal. Despite the humiliated posture of the bull, Chinese tradition remembered the transition of power recorded in Seal 685 as the accession of Emperor Yao,[9] their version of Yawan or Javan.

In 2357, the Sino-Tibetan stock did not yet exist but was scheduled for formal establishment at the next epoch. In the system of Seal 685, Javan governed the Mongoloid Ural-Altaics, from whom the Tibetans derived. The Chinese, who owed much of their genetic character to Javan's father, Gomer, could logically trace their origin back to 2357, especially if Javan, like Shem, introduced the new language prematurely. In any case, Sino-Tibetans have the distinction of coinciding in origin with the "Confusion of Tongues" at Babel.

Because Genesis 11:8 states that the builders of the Tower were "scattered abroad from there over the face of all the earth," some process of dispersion intervened between the fivefold order of the First Ennead and the elevenfold or twelvefold order of First Kish. When Javan came to power as "Emperor Yao," the human race was located in the five regions of the First Ennead: Sippar, Agade, Babel, Nippur, and Erech. The design of Seal 685 suggests that the immediate response to the Tower of Babel judgment was to spread northward beyond Sippar and Agade toward the primitive homeland of Syrian Mesopotamia.

The figure of Sha, at the right end of the seal, establishes Elishah's character as Lelex, the "Second Semitic Japhethite," in control of the Semitic linguistic stock after 2357. We are safe in assuming that the Semites remained at Nippur, the seat of Enlil, where they appeared as the dog of Cernunnus after 2338. Thus the right end of the seal corresponds to the southeastern limit of Sidon's new order at Nippur. All of the populace south of Nippur had been withdrawn to build the Tower of Babel. The figure of Enki, with the kneeling bull, represents the Sumerians and Ural-Altaics at the existing camps of Sippar and Agade.

The two remaining stocks of the First Ennead migrated farther north to the positions at the left end of the seal. Their dispersion camps appear as the symbolic mountain of the rising sun god and grain goddess and the figures of a hunter and lion. The chief mountain of early Noahic tradition was the Jebel el Bishri, from which Noah's daughter Arvad took the Satem Aryan name Parvati, "From the Mountain."[10] Inanna holds a sheaf of grain atop the symbolic mountain to signify her substitution for Arvad, the Sumerian grain goddess Nissaba. She and her son Salah, the sun god Surya, divided the Indo-European stock into its Centum and Satem divisions at parallel camps west and east of Jebel el Bishri. These positions, to the north of Martu, explain why the Indo-Europeans of the Cernunnus panel appear to the west of the Euphrates in Martu.

The offending Hamites were banished farthest from Mesopotamia toward their ancestral fief of Syria. One division of the stock under the "hunter" Nimrod took Camp 7 of his wife Bau-Isin at Tuttul. The other, under Canaan, took Camp 6 at the Taranis serpent, Emar. In settling in or near the Syrian fief, however briefly, the Hamites deepened the Egyptian claim to Syria in an ancestral process culminating in the Battle of Carchemish.

The Hamites and Indo-Europeans were banished to the remote end of the post-Babel order because open hostility between them had punctuated the effort to build the Tower of Babel. We have seen one evidence of this hostility in the Imdugud Bird of the Two Lions. More literalistic evidence derives from Mesopotamian Seal 690.

The seal shows how the nine foundational stocks of the First Ennead were occupied while the Tower of Babel was being built. Of the nine anthropomorphic figures, six work on a temple tower, a god stands in the "Ka" posture, and two additional gods are in conflict, one striking the other down. These details have a decidedly "Egyptian" value, not only because of the pan-Hamitic Tower, but because the tableau of gods in conflict matches the climactic ritual of the Egyptian Sed festival,[11] just as the correlative Mesopotamian Seal 684 depicts the Sed pole itself. The three gods to the left of the tower are the three elders of the Ennead: Obal (Ra), Nimrod (Shu), and Japheth (Geb). Obal adopts the same "Ka" posture as he does in the Trinity panel nineteen years later. Japheth lies prone as he does in the Geb-Nut Cosmogony; and Nimrod duplicates his image as Shu, standing above him. But there is a rather horrifying difference between Seal 690 and the Cosmogony.

Seal 690 is more literalistic than the Cosmogony; and its message is embarrassing, if not shocking. Genesis 10:21 labels Japheth *ha-gadol*, "the great one," as though he were the tallest and strongest of the male survivors of the Flood. But the mulatto Nimrod was taller and stronger yet. The history of postdiluvian warfare began as a physical duel between the two, Nimrod championing Canaan's faction and Japheth, Shem's faction. The crisis came when Japheth refused to evacuate Sumer in order to add its Indo-European populace to the builders and worshippers of the Tower. Because the Tower scheme demanded the symbolic participation of all mankind, Japheth knew that he could thwart the scheme by refusing to send laborers northward to Camp 12. Nimrod acquired his image as "mighty hunter of Yahweh" (and as the captor Varuna), by leading one of the Hamite divisions southward to subdue Japheth's populace, Indo-Europeans of the Storm God. As in the Erech-Aratta War, the battle took form chiefly as a duel between champions. Nimrod literally battered Japheth into submission and carried the separatistic populace off to the "plain in Shinar."

Japheth survived the duel but never forgave this humiliation; and his hatred for Nimrod triggered the confusing political circumstances of the Erech-Aratta War, when the loyalist Peleg formed a temporary alliance with Nimrod, split the loyalist faction, and provoked Japheth into supporting Salah's Erechite version of Canaan's rebel cause. Because of their roles in the conflict of Seal 690, the Indo-Europeans and Hamites were banished from Mesopotamia to the Upper Euphrates in 2357.

The First Kish Order

Chinese tradition emphasizes the century-long reign of "Emperor Yao" because the First Kish epoch, in the nineteenth year of this period, meant the birth of the Sino-Tibetan linguistic stock. This stock was distilled from the Mongoloid population of existing stocks and made their way to Camps 14 and 15 of the Fish and Rider on the Tigris not far from Mesopotamian Larak. This process, which meant birth to the Chinese, meant death to the First Ennead regime, in fact, the mythological death of Osiris on the "seventeenth day of Athyr."[12]

The "death of Osiris" occurred in November, 2338 B.C., and was nothing more nor less than the First Kish epoch with all its political, religious, and ethnological implications. A mythological version of the same event was the East Indian Feast of Daksha, stressing conflict between Osiris (Shiva) and Daksha, Arphaxad I, the bearded face of the Trinity panel. The Sumerians remembered the same event, not only as the Flood epoch of their First Kish dynasty, but also in their Myth of Adapa, in which the protagonists are Enki, the reigning figure of Seal 685, and the ritual sinner Adapa, another version of the same Seba-Osiris-Shiva.

In 2338, Sidon managed to single out Seba as scapegoat for the guilt incurred in the Tower of Babel scheme. Sidon's father-in-law Arphaxad, as Daksha, vilified Seba as an unworthy suitor to his daughter Sati,[13] a sister of Inanna and personification of the newly formed Chinese race. The Chinese were chiefly the Mongoloid contingent of the existing Hamitic stock, derived from the Mongoloid prince Gomer, Hamitic Khufu. The Chinese distillation was interpreted as the "death of Osiris" because the Hamitic stock had inhabited Seba's Camp 12, the immediate scene of the Tower of Babel. The same circumstance explains why Seba was singled out as scapegoat for the guilt of the Tower of Babel.

The Egyptian Legend of Osiris claims that the god reigned twenty-eight years before being slaughtered by Seth.[14] This detail means that the Hamites of Babel had begun to construct the Tower twenty-eight years before the First Kish epoch or two years after the Tower epoch in 2366. Another detail is that Seth cut Osiris' body into fourteen or more pieces, a reference to the subdivision of Noahic mankind at the First Kish epoch. The total of fourteen represented the sum of eleven provinces of the Cernunnus system and the temporary colonies of Seal 685 at Camps 6, 7, and 8 in Syria.

We have seen that Seals 690 and 685 represent the Mesopotamian world order before and after the Tower of Babel judgment in 2357. All of the seals derived from Canaan's rebel faction and reflected its viewpoint, the classic Mesopotamian viewpoint of Sidon and Salah. Because the Tower of Babel era belonged to the rebel faction, there was no difficulty in matching the rebel viewpoint with the political realities of the period. But the loyalist order of First Kish posed a problem. How could the rebels lay memorial claim to a political order created by their adversaries? The answer lies in Seal 684, where the rebel sphere of influence, instead of being abolished in the First Kish period, is simply contracted.

Seal 684 represents a geo-political fraction of the Cernunnus system granted to the rebels in order to maintain peace throughout the period from 2338 to 2308. The classic Mesopotamian rebels remembered it as their version of the First Kish order, forgetting the larger context of the Cernunnus panel. Thus Seal 684 and the Cernunnus panel are cognate variations of the same system, variations indexed by the contrasting male deities of the Trinity panel, the loyalist Arphaxad I and his son Obal (Ra of the First Ennead). The interpretive challenge is to coordinate Seal 684 with the Cernunnus panel and with the underlying Noahic camps of Mesopotamia reflected in the Cernunnus panel.

The fish to the right of the Cernunnus panel matches the enthroned water god Enki to the right of the seal. The kneeling figure to the left of the seal holds a Mesopotamian version of the Sed pole, sign of Osiris of Camp 12, equivalent to the Hamitic lion of Cernunnus. Because we have identified the Fish and Rider complex with the Sino-Tibetan stock at Camps 14 and 15, the four figures of the seal represent Camps 12-15 inclusive, the contracted rebel sphere of the period. The Sino-Tibetans, symbolized by Arphaxad's rebellious daughter Sati, belonged to the rebel sphere because of their debt of origin to the older Hamitic stock. Sati's self-immolation on the funeral pyre of Shiva meant the willingness of the Sino-Tibetan stock to share in the contracted system together with Seba's Hamitic stock, the stooping figure to the left.

In the seal, two sun gods intervene between Seba and Sidon at either end. Because Camp 13, Lagash, belonged to Nimrod, the sun god to the left represents Nimrod-Helius, the personified Sun of Hellenic tradition. We might have supposed that the other sun god represents the Hellenic Apollo, the classic sun god Obal-Ra; but no link exists between Camp 14 and Obal. Instead the sun god of Camp 14 is the Chinese Emperor Yao, Gomer's son Javan, whose Hellenic identity coalesces with Nimrod's in the curious name "Ion" of Ionia. Camp 14 originally belonged to Mizraim, who transferred it to his maternal grandson Javan as lord of the newly formed Chinese race at the sign of the fish. Sidon-Enki, at the right end, answers to the Tibetan fish rider, the second anthropomorphic figure of the panel, diminished rebel counterpart to the anthropomorphic Peleg-Cernunnus.

In other words, the seat of rebel power in the First Kish period extended from the site of the Tower of Babel southeastward to Lagash and eastward to a pair of camps on the Tigris near Al Kut. These sites encompassed four populations: Hamites and African blacks at Babel and Lagash and Chinese and Tibetans on the Tigris. The rest of the nations belonged, for the time being, to a larger loyalist sphere, under the imperial rule of Cernunnus, Peleg the

Divider.[15] The two halves of the Indo-European stock returned from Jebel el Bishri to join him at Camp 11. Japheth, as the serpent Ningishzida, now reigned over the Sumerians on the Lower Euphrates, the serpent of Cernunnus. In reunifying under Peleg, the Indo-Europeans reduced the number of stocks by one unit; but this was replaced by the subdivision of Obal's colony at Sippar into Finno-Ugrians (Subarians) and Sumerians. As the eldest linguistic stock, the Ural-Altaic had now been subdivided into three nations: Subarians at Camp 9, Mongols at Camp 16, and Sumerians at Camp 25 in their homeland of Sumer.

The second Noahic stock, the Hamitic, had now been divided five ways into the Lower or "red" Egyptians at Camp 12, Cushite blacks at Camp 13, Chinese at Camp 14, Tibetans at Camp 15, and Upper or "white" Egyptians at Camp 21 (outside the Cernunnus zone). A correlation existed between these five divisions and the five males of the First Ennead. The two proto-Egyptian stocks, who remained Hamitic speakers, derived from Osiris' colony at Babel and Geb's colony at Erech where Nimrod had conquered Japheth. The Cushites derived from the Mongol sphere under Seth at Agade. After the ninetieth year, Cush had governed the Mongols as Kara Khan, the "Black Prince." The Tatars remembered the separation of Mongols and blacks, in 2338, as the expulsion of Kara Khan out of "heaven,"[16] the northern realm of the heaven goddess Nut. The two Sino-Tibetan divisions probably originated as Hamitic subdivisions who had left Babel to replace Sumerians and Semites at Sippar and Nippur when the latter sent workmen to build the Tower of Babel.

To simplify this rather complex picture, we can outline the immediate geographic source of each stock and trace it to its appointed place in the system of the Cernunnus panel:

Stock	Location Before 2338	Location After 2338
Subarians (Ural-Altaic A)	Sippar	Camp 9 (Martu)
Amerindians (Semitic Conversion A)	Nippur	Camp 10 (Martu)
Indo-Europeans	Jebel el Bishri (exile from Sumer)	Camp 11 (Martu)

Stock	Location Before 2338	Location After 2338
Red Hamites	Syria (exile from Babel)	Camp 12 (Babel)
Black Africans (Hamitic Conversion A)	Agade	Camp 13 (Lagash)
Chinese (Hamitic Conversion B)	Sippar (from Babel)	Camp 14
Tibetans (Hamitic Conversion C)	Nippur (from Babel)	Camp 15
Mongols (Ural-Altaic B)	Agade	Camp 16 (Elam)
White Hamites	Syria (exile from Babel and Sumer)	Camp 21 (Hamazi)
Dravidians (Semitic Conversion B)	Nippur	Camp 23
Semites	Babel (from Nippur)	Camp 24 (Nippur)
Sumerians (Ural-Altaic C)	Babel (from Sippar)	Camp 25 (Sumer)

These twelve colonies were the Pelegite division of the earth named in Genesis 10:25 and celebrated in the Cernunnus panel. The twelve were colonized at intervals of thirty months in precise correlation with the first twelve reigns of the "Ayodhya" dynasty. The twenty-three reigns of the First Kish dynasty ran concurrently in terms of fifteen months each. Gaur,[17] the first king of the dynasty, was Gether, patriarch of the Finno-Ugrian Agathyrsians. After reigning fifteen months at Kish, he led the Subarians from Akkad to Camp 9 in accordance with the first "Ayodhya" epoch of thirty months in the spring of 2335. Thus the "earth was divided" in twelve stages; and a few of these colonies, such as the Sumerian on the Lower Euphrates, were destined to last for many centuries, confirming the Noahic intention to make the twelve provinces the first step in a colonization program aimed at the "uttermost parts of the earth."

The anachronistic Mesopotamian "Ayodhya" cannot be identified with Kish if only because Ikshvaku, the contemporary first ruler of Ayodhya, cannot be identified with Gether of Kish. By the time of Haryashva, "Ayodhya" represented Lagash of Ur-Nanshe; and we have every reason to identify "Ayodhya" with Lagash from 2338 forward. The "solar" character of the Ayodhya and Videha lines points directly to the two sun gods of Seal 684 and their Camps 13 and 14, as though Ayodhya and Videha were Lagash and Camp 14 on the Tigris. Sons of Canaan dominated Lagash in every period. His mulatto son Nimrod was the god of the city, both as Ningirsu and as the sun god to the left of Seal 684. The integrity of Canaan's Olympian family suggests that Ikshvaku, founder of the Ayodhya regime, was the second son Heth, whose brothers Jebus and Sidon founded later regimes at Lagash.

The opposing lunar lines of Puru and Yadu[18] corresponded to loyalist regimes at Kish and Agade, under the domination of Peleg as Puru-ravas. In this way, Peleg and Heth, as Puru-ravas and Ikshvaku, acquired their analogous values as Nergal and Hades, Mesopotamian and Olympian gods of an underworld correlative with the one into which Kara Khan was expelled after 2338. Rebel mythologists, devoted to the celestial ideal of the Tower of Babel, interpreted the transition of power in 2338 as a kind of descent into hell.

Most of the dynastic names from the First Kish period remain mere names. More significant are the regional governorships of Peleg's empire as distinguished by the various figures of the Cernunnus panel and Seal 684:

Chronology	Figure	Location	Governor
2335	Western Bull (Finno-Ugrians)	Camp 9	Gether (Gaur)
2333	Stag (Amerindians)	Camp 10	Sabtechah (Alulim)[19]
2330	Cernunnus (Indo-Europeans)	Camp 11	Peleg (Cernunnus)
2328	Lion (Red Hamites) Seal 684: Left (Seba)	Camp 12 (Babel)	Seba (Osiris)
2325	Western Lion-Ram (Black Africans) Seal 684: Left Center (Sun God A)	Camp 13 (Lagash)	Nimrod
2323	Fish (Chinese)	Camp 14	Javan (Yao)

Chronology	Figure	Location	Governor
	Seal 684: Right Center (Sun God B)		
2320	Rider (Tibetans)	Camp 15	Sidon
	Seal 684: Right (Enki)		
2318	Eastern Bull (Ural-Altaics)	Camp 16	Ashkenaz
2315	---------- (White Hamites)	Camp 21 (Hamazi)	Obal (Hatanish)
2313	Eastern Lion-Ram (Dravidians)	Camp 23	Riphath
2310	Dog (Semites)	Camp 24 (Nippur)	Magog (Kalibum)
2308	Serpent (Sumerians)	Camp 25 (Lower Euphrates)	Japheth (Atab)

The First Kish order inaugurated the history of nationhood on earth. No actual nations existed before 2338 because no earlier social groups met the spiritual criteria essential to nationhood. Before nationhood came empire. A universal imperium had existed at least as early as 2368. Seal 690 shows Obal in the "Ka" posture because he was a true emperor, the Hamitic Ra, chronological prototype of all the imperial sun gods and immediate predecessor to the Emperors Yao and Shun. Empire preexisted nationhood because the latter depended on a spiritual division of the former. Every nation is a fraction of the universal imperium.

The design of the Cernunnus panel recalls the motif of Adam's naming the creatures (Genesis 2:19). As the crown of creation, Adam named the creatures in order to complete the creation of Elohim through the subjective medium of human culture. The same logic applied to the new cosmos of human government. The new nations demanded names, animal symbols, lands, and distinct shares of the imperium. As Cernunnus, embodiment of the Indo-European stock, Peleg functioned as a priest of Yahweh proper, the Storm God, analogous to the Yahweh Elohim of Genesis 2:18. A primary motive of the Storm God was to distinguish one nation from another as peculiar agent of justice.

The classic Mesopotamian mythologists so hated Peleg that it is difficult to determine, from gentile tradition, just what practical form his privileges took. The Marduk Epic acknowledges that he had something to do with a system of creatures, at least that his mistress Tiamat did:

> She set up the viper, the dragon, and the *lahamu,*
> The great lion, the mad dog, and the scorpion-man,
> Driving storm-demons, the dragon-fly, and the bison,
> Bearing unsparing weapons, unafraid of battle.

> ★   ★   ★   ★   ★   ★   ★

> Altogether eleven kinds of monsters of this sort
>   she brought into being.
> Of these among the gods, her first-born, who formed
>   her assembly,
> She exalted Kingu (I, 11.140-47).[20]

Because Kingu is the epic's version of Peleg, this coincidental introduction of Kingu in company with "eleven kinds" furnishes a strong analogy to the elevenfold Cernunnus panel. The "great lion" and "mad dog" match the lion and dog at the Akkadian northern sector of the panel.

Peleg's privilege was analogous to Jacob's assignment of animal symbols to the twelve tribes in Genesis 49. Jacob's animals include several of the ones featured in both the Cernunnus panel and the Marduk Epic: the lion (Judah), the viper (Dan), the deer or stag (Naphtali), and the dog or wolf (Benjamin). The practical function of the tribes was to divide the land of Israel into permanent holdings analogous to the twelve provinces of Peleg. Jacob's animal symbols were specifically prophetic because the tribes of Israel, like the nations of Peleg, claimed a specific share in the spiritual matrix of the third heaven, authoritatively represented by animal forms originating in the mind of God.

Peleg's duty was to assign a predetermined set of animal symbols to the existing linguistic stocks of Noah's family. The serpent form, for example, was calculated to represent the Lower Euphrates a priori. By assigning this form to the Sumerians, Peleg defined the Sumerian homeland and created the Sumerian nation. The generic symbol of nationhood proper to the Gundestrup Caldron is the Celtic torc, the interrupted neckband, which Cernunnus not only wears around his neck but holds upward in his free right hand. The torc around his neck symbolizes the nationhood achieved by the Indo-Europeans; the torc in his hand, his power to confer nationhood on other stocks.

The torc design appears ten times in the extant panels of the Caldron: twice, as indicated, in the Cernunnus panel; twice in the Trinity panel of the same First Kish epoch, around the necks of the Yellow Matriarch and the smooth-shaven god, her grandson Obal; twice in the Braided Goddess panel, around the necks of the chief subject and the facing, African version of the Black Matriarch; and once each around the necks of Ham, Japheth, Medb (Inanna), and the White Matriarch. We can only guess at whether the image appeared in the missing panel of the Black Matriarch; but extrapolation suggests that there may have been two torcs in that panel, as in the preceding panels of the Red and Yellow Matriarchs.

In any case, the total number of torcs pictured in the Caldron approaches the eleven or twelve proper to the system of nations created by Peleg, the bestower of torcs. To complete our picture of the First Kish order, we require a correlation between the nations of the Cernunnus panel and the various torcs throughout the Caldron. These correlations yield a new pattern of national principalities:

Nation	Torc	Prince
Subarians	God of the Boxer-Dancer panel	Japheth (Tasmisu)[21]
Amerindians	Hand Torc of Cernunnus	Reu son of Peleg
Indo-Europeans	Neck Torc of Cernunnus	Peleg (Cernunnus)
Red Hamites	God of the Dragon panel	Ham
African Blacks	Western Attendant of the Braided Goddess panel	Black Matriarch
Tibetans	---------	---------
Chinese	Goddess of the Trinity panel	Yellow Matriarch
Ural-Altaics	Medb	Inanna
White Hamites	Smooth-shaven God of the Trinity panel	Obal (Ra)
Dravidians	---------	---------

Nation	Torc	Prince
Semites	Braided Goddess	Red Matriarch (Adum)[22]
Sumerians	Goddess of the Sphinx panel	White Matriarch (Ningal)

The governorships of the "twelve provinces" were temporary, confined to the First Kish era only; whereas the principalities of the torc series were permanent enough to establish the political context for the Erech-Aratta War. Perhaps the most telling characteristic of the torc series is the exclusion of the chief antagonists of the two political factions: Noah, Shem, and Arphaxad I on the loyalist side and Canaan, Sidon, and Salah on the rebel side. The Gundestrup versions of Noah, Shem, and Arphaxad do not, in fact, wear the torc. Those who do wear it were originally conceived as agents of compromise. Peleg, for example, despite his loyalist polarity, was a grandson of Salah; and his loyalist militancy did not emerge until after 2308. Ham himself belonged to the compromising faction as the son of Noah and father of Canaan.

The torc signified nationhood, as opposed to language and genetics. Japheth, for example, remained the linguistic father of the Hamites according to his place in the octad of the exterior panels; whereas he made no claims to the nationhood of the two Hamitic stocks destined to inhabit Egypt. In the normal course of affairs, Japheth might have been expected to claim the torc of the Indo-Europeans, lost to Shem through factional strife. Instead, Peleg claimed the Indo-European torc for himself and granted Japheth the torc of the Finno-Ugrians, twin stock to the Sumerians of Japheth's mother. Whatever Peleg's justification in claiming the Indo-European nation, there is little question that this claim precipitated the Erech-Aratta War,[23] the strangest and most momentous event of Noahic history outside the Bible.

The Erech-Aratta War

Peleg's authority to bestow the torc of nationality was as authoritative as Noah's power of the curse. In claiming the Indo-European torc for himself, he left a peculiar mark on gentile tradition. In Teutonic mythology Peleg and Joktan head two divisions of the gods, Vanir and Aesir.[24] The tradition fails to identify the two princes, Frey and Odin, as brothers. The tradition testifies to some source of radical incoherence in formative Indo-European experience. The Vanir-Aesir distinction cannot be identified with any structural distinction such as between the Centum and Satem speakers. Instead, it refers to two stages in Indo-European protohistory before and after the Eanna epoch in 2308, when the center of power shifted from Peleg, Cernunnus, to Joktan, Enmerkar of Erech.

By assigning himself the Indo-European torc, Peleg planted that nation in his birth camp west of the Euphrates in Martu. If he had assigned this torc to Japheth, the latter would have re-planted the Indo-Europeans in Sumer at Camp 25 (Enegir) in Sumer. In this case, Japheth would have acted logically as representative of his mother in claiming her Sumerian fief. As corollary, the Sumerian nation, based on the same stock as the Finno-Ugrian, would have settled Camp 11. Because Sumer was more desirable land than Martu, the Indo-Europeans had reason to resent Peleg's decision.

This decision was all the more offensive because the Indo-Europeans, together with the Semites, had been the first to colonize Sumer, creating the very cult centers which the Sumerians treated as their own. The decision was so vitally important to Sumerian origins that it formed the cryptic basis of two leading Sumerian traditions, the Myths of Etana and Adapa. Both attribute a strong guilt motif to Peleg for the same decision which benefited the Sumerians with their grain-rich homeland.

The historical process of the Myth of Etana commenced in Peleg's First Kish era when Noah reigned as Etana. In it, Peleg appears as a mythical Eagle,[25] who incurs guilt by raiding and carrying off a Serpent's brood. The Serpent refers to the serpent prince Japheth (Ningishzida) and the brood, to the Indo-European stock, whom Peleg transferred, in effect, from the serpent colony of the Lower Euphrates to Camp 11 in Martu. After the Eagle is consigned to a pit for his crime, Etana liberates him and is rewarded by enjoying a flight into heaven on the Eagle's back. This latter stage of the myth refers to Peleg's alliance with Noah's Ural-Altaic stock at Aratta (birth camp of the heaven goddess Inanna) after 2308.

The Myth of Adapa approaches the same political events from a different, more revealing angle. In the first place, the myth confounds Peleg with Seba (Adapa) according to the same conceit which identified the East Indian Shiva (Seba) with Dravidian Pashupati (Peleg). In reality, Peleg was Seba's nephew, identified in the Egyptian pantheon as Har-Iset, a son of Isis (Panthrus-Nephele), by Eber rather than by her brother Osiris (Seba). Another ground for identifying the two was the immediate sequence of their respective Camps 11 and 12. For whatever reason, the Sumerian myth conceals Peleg under his uncle's name Adapa, at the same time that it blends the characters and motives of the two.

The myth interprets Adapa as a protege to Enki, much as Seba appears, as the Sed-holder, before Enki's throne, in Seal 684. In reference to Peleg, the myth signifies that the Divider enjoyed his authority throughout the First Kish era as a specious subordinate to Sidon. As Sidon's great-grandson, Peleg made a rather logical subordinate. Adapa incurs guilt through the cryptic act of "breaking the wing of the south wind," in retaliation for its capsizing his boat during a fishing trip.[26] Enki instructs him to curry favor with the gods and atone for his sin by flattering the "two gods who disappeared from the land," Gishzida and Tammuz (Ningishzida and Dumuzi the Shepherd), Japheth and Togarmah, the two princes whose nations were juxtaposed by Peleg's decision. In effect, the Sumerians of Togarmah "disappeared" from Camp 11 to Camp 25 and the Indo-Europeans, from Camp 25 to Camp 11. The myth confirms that Peleg met political confusion in dealing with the Sumerians and Indo-Europeans and that he or his political interests were manipulated by Sidon.

At the same time, between 2308 and 2305, Sidon (Teutonic Loki and East Indian Kasyapa) gained the confidence of the Indo-Europeans and persuaded them that, if they would accept Joktan rather than Peleg as their national leader, they could return to Sumer to stay. As a consequence, they helped build the city of Erech and the Eanna regime, under Eber (Meskiaggasher), father of both princes. Sidon chose Joktan as a closer relative, a son of his wife Inanna (Hellenic Ino). The Indo-Europeans were now allied with the Semites and Sumerians in Mesopotamia, under the dominance of its new, southern capital of Erech.

Peleg remained too prestigious to be pushed aside without compensation. Because he had lost the Indo-Europeans to Inanna's son, she granted him the privilege of governing a new empire in her Iranian Medb zone, analogous to the Cernunnus system of the previous era but smaller in compass and in ethnic importance. The White

Egyptians had already settled in one of the six Medb camps and were incorporated outright. To balance the two empires, Peleg carried five additional stocks from the Cernunnus zone into the remaining five camps of the Medb zone: Amerindians, Dravidians, Chinese, Tibetans, and Ural-Altaics. Such was the Iranian alliance of Kingu, enemy of Marduk.

The division of Noahic mankind into two empires proceeded swiftly, setting the stage for the Erech-Aratta War in the "336th year of Ra-Harakhte," 2302 B.C. The six camps of the Iranian empire were governed by members of the "Austronesian" or proto-Cushite clan as follows:

Empire of Kingu and Tiamat: 2305 B.C.

Location	Stock	Governor
Camp 17 (Anshan)	Amerindians	Sabtechah son of Noah
Aratta (Isfahan)	Ural-Altaics	Nimrod (Ninigi)[27] vassal of Peleg (Kingu)
Camp 19	Tibetans	Dedan (Noah)
Camp 20 (Marhashi)	Chinese	Raamah (Shem) son of Noah
Camp 21 (Hamazi)	White Hamites	Seba (Osiris)
Camp 22 (Elam)	Eastern Blacks	Sabtah son of Seba

The six governors included all of the Cushite clan except Havilah II and Sheba II, Ham and Japheth, who cast their lot with the Mesopotamians. Because the Iranian alliance pre-existed the Cushite clan per se, it formed the basis of it. The governors, together with Peleg and the Red Matriarch (Kingu and Tiamat) constituted the inner circle of the loyalist faction as it existed in 2305. Noah and Shem took command of the Sino-Tibetans precisely because this stock had belonged to the rebel alliance of Seal 684 in the previous era. Their goal was to re-indoctrinate this stock, but their influence over them was shortlived owing to the chaos of the Erech-Aratta War. They lifted Seba directly out of the context of Seal 684, consolidating the Egyptian alliance of Osiris with Har-Iset (Peleg).

The new language of the era and of the Iranian empire was Austronesian, a language shared by a wide range of Mongoloid and Negroid people from Malagasy in the west to Polynesia in the east.

Austronesians were distilled from all six of the new colonies of the Medb zone. From the Amerindians came the Polynesians, destined to inhabit the middle Pacific just beyond the verge of the Americas; from the Ural-Altaics, the Japanese, clinging to an exotic variety of Ural-Altaic but with geographic and racial affinities to the Polynesians; from the Sino-Tibetans of Camps 19 and 20, Malays, Indonesians, and other Pacific Mongoloids; from the White Hamites of Hamazi, the people of Malagasy, akin to the Malays but inhabiting an island off the coast of Africa; and from the Dravidians of Camp 22, Papuans, Melanesians, Andamese, and other black Austronesians.

The opposing empire of Joktan included the historical regimes of Erech and Kish in the Eanna period. It consisted of the six remaining stocks of the First Kish order: Finno-Ugrians (Subarians), Indo-Europeans, Sumerians, Semites, Red Hamites (Lower Egyptians), and the blacks destined for Africa. The Sumerians remained on the Lower Euphrates; and the Indo-Europeans joined them at Erech, under the new arrangement between Sidon and Japheth. The Red Hamites remained in Akkad to serve Ham and Canaan, Enmebaraggesi and Aka of the extended First Kish dynasty. This regime at Kish, contemporary with the one at Erech, explains why the Eblaites remembered the Erech-Aratta War as the Kish-Hamazi War. The other stocks probably remained in their former camps until the demands of the war drew them eastward.

The local governors of the Mesopotamian alliance became commanders of the respective divisions of Marduk's army. They emerge in gentile tradition as four war gods and the two destroying heroes of the Erechite Epic of Gilgamesh, Elam (Gilgamesh) and Elishah (Enkidu). The structure of the empire was as follows:

Empire of Marduk: 2305 B.C.

Location	Stock	Governor
Camp 9	Finno-Ugrians (Subarians)	Elishah (Enkidu)
Erech	Indo-Europeans	Meshech (Karttikeya)
Lower Euphrates	Sumerians	Elam (Gilgamesh)
Lagash	Western Blacks	Girgash (Ares)

Location	Stock	Governor
Nippur	Semites	Salah (Marduk)
Kish	Red Hamites	Gomer (Anhur)

In the Epic of Gilgamesh, the protagonist and Enkidu form a team in combating the mythological enemies of Erech; but, as it happens, Enkidu slays the first enemy, Elamite Huwawa, and Gilgamesh, the second, the Gutanu (Bull of Heaven).[28] These individualized killings symbolize two out of six Mesopotamian invasions and conquests in Iran. In the first case, Elishah's followers, the Subarians, crossed Mesopotamia to attack and conquer the Eastern Blacks at Camp 22. In the second, Gilgamesh led an army of Sumerians against the Chinese (the Gutanu) at Camp 20 further east.

In another Sumerian tradition, Enmebaraggesi of Kish "smote the weapons of the land Elam."[29] In this case, the Red Hamites from Kish invaded and conquered the White Hamites at Hamazi. Thus the Sumerian traditions of the epic and kinglist account for the overthrow of the three colonies in the lower row of the Medb panel: Dravidians, Upper Egyptians, and Chinese. Yet the central target of the Mesopotamian alliance lay at the capital of Aratta in the upper row. The conquest of Aratta itself concerns the Erechite legends of the reign of Enmerkar (Joktan) and forms the climax of the Babylonian Epic of Marduk (Salah).

The three Mesopotamian stocks available to attack the upper row of colonies were the Africans, Indo-Europeans, and Semites. The various traditions of "Cush and Havilah," including the Meso-American painting of reds and blacks at war, suggest that the Western blacks left Lagash to attack the Amerindians at Camp 17 of the Zagros. The remaining armies, Semites and Indo-Europeans, were the proper force of the Marduk Epic and the Erechite legends, the Semites under Salah (Lugalbanda-Marduk) and Indo-Europeans under Joktan (Enmerkar-Odin). They obviously struck at the "belly of Tiamat," the inner camps of the upper row, Ural-Altaics at Aratta and the Tibetans under Noah[30] at Camp 19 in the remote northeastern corner of the Medb system.

Kramer discusses four Sumerian legends concerning the Erech-Aratta War. Of these, "Enmerkar and the Lord of Aratta" makes a striking contribution to the logic of the two imperial sextads. The

Lord of Aratta arranges a duel between the two powers:
This time he demands that Enmerkar select, as his
representative, one of his "fighting men" to engage in
a single combat with one of his own "fighting men."
Thus "The stronger will become known." The challenge,
in riddle-like terms, asks that the selected retainer be
neither black, nor white, neither brown, yellow, nor
dappled—which seems to make little sense when speaking of a man.[31]
Whether these colors refer to skin-color or garments makes little difference; the symbolic value remains the same. Because the Lord of
Aratta negates five colors, his demand requires a sixth. The logic
is consistent with the two sextads of Iran and Mesopotamia.

All five of the specified colors are applicable to racial skin-color
in a conventional or symbolic sense; and the missing color is clearly
red. Because the Red Matriarch personifies the Iranian empire in
the Marduk Epic, the Lord of Aratta's challenge reflects Peleg's
alliance with the Red Matriarch. The red Amerindians held the position of Camp 17 under Sabtechah, postdiluvian son of the Red
Matriarch and Noah, governor of Camp 19. The Lord of Aratta,
as head of the entire upper row of Camps 17-19, demanded a champion qualified to challenge the family of Noah, Havilah I, and
Sabtechah. Because the founder of the Erechite regime was Salah's
son by the Red Matriarch, the challenge aimed at the heart of that
regime, the Red Matriarch's Messianic husband Salah, Marduk the
Great, the Erechite Lugalbanda.

The outcome of the challenge is celebrated graphically in
Mesopotamian Seal 687. Like Seal 684, this one pictures Enki on
his sea throne at one end of the frame but this time to the left as
though to welcome the three other figures as conquering heroes from
the east.

The first figure to Enki's right is his double-faced vizier Sha-Usmu,
his son Elishah, the legendary Enkidu, conqueror of Camp 22. The
second figure holds over his shoulder a curved stick with a branch
hanging from it. The branch symbolizes the Iranian colony of Camp
21, the Upper Egyptians, whose heraldric sign was a flowering rush.[32]
The Mesopotamian leader of the Red Hamites was Gomer, as the
Egyptian war god Anhur. Thus the first two figures symbolize successful victories over the Eastern Blacks and White Hamites by

Elishah and Gomer respectively.

The figure to the far right has defeated and captured a "bird man," logically a variation of the Zu bird Shem, as Raamah, lord of the Chinese Gutanu at Camp 20. The captor, therefore, represents Gilgamesh, who must have penetrated as far east as Camp 20 in order to encounter Ziusudra of Camp 19. Seal 687 includes the entire lower row of the Medb panel and celebrates both heroic victories of the Gilgamesh Epic. In fact it adds to these victories of the Kish-Hamazi campaign Enmebaraggesi-Ham's conquest over Camp 21, in a personal alliance with Gomer at the head of a Lower Egyptian race destined to accept both Ham and Gomer as Zoser and Khufu of Memphis.

In sending the Red Hamites of Kish against the White Hamites of Camp 21, Ham forced, in effect, a union of the "Two Egypts" at a time when the two peoples were still remote from Egypt. More particularly, the attack on Camp 21, in 2302, defined the "War of Horus and Seth" in Egyptian tradition. Because Seth was originally reckoned the Lord of Upper Egypt, there is no question that his name symbolizes the White Egyptians of Camp 21 and the Iranian alliance generally, thus identifying the ubiquitous name "Horus" with the Mesopotamian alliance.

To gauge the incoherence of the Egyptian mythology, Peleg-Kingu, head of the Iranian alliance of "Seth," is known to the Egyptians as "Horus son of Isis," as though he were the Horus who made war against "Seth" and, therefore, against himself! Behind this seemingly bad logic, however, is an actual mystery of Peleg's political role in the war era. To the Sumerian pantheon, Peleg is known as Nergal and given the same two parents as Ninurta, namely, Enlil and Ninlil, Canaan and Lehab. In Peleg's case, this parentage is erroneous but serves to identify Peleg with Nimrod as Iranian ally. Because Nimrod, a son of Canaan, had been an arch-rebel and Peleg a loyalist symbol in earlier times, their alliance was paradoxical, at best, and was not destined to last.

Peleg and Nimrod had embraced at the outset of the era as common adversaries to Japheth, who had been humiliated by Nimrod in the Tower of Babel era and by Peleg in the First Kish era. When Peleg was stripped of the Indo-European torc, he took refuge with Japheth's old enemy realizing that the Indo-Europeans who rejected his leadership did so because they had been deeply attached to

Japheth, their lord at proto-Erech in their heroic stand against Nimrod's Tower of Babel. The Hellenic Argonautic tradition claims that Peleg (Phrixus) fled the murderous machinations of his stepmother Ino (Joktan's mother Inanna) and took refuge with Colchian Aeetes,[33] a son of Helius, the Titan version of Nimrod. If the Hellenes can be believed, Peleg closed hands with Nimrod as a fugitive in defense of his life.

If so, Peleg's sense of loyalty toward Nimrod could not have run deep. At the outset of the era, he had formed the Iranian alliance to maintain some degree of self-respect and political power, not to help Nimrod execute a new stage in the rebel program to undermine the authority of Noah and Shem. His conflict with Japheth meant a rift within the loyalist faction, not his recruitment to the rebel cause. When hostilities began, his complex political career took a new turn.

A detail of Seal 687 suggests the true course of affairs. The figure of Sha-Usmu holds nothing over his shoulder comparable to the branch and bird man held by the two deities behind him. Sha's point of attack was Camp 22, whose black inhabitants included the Andamese, who remembered Peleg so well as Puluga. We are faced with two implications: (1) Peleg made Camp 22 his personal seat, and (2) he either eluded capture or gained his freedom by negotiation.

Because Peleg's personal alliance with Nimrod was feeble at the outset, his early defeat at Camp 22 freed him from obligation to defend the Iranian colonies of the upper row. Under normal circumstances, he would have supported Nimrod; but the capture of Seba and Shem altered his strategy. The Egyptians remembered him as Har-Iset, a powerful ally to Osiris because, having eluded captivity, he ransomed Seba and Shem by agreeing to join the Mesopotamian alliance against the forces of Aratta. He momentarily rejoined the family of Eber and Joktan and helped them overthrow the remaining Iranian forces.

The plan of the "Huwawa-Gutanu" campaign, in avoiding Aratta itself, implies that the Mesopotamians feared the Ural-Altaic force garrisoned there and its leader, the physically powerful Nimrod, chief priest of the War God, El Gibbor, the "Strong God." Nimrod was the Samson of the early postdiluvian world and a formidable enemy in an age when battles were still being determined by personal duels. Peleg's conversion, however, brought new courage to the Mesopotamian alliance because of the formal dualism of Ninurta and Nergal.

As Nergal, Peleg was a second war god akin to the first and able to match Ninurta spiritually if not physically. The Mesopotamians freed Peleg on the stipulation that he lend the spiritual charisma of the loyalist faction to the Mesopotamian alliance by becoming a feudal son to Enlil and Ninlil, dissolving his feudal clan, replacing the maverick Nimrod as chief priest of the War God, and taking the field against him in the Mesopotamian campaign against the remaining colonies.

Nergal's status as Ninurta II is quite apparent in Seal 699, where his mace of the two feline heads[34] matches Ninurta's Imdugud of the Two Lions. And the two cats have the same symbolic value as the two lions, representing the two Egyptian stocks, reunited under Nergal, Peleg, "Horus son of Isis." Nergal tramples on a defeated enemy lying on a mountain, symbolic of one of the three leaders and armies of the northern sequence of Camps 17, 18, and 19.

The nations conquered at Camps 17, 18, and 20 were the ones destined for the most remote regions of the earth: the "landbridge" nations of the Far East and the Americas and intervening islands of the Pacific. The Iranian alliance had degenerated into a rebellion within a rebellion and served, among other things, to discredit the loyalist cause by discrediting Peleg's role as Kingu. The geographic destinations of the defeated stocks were punitive. The Erech-Aratta War altered the structure of Genesis 10; but, more important, it altered the ethnographic structure of the world. The mythological slaughters of "Huwawa" and "Gutanu" triggered a mysterious process of distant colonial migrations, superintended by the Mesopotamian rulers of the Akkadian Age. These migrations drove the various stocks of the Noahic cosmos so far apart that their locations have fed the delusions of polygenetic thought ever since. By purging the Sumero-Akkadian world of "dissident elements," the Erech-Aratta War secured not only the rapid development of Middle Eastern civilization but also an agnosticism concerning origins essential to the great secular lie.

NOTES

[1] The vertical tripartite design isolated by Grosse in the Gundestrup floor panel is topped by a triangle. If the lunar crescent stands at Ur and the sunburst at Sippar, the triangle takes the relative position of the Subarian fief. Because that fief correlated with Noah's Heaven God, the triangle (like the solid pyramid) symbolized heaven.

[2] Roland B. Dixon, *Oceanic Mythology, Mythology of All Races* (New York: Cooper Square, 1964), IX, 33.

[3] Moret, p. 61.

[4] Kramer, *The Sumerians*, p. 328.

[5] Beek, *Atlas of Mesopotamia*, p. 66.

[6] See discussion of Seal 690 below.

[7] The numbers assigned to the various Mesopotamian seals are from Pritchard, *The Ancient Near East in Pictures*, pp. 220-22.

[8] Frankfort, p. 28.

[9] The traditional accession date of Yao was 2357. De Bary, xix.

[10] Ions, p. 91.

[11] Adolf Erman, *Life in Ancient Egypt* (New York: Benjamin Blom, 1969), p. 279. The details of the festival are analyzed later.

[12] Moret suggests the identity of the month Athyr with November. *The Nile and Egyptian Civilization*, p. 88.

[13] The dispute over who should marry Sati originated as a dispute over where the newly formed Chinese stock should settle at the Sino-Tibetan epoch of First Kish. The stock originated at the Tower of Babel, Seba's Camp 12, hence Sati's premature "marriage" to Shiva. Sati's familiar self-immolation motif derived from a synthesis of two circumstances: (1) the Tower of Babel judgment and (2) the decision of the Noahic council to settle the Chinese at Camp 14 rather than Camp 12. The details of the Shiva-Daksha-Sati myth are found in Ions, pp. 44-46.

[15] Moret, loc. cit.

[15] The Hebrew verb root *palag* means to split or divide, hence Peleg's role as divider in Genesis 10:25. Francis Brown, S. R. Driver, and Charles Briggs, *Hebrew and English Lexicon* (Oxford: Clarendon, 1962), p. 811.

[16]Uno Holmberg, *Finno-Ugric and Siberian Mythology,
Mythology of All Races* (New York: Cooper Square, 1964), IV, 405.

[17]Variant readings for the kings of First Kish are given by Kramer,
p. 328, and Hallo and Simpson, p. 41. Hallo and Simpson read the
first king of Kish Mashkakatu, the "Harrow." We prefer Kramer's
"Gaur" because of the analogy to Gether, Agathyrsus, or Gasur.

[18]Waddell, p. 523.

[19]Hallo and Simpson (p. 32) translate the name Alulim, "Stag."
Olcott and Putnam, p. 144, mention a Mesopotamian Alula, meaning "Eagle." We favor a synthesis of both values because the constellation of Aquila, the Eagle, stands to the left of Ophiochus, the
Serpent-Bearer, in the same way that the stag stands to the left of
the serpent-bearing Cernunnus in the Cernunnus panel. Peleg-
Cernunnus himself gains identity with an Eagle in the Myth of Etana
discussed below.

[20]Heidel, pp. 23-24.

[21]The Hittite (originally Subarian) versions of Shem, Ham, and
Japheth were Teshub, Aranzah, and Tasmisu, sons of Anu (Noah)
through the magical intervention of Kumarbi (Canaan). Beyerlin,
p. 154.

[22]The West Semitic goddess Adum, wife of Resheph, took her
name from a word meaning "red." As an underworld goddess she
was equivalent to Ereshkigal, Sumerian version of the Red Matriarch.
For Adum, see Albright, *Yahweh and the Gods of Canaan,* p. 140.

[23]The Erech-Aratta War can as justifiably be labeled the Kish-
Hamazi War. These two pairs of cities were the termini of two
distinct campaigns of the same Mesopotamian-Iranian War fought
in the Eanna period after 2308 B.C.

[24]George W. Cox, *The Mythology of the Aryan Nations,* I (Port
Washington, NY: Kennikat, 1870), 372-81.

[25]Pritchard, *Ancient Near Eastern Texts,* pp. 114-118.

[26]Ibid., p. 101.

[27]*Larousse Encyclopedia of Mythology* (London: Paul Hamlyn,
1959), p. 419. The Japanese name resembles Nigi, one of two rulers
of Aratta given by Hallo and Simpson, p. 47. Nimrod's vassalage
to Peleg is given by Slavic tradition where Varpulis is subordinate
to Perkuna.

[28]Pritchard, *Ancient Near Eastern Texts,* pp. 79-85.

[29]Kramer, p. 328.

[30]The Epic of Gilgamesh identifies Noah as Ziusudra "the Faraway" for this reason.

[31]Kramer, p. 269.

[32]Erman, p. 17.

[33]Zimmerman, p. 209.

[34]Pritchard identifies the feline heads as such. *Ancient Near East in Pictures,* p. 333.

Chapter 6

The Imperial Age II: General Dispersion

The Sumerian Era

Sixty years intervened between the foundation of the Erechite regime in 2308 and the rise of Sargon in 2248. The Erech-Aratta War consumed only a fraction of this period. After defeating Nimrod at Aratta, Peleg spent the remainder of the Eanna era stabilizing the Iranian empire from Aratta, where he appears as Nigi's successor Suhkeshdanna. His modified version of the Iranian empire forms the subject of the Dravidian seal of Shiva Pashupati[1] showing the same system as the Medb panel in variation. The horns of the seated figure lie in the upper middle position of Aratta with the two flanking elephants reproduced by another elephant at Camp 17 and a rhinoceros at Camp 19. The head and body of Shiva interrupt the lower row; but a tiger, as in the Medb panel, holds what would have been the middle lower position, with a human figure to the left at Camp 22 and an ox to the right at Camp 20.

A row of six pictographic letters, along the top of the seal, suggests a further elaboration of the empire as outcome of the war. Each of the six colonies of the Medb zone included both Austronesians and original stocks: Amerindians, Mongols, Tibetans, Chinese, White Hamites, and Dravidians. Because four of these stocks were destined for the most distant lands on earth, it is reasonable to assume that they were the first to abandon the Medb colonies, leaving these in the hands of the Austronesians. Two of these elder stocks, White Hamites and Dravidians, were soon to inhabit the eastern lands of Magan and Meluhha, that is, Makran and the Indus. From the Dravidian civilization of the Indus came the seal itself, as though to connect that civilization as directly as possible with political changes in the Medb zone.

If the six colonies of the Iranian empire had been subdivided into twelve by the next epoch of 2278, the same was necessarily true of the six victorious stocks of the Mesopotamian empire. Of these, the Sumerians, Subarians, and Red Hamites were already subdivisions of larger stocks dating back to the twenty-fifth century. The time had now come to subdivide the remaining stocks: Semites, Indo-Europeans, and Western Blacks. Thus the Mesopotamian empire arrived at its total of twelve stocks, not by dividing six members once, but by leaving three members whole and dividing the others twice. The Semites, Indo-Europeans, and Western Blacks were divided into three stocks each.

Aside from the Khoisans, classic black Africa consists of three stocks: Nilotes, Cushites, and Congo-Kordofanians, the common stock to which both Bantus and Sudanics belong. As for the Indo-Europeans, a strong case can be made that the Anatolians form a group distinct enough from the Centum and Satem groups of Europe and the East to be reckoned a separate third. With the Semites, a regional distinction existed among the Aramaeans in the west, Amorites in the middle, and Akkadians in Mesopotamia. Linguistically, the Semites of Ebla spoke a tongue similar to the Palestinian "language of Canaan"[2] but distinct from the Amorite; and archaeologists have shown a clear cultural distinction between the Palestinian Canaanites and the Amorites east of the Jordan.[3] If we add these two western groups to the Semites of Mesopotamia, we define a Semitic triad.

For the sake of convenience, these nine subdivisions can be labeled Nilotes, Cushites, Sudanics, Centum Aryans, Satem Aryans, Anatolians, Canaanites, Amorites, and Akkadians. These complemented the Sumerians, Subarians (Hurrians), and Lower Egyptians; and all twelve complemented the twelve conquered peoples of the empire of Aratta. By the culminating Sumerian era between 2278 and 2248, the Noahic world had been divided into twenty-four ethnic units.

This period was the age of the city state, when independent regimes arose at Kish, Adab, Awan, and other specific locations of the greater Sumerian world. Hallo and Simpson chart eleven such locations: Kish, Erech, Ur, Aratta, Lagash, Adab, Hamazi, Mari, Umma,

Akshak, and Awan. To these can be added Ebla where Igrish-Halam reigned contemporaneously with Urukagina[4] of Lagash before the rise of Sargon. Another consideration is the eight lands of Lugalannemundu, who reigned at Adab in the same period. All these are the scattered limbs of a cosmos made up of twenty-four elements.

At some time in the latter third milliennium, the Dravidians of Camp 22 migrated to the Indus Valley and established the civilization which left the seal of Shiva Pashupati at Mohenjodaro, one of three points on the Indus including Harappa and Udyana.[5] The intimate connection between the seal and Peleg's Iranian empire suggests that these three colonies were established at some time before the rise of Sargon. If each possessed a separate political identity, the Indus civilization constituted an eighth of the postwar cosmos.

In the absence of a comprehensive documentary guide to this cosmos, it can only be synthesized from empirical data. On such a basis, eight triads can be suggested as follows:

Sphere of Ebla:	Ebla (Syria)
	Mari (Martu)
	Kaniesh (Anatolia)
Sphere of the Kish-Akshak Alliance:	Kish
	Akshak
	Agade
Sphere of the Lower Tigris-Euphrates:	Erech
	Ur
	Lumma (Elam)
Sphere of the Lagash-Umma War:	Lagash
	Umma
	Adab
Sphere of Iran:	Aratta
	Hamazi
	Awan
Sphere of Subaria:	Subir
	Gutium
	Anshan[6]
Sphere of the Persian Gulf:	Marhashi
	Magan
	Dilmun
Sphere of the Indus (Sumerian Meluhha):	Mohenjodaro
	Harappa
	Udyana

Of these twenty-four names, six or seven refer to regions rather than cities; but the example of Eanna-Erech shows how easily a city state could define a region as well as a city.

While admitting the absence of a systematic guide to this cosmos of twenty-four components, it is impossible not to mention the empire of seventeen lands given by Pettinato from a "school text" found at Ebla.[7] If the empire of Ebla pre-dated the Akkadian, our synthesis requires that it arose after the Erech-Aratta War, which was precisely the "great encounter" between Kish and Hamazi named by Pettinato. The specific names of the seventeen lands are unidentifiable except for Kanishu, which Pettinato identifies with Anatolian Kaniesh.[8] This last detail is especially intriguing because "Khutuni King of Kaniesh" appears in the list of seventeen kings conquered by Naram Sin in a document translated into Hittite.[9] The sum of seventeen is explicit in the Hittite document as in the document from Ebla.

In other respects the two lists fail to match; but the important point is the duplication of empires formed of seventeen units, both including northern Kaniesh, from two successive ages. This total of seventeen fell one unit short of the eighteen we would expect from the traditional Noahic subdivision of a given imperium into ratios of two thirds to one third. We have seen that Seal 684 isolates a rebel third of the First Kish order from the loyalist majority of two thirds. The same logic may apply to the empire of Pettinato's "school text." What we have called the "Sumerian era" was another cyclical loyalist era as opposed to the rebel era of the Erech-Aratta War. Consequently, the empire of Ebla seems to have originated as the loyalist two-thirds of an imperium of twenty-four. Mari fails to appear in this school text because it belonged to the rebel third and was inimical to Ebla throughout much of its history; in fact, it may well have been the ninth rebel unit carried over from the loyalist two thirds to reduce the latter from eighteen to seventeen units.

Because the Eblaite names are so obscure, it is pointless to match them either with the city states above or with the corresponding ethnic stocks listed below. An exception is that Kaniesh belonged to a twenty-fourth division, the Anatolian Aryans. Our theory suggests, however, that the Semitic names listed by Pettinato symbolize two-thirds of the human race in seventeen entirely distinct ethnic stocks between the years 2278 and 2248 B.C.

At this point the monogenetic and polygenetic theories of human origins collide head on. According to the polygenetic logic of the evolutionary philosophy, Kish, Akshak, Lagash, Erech, Ur, Umma, and Adab were exclusively Sumerian cities, built by Sumerian speakers, and inhabited by the same brachycephalic Caucasoid race in the middle third millennium as in later times. Likewise, the three cities of the Indus Valley were supposed to have been linguistically and racially uniform from the instant of their origins. According to polygenesis, both races, white Sumerians and black Dravidians, dropped from the womb of Mother Nature from time immemorial and from geographic regions half known and historically anonymous because subhuman in essence. On the contrary, our monogenetic theory requires that the inhabitants of these twenty-four states were the last version of the Noahic racial plenitude before the authorities of the Akkadian age sent Africans to Africa, Chinese to China, and Amerindians to America.

Some idea of which stock inhabited which state can be gained from the synthetic kinglists of the period given by Hallo and Simpson. Shortly after the war, Shem reappeared at Kish under the name Dadasig[10] compounding his Syrian and Teutonic names as storm god. A few years after the new epoch, he appeared at Elamite Awan under the name Tata,[11] the familiar designation of the Ural-Altaic race of Genghis Khan. From these definitive names, we gather that the Centum Aryans were at Kish and the Ural-Altaics at or near Awan. The East Indian fixation on "Ayodhya" places the Satem Aryans at Lagash before "Ayodhya" acquired its identity with Agade at the rise of Sargon. In general, the cosmos outlined here coincides with the empire of Lugalannemundu and with the sequence of lands outlined in the Sumerian tradition of the decrees of Enki:[12] Sumer, Ur, Meluhha (the Indus), Dilmun (Bahrein Island), Elam, Marhashi, and Martu.

From the best evidence we can gather, the pre-Akkadian world empire was as follows:

Location	Stock	Princes
Ebla (Syria)	Canaanites	Gomer (Gumalum)
		Magog (Igrish-Halam)
Mari (Martu)	Amorites	Nimrod (Ilshu)

Location	Stock	Princes
Kaniesh	Anatolian Aryans (Hattians)	Shem (god Taru)
Kish	Centum Aryans	Salah (Tuge-Tue)
Agade	Akkadians	Reu (Sargon)
Akshak	Amerindians	Zud (Zuzu-Tupan)
Erech and Adab	Sumerians	House of Sidon: Salah (Lugalbanda) Elam (Gilgamesh) Elishah (Elilin) Khetm (Lugal-kitun) Tarshish (Lugal-Tarsi)
Lagash	Satem Aryans	Jebus (Haryashva-Ur Nanshe)
Umma	Cushites	House of Ham: Cush (Ush) Mizraim (Enakalle) Canaan (Ukush) Nimrod (Lugalzagesi)
Shuruppak	Bantus	Lehab (goddess Ninlil)
Ur	Nilotes (Shilluks)	Canaan (Shulgi of Third Ur period)
Mohenjodaro	Dravidians	Sabtah (god Ganesa)
Harappa	Black Austronesians	Riphath (god Olifat)
Udyana	Tibetans	Noah (Etana)[13]
Dilmun	Polynesians	Ham (Raki): Gurmu of Lagash
Elam (Lumma)	Malays and Hovas	Masluh (Ur-Lumma of Umma)
Marhashi	Indonesians	---------
Awan	Chinese	Peli (Peleg) Arphaxad I (Shushuntarana of Awan-Emperor Shun)[14]
Anshan	Ural-Altaics	Girgash: Akurgal of Lagash (Gal of Anshan)[15]
Subir	Subarians (Hurrians)	Hiv: Mugamimla of Lagash
Aratta	Japanese	Mizraim (god Amenominakanushi): Enakalle of Umma
Hamazi	Red Egyptians	Obal (Hatanish)
Magan	White Egyptians	Ashkenaz (god Nintulla son of Ninhursag)[16]

The Sumerians shared the land of Sumer, at first, with the African blacks of Camp 13 and Satem Aryans from Camp 11. The blacks left Lagash to the Satem Aryans and spread along the north-south axis from Umma to Shurruppak and Ur. The Sumerians remained in the western land of Erech and the Lower Euphrates north of Ur. The racial distinction between the Sumerians and blacks explains the curious sequence of Sumer, Ur, and black Meluhha in the tradition of Enki's decrees. In fact, these three lands recapitulate what had been the sequence of the serpent and two lion-rams in the Cernunnus panel where the Dravidian race of Meluhha had camped at the sign of the eastern lion-ram (Camp 23) east of Lagash.

A footnote to this scheme of twenty-four nations concerns the formation of six additional linguistic stocks in celebration of the epoch of the Water God in 2278. Thirty years earlier, in celebration of the War God, all six colonies of the Iranian empire had generated new stocks of Austronesian speakers. In 2278, the six victorious colonies of the Mesopotamian empire, in addition to the subdivisions already noted, generated an analogous set of new stocks. From the Subarians and Sumerians came Lullubians and the related Elamites of Susa; from the Western Blacks, Khoisans; from the Ural-Altaics, Caucasian Japhetics (Georgians); from the Semites, Etruscans; and from the Indo-Europeans, Gutians. These six stocks raised the total of such nations from twenty-four to thirty, matching the total of the first thirty Noahic camps. The goal of most of these new stocks was to colonize an Iran evacuated by the defeated nations.

A correlation exists between this last set of languages and the ubiquitous Japhethite A clan destined to establish the regime at Ebla before the close of the era. The Caucasian Japhetics, for example, are the people of Tubal (Ebrium); and the Etruscans (Rasena or Tyrsenoi), the people of Tubal's son Tiras (Shura-Damu). As an offshoot of the Semites, the Etruscans were logically attached to the Canaanites of Ebla, whose tradition was carried into the Asianic sphere of western Asia Minor after the fall of Ebla to Naram Sin. The Caucasian Japhetics of Tubal derived from the Ural-Altaic colony in Anshan, a region of the Zagros Mountains north of Elam, where they complemented the Elamites, Lullubians, and Gutians. The Gutians derived from the Anatolian third of the Indo-Europeans.

Because the modern Khoisans inhabit Southwest Africa and are insulated by the Bantus from the other two major black African stocks, they must have derived from the Bantu-Sudanic colony at Shuruppak. Girgash, Akurgal of Lagash, gave his name to the Khoisan Kora (Hottentots); and Urukagina of Lagash yielded his to the Khoisan deity Cagn. In deriving from Shuruppak of Sumer, the Khoisans were analogous to the Elamites, who derived from the Sumerian stock itself, taking their Hebrew name Elam from the Sumerian hero Gilgamesh. An apparent traditional link between the Elamites and Khoisans is the resemblance between the Elamite goddess Usan and the Khoisan tribe Nusan of the Kalahari Desert. Usan is believed to be the Elamite version of Inanna.[17]

For the Sumerian era, Kramer is able to show patches of sober-looking history based on the comparative wealth of documentation discovered at Lagash from this period. Aside from the self-proclaimed empire of Lugalannemundu, the chief events of the period were a war between Lagash and Umma, an alliance of Kish and Akshak against Lagash in the time of Urukagina, and the final defeat of Lugalzagesi by Sargon at the outset of the next era.

We term the period from 2278 to 2248 the "Sumerian era" because the chief rulers of most of the regimes from this period claimed Sumerian names, fueling the polygenetic assumption that the populations under all these regimes were racially and linguistically Sumerian. Despite the wealth of linguistic stocks existing in and near Mesopotamia at this time, the Sumerian tongue was sacred to the Water God, whose ritual dispensation had come. The Sumerian language functioned, as the Hamitic had in the Tower of Babel era ninety years earlier, as a sign of theocratic authority. No attempt was made to teach all the Noahic populace Sumerian; but this language gained a status comparable to the French of Norman England.

Akkadian Colonization

The great work of the Akkadian Empire was to colonize the earth with the nations produced by Noah's family. From Noahic precedent, they obtained the privilege to carry out this task in four successive eras, totaling the same formal 120 years which God had allowed Noah for building the ark. This imperium lasted from 2248 to 2128 B.C. For good or for evil, the Akkadian emperors carried out their task so efficiently that the nations of mankind have displayed a certain polygenetic image ever since, each treating its homeland as the center of the earth in the absence of explicit traditions of migration from Mesopotamia. The first law of polygenetic reasoning is that the Egyptians could not have originated anywhere else except in Egypt. The philosopher Herder planted this idea in the minds of scholars two centuries ago; and so great is its cultural appeal that the monogenetic implications of an ancient empire such as the Akkadian have gone unheeded. Modern scholars define the Akkadian Empire, not in terms of its great commission, but in terms of the ancient soil surrounding Agade or the peculiarities of Semitic culture.

The Akkadian emperors were not mere Mesopotamians or Semitic speakers but men, created in the image of God, capable of mighty exploits, and bounded only by the finite sphere of the earth. As with all third millennium phenomena, not a great deal is known about them; but their works are manifest in a world of nations. Their commission extended to four eras because they, like their Sumerian predecessors, interpreted the earth as a tetrad of ordinal directions.[18] In each generation, they were to colonize a quarter of the earth. They constituted a tribal dynasty four in number: Peleg's son Reu, the Emperor Sargon; two sons of Sargon, the next heir Serug, Manishtushu, and his brother Rimush; and Serug's heir Nahor I, the Emperor Naram Sin. Following the process of the four Tezcatlipocas, Sargon was to colonize the red East; Rimush, the yellow south; Manishtushu, the black west; and Naram Sin, the white north. They were to approach this process, however, in accordance with Marduk's great victory over the Iranian empire; and that meant, through the sign of the god Surya, the Swastika.[19]

The adoption of a clockwise Swastika design meant that Sargon's expedition was to approach the East after reaching the terminus of a northern axis:

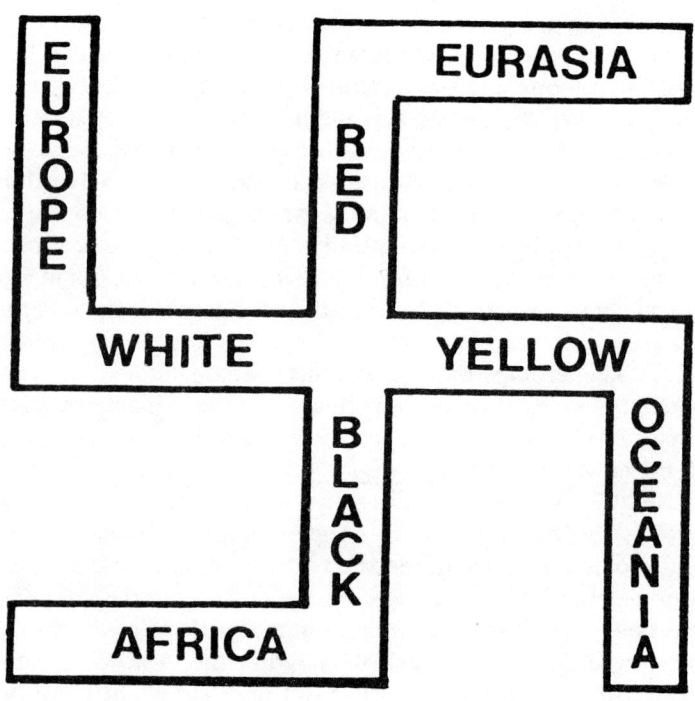

The Akkadian emperors chose as their agents in this great scheme the fraternity of Genesis 10:6, four sons of Ham, who had reigned as ensis of Umma in the Sumerian era. Sargon rose to power at the overthrow of Nimrod as Lugalzagesi son of Ukush, Canaan, the last in a series of Hamite ensis at Umma, seat of the Cushites. The four Hamites are defined as a tetrad unit in all four branches of the Swastika: to the Tatars of Kudai Bai Ülgön, Kara Khan (Cush), Pyr-shak Khan (Mizraim), Suilap (Phut), and Tös Khan (Canaan); to the Polynesians of the yellow branch, Tane-mahuta (Cush), Tangaroa (Mizraim), Tawhiri (Phut), and Tu-matauenga (Canaan); to Egyptian Dynasty III of the black branch, Zoser II (Cush), Sezes (Mizraim), Nebkara (Phut), and Neferkara Huni (Canaan); and to the Hellenes of the white branch, the Titans Hyperion (Cush), Oceanus (Mizraim), Iapetus (Phut), and Cronus (Canaan).

The Hamite role in the great Akkadian colonization program ex-plains the Hellenic myth of the Titan banishment to "Tartarus,"[20] mythic Tataria, intermediate terminus of the opening Red Branch. The Titans suffered this fate after their defeat by Zeus in the Titan-Olympian War, precisely the historical struggle between Lagash, under the house of Zeus (Ur-Nanshe) and Umma of the four ensis. The Hellenes viewed the colonization program as punitive, a righteous judgment against Ham's family for Canaan's attempt to control Mesopotamia from Lagash. The animosity between Shem and Canaan remained strong enough to determine the political logic of Shem's ancient Indo-European stock in their interpretation of the inchoate Akkadian Empire; and this meant that the Akkadian emperors came to power, not only as sons of Peleg and Semitic speakers, but as specious servants of the loyalist cause. When Sargon humiliated Lugalzagesi,[21] he duplicated his father's act as Nergal of Seal 699 in overthrowing the same Nimrod at Aratta. The horrendous Mithraic conflict between the loyalist leaders and Naram Sin resulted from Akkadian betrayals of the original sanction of the imperium.

A series of coincidences reveals the systematic process of the colonization scheme. All four Hamites reigned together as Pharaohs of the Egyptian Dynasty III at Memphis. Because the African branch was the third of the scheme, we can draw two conclusions: (1) the Hamites remained together in pursuing the first three expeditions and (2) the first four Egyptian dynasties arose in succession in each of the four Akkadian eras. The development of Egypt ran a parallel course to the entire colonization process; and the great pyramid tombs of Dynasty IV symbolized the final exhaustion of Noahic world enterprise after the epoch of the 360th postdiluvian year beginning a decade after Noah's death.

The Akkadian emperors taxed Ham and his sons to the limit. The Tatars recall the beginning of the colonization process, with their own branch, as a going forth from the "great mountain" of Sumerla,[22] precisely the land of Sumer, known as Kurgal, "Great Mountain," to the Sumerians themselves.[23] Because Ham accompanied his four sons, as Zoser I, at Memphis, the scheme called for a fivefold elaboration of each branch beyond the heartland of Mesopotamia, like five tiers of an artificial mountain or zigurrat, descending from the apex of Sumer into the four sides of the earth. The central pinnacle itself represented a sixth point in each branch raising the total of points to twenty-four. Into these, the Akkadians poured all twenty-four Noahic stocks developed by the Sumerian age. Because the Akkadians were Semitic speakers allied to the Sumerians, they designated as the four stocks of the pinnacle or center, the three Semitic nations of Ebla, Mari, and Martu, and the Sumerians themselves.

From the Sumerians came the opening Red Branch, including their linguistic kinsmen, the Subarians and Ural-Altaics of Tataria. Symbolically, the Yellow Branch of Rimush commenced from the Akkadians; the Black Branch of Manishtushu, from the Amorites; and the White Branch of Naram Sin, from the Canaanites of Ebla. The ethnic contents of each branch were as follows:

Red Branch:	Domestic stock.	Sumerians
	First colony.	Subarians (Hurrians)
	Second colony.	Ural-Altaics
	Third colony.	Tibetans (incorporated from Udyana)
	Fourth colony.	Japanese
	Fifth colony.	Amerindians
Yellow Branch:	Domestic stock.	Akkadians
	First colony.	Polynesians
	Second colony.	Black Austronesians
	Third colony.	Indonesians
	Fourth colony.	Malays
	Fifth colony.	Chinese
Black Branch:	Domestic stock.	Amorites
	First colony.	Dravidians
	Second colony.	Hovas
	Third colony.	Cushites
	Fourth colony.	White Hamites
	Fifth colony.	Red Hamites
White Branch:	Domestic stock.	Canaanites
	First colony.	Nilotes
	Second colony.	Bantus
	Third colony.	Centum Aryans
	Fourth colony.	Satem Aryans
	Fifth colony.	Anatolian Aryans

Drawing on East Indian sources, Waddell claims that Manishtushu (Asa-Manja) established the White Hamites in Upper Egypt, prematurely, through a rebellion against his father Sargon.[24] In any case, Manishtushu could hardly have waited until the third Akkadian era to colonize Upper Egypt if, in fact, the Egyptian dynasties synchronized with the four Akkadian eras. The first Upper Egyptian dynasty was Dynasty I and had to have been created in the first Akkadian era. The chronology of the colonization program requires close inspection.

The Hamitic integrity of Egyptian Dynasty III means that Ham and his four sons reigned in succession during all or part of the era of the Black Branch from 2188 to 2158. Their seat at Memphis constituted the fifth and last colony of that branch. If all five princes had worked their way as a body from one colony to the next throughout the era, their time spent at Memphis would have been too brief to identify Dynasty III with the whole era. But such was not necessarily the case if Ham brought the Red Hamites to Lower Egypt in advance of his four sons. Ham could have reigned at Memphis as Zoser I while Cush was in the fourth colony of Upper Egypt, Mizraim in the third colony of Ethiopia, Phut in the second colony of the Hovas, and Canaan at the Indus with the Dravidians.

The Black Branch differed from the other three branches in that all of its locations had been explored and two of them colonized before the start of the age. After 2188, Ham could advance swiftly to Lower Egypt on the basis of existing knowledge. In contrast, the advanced colonies of the other three branches lay in terra incognita. In order to coordinate the exploration and colonization of such vast regions, it was essential to adopt a predetermined sequencing device distinct from the overall design of the Swastika.

The Egyptian heritage of the twenty-second century identifies that device as the rambling and convoluted stellar asterism of Draco the Dragon. At some time in that century, Pharaoh Khufu of Dynasty IV aligned the open tunnel of the Great Pyramid to the alpha star of Draco, Thuban, the pole-star of the age.[25] Furthermore, the Gundestrup Caldron characterizes the pentad of Ham and his sons in a Dragon panel. The design of Draco has no capacity to reproduce the spatial proportions of Ham's colonial activity; but it does reveal two aspects of the colonial scheme. First, it shows that the various branches of the scheme were colonized continuously without any returns to Mesopotamia. Second, it groups each set of five colonies into a separate sequence of stars, suggesting how the first three branches were linked, first in the Pacific and later at the Indus.

In the first place, the Yellow Branch was colonized in reverse, from

Polynesia to the Indus, where the Dravidians and black Austronesians had already been planted. The Yellow Branch corresponds to the interior loop of the Dragon, a set of stars running from Delta to Phi.[26] Thuban lies third star from the tail and represents Lower Egypt as fifth colony of the Black Branch, third of the series. The asterism contains only nineteen stars of the fifth magnitude or brighter and is not populous enough to represent the European colonies of the White Branch. The sequence begins at the bright head of Eltanin and Rastaban and represents the Mesopotamian source of "Kurgal" in the white star Al Rakis, the "Dancer,"[27] logically the dancer of the Sumerian Sphinx and Lower Egyptian Boxer-Dancer panels, furnishing the theme for both lands, at head and tail.

In order to colonize the Red and Yellow Branches, Ham's family carried out of Mesopotamia eight of the ten nations required for these regions. An apparent exception was the black Austronesian nation, who had already colonized the Indus and would appear to have colonized the Austronesian zone from the Indus rather than the Pacific. Nevertheless, Ham's expedition rendezvoused with the Indus colonies at Udyana in order to incorporate the Tibetans; and it is reasonable to assume that they drew the black Austronesians from Harappa at the same time.

Ham's followers created a new colony at each fifth of a Noahic era, that is, every six years. They began by creating a new Subarian or Hurrian colony six years after the rise of Sargon in 2242. The colonies of the Red Branch were assigned to the Hamites of 10:6 in reverse order, beginning with Canaan as feudal lord of the Hurrians or "Hivites" in the Canaanite clan.[28] A second colony, based on the Ural-Altaic populace, was formed by 2236 somewhere near the Ural River, where Phut's sons in Hellenic tradition accounted for a variety of Ural-Altaic (or Finno-Ugrian) peoples: Halmus, for the Kalmuk Mongols; Macareus, for the Magyars or Hungarians; and Salmoneus, for the Samoeds. Mizraim adopted the Tibetans of Udyana, forming the next colony in or near Tibet; and Cush completed the continental process by establishing his identity as Kara Khan or Mandaru among the Manchus and Japanese in Manchuria.

The four continental colonies were programmed by the four stars of the Dragon's head. The full sweep of colonies from Sumer to Lower Egypt was as follows:

Empire of Draco: 2242-2158

Star	Location		Nation	Prince
Rastaban	Caucasus:	2242	Hurrians	Canaan (Tös Khan)[29]
Eltanin	Urals:	2236	Ural-Altaics	Phut (Suilap)
Nu Draconis	Tibet:	2230	Tibetans	Mizraim (Pyrshak Khan)
Grumium	Manchuria:	2224	Japanese	Cush (Kara Khan)
Omicron Draconis	America:	2218	Amerindians	Ham (Kudai Bai Ülgön)

Yellow Branch:

Star	Location		Nation	Prince
Delta Draconis	Polynesia:	2212	Polynesians	Ham (Raki)[30]
Epsilon Draconis	Melanesia:	2206	Black Austronesians	Cush (Tane-mahuta)
Tau Draconis	Indonesia:	2200	Indonesians	Mizraim (Tangaroa)
Chi Draconis	Malaysia:	2194	Malays	Phut (Tawhiri)
Phi Draconis	China:	2188	Chinese	Canaan (Tu-matauenga)

Black Branch:

Star	Location		Nation	Prince
Zeta Draconis	Indus:	2182	Dravidians	Canaan (Neferkara Huni)[31]
Eta Draconis	Malagasy:	2176	Austronesians of Malagasy	Phut (Nebkara)
Theta Draconis	Ethiopia:	2170	Cushites	Cush (Zoser II)
Ed Asich	Upper Egypt:	2164	White Hamites	Mizraim (Sezes)
Thuban	Lower Egypt:	2158[32]	Red Hamites	Ham (Zoser I)

The Mithraic Vendetta

The develoment of the European White Branch was complicated by the chaotic and violent career of Naram Sin, culminating in the Mithraic vendetta against him. At some point in Akkadian history, the regime of Agade lost the sympathy of the loyalists Shem and Peleg and of their race, the Indo-European linguistic stock. We have noted that the chief theme of the Gundestrup interior panels is the overthrow of the Akkadian Empire. This theme necessarily depended, to some extent, on the history of the White Branch.

The loyalist grievances against Naram Sin were fivefold: (1) he came to power prematurely, (2) he enforced the dispersion of the

White Branch prematurely, (3) he favored two black nations, rather than Indo-Europeans, with the inner positions of the White Branch, (4) he forced loyalist princes, rather than the Hamites, to undertake the expedition of the White Branch, and (5) he murdered ten princes of Genesis 10 at the nome of Metelis in Lower Egypt.

Manishtushu's colonization of Upper Egypt triggered a rebellion among the leaders of the same Noahic world which had sanctioned his father's imperium. He left an inscription proclaiming victory over thirty-two kings across the Lower Sea (Persian Gulf).[33] The total of thirty-two, at this point in history, suggests a substantial fraction of the entire Noahic council of Genesis 10, alienated from the Akkadian regime and uniting their forces somewhere in Arabia or the greater sphere of the Braided Goddess panel. If we add these thirty-two to the ten victims at Metelis and the seventeen kings later overthrown by Naram Sin, the total of fifty-nine, leaves just eleven from the system of seventy outlined in Chapter Three. Nine of these eleven were necessarily the inner circle of the Akkadian regime: the three emperors of the line of Peleg, Nimrod, and Ham and his four sons. In chronological terms, the Akkadians subdued, first the thirty-two of Manishtushu, then the ten of Metelis, and finally the seventeen of Naram Sin. The ten of Metelis fell victim to Nahor I (Naram Sin) in his Egyptian Dynasty I character as Pharaoh Narmer during the formative years of the White Branch.

Thus the chronology of the White Branch depends on the chronology of Naram Sin's Egyptian reign as Narmer. Because Narmer was an early Pharaoh of Dynasty I,[34] he came to power at some time in the first Akkadian era while his grandfather Sargon was still on the throne of Agade. A further consideration is that he destroyed his ten victims at the nome of Metelis in Lower Egypt as though transferring his regime from the south to the north at some intervening time. A logical explanation is that he established a regime in Lower Egypt when a distinct group of princes came to power as Dynasty II in Upper Egypt at the second Akkadian epoch in 2218. He then seized the opportunity to form the White Branch, beginning with a location in North Africa just west of Lower Egypt, under the pretext of coordinating the horizontal axis of the cosmic Swastika by forming the White Branch at the same time that Ham was beginning to form the Yellow Branch in the Pacific.

The construction of the White Branch was as follows:

Location		Nation	Prince
Libya:	2212	Nilotes	Japheth (Lugh)
Algeria:	2206	Bantus	Arphaxad I (Taranis)
Baltic:	2200	Centum Aryans	Joktan (Esus)
Sarmatia:	2194	Satem Aryans	Shem (Teutates)
Anatolia:	2188	Anatolian Aryans	Peleg (Cernunnus)

Nahor's authority to banish the loyalist leadership in this way was as absolute as Sargon's authority to use the Hamites of the Dragon system. The loyalists could hardly reject a political principle as working to their disadvantage after seeing it work to their advantage against Ham. Yet Nahor's use of this authority was an act of lawless tyranny, forcing the Indo-European dispersion sixty years too early and betraying the loyalist premise of the Akkadian imperium.

Nahor sealed his tyranny by executing the ten victims of the Narmer palette at Metelis. The simplest explanation of the victims of Metelis is that they were Genesis 10 princes held hostage to secure the successful completion of the White Branch. Certain princes whose longevities should have carried them through the twenty-second century disappear from the political scene at that time. For example, the Japhethite A clan, which had ruled as a unit at Ebla, reappeared as a defective unit in Egyptian Dynasty IV, which included Gomer, Javan, Tubal, and Meshech but none of the other three. Japheth's colony had taken the lead position in the White Branch, and it was logical to take hostages from his family.

The total of ten victims, arranged in rows of five,[35] suggests that two hostages were held for each of the five colonies of the White Branch. The most probable identities of the ten victims were as follows: for Japheth's colony, his sons Magog and Madai; for Arphaxad's colony, his sons Obal and Diklah: for Joktan's colony, two of his Aramaean vassals (sons of Shem) Uz and Mash (Eddic Magni and Madhe); for Shem's colony, the other two sons, Hul and Gether (Hellenic Hyllus and Agathyrsus); and for Peleg's Anatolian colony, two princes linked both to Peleg and Japheth, the seventh Japhethite Tiras (Peleg's brother) and Peleg's vassal Abimael, a son of Javan.

Nahor's motive, both in forming the White Branch prematurely and in executing the hostages, was to rid the Fertile Crescent of rival power. Every colonial exile or death by a member of Noah's family meant the dissolution of a visible Noahic cosmos and the consolidation of a conventional empire well-adapted to secularistic ideas. Nahor's tyranny helped to breed the polygenetic and agnostic delusions of modern times by converting the image of the Noahic aristocracy into a field of decapitated corpses in a purely Egyptian Egypt world without end. The Akkadian Empire had degenerated into the archetype of all secular governments based on "existing power," devoid of any real science of origins, and at odds with any sense of apocalyptic accountability to God.

After launching his reign of terror in 2188, Nahor had only eleven years to live down to the death date of 2177 established by Genesis 11:25. If his death resulted from a loyalist vendetta spearheaded by the Gutians, the loyalist leaders of the White Branch must have moved swiftly to undermine the empire once they got word of the executions at Metelis. Under these circumstances, the scheme of the Taranis panel took on a new dimension of historical meaning.

The lower row of the Taranis panel consists of three identical griffin birds, all turned toward the left of the panel, together with a serpent. Because a serpent symbolizes the Sumerian nation in the Cernunnus panel, the lower row represents, in some sense, the four favored stocks of the Akkadian empire, the Sumerians and three nations of the Semitic linguistic stock. The griffins face toward the sea as though to repel an invasion from the Anatolian northwest. The upper row includes both Lugh and Taranis, two of the loyalist princes of the White Branch. The two leopards on either side of them march to the right as though invading Syrian Mesopotamia and Subaria.

After 2188, the loyalists countered the four nations of the Akkadian Empire with four nations of their own and even succeeded in wrenching one of the three Semitic nations, the Amorites, out of the grasp of the empire. Of the four invading nations from the north, historians have identified the Gutians and Hurrians.[36] To add further nations from the White Branch meant a violation of integrity in the original colonization scheme. The structure of world ethnology suggests two such violations. The first and fourth nations of the Taranis invasion row were the Anatolian and Satem Aryans, destined to inherit Anatolia, Gutium, and the rest of Iran and India.

The loyalist leadership reasoned from ritual parity between the four nations of the empire and four opposing nations available to them. Through the tradition of "Indra of the Maruts," we have learned to connect the Satem Aryans with Amorites as if the Satem group were designated to match the Amorites before winning them to the loyalist cause. The Gutian interplay with the Sumerians is a matter of record.[37] The Hurrians, who belonged to the Canaanite section of Genesis 10, opposed the Canaanite wing of Naram Sin's defenses; and the Anatolians, possessing all the land in the rear of the invasion, opposed the Akkadians as national rulers of Mesopotamia.

The Taranis panel pictures all eight of these nations or, at least, their fighting men as drawn up ritually into the eight primeval camps of the Taranis zone. Because the Anatolian Hittites remembered Naram Sin's northern campaign, there is no reason not to take the Taranis scheme literally, at least to the extent that representative armies of the eight nations had gathered in the north:

Scheme of the Mithraic Vendetta: 2188-77 B.C.

Taranis Figure	National Army	Prince
Western Leopard	Anatolian Aryans	Shem (Sahlamu)[38]
Lugh	Gutians	Japheth (Zuabu)
Taranis	Hurrians	Arphaxad I (Harharu)
Eastern Leopard	Satem Aryans	Noah (Didanu)
Western Griffin	Akkadians	Nimrod (Iangi)
Serpent	Sumerians	Joktan (Emsu)
Middle Griffin	Canaanites	Zud (Tudia)
Eastern Griffin	Amorites	Seba (Adamu)

The Amorite names assigned to the eight princes reveal the underlying political logic of the Taranis scheme. The figures of the lower row are shown as facing the sea because they represented the ethnology of the Akkadian Empire under invasion. But these four armies could not have camped in such orderly array without being allied to the invaders. Nimrod, Seba, and the others were so appalled at the executions at Metelis that they abandoned Naram Sin, drew recruits from each Akkadian nation, and joined the invaders in the Taranis Zone. The Sumerian recruits, remembering Joktan as their great King Enmerkar, submitted to him at Emar. Nimrod, despite

having helped to build the empire, still smarted from his humiliation by Sargon and willingly governed a detachment of Akkadians
at Camp 5. The eight captains, including most of the Amorite
Kinglist, now constituted an Amorite imperium, a prototype of the
Babylonian empires of Hammurabi and Nebuchadnezzar sworn to
the destruction of Naram Sin.

In order to avenge the ten victims of Metelis, the Amorite chiefs
recruited two more allies, Zud's son Anam, as Hanu, and Nimrod's
feudal father Cush, after his return from the East, as Mandaru. The
construction of the Yellow Branch ended in 2188, freeing Cush to
join the alliance as head of the Elamites from the southeast. Anam-
Hanu appeared in Akkadian history as Anu-Banini,[39] chief of the
Lullubians, whom Naram Sin managed to overthrow. The exact sequence of these events is difficult to follow; but all occurred between
2188 and 2177 as the Amorite alliance encircled the empire with its
various divisions.

The Amorite alliance was not only tenfold but required just ten
years to effect the death of Naram Sin after the beginning of an annual process in 2187. Because Noah's primitive camps were annual,
the re-occupation of the Taranis camps meant the re-adoption of
an annual process of political action. The Gundestrup floor panel
pictures the Akkadian Empire as pinned between two forces, the Gutians to the northeast and Amorites to the southwest. For some
reason, these two nations succeeded where the other eight nations
failed. Japheth, head of the Gutian force which finally succeeded
in sacking Agade, appeared in the Amorite Kinglist as Zuabu, tenth
and last of the series as listed by Hallo and Simpson. This coincidence
implies that the sequence of the Amorite Kinglist took rise from the
invasion scheme. If so, the chronology of the Mithraic vendetta was
as follows:

Year	Prince	Army
2187	Tudia (Zud)	Allied Canaanites
2186	Adamu (Seba)	Amorites
2185	Iangi (Nimrod)	Allied Akkadians
2184	Sahlamu (Shem)	Anatolian Aryans
2183	Harharu (Arphaxad I)	Hurrians
2182	Mandaru (Cush)	Elamites

Year	Prince	Army
2181	Emsu (Joktan)	Allied Sumerians
2180	Didanu (Noah)	Satem Aryans
2179	Hanu (Anam)	Lullubians
2178	Zuabu (Japheth)	Gutians

This chronology means that each of the allied forces launched its attack in the year indicated and that each was defeated or driven off until the Gutians finally succeeded in 2178. Waddell translates a Hittite document in which Naram Sin is reported to have conquered an alliance of seventeen kings of seventeen nations or city states, including "Akwaruwash King of the Amorites."[40] Because the list begins with the conquest over "the Western Land," it would appear to include the ten victims of Metelis except that the majority of kings appear at known locations in Syria, Anatolia, Mesopotamia, and Iran far from Egypt.

If the Hittite inscription captures a specific moment in Naram Sin's career, the logical moment was 2181 after he had defeated the allied Sumerian force at Larak ("Urlarag of Larag") but before he encountered the Satem Aryans, Lullubians, or Gutians. He chose this moment because of the predetermined symbolic value of seventeen conquests. In the following year, whether or not the Satem Aryans met with success, their leader Noah, as "Indra of the Maruts," seems to have inspired the Amorites to undertake the role attributed to them in the Gundestrup interior panels. A year later, Naram Sin conquered the Lullubians in an event celebrated in the Naram Stele; but within the next two years, he met his doom at the hands of the Gutians.

So intense was the moral fervor of the loyalists who overthrew Naram Sin that their tradition and spirit lived on to become Iranian Mithraism, a religion stressing eternal military glory.[41] The geographic name Iran is a metaphor for separatistic fervor, the moral impulse to strike a death blow at the heart of a corrupt and pseudo-sophisticated world order. Nothing appeals to the human spirit quite like the prospect of a good fight in a righteous cause. The leaders of the Gutian or Amorite alliance stood, for a brief historical moment, at the ecstatic pinnacle of such a cause because of what the Akkadian Empire had come to mean by the year 2178.

The Later Third Millennium

When the loyalist leaders executed Nahor in turn in 2177, they introduced a period of relative anarchy, the Gutian interregnum. They realized that Noahic precedents must be modified to fit existing circumstances; but they determined to respect the predetermined Akkadian chronology, which required forty-nine more years to pass before the close of the 120th year in 2128. The Sumerian Kinglist states that precisely forty-nine years elapsed during the reigns of Naram Sin's successors through Dudu: twenty-five years for Sharkalisharri, three years of anarchy, and the remaining twenty-one years for Dudu.[42] Clearly, Sharkalisharri reigned according to a predetermined half of the Akkadian remnant of time from the Gutian attack in 2178 to 2128; and Dudu, once he came to power, simply consumed the last remnant of the age. The Kinglist testifies to a Noahic thirst for order in the midst of chaos.

As a son of Naram Sin, Sharkalisharri was either a brother to Abram's father Terah or Terah himself. The chronology of Terah's family weaves intriguingly throughout the Akkadian age. When Sargon came to power, Terah was forty-eight; he begat the eldest of the three sons in Genesis 11:26 twenty-two years later; so the Akkadian epoch occurred roughly two-thirds of the interval from Terah's birth to his first heir's birth at a time which was also nearly two-thirds of the respective Noahic era. If we reckon Sargon's reigning generation twenty-eight rather than thirty years, in accordance with his double-reign of fifty-six years, he began to reign when Terah was an even fifty; and Terah's first heir was born in the twentieth year of this reign. The second heir was born in the twentieth year of Sargon's second reign; and Abram, the third heir, in what would have been the twentieth year of Naram Sin.

Furthermore, Terah named one of his sons Nahor II, as though he expected him to succeed Naram Sin. The most important consideration is that Terah was Naram Sin's imperial heir born when the latter was approaching the standard age of thirty. Terah delayed his own series of imperial heirs until he reached seventy because of the expanding chronological horizon of the Akkadian imperium, with its grandiose reigns of fifty-six years. Given Terah's status as imperial heir in Genesis 11:24, it is more likely than not that Sharkalisharri was Terah.

One objection to this view of Abram's family is that their early seat, in Genesis 11:28-31, is clearly Sumerian Ur rather than the capital of Agade. The fact is, however, that the royal house of Agade was deeply devoted to the lunar cult at Ur, both Sargon and Naram Sin making their daughters Enheduanna and Enmenanna high priestesses of that cult.[43] The strong connection between Agade and Ur is a matter of record; and Terah's relationship to the two cities is a matter of detail. The migration from southern Ur to northern Harran makes all the more sense in the light of Terah's familiarity with the intervening Agade. The premise behind the migration was the close of the imperium in 2128; and the premise behind Terah's residence in Ur, at that time, was the close of his imperial reign at Agade twenty-four years earlier.

Terah died and Abram left Harran for Palestine in the year 2091 after a sojourn of thirty-seven years at Harran. These years were the first Noahic generation after the close of the Akkadian imperium. The sequence of the Gutian kinglist had begun much earlier because Van Der Meer shows a contemporaneity between Sharkalisharri and Sarlagab, fourth king of the Guti.[44] In running concurrently from Nahor's death, the ninety-one years claimed for the Guti dynasty would have carried it no further than 2086, about thirty-five years too early to agree with Van Der Meer's date of 2044 for the accession of Ur Nammu. The true state of affairs was as follows:

Gutian attack on Agade:	2178
Gutian counter-imperium:	− 120
	2058
Reign of Utuhegal	− 7½
Accession of Ur Nammu	2050

By positing a Gutian counter-imperium of 120 years, in answer to the corrupt imperium of Agade, we arrive at precisely the same discrepancy of six years higher than Van Der Meer as in our date of 2248 (rather than 2242) for the accession of Sargon.

This chronology means that, when Abram journeyed to Palestine, some thirty-three years remained to the Gutian imperium; and the world of Genesis 14 was now convulsed by a struggle for supremacy between the two victorious powers of the Gundestrup interior panels, eastern Gutians and western Amorites. The Abrahamic war of Genesis 14 reveals the political stalemate which served as background for the Sumerian revival of Utuhegal and Ur Nammu.

In Genesis 14:1, the Gutians appear under the West Semitic name "Goyim," the generic Hebrew word for "gentiles." It is clear that the West Semites remembered the foundational role played by the non-Semitic Gutians in overthrowing Naram Sin and conceived of these "Goyim" as representatives of the entire non-Semitic world. One reason that the Javanites are said to have populated the "coasts of the gentiles" in Genesis 10:5 is that Javan appeared late in the Gutian kinglist as Ibranum (Bran). In Genesis 14:1, "Tidal King of the Goyim" is logically allied to his fellow-Iranian "Chedorlaomer King of Elam." We have shown that the Gutians and Elamites were cut from the same historical cloth as members of the last six stocks to be formed in the Sumerian era.

If, as Zuabu, Japheth entered the old Amorite alliance as chief of the Guti, he and his grandson Javan belonged to the Iranian world, where the people of his son Madai took root in Media, the Gutium of later times. After 2188, Japheth had to be the angriest man on earth, after learning that Naram Sin had murdered his sons Magog and Madai and his vassal Tiras. His undying wrath was eventually incorporated into the Mithraic cult of Iran. Abraham and Lot were a son and grandson of Naram Sin's imperial heir and, therefore, Japheth's hereditary enemies.

In the war of Genesis 14, Abraham found himself caught in a crossfire between a Semitic Ham, Bera of Sodom, and an Iranian Japheth, Chedorlaomer King of Elam. He was obliged to fight against Japheth, the eternal enemy of his grandfather Naram Sin. The glorious vocation of Noah's antediluvian sons had degenerated to this extent; and the history of the Judaeo-Christian heritage began the instant Abraham won his symbolic victory over the wrathful Iranian Japheth, who had lived so long and endured so much. Immediately after the battle, Shem, as Melchizedek, blessed the founder of the Jewish faith in the name of Noah's god Anu, El Elyon, divine founder of the legitimate Noahic cosmos, the El Elyon of Psalm 82, creator of the human "elohim," gods of the third millennium:

> Blessed be Abram of El Elyon
> Possessor of heaven and earth;
> And blessed be El Elyon,
> Who has delivered your enemies into your hand
>   (Genesis 14:19-20).

Standing midway between Ham's immoral Sodom and Japheth's wrathful Iran, Shem pointed out to Abraham the lawful course, which is "neither violent nor casual."

The twilit denouement of Noahic history was Ham's reign as Ur Nammu of Ur and his construction of the beautiful and numinous lunar temple there. Ham's final transition from Abraham's Palestine to Abraham's Ur was a matter of some twenty-three years, from the war in Palestine to the epoch of Third Ur. Genesis 14:4-5 contains a relative chronology, claiming that the Amorites served the king of Elam twelve years, rebelled in the thirteenth year, and were invaded in the fourteenth. Logically the epoch for these terms was the ninety-first year of the Gutian imperium, 2087, the close of Gutian power specified in the Sumerian Kinglist. It is quite apparent in Genesis 14 that the Elamites have gotten the upper hand over the Gutians, Japheth having determined to close out the Gutian imperium in Elam. The Sumerian Kinglist refuses to name this Elamite interval between eras of Gutian and Sumerian rule because of the Sumerian prejudice against Elam. If Japheth came to power as Chedorlaomer in 2087, the Abrahamic War occurred in 2073; and Ham came to power twenty-three years later as Ur-Nammu in 2050.

A prelude to Ham's Sumerian regime was the Lagashite regime of Gudea in the Gutian period. The regime included Arphaxad I (Ur-Bau), Arphaxad's son-in-law Sidon (Gudea), and Sidon's son Salah (Ur-Ningirsu).[45] The dominant political figure of the Gutian age was Japheth; and both Arphaxad and Sidon were closely connected with Japheth in a variety of ways, Arphaxad as Taranis coupled to Lugh in the Taranis panel and Sidon as the father or grandfather of all the vassals of Javan, Gutian Ibranum. Hallo and Simpson date the accession of Gudea as contemporary with the end of Dudu's reign, giving an absolute date of about 2137,[46] just nine years earlier than our date of 2128 for that event (close of the Akkadian imperium).

Ham came to power in the twilight hour of Noahic history. After their reigns at Lagash, Arphaxad I and Salah were destined to die, respectively, in 2078, four years before the Amorite rebellion against

Elam, and 2048, two years after Ham's accession. Because Arphaxad was one of the oldest postdiluvian males, his death symbolized the end of an age of genetic nation-building; and, because Salah was Marduk the Great, his death symbolized the end of the high mythology or of events capable of generating such mythology.

Ham must have designed the lunar temple with a view to these elegiac changes, as a final monument to early postdiluvian cosmic vision. The temple was necessarily devoted to the image of the moon, that pale and austere vessel of stone which floats endlessly from one evening horizon to another. We have discussed the features of Ur Nammu, a Sumerian study in elegiac mystical sentiment. The design of the lunar temple was a poetic conception in its own right, its three stairways converging like the wings and torso of an ascending swan.[47] The central stairway ascended along an axis from northeast to southwest, like the geographic axis of Puluga and Darya, running from Mesopotamia to South Arabia where all the woes of Noah's family originated in Ham's sin. As worshippers climbed this flight to the pinnacle, it was as though they reversed the sequence of events which had doomed the millennial dream of the Tower of Babel and of one world united by benevolent despotic power.

One hundred-twenty years earlier, Ham had set his hand to a more heroic edifice, the Step Pyramid of Sakkara, during his Egyptian reign as Zoser I. Lauer's model of the Step Pyramid[48] shows five tiers, aside from the top level, one for each member of the Titan family of Dynasty III, Ham and his four sons. The six levels, including the top, celebrated the "great mountain" of the cosmic Swastika, the radiation of five colonies in four directions from a common center. Having completed the fabrication of "the world that now is," Ham and his sons recorded this achievement in a tower of brick, akin to the one they had sought to construct at Babel. The Step Pyramid still stands; the world they created still stands. The Amerindians inhabit America and the Chinese China because the builders of the Sakkara pyramid put them there.

NOTES

[1]MacCana, *Celtic Mythology,* p. 38.

[2]Pettinato, *The Archives of Ebla,* p. 7.

[3]Kathleen M. Kenyon, *Archaeology in the Holy Land* (New York: Frederick A. Praeger, 1960), pp. 159-60.

[4]Matthiae, "Ebla in the Late Early Syrian Period," 106.

[5]Udyana lay on the upper River Sindhu north of Harappa and defined a region not a city. Waddell, p. 116.

[6]Beek and Kramer disagree over the location of Iranian Anshan, Beek placing it northeast of Susa, the Elamite capital, and Kramer locating it south of Elam toward the Persian Gulf. Waddell identifies the name with the whole of Iran. We accept Beek's location because Kramer himself notes that the messengers of Enmerkar must "cross the imposing mountains of Anshan" to reach Aratta. *The Sumerians,* p. 270.

[7]*The Archives of Ebla,* pp. 106-07.

[8]Pettinato's "Kanish in central Turkey" (loc. cit.) is equivalent to Waddell's "Kaniesh" and Hallo and Simpson's Kanish near the upper River Halys. *The Ancient Near East,* p. 76.

[9]Waddell, pp. 206-07.

[10]Hallo and Simpson, p. 47.

[11]Ibid., p. 53.

[12]Kramer, p. 173.

[13]Waddell finds evidence for associating Etana with the Indus Valley. Waddell, p. 167.

[14]According to Chinese tradition, Emperor Shun succeeded Emperor Yao in the year 2255, just seven years before the rise of Sargon. De Bary, xix.

[15]Waddell identifies Akurgal (or "Madgal") of Lagash with "Gal of Anshan." Waddell, p. 169.

[16]Kramer, p. 227.

[17]T. G. Pinches, "Elam," *The International Standard Bible Encyclopedia,* 1939.

[18]Like Sumerian Lugalannemundu, Manishtushu of Agade claimed

to be "King of the four quarters." Kramer, p. 62.

[19]The swastika was a universal cosmic design, observable among three peoples located at points of geographic transition in the colonial universe described below: the North American Hopi, at the transition from the first to the second colonial branch; the East Indians, at the analogous point from the second to the third branch; and the Hittites, at the Anatolian terminus of the scheme. Furthermore, the Hopi connected the swastika design with ancient traditions of migration. Frank Waters, *Book of the Hopi* (New York: Ballantine Books, n.d.), p. 42.

[20]Zimmerman, p. 253.

[21]Kramer, p. 60.

[22]Holmberg, *Finno-Ugric and Siberian Mythology*, p. 341.

[23]Samuel Noah Kramer, *Sumerian Mythology,* rev. ed. (New York: Harper and Brothers, 1961), p. 76.

[24]Waddell cites an East Indian tradition of Asa-Manja's rebellion against his father Sagara. *Makers of Civilization,* p. 259.

[25]Joseph A. Seiss, *A Miracle in Stone* (Philadelphia: General Council, 1877), p. 83.

[26]Olcott, *Field Book of the Skies,* p. 129.

[27]Ibid., p. 421.

[28]The Septuagint replaces the "Hivite" of Joshua 9:7 with "Horite," the biblical counterpart to "Hurrian." A. H. Sayce, "Hivite," *The International Standard Bible Encyclopedia,* 1939.

[29]The sons of Kudai Bai Ülgön appear in Holmberg, p. 405.

[30]Dixon, *Oceanic Mythology,* p. 6.

[31]The five Pharaohs of Dynasty III are listed in Moret, p. 148.

[32]The dates listed here for the Black Branch obviously do not correspond to the accession dates of the respective Pharaohs. Instead, they record the years when each respective land received geographic nationhood in the names of the corresponding princes.

[33]Kramer, *The Sumerians,* pp. 61-62.

[34]Hallo and Simpson, p. 203.

[35]See details of the Narmer palette. Ibid., p. 200.

[36]Ibid., pp. 64-65.

[37]Kramer, p. 67.

[38]The Amorite names listed here are from Hallo and Simpson, p. 67.

[39]Ibid., p. 63.

[40]Waddell, pp. 306-07.

[41]Vermaseren, *The Secret God,* p. 30.

[42]Kramer, p. 330.

[43]Hallo and Simpson, p. 58.

[44]Van Der Meer, p. 47.

[45]Hallo and Simpson, p. 67.

[46]Ibid.

[47]Eva Strommenger, *Art of Mesopotamia* (New York: Harry N. Abrams, n.d.), pp. 406-09.

[48]Hallo and Simpson, p. 219.

Chapter 7

The Mythological Heritage

Human Deification

Although Christian euhemerists of the eighteenth century were iconoclastic, they turned to euhemerism for guidance in studying Noah because of their intuitive Christian understanding of the resources of deity available to mankind. As long as we distinguish between the Creator and His creatures, it is almost impossible to exaggerate these resources. Even the blasphemy of Antichrist depends, not so much on claiming deity, as on denying it to others.[1] Evidence for the limited deification of mankind appears in Exodus 7, Psalm 82, John 10, and I Corinthians 8. Each of these passages deals with a type of nominal deity distinct from the unique Deity of Jesus Christ. The orthodox, in their zeal for defending Christ's Deity, have not always displayed insight in coping with this other sort of deity.

The logic of Christian orthodoxy is complicated by striking spiritual paradoxes. One of the most difficult concerns what Christians call "resurrection power." They teach that, because of Christ's Resurrection, a certain charisma is available to them despite their failure, thus far, to have gained a resurrection body like His. They testify to immortal powers out of a context of mortality. This paradoxical circumstance creates any number of cultural anomalies; and one of these influences the Christian understanding of the human "elohim" of Exodus 7 or Psalm 82.

Our feeling for deity, in general, is clouded by mortal fear, uncertainty, skepticism, and the necessity for a repentance process. It is no coincidence that the high-spirited poet Percy Shelley, who understood the nature of artistic charisma so well, wrote slightingly of repentance at the close of *Prometheus Unbound.*[2] Immortals do not repent. In fact, they cannot repent. Fallen angels have no opportunity to repent; and the resurrected humanity of Revelation 22:11, both good and evil, are beyond the reach of any repentance process. If we understand what the biblical term "repentance" means, we can appreciate why it is so difficult for Christians, involved in sharing their repentant logic with others, to deal objectively with the logic of a non-repenting eternal state.

The New Testament word for repentance, *metanoia,* means "change of mind." Mortals live in a context of change: improvement, on the one hand, and degeneration, on the other. To improve our minds, we must change them; and, to change them, we must become intellectually dissatisfied or skeptical. Every mind given to skepticism either experiences or promotes repentance of one kind or another. The general ministry of repentance passes under many names: "iconoclasm," "the analytic habit," "disillusionment," "openmindedness," or "criticism." Opposed to all these is the quality of life and thought known as "superstition," which simply means inadequate or false charisma, immortality falsely so-called, or false mysticism.

Adolf Erman shows that the ancient Egyptians lived in a definitive state of "superstition"; that is, they professed a striking but inadequate sense of immortality. Living in a condition of numinous awe, they had arrived at something more or less eternal; but whatever it was satisfied neither the Jewish fathers nor the founders of the Christian Church. Obsessed with the glory of their gods, the Egyptians lived in a state of "perfect unrepentance," changeless mystical insight, like "ineffectual angels beating their wings in vain":

> The magical formulae used by the Egyptians were founded chiefly on the following idea. The magician would recollect some incident in the history of the gods, which had brought good luck to one of the heavenly beings. In order to reproduce the same good luck he would imagine that he himself represented that god, and he would therefore repeat the words the god had spoken in that incident; words which had formerly been so effective would, he felt sure, be again of good service.[3]

Aside from suggesting how euhemerism arose, such behavior was obsessive. What had inspired such obsession? Erman accurately names the cause, "the history of the gods."

The devotees of Egypt were still sharing in the unspeakable glory of Noah's family, the human gods, their own kinsmen. It is quite normal and reasonable to be obsessed with sublime things. The power of Egyptian art speaks for itself. The Egyptian religion was both concrete and numinous and grounded in historical realities both concrete and numinous.

The details of early Egyptian culture make good sense, if we assume that this culture reached complete fruition in the early postdiluvian period when Noahic "gods" walked the earth. Take, for example, the indifference to genealogy and family name noted by Erman.[4] Genealogists recall past glory as past, genealogy serving as a causal link to a world which might otherwise be lost and forgotten. To the Egyptians, on the contrary, the early postdiluvian age had never ceased. Each Pharaoh was the latest version of the gods of Genesis 10: gods linked to an eternal community, not by genealogy, but by mystical rites of feudal vassalage through the medium of spirit, the divine essence of the "Ka." Israel, with its powerful historical sense, claimed descent from the genealogical world of Genesis 11; Egypt, from the non-genealogical quasi-angelic host of Genesis 10.

By acknowledging the deity of the man Jesus, Christians have always involved themselves in a variation of these principles. Because they are not pagans, they have been quick to distinguish between their conception of Christ and pagan gods. The Apostle Paul, for example, does so in dealing with the issue of food offered to idols:

Therefore concerning the eating of things offered to idols, we know that an idol is nothing in the world, and that there is no other God but one. For even if there are so-called gods, whether in heaven or on earth (as there are many gods and many lords), yet for us there is only one God, the Father, of whom are all things, and we for Him; and one Lord Jesus Christ, through whom are all things, and through whom we live (I Corinthians 8:4-6).

Paul's statement is boldly monotheistic but pragmatically so, limiting the range of his monotheism by the phrase "for us," in the sense that "we" practice the knowledge of only one God. Aside from such Christian pragmatism, the universe includes, in some sense, "many gods and many lords," an apt characterization of the world of

Genesis 10. The Apostle realized that lords and gods existed somewhere in human experience, outside the pale of the Christian dispensation. He also realized that these lords and gods formed a loose analogy to the "Lord Jesus Christ" and "God the Father." The Apostle's task was to stabilize Christian doctrine; and, in doing so, he often diverted his reader's attention from one reality to another. A normal reader of I Corinthians would conclude that "many gods and many lords" are a thing of the past, an eccentric variation of the one true God and Lord, and not worthy of much attention. But such is not the case in John 10 where Christ Himself takes up the issue in greater depth. An eternal Being, Christ is free of pragmatic limitations, and, as such, perfectly familiar with the relationship between "many gods" and Himself.

Pressed by His Jewish adversaries to defend His Deity, Christ did so through an appeal to Psalm 82, where God, as El Elyon, addresses a group of lesser "elohim" or "gods" distinct from Himself.[5] A careful study of the logic of Christ's defense will illumine, once for all, the peculiar glory of Noah's third millennium:

> Jesus answered them, "Is it not written in your law, 'I said, "You are gods." ' If He called them gods, to whom the word of God came (and the Scripture cannot be broken), do you say of Him whom the Father sanctified and sent into the world, 'You are blaspheming,' because I said, 'I am the Son of God'?" (John 10:34-36).

Although Christians realize that Christ's Deity is totally unique, Christ's argument, in this passage, does not aim at uniqueness. Instead, He shows that, in the light of Psalm 82:6 (as in Exodus 7:1), there is no blasphemy in applying the term "elohim" (our "gods") to humanity, Himself included. The criterion of deity in Psalm 82 is the Noahic principle of governmental empowerment, not sanctity, because the "elohim" of the Psalm are rebuked for their sins.[6]

The gods of Egypt will never be understood until Christians perceive and develop the analogy between these gods and themselves, in the future immortal condition of the general resurrection. We must learn to conceptualize immortality as a concrete given. Once this is done, the critical notions of "mythology" and "superstition" will take a more subordinate position in our thinking, giving way to an aggressive, confident mysticism of our own. Otherwise, the logic of progressive repentance causes us to envision the resurrection as a distant goal, a vague abstraction, rather than a concrete reality and logical premise. Once we envision the universal scope and inevitability of resurrection, we grasp the full force of Christ's argument in John 10. Despite the uniqueness of His Deity, Christ found it a simple matter to compare Himself with a general class of "elohim" because He understood the immortal destiny of the human race as a whole, through the resurrection of the just and unjust.[7] The distinguishing marks of deity in John 10 seem rather ordinary. The "elohim" of Psalm 82, Christ tells us, were called "gods" because "the Word of God" came to them; whereas Christ belongs to such a class because God "sent Him into the world." As a matter of fact, the Word of God has come to many; and others have been "sent into the world," in the apostolic sense.

Noah certainly belonged to such a class. The "Word of God" came to him in the antediluvian period; and, as a consequence, he was "sent" into the postdiluvian age to build the world itself. His privileges included a plan for introducing the Semitic and Indo-European languages in which the Bible, the written "Word of God," is incarnated; and they also included the genetic authority to act as ancestor to the Messiah, the living "Word of God." If our thinking had not been clouded by mortality, we would have realized the magnitude of these Noahic privileges long ago. These privileges were more than sufficient to meet the criteria of deity established in John 10.

The Mythological Worldview

The iconoclastic repentance motive translates, almost as once, into the evolutionary philosophy, the stress on development. A developing mind naturally see development in anything it studies. Sequences of development can be discovered in any period of history, including the Noahic third millennium. Pyramid architecture, for example, "evolved" over the relatively brief sixty years of Dynasties III and IV. One man, Noah's son Ham, was largely responsible for the whole pattern of architecture in the third millennium; but Ham was capable of being resourceful and changing his mind once or twice.

It goes without saying, however, that evolutionists exaggerate the importance of development and underestimate the eternality of certain images. The whole point of the Creationist-Darwinian debate is whether the leonine form, for example, originated as a perfect idea in the mind of God or as a casual exercise in feline development. The Darwinian conscience acknowledges that it does not yet possess the truth and invites animal forms to "repent" along with it. To the Creationist, a lion expresses feline truth; whereas the pure Evolutionist acknowledges no ideal truth, having rejected a priori all perceptions of immortal form or stable idea.

The evolutionary philosophy begins to lose its appeal the instant that a mind begins to suspect that certain visible forms have eternal value; but, then, the risk is a return to some form of pagan idolatry, the worship of imperfect visible forms. Our goal is to strike a just balance between the opposite extremes of iconoclastic evolutionism, on the one hand, and idolatry on the other.

To achieve that balance depends on acquiring just views of mythology and the mythological worldview characteristic of the literature and traditions of the third millennium. We must learn to combine criticism with admiration. The Marduk Epic, the Myth of Etana, the Osiris Legend, and other myths are sublime if only because of their high antiquity. Above all, they are sublime in origin, as sourced in Noah's family, and in symbolic imagery, as sourced in the angelic cosmos of the third heaven. The orthodox who despise mythology necessarily despise the prophecies of Jacob in Genesis 49, as well as the apocalyptic imagery of Daniel, Zechariah, and Revelation. In fact, such minds despise the supernatural in one of its chief manifestations.

The general term for a healthy mythological consciousness is "idealism." The basic premise of all idealism is that ideas determine reality rather than approximating realities. To the idealist, the mind is an authoritative power to confer reality rather than a passive device for recording impressions.[8] On the face of it, idealism seems "superstitious" because it implies an "omnipotence of mind" beyond the reach of correction and repentance. "Mythology," then is simply idealistic history, shaped by subjective ideas rather than objective impressions originating outside the mind. The value of mythology rises or falls according to the authority of the ideas which inspire it.

In this sense, Nature itself is a "mythology" arising from the formative ideas of God at the Creation. Because God has the power to enact His ideas, there is no gap in His experience between the subjective and objective. Whatever He knows exists, either actually or potentially. His creative authority abolishes the distinction between myth and sober history. Instead of passively recording events, He actively determines them; and they take whatever substance they possess from various dimensions of His own mind.

The critical case against mythology derives from the gulf separating God from man, who often seems powerless to enact his ideas and whose ideas are sometimes defective in the first place. Our critical suspicions and doubts express an inner sense of creative powerlessness, an inability to conceive ideas worthy of objective execution. With God, all things are possible. With man, many things are unlikely.

If we grasp this logic, it is obvious why mankind, in the third millennium, generated so much mythology and so little sober history. The life history of a high-spirited, creative human being is never "soberly historical" in any case. In proportion as heroic men resemble the living God, they enact ideas, leaving historical sobriety to low-spirited scribes. Jesus Christ "spoke with authority and not as the scribes" because He possessed the divine privilege of fusing idea with action, bringing His ideals to fruition. Noah's family shared in such creative privileges but were tactless, disobedient, sinful men; and their curious blend of power and lawlessness bred precisely what we see in the world of pagan mythology.

Because we see an explicit blend of divine privilege with sinfulness in Psalm 82, every sensitive reader of that psalm has looked into the ethical foundation of world mythology. The Marduk Epic, for example, offers a splendid illustration of divine privilege, on the one hand, and contemptible pride, on the other. The complex historical event celebrated in this epic raised both principles to a definitive height. The antagonistic Iranian alliance of "Tiamat and Kingu" was a counter-revolutionary rebellion triggered by the alienation of the loyalists Peleg and Japheth. Peleg (Kingu) had refused, in effect, to accept the political due process which brought Canaan's faction to power at the epoch of the Eanna regime. Pious or separatistic violations of due process are familiar to any student of the Puritan seventeenth century, when they had much the same moral effect as Peleg's rebellion. Canaan's champion Salah, the great god Marduk, possessed the same sort of theocratic and ethical value as the Restoration King Charles II or his spiritual ally, the French "Sun King" Louis

XIV. Salah, Charles II, and Louis XIV were all "gods of this world," masters of legitimate due process in advancing causes of sinister origin, proud disposition, and uncertain destiny. Mythology formed an appropriate vesture for the conflict of Salah and Peleg because of the vast archetypal power wielded by both men. Such power simply cannot be rendered in "plain prose"; and it is apparent to students of literature that "plain prose" studies of kings such as Louis XIV belie the subject through democratic sentiment, excessive analysis, and petty envy. Like Ur Nammu's temple, Louis XIV's Versailles Palace speaks for itself and "silences our belittling criticisms."

Plain prose is nothing more nor less than the literature of the repentance process, mortal human sentiment groping for progressive improvement. Historical sobriety is the cultural result. Prose is the literary essence of progressive democracy. In Shakespeare's tragedies, nobles speak the empowered language of blank verse; commoners (or nobles in their unempowered moments) speak the rambling trial and error of prose.

Mythology, poetry, and aristocratic consciousness are all much the same. All express the nature of the "Ka" or human spirit as opposed to the "Ba" or soul.[9] Frankfort accurately equates the "Ka" with the Latin term "genius":

> The best equivalent for the Ka is the *genius* of the Romans, though the Ka is much more impersonal. But in the case of the *genius,* as well as in that of the Ka, there is the recognition of a power which transcends the human person even though it works within him.[10]

The power to transcend human personality is as basic to human experience as the image of the rising sun. Our popular English use of the word "genius" shows the result. A "genius" is anyone who has the good fortune to get involved in a task which draws him beyond the limitations of private consciousness. We all experience such activity from time to time but reserve the term "genius" for anyone who sustains such activity long enough to alter the course of history, usually in a beneficent way. The works of "genius" or high spirit invariably result in "legend" or mythology, memories of high achievement which stand out above the ordinary context of mechanical causes and effects.

None of the Bible is mythological in the pejorative sense; but some

of it resembles pagan mythology because of the inherent demands
of the subject. A classic case is Ezekiel's "King of Tyre" passage,
which literally gives the devil his due. We have seen that Tyre was
the birthplace and nominal seat of the mighty "Sun King" Salah,
god of the Swastika, founder and personal incarnation of the gentile cosmos, as modified by Canaan's faction. Accordingly, Ezekiel
pictures Satan in his glorious prelapsarian state through the symbolic medium of a "King of Tyre," more or less equivalent to Tyre
personified, Lord Salah:

> You were the seal of perfection,
> Full of wisdom and perfect in beauty.
> You were in Eden, the garden of God;
> Every precious stone was your covering:
> The sardius, topaz, and diamond,
> Beryl, onyx, and jasper,
> Sapphire, turquoise, and emerald with gold.
> The workmanship of your timbrels and pipes
> Was prepared for you on the day you were created
> (Ezekiel 28:11-13).

The description fits the jewel-encrusted Hoysala version of Surya.
The passage is quintessential "poetry," "legend," or "mythology"
because its subject is inherently poetic, legendary, or mythological.
To call it factual understates the case. It is perfectly factual; but it
is far more than mere fact.

The cornerstone of poetic vision or mythological consciousness
is the power to imagine or reason synthetically. Poetry "regards the
similitudes of things."[11] It subordinates differences to similarities.
Ezekiel's passage tacitly fuses the king of Tyre with the prelapsarian
Satan and the Garden of Eden with some "garden of God" existing
in the angelic cosmos before the creation of the physical universe.
Tacit identifications of this kind are the bedrock of poetry and
mythology; but they are as objectively real as anything we know.
They seem dreamlike or unreal to us only because of the limitations
of mortal consciousness: our instinct to plod from one reality to
another without perceiving the ideal symbolic connections.

The mortal repentance process wreaks havoc on poetry or
mythology by giving instinctive preference to "the differences of

things." To repent, a mind must discover differences and abide by them, rejecting evil terms and accepting good ones. This exercise dictates an extremely faulty view of the value of symbolism. Because the analytic or repentant mind shuns similarities, it clings to the view that symbolism is a kind of pragmatic trickery of words. No matter how hard an instinctive analyst tries to appreciate the similitude of the "King of Tyre" with Satan, he still feels that he has been tricked. He reasons with himself, "Because the purpose of intellectual life is to draw distinctions, the identity of Satan with the king of Tyre must be a useful sort of temporary delusion."

The poetic mind realizes that the king of Tyre and Satan were entirely distinct persons but that Ezekiel reveals a compelling ideal identity between them. Identities of this sort are a groundrule of poetic or "mythological" consciousness. At one point, for example, Christ identifies John the Baptist with Elijah.[12] Such identities owe nothing to verbal pragmatism. They reveal the existence of a harmonious spiritual world, in which the distinction of soul between a John the Baptist and an Elijah takes second place to an identity of "Ka" or divine vocation common to both men.[13] The special world of Christian typology, for example, is nothing but a sample of a harmonious spiritual universe reinforced by symbolic identities from top to bottom.

The synthetic nature of mythology has a profound effect on the logic of euhemeristic identifications, for example, between Marduk and Salah. In an analytic sense, we isolate Salah, as the personal Marduk, because of the specifics of Marduk's genealogy in its third millennium setting. Both the genealogies and military achievements of Salah and Marduk agree in an exclusive way. No other member of Noah's family fits either the genealogical or political specifications of Marduk so well. Nevertheless, the full symbolic value of Marduk cannot be confined to Salah's private identity or personal soul. The name Marduk refers to Salah's spirit, empowered self, or "Ka" at the time that he undertook the conquest of Iran. For this reason, the god name, as a spiritual entity, can be extended to Canaan's entire faction, its cause, the religious culture of Mesopotamia as opposed to Iran, the cult of astrology, the cosmos of the Swastika, or any other value which Salah embodied when he led his Mesopotamian army into Iran.

Euhemeristic Verification

Some source of intellectual stimulation caused Bochart, Pezron, Bryant, Jones, and others to identify specific gods with specific men. They were often mistaken and realized the possibility of error in making such judgments; yet they made them anyway. Their scientific consciences worked in a peculiar way, finding the identities of gods with men more probable than not. If we can retrace the source of their assurance in such matters, we can begin to furnish an apology for euhemeristic science.

Especially useful, in this regard, are the works of Sir William Jones, who came late enough in the history of the euhemeristic movement to entertain some of the doubts which destroyed the cause during the course of the nineteenth century. In a review of Bryant's *New System*, for example, Jones objected to the subtitle, "An Analysis of Ancient Mythology," because Bryant's intellectual method seemed less analytic than synthetic.[14] This objection anticipated the general trend toward scientific analysis as the guiding light of historiography after 1800.

Jones' definitive "On the Gods of Greece, Italy, and India" appeared in 1784. In it, Jones lists "four principal sources of all mythology": (1) the perversion of "historical or natural truth," (2) an excessive enthusiasm for the sun, moon, and stars, (3) the "magic of poetry," and (4) the "metaphors and allegories of moralists and metaphysicians."[15] Because euhemerism traces mythology to "historical truth," Jones typed himself as a euhemerist by placing this term at the head of his list; yet euhemerism was soon to perish through the logic of nineteenth-century anthropologists who shared the conviction that mythology originates in "natural truth," which Jones couples with the other term. Something in eighteenth-century culture prompted Jones to give priority to "historical truth" despite his recognition of other factors. In the same century, iconoclasts such as Voltaire and Paine were inclined to trace mythology and religion generally to "priestly imposition" and, therefore, to Jones' fourth factor of moralizing allegory.[16] The suspicion against priestcraft persisted long enough to influence the anthropological tradition of the nineteenth century but lost ground to the growing tendency to attribute all things to the "analogy of nature," especially through the medium of blind human instincts at work on the elemental forces of life. Jones touches on this explanation in his second term, the "wild admiration of the heavenly bodies"; but the term is too specialized to satisfy those modern students of human nature who divert attention from the stars to blood and urine.

Jones' third term, the "magic of poetry," merely describes mythology as a cultural mode distinct from scribal or analytic historiography. Neither it nor the second point offers any comprehensive explanation of the origin of mythology. The strength of the list lies in "historical truth," "natural truth" (or the forces of nature as channeled through the human psyche), and "moral allegory" or priestly imposition. The general trend of anthropology has been to suppress the first, exalt the second, and incorporate the third as a reminder that, although "religionists" are colorful, they remain inimical to science.

A mystery of nineteenth-century philosophy is how and why so many scholars agreed to eliminate "historical truth" from consideration. To ground mythology in "natural truth" meant to envision its causative events as "natural," that is, recurrent, individually insignificant, and unremembered except in their effects. The "historical" alternative identified specific causes important enough to have been remembered by large numbers of people, even by different nations. In short, the debate between anthropology and euhemerism depends on whether to ground mythology in private or in public experience.

One soon discovers why Jones preferred the public explanation. It was a matter of religious conviction linked to political esprit, the theocracy of the Church of England:

> Either the first eleven chapters of Genesis, all due allowances being made for a figurative Eastern style, are true, or the whole fabric of our national religion is false; a conclusion which none of us, I trust, would wish to be drawn.[17]

Nineteenth-century German adversaries of euhemerism, such as Friedrich Max Müller, were quick to link British scholarship, including British euhemerism, to an Anglican Church which they accused of abridging liberty of conscience.[18] In laying the groundwork for anthropology, the Germans found a common ground between liberty of conscience and the private or "natural" explanation of mythology. On the other side, Anglicans such as Stukeley, Bryant, and Jones sought for the historical or public explanation of mythology because of the high value placed on public consciousness and religious historicity among members of a national or public church.

Euhemerism, therefore, depends strongly on the value of public religiosity and on the primary historical question of whether a public religious consciousness existed in high antiquity. To Herder and his disciples all nations are locally determined "folk" bound by the limitations of "folklore" or private religious experience. George Grote, the nineteenth-century historian of Greece theorized that public consciousness originated in the Athenian democracy of the latter first millennium.[19] In this way, Grote confirmed the German belief that the name Noah belonged to the earlier, harmless world of folklore.

Jones and his Anglican brethren could reason as they did because they regarded Noah as a fellow man, capable of some degree of public consciousness, akin to their own. Euhemerism reverses the polarity of folklore anthropology. Instead of grounding alleged history in the blind womb of natural folklore it traces folklore itself to the Noahic cosmos, the dispensation of human government, fountainhead of all national existence and public consciousness.

The case for euhemerism, therefore, rests with the strength of Genesis 1-11 as an expression of public consciousness, the historical view of life. The euhemerists saw themselves as Christian agents of biblical historical consciousness in supplying the Noahic context to the substance of pagan mythology or "Asiatic fiction." Jones realized that this activity was an exercise in probability, the intellectual counterpart to faith in supplying the "substance of things not seen":

> Now it seems not easy to take a cool review of all these testimonies concerning the birth, kindred, offspring, character, occupations, and entire life of Saturn, without assenting to the opinion of Bochart, or admitting it at least to be highly probable, that the fable was raised on the true history of Noah.[20]

Jones' rhetoric is highly significant. He tells us that he finds it "not easy to take a cool review" of the apparent analogies among Noah, Saturn, and Manu. In the modern, Laodicean world, many find it quite easy to take a "cool review" of almost anything. In contrast, the public consciousness which Anglican euhemerists discovered in Genesis 1-11 and in pagan mythology rested on a foundation of enthusiasm, a spiritual fact. No argument for or against euhemerism is possible without considering the quality of this enthusiasm.

One does not read far in Jones' essay before he discovers a major source of this enthusiasm in the standard neoclassical zeal for the Roman Empire. In summarizing the comparatively unfamiliar gods of the East Indian pantheon, Jones clothes them in a steady stream of analogies taken from the Roman pantheon, the enveloping presence or atmosphere of his work.[21] Thus the public consciousness which the euhemerists affirmed and folklore anthropologists denied was the general ideal of empire, so well represented by Rome. Ultimately, euhemerism is the imperial reading of world mythology: folklore read by the light of the sun, not as lunar folklore, but as imperial myth.

An empire, like a temple or poem, is a synthesis, a fabrication. All vital synthesis derives from enthusiasm, just as surely as infants originate in the sexual enthusiasm of their parents. The enthusiasm which animated the British euhemerists was essentially the same enthusiasm which created the British Empire; and to cavil against it, as some Germans did, is to question whether such empires should ever have existed; whether the dispensation of human government should have occurred; whether Noah should have survived the Flood; or whether God should have dared to create mankind.

Although we can criticize Jones' equation of Noah, Saturn, and Manu, the motive to establish these identities lies beyond the reach of criticism. To reject synthesis, on principle, is to reject life itself. Our own studies suggest that Jones' equation involved four different persons: Hebrew Noah; Latin Saturnus, Hebrew Arphaxad I; Greek Cronus, Hebrew Canaan; and East Indian Manu, Hebrew Asshur. But all this is a matter of analytic detail. The Bochart-Tooke-Jones perception remains secure: the fable of Saturn was "raised on the true history of Noah" in one way or another, that is, if we accept the premise that Noah stood at the cornerstone of a universal imperium.

In accepting this premise, we learn to tolerate any number of hypothetical euhemeristic errors in order to make progress toward an inevitable goal. Historical science exhibits a full spectrum of different degrees of certitude. The goal of euhemeristic study is to observe, test, synthesize, and interpret as many coincidences as possible. Each new hypothesis refracts the sunlight of the Noahic imperium to a greater or lesser degree. Error blocks the light altogether and is soon recognized as such. No attempt is made to deceive anyone. At the very least, euhemerism reports the existence of certain coincidences; and each coincidence lives or dies in its results.

NOTES

[1] In II Thessalonians 2:4, the "man of sin" manifests himself as God only after "opposing and exalting himself above all that is called God or that is worshiped."

[2] The concluding four lines of Shelley's *Prometheus Unbound* read as follows:

Neither to change, nor falter, nor repent;
This, like thy glory, Titan, is to be
Good, great, and joyous, beautiful and free;
This is alone Life, Joy, Empire, and Victory.

John L. Mahoney, ed., *The English Romantics* (Lexington, MA: D. C. Heath, 1978), p. 503.

[3] Erman, *Life in Ancient Egypt,* p. 353.

[4] Ibid., p. 158.

[5] "God stands in the congregation of the mighty; He judges among the gods" (Psalm 82:1).

[6] "How long will you judge unjustly and show partiality to the wicked" (Psalm 82:2).

[7] Acts 24:15.

[8]For Coleridge, human perception is the result of an active power rather than a passive experience. In the thirteenth chapter of *Biographia Literaria,* he writes, "The primary Imagination I hold to be the living Power and prime Agent of all human Perception, and as a repetition in the finite mind of the eternal act of creation in the infinite I AM." Mahoney, p. 244.

[9]The "Ba" is defined in Frankfort, *Kingship and the Gods,* pp. 63-64, and Erman, p. 307.

[10]Frankfort, p. 65.

[11]Percy Shelley, "A Defence of Poetry," Mahoney, p. 535.

[12]Matthew 11:14.

[13]The context of Matthew 11 involves the universal principle of "taking" the "kingdom of heaven" by "violence" (11:12), the Noahic principle of forming a unified cosmos through processes such as the Erech-Aratta War. Elijah and John the Baptist shared in the separatistic initiative of Israel to create this cosmos through sectarian resistance against the larger gentile process of violence. Because of their own, unavoidable sectarian violence, Christ states plainly that the "least in the kingdom of heaven is greater" than John (11:11). Elijah and John were identical in separatistic motivation, sharing in the "eye" of Yahweh, the eternal spirit of judgmental separatism.

[14]Nevertheless Jones was capable of appreciating Bryant's synthetic method, which he described as "an assemblage of numberless converging rays from a vast circumference." Sir William Jones, "Third Anniversary Discourse, 2 February, 1786," *The Works,* ed. Anna Maria Jones (London: John Stockdale and John Walker, 1807), III, 25.

[15]Sir William Jones, "On the Gods of Greece, Italy, and India," *Asiatick Researches* (London: J. Sewell, 1801), I, 222-23.

[16]The notion of priestly imposition is basic to Paine's attack on Christian orthodoxy in *The Age of Reason,* a work vaguely analogous to the Bryant-Faber school in its subtitle "An Investigation of True and of Fabulous Theology." Early in his work, Paine makes iconoclastic use of pagan euhemerism in order to discredit the Christian belief in the Deity of Christ. A little earlier, he had defined national churches as "inventions set up to terrify and enslave mankind and monopolize power and profit." Harry Hayden Clark,

ed., *Thomas Paine,* rev. ed. (New York: Hill and Wang, 1961), pp. 235-38.

[17]Jones, "On the Gods of Greece, Italy, and India," 223.

[18]Throughout the 1850's, Müller saw his role in Britain as an effort to illumine Philistines. His attitude toward Anglicanism anticipated Matthew Arnold's critique of British Evangelicals. He was convinced that the religionists of Britain had traded intellectual integrity for political favor. In 1855, for example, he found Edward Pusey "very dangerous," that is, a political threat to his intellectual goals. Georgina Max Müller, *The Life and Letters of the Right Honorable Friedrich Max Müller* (London: Longmans, Green, 1902), I, 174.

[19]Grote traced the modern spirit of historical objectivity to the Greek "strong desire of the public applause." George Grote, review of Henry Fynes Clinton's *Fasti Hellenici, Westminster Review* 5 (April, 1826), 270.

[20]Jones, "On the Gods of Greece, Italy, and India," 229.

[21]Ibid., 241.

Chapter 8

The Apologetics of Noahic Science

Polygenetic Secularism

To those who actually believe it and understand its implications, the story of Noah is a devastating weapon against secularistic thought. It undermines the secular synthesis of modern times in five ways: (1) by precedenting a threat of judgmental world annihilation, (2) by reducing the powers of world civilization to unstable principles of charismatic inspiration, (3) by reducing world history to a single, symbolically reinforced intrigue, (4) by reinterpreting political and intellectual freedom as divinely appointed privilege, and (5) by indicting all nations and cultures of unatoned high crimes against their own formative principles of life. The story of Noah is the very "scourge of Nergal," a separatistic baptism of intellect. In the day that it stands, much secular logic will fall.

Accordingly modern scholars have developed an effective system of defenses against it. For the lack of a better term, these defenses can be called "polygenesis," the doctrine of the many origins of mankind. In reality, polygenesis is not so much a doctrine or even a theory as it is a gentleman's agreement about how to study antiquity. The leading scruple is never to give undue importance to any one document or tradition but to distribute the power to define antiquity among many sources in the same way that a democratic electorate distributes power. Essentially, this policy means the avoidance of despotism or centralized power in doctrine. Biblical fundamentalism lies outside the intellectual mainstream because it gives so much importance to a single set of documents from a single culture.

Polygenesis is a specialized synonym for empiricism, as it relates to the study of antiquity. Empiricism means the preference for observation above interpretation in science. To avoid the dangers of premature interpretation, an empiricist keeps gathering more evidence; and to avoid the crisis of interpretation, he makes the gathering of evidence an end in itself. Such policies are a kind of conservative wisdom. However, if premature interpretation is foolhardy, excessive empirical policy is scientific cowardice, a shirking of intellectual responsibility. Cowardice is always rooted in faithlessness; wherever men honestly believe the Bible, they have the power to interpret experience and do so.

The polygenetic approach to antiquity was worked out during the course of the nineteenth century in step with the decline of Bryant's school of Noahic study. For British writers such as Charles Darwin and Frederick Farrar, the chief stimulus toward polygenesis was simple culture shock through the contrast between civilized Europeans and ultra-primitives such as the Tierra del Fuegans or Bushmen. Darwin, in *The Voyage of the Beagle,* confessed his astonishment at such primitives:

> One's mind hurries back over past centuries, and then asks could our progenitors have been men like these?. . . .I do not believe it is possible to describe or paint the difference between savage and civilized man.[1]

Darwin's question was pregnant with the doctrine of evolution; but his assertion, with polygenesis. Either the prevailing conception of "our progenitors" must be changed; or these savages must be disinherited from the European genetic community. Either we descend from brutal savages; or such savages derive from a source distinct from our own.

Victorian racists such as John Crawfurd adopted the second view; and Crawfurd's harsh brand of polygenesis reached fruition in Waddell's twentieth-century Nazism. The humanitarian alternative lay in the type of Darwinism espoused by the clergyman Frederick Farrar, a Victorian prototype of the humane Darwinian status quo achieved after the fall of the Nazis in 1945. Farrar read his definitive "Aptitudes of Races" to the Ethnological Society of London on March 27, 1866.

Farrar's argument began with an analysis of mankind into civilized, semi-civilized, and savage races. These he called, "three distinct strata or stages of humanity."[2] The word "stages" implied evolution; and Farrar added, "The only scientific choice appears to be between the doctrine of development, on the one hand, or polygenism on the other." Although Darwin's principle of natural selection tends to be polygenetic in casual operation, Farrar distinguished between evolution and polygenism, on humanitarian grounds, by contrasting the harsh racism of Crawfurd with the humble idea that we have all descended from the same apes. Farrar's paper concluded on a note of Darwinian-styled charity: "We believe that the lowest of them are the eldest brothers of our race. . . . I do not require the notion of a physical or genetic unity in a motive to philanthropy."[3]

In a sense, Farrar was merely echoing the Apostolic commission to preach the Gospel "to every creature," without having to trace the pedigrees of the Chinese or Teutons or Bushmen to Adam or Noah. Darwinian evangelicals exist; and their logic must rest with Farrar's conviction that we "do not require a notion of a physical or genetic unity in a motive" to evangelistic zeal. Furthermore, it is always possible to trace all existing races from the same primate species, giving primitive and civilized nations the abstract letter of genetic unity, as some anthropologists have done since 1945.

Farrar's statement was a key precedent because it combined humanitarian sentiment with an agnostic attitude toward origins. These are the key components of modern polygenesis, especially throughout the Christian world since 1945. The development of a humanitarian version of Darwinism has been extremely important to Christians who compromise with the evolutionary viewpoint because such Christians are at least dimly aware of the fascist uses of "survival of the fittest." Robert E. D. Clark, in *Darwin: Before and After,* makes a convincing case that the whole pattern of late Victorian bloodlust reflected in the two World Wars can be traced to the logic of Darwinian evolution.[4] Christian Darwinians and liberal humanists have joined in a common cause to refute Clark by showing that the "doctrine of development" is either kindly in itself or can be rendered kindly by the right sort of emphasis.

In reality, neither Darwinism nor its Creationist alternative is a kindly doctrine in its present ideological function. Experiments in humanitarian Darwinism obscure the real issue. Despite the truth of Clark's thesis, both the destructive and humanitarian aspects of Darwinism are secondary. Its chief function, especially since 1945, has been to buttress the defenses of secularism against the vast destructive power of biblical truth and justice. The God who creates also destroys; and the apostate civilization which denies His creative power must feel the full weight of this other, destructive power. To appreciate such destructive power, one must interpret its target, the secular synthesis as held together by the evolutionary philosophy. Darwinism could not have supplanted vital Christianity if it lacked the characteristic powers of a post-Christian religion. Its most powerful spiritual resource is civilization itself. The classic Victorian progress myth, sourced in Thomas Babington Macauley's interpretation of British economic history and fortified by Darwin, is little more than implicit worship of civilization. Because the powers of civilization are visible and manifestly excellent, the faithless instinctively worship them; and such worship is more reasonable than some suppose. The powers of civilization derive from Noah's theocracy. Relative to Noah, world civilization is a sacred thing; and those who give their lives, conscientiously, to the arts of civilization can sense the power of God in them. To the secularist, this principle means that men and women can labor and plan, temporarily, with a high sense of purpose and hope without any explicit devotion to the God of religion.

In other words, civilization, like nature and art, operates as an implicit "means of grace." The refined secularists of the Soviet Union or of the post-Christian Western universities surround themselves with beauty, discipline, and high social ideals. They engage in the same sorts of utopian exercises as the sons of Noah and meet with successes glorious in themselves and useful to mankind. Because God overrules their work, they can sense His presence in all of their best efforts. They, like the rulers of nations, serve God through the Noahic medium of "human government"; and their neglect of Judaeo-Christian religion is quite understandable. Advanced physics, the space program, and medical research all testify to the grandeur of Noahic enterprise, the will to build and maintain a progressive human cosmos.

The Abrahamic, Mosaic, and Christian dispensations succeeded the Noahic in order to satisfy needs beyond the limitations of human civilization. If the glory of civilization is manifest, its spiritual limitations should be painfully obvious to any sensitive conscience. As Thomas Carlyle put it, all the commissions and committees are inadequate "to make one shoeblack happy." Darwinian secularism is a desperate attempt to prove Carlyle wrong: to conceive of the universe in a way which will enable the powers of civilization to stand alone as an adequate substitute for the eternal God of religion. To accomplish this end, the secular philosophy must furnish a substitute for eternity within range of civilized power: hence the strategic importance of high chronology to the Darwinian theory of origins. To dispute chronology with a Darwinian is like blaspheming against the idea of eternity. Secularists lead spiritual lives; and their engagement with the idea of immense oceans of time is a spiritual fact. Darwinian chronology has become a vital cultural metaphor for eternity.

Once eternity is redefined as an immensity of natural time, the metaphor expands to include every branch of theology. The Victorian apostates who fostered the doctrine of development knew Christianity well. What is more, they worked from an authoritative series of analogies which God has incorporated into the physical universe. Apes certainly resemble men for the same reason that all animals resemble men to a greater or lesser degree: the form of the human body is a divine archetype for the visible definition of life. The Pauline "second heaven" of outer space serves as a convenient substitute for the "third heaven" of the angels, who yield, in turn, to superhuman "space invaders," products of parallel evolution. Natural selection answers to elective grace; survival of the fittest, to individual redemption; mutation, to regeneration; the progress of civilization, to growth in grace; and an eschatology of superhuman evolution, to the metaphysics of the resurrection body.

So potent are these analogies, that the general erosion of Christian idealism has weakened their general appeal. The high enthusiasm for parallel evolution expressed in the classic Hollywood science fiction films of 1951-56 has grown steadily weaker because secularists are less and less aware of the residual Christian concept of superhuman angels. Of course, these enthusiasms can be revived at any moment; but secularists can sense that by reviving enthusiasm for parallel evolution they run the risk of reviving serious, metaphysical conceptions of angels. Because such conceptions are vital to Christian logic, the secularists have more to gain by riveting their attention on past evolution than by returning to sensational images of future evolution and provoking the masses to revived

Christianity.

Hence the strategic secular importance of the unimaginative neutrality of polygenesis. Modern Darwinism is no longer an insurgent intellectual cause but an established, conservative consensus, featuring a placid ideal of powerless origination, a kind of comforting bee-swarm of haphazard causes operative over endless millennia of droning "steady state" punctuated by occasional bee-stings of genetic mutation. Without pressing the image of human descent from apes or forcing the premise that God does not exist, secularists have won a wide following among Christian academics by circulating the simple polygenetic idea that, "We may never know the origin of the Chinese." Preying on the conservative instinct for unimaginative bathos, they have successfully reduced the name of Noah to a conceptual nullity.

The Epic of Gilgamesh as Secular Archetype

If the story of Noah is such a potent antidote to secularism, the Epic of Gilgamesh, by undermining the logical force of that story, stands as an archetype of the secular worldview. The epic replaces the reality of a Noahic cosmos with the standard secularistic ideal of an existing urban civilization without beginning and without end. The Noah figure Ziusudra is the ancestor of neither Gilgamesh nor anyone else. The hero Gilgamesh's motivation owes as much to human pathos as to any divine principle of empowerment; his achievements are altogether cryptic; the story features a hoodwinked and debauched farm boy; the actual theme is the glorification of a city world without end; and the world of the epic is in control of politicians, prostitutes, and bullies.

The secret of corrupt power is the same principle that operates in polygenesis: anonymity of origin and vagueness of purpose. Christianity is a holy faith because, among other things, Christ's origin is so firmly established and His purposes in life so clearly defined.[5] Factual mysteries exist in Christianity but the historical and moral context is clearly established. In the secular city, nothing except the city itself possesses any clarity of definition. Characteristically, the prostitutes, pimps, and hoodlums have forgotten their parents and are known by their function rather than by morally coherent career goals. Although the Erech of the Epic of Gilgamesh is not quite criminal Chicago or London, its prototypical tendency toward "polygenetic" anonymity is quite apparent.

After a few introductory remarks on the unnamed hero, the epic opens as a hymn of praise to the city itself:

> Of ramparted Uruk the wall he built,
> Of hallowed Eanna, the pure sanctuary.
> Behold its outer wall, whose cornice is like copper.
> Peer at the inner wall, which none can equal
> (I, i, 11. 9-12).[6]

Noahic mankind was certainly proud of architecture, with a pride intense enough to be featured in the climactic story of the Tower of Babel, as in the mighty pyramids of Egypt. Because of the overwhelming need to create civilization after the Flood, this pride was understandable and blameless in itself. The evil of it lay in what was missing: an historical context such as the one offered in Genesis 9-11. In the absence of such a context, the city became a mythic absolute in abstraction from any sort of moral purpose.

The opening section on the glory of Erech concludes with an exception that proves the rule, a note of contextual origin:

> Go up and walk on the walls of Uruk,
> Inspect the base terrace, examine the brickwork:
> Is not its brickwork of burnt brick?
> Did not the Seven Sages lay its foundations?
> (11. 18-19).

Instead of an explanation, the "Seven Sages" are a bit of allusive folklore. We cannot blame the author for depending on allusion, a common practice in literature. Nevertheless, allusion of this kind points up the interplay between ancient and modern secularism. Allusive folklore is the concrete substance of polygenesis, every culture claiming its own quaint traditions, none of which is supposed to possess international scope or historical authority. To the standard secularist, the "Seven Sages" are an ancient phrase and mental image, not seven anthropomorphic beings engaged in historical enterprise. The dainty alliteration of the English translation makes the point; the "Seven Sages" are no less decorative than the "cornice like copper."

The next section of the epic, the urbanization of the wildman
Enkidu, expresses an archetypal understanding of the difference between farm boys and city slickers, the one class in communion with
nature, the other attached to the will of the city through union with
its prostitutes. Gilgamesh instructs his agent, the "hunter," to in-
troduce Enkidu to a prostitute and thus subdue him to the urban
way of life, reducing the threat he poses to the city:

"Go, my hunter, take with thee a harlot-lass.
When he waters the beasts at the watering-place,
She shall pull off her clothing, laying bare her ripeness.
As soon as he sees her, he will draw near to her.
Reject him will his beasts that grew up on his steppe!"

(I, iii, 11. 41-45).

The episode celebrates the transition from the Nomadic to the Imperial Age. Gilgamesh's Eanna regime commenced some fifty years
after the Tower of Babel and consolidated the urban and imperial
ideal of Mesopotamia in the Erech-Aratta War. We have seen that
the Sumerian Kinglist refuses to acknowledge a nomadic age between
the Flood and epoch of First Kish. The Enkidu episode reveals the
spiritual climate surrounding this suppression of the nomadic
heritage.

What sort of magic does prostitution exercise in creating and main-
taining the secular city? If marriage is a metaphysical absolute, prostitutes are married to all of their patrons. Their careers are the
physical embodiment of polygenesis. Every marriage, like that of
Adam and Eve, is an origin; and the prostitute's anonymous swarm
of marriages embodies the polygenist's vague swarm of origins. In
Noahic times, prostitution represented a corrupt variation of
polygamy. Noah's polygamous goal was to generate a millennial
plenitude of nations; his enemies managed to replace polygamy with
prostitution and reduced the gentile world to a spiritual condition
both "common and unclean." Marriages, in particular, degenerated
into sex in general; nations lost their status as explicit fractions of
a universal community; and history lapsed from a single, purposeful
intrigue into the casual rote variations of prostitutes' memoirs.

The apocalyptic phrase "Harlot of Babylon" is an apt
characterization of a polygenetic world order governed by conflict-

ing beliefs and agnostic science. The pride of Erech, the Eanna temple, was devoted to the goddess Inanna, Semitic Eshtar, whom the iconoclastic Hislop singled out as prototype of the Harlot of Babylon. One of Hislop's chief insights concerning the Inanna-Eshtar-Astarte figure is that she was a goddess of urbanization, the mythic source of walled cities:

> These testimonies in regard to Astarte, or the Syrian goddess, being, in one aspect, Semiramis, are quite decisive. The name Astarte, as applied to her, has reference to her as being Rhea or Cybele, the tower-bearing goddess, the first, as Ovid says, that "made towers in cities"; for we find from Layard...that in the Syrian temple of Hierapolis, "she was represented standing on a lion crowned with towers."[7]

Unlike Hislop, we have interpreted Inanna as a very great and legitimate power in Noah's original order. Her divine son was not, in fact, Nimrod but the great god Marduk, the Messianic heir Salah, Lugalbanda of Erech, father of Gilgamesh and of the next heir Eber, Meskiaggasher, founder of Erech. As granddaughter of Shem and mother of the Messianic line below her father Arphaxad I, Inanna belongs to sacred history as well as profane. In dealing with her reputation as a prostitute, we must consider the possibility of calumny or obscure political allegory. In her, as in her mighty son Salah, apocalyptic streams of good and evil meet at the source.[8]

The Epic of Gilgamesh boldly asserts Inanna's reputation for whoredom at the foundation of the Gutanu or "Bull of Heaven" episode. We have suggested that the heroic slayings of Huwawa and Gutanu symbolized the two campaigns of the Mesopotamian-Iranian war, a bizarre affair in which Sumerian legend identified Inanna as the chief goddess of both antagonistic powers, Mesopotamian Erech and Iranian Aratta. The epic captures the same ambivalence, picturing Inanna, goddess of the temple of Erech, as creator of the Gutanu,[9] one of the enemy factions of Iran. Beyond all this, we have identified Inanna with the Celtic war goddess Medb, comprehensive ruler of the Iranian order constructed by Noah's family around her birthplace at Aratta. In accusing Inanna of prostitution, the Sumerian epic serves to discredit the Iranian cause in much the same way that the Babylonian epic discredits the same cause through its portrait of the Red Matriarch as Tiamat, goddess of chaos.

If prostitution lies at the cornerstone of the secularization of Noahic mankind, the Gutanu episode is a key to the spiritual destiny of the gentiles. At the outset of Tablet VI, Inanna invites Gilgamesh to become her husband:

> Thou shalt be my husband and I will be thy wife.
> I will harness for thee a chariot of lapis and gold,
> Whose wheels are gold and whose horns are brass.
>   (11. 9-11).

Because chariot wheels dominate the imagery of the Medb panel, Inanna's offer is tantamount to the possession of Iran, a land destined to bear Gilgamesh's Hebrew name Elam. The epic apparently means that Inanna's influence over Iran remained great enough to have appeased the Iranian forces through a royal marriage to Gilgamesh.

In a fit of monogamous indignation, the hero rejects the offer by questioning the goddess' value as a loyal wife in view of six former husbands, all of whom she has ruined: "Tammuz, the lover of thy youth," "the dappled shepherd-bird," "a lion," "a stallion," "the keeper of the herd," and "Ishullanu, thy father's gardener" (11. 46-64). Because of its combined zoomorphic and anthropomorphic membership, the list reads like a variation of one of the Gundestrup interior panels. The details match none of the panels; but the total of six suggests the six points of Inanna's own Medb panel, the Iranian empire at issue.

What is not so clear is the justice of Gilgamesh's case against Inanna's polygamous career. If the four female survivors of the Flood practiced systematic polygamy in order to generate nations, how did Inanna's career differ from theirs? According to the letter of the epic, she was unable to dispute the charges against her. She complains to the god Anu, not that Gilgamesh's claims are false, but that he has offended her by naming them:

> "My father, Gilgamesh has heaped insults on me!
> Gilgamesh has recounted my stinking deeds,
> My stench and my foulness"   (11. 83-85).

Neither she nor Anu disputes that her deeds are, in fact, "stinking."

The answer to our question lies in the polygenetic spirit of the whole work. Inanna's polygamy can find no excuse in the duty of generating nations because, in Sumerian tradition, neither gods, demigods, kings, nor ordinary men generate nations. The true polygenist cannot conceptualize the origin of anything; that is, he prefers not to and, therefore, does not. As far as the epic is concerned, Inanna's amours remain fruitless; and her cultic status as mistress of "pleasure-lasses and temple-harlots" remains unexplained, a traditional given. We are still faced with the question of how an acceptable principle of polygamy had degenerated into harlotry.

In the light of Kramer's *The Sacred Marriage Rite,* the issue of Inanna's morality seems irrelevant because she represents an idealization of sexual power among a people innocently preoccupied with physical wealth: "grain-laden fields, vegetable-rich gardens, bulging stalls and sheepfolds, milk, cream, and cheese in profusion."[10] From our fundamentalist understanding of the universal Flood and the need to regenerate the human race, the Sumerian obsession with procreation and productivity was perfectly understandable. As long as Inanna's cult can be viewed in such a light, there is no moral issue. But the Gutanu episode does, in fact, raise an explicit issue of sexual morality. In it, we have passed from Kramer's world of innocent pastoralism to the worlds of epic and tragedy, where sexual misconduct connotes treason. Noah's family did not merely survive and procreate their kind; they created nations and experienced the peculiar ethics of high political intrigue.

In biblical tradition, the focal point of sexual irregularity is Noah's son Ham, who began his political career as Enmebaraggesi of Kish and concluded it as Ur Nammu of Ur. Ham's regime of Third Ur holds the key to the sacred marriage rite and to its political and spiritual correlatives. The dynasty claimed an all-star cast from the great rebel faction: Ur Nammu, Ham; Shulgi, Ham's cursed heir Canaan; Shu-Sin, the "Mighty Hunter" Nimrod; and Amar-Sin, Jebus, the great god Zeus. Shulgi, as it happens, was the first fully documented "husband" of the sacred marriage rite as political ritual.

Reasoning from the standard, leisurely evolutionary chronology, Kramer explains that, at some unknown point in the third millennium, "the king of Sumer, whoever he may have been, had to become the husband of Inanna, as a kind of Dumuzi incarnate."[11] Dumuzi was the patriarch Togarmah, Noah's son by the White

Matriarch and father of the Sumerian race. As Ham's son by the White Matriarch, Canaan was Dumuzi's logical counterpart, especially if we recognize Ham's desire to supplant Noah as first father of postdiluvian mankind. The regime of Third Ur commenced after Noah's death. Whether or not the practice of the sacred marriage rite originated at Third Ur is beside the point because it arose from Ham's primitive motive to supplant Noah. Coming into his own at latter-day Ur, Ham made Canaan the definitive "Dumuzi incarnate," spouse of the goddess Inanna, who would confirm Canaan's legitimacy despite all the curses that Hebrew tradition could summon against him:

> "In battle I am your leader, in combat I am your
>   helpmate,
> In the assembly I am your champion,
> On the road I am your life.
> You, the chosen shepherd of the holy house,
> You, the sustainer of An's great shrine,
> In all ways you are fit."[12]

The voice of Inanna in this crux passage carries the weight of the "Ka," even the Christian *Paraclete,* a point made repeatedly by Hislop in regard to the cult of Astarte. Through Ham's logic, femininity replaced the "Ka" altogether. Enkidu of the Epic of Gilgamesh lay with a prostitute because sexual contact was supposed to have opened his eyes to the powers which distinguish urban civilization from rural savagery. Ham had experienced the great revolution of the dispensation of human government and realized, in the depth of his soul, the spiritual difference between antediluvian and postdiluvian life. He and Canaan lacked the faith to attribute this great revolution to the will of an invisible God. Instead, they found what seemed to them the ultimate explanation of civilized glory in the distinctive sexual privileges of Noah's early postdiluvian family. Polygamy degenerated into prostitution when sexual privilege became a medium of free and casual power hunger. Secular world civilization is built on such a foundation of prostitution, polygenetic amnesia, and an endless process of political manipulation and improvisation. The explicit Noahic charter is gone; instinctive power hunger remains.

The Texture of Modern Apologetics

The Protestant Reformation of the sixteenth century triggered the climax of the present age of the Church both for good and evil. It took effect in three ways: (1) by placing the Bible and the privilege of interpreting biblical doctrine in the hands of Christian laymen; (2) by promoting liberty of conscience and, therefore, general liberalism, as an ethical ideal; and (3) by giving scientific prestige to empirical investigation, rather than tradition, in determining issues of fact and truth.

The Protestant phase of the Church Age climaxed two centuries later in the Great Awakening and Evangelical movement of eighteenth-century Britain and colonial America. Evangelicals modified all three of the Protestant tendencies: (1) by achieving a new catholic consensus through key salvation doctrines too humane and popular to be neglected or opposed by the Protestant world; (2) by redirecting Protestant moral energy from liberty of conscience to missionary zeal; and (3) by re-focusing empirical thought on the concrete phenomenon of New Birth and on the casual growth of Church population. In short, evangelicals treated the sixteenth-century revolution as a means to specific Gospel ends rather than a liberal end in itself.

The Great Awakening, however, coincided with the Enlightenment, the foundational movement toward secularistic apostasy throughout Christendom. John Wesley and Voltaire were contemporaries. The Enlightenment simply meant the Reformation stripped of its religious premises, subject matter, and motivation. Because of the variety of religious opinions which resulted from the Protestant ideal of lay Bible study, "enlightened" Deists concluded that the Bible was too specific in contents and too peculiar in its impact on diverse readers to inspire religious consensus. Ignoring the evangelical answer, they rejected peculiar Bible doctrine in favor of the general truths of natural revelation. These Deists now treated liberty of conscience as a humanitarian moral absolute superior to any purely religious consideration. In fact, they put religion on the defensive to prove its humanitarian value. Trends in science followed suit. By the early nineteenth century, "enlightened" minds of the logical positivist kind began to treat methodologies for gathering fact as more authoritative than any conclusions drawn by these or any other methods. Secularists now began to conceive of science, not as knowledge, but as an endless quest for knowledge, that is, a set of learned rituals for confirming agnosticism.

In sum, the Enlightenment implied three principles: a distrust of religious orthodoxy based on a fear of being misled by doubtful specifics; an absolute humanism, the ethics of humanity for humanity's sake; and a curiously self-contradictory agnostic science. In religious terms, these principles meant a distrust of the Bible, a distaste for the doctrine of hell (as inhumane), and a commitment to be "ever learning and never coming to the knowledge of the truth." No matter what the vicissitudes of philosophical or religous opinion, these three principles remain the foundation of secular learned consensus.

Because these principles are neutral and colorless in themselves, they required concrete embodiment and received it from the Victorian thinkers Karl Marx, Charles Darwin, and Sigmund Freud. Marxism, Darwinism, and Freudianism represent more than the specific subject matters and issues of *Das Kapital, Origin of Species,* or *The Ego and the Id.* Marx and Lenin gave the secular principle of humanity for humanity's sake a concrete revolutionary image by identifying the cause of humanity with the economic interests of a specific social class. Freud took a lesson from Shakespeare's character Queen Gertrude of *Hamlet* and applied to the souls of millions the "flattering unction" that human psychology, rather than spiritual power, accounts for the affairs of men. By explaining the spiritual away, Freud confirmed the "enlightened" distrust of religion by dismissing transcendental symbolism as earthy dream imagery, colorful and compelling but devoid of objective authority. Darwinism completed the process by anchoring the secular ideal of the endless quest in a colorful theory of origins. Darwinism buttressed Freudianism (and largely inspired it) by re-defining animal species as casual variations rather than complete manifestations of God's creative ideas, thus establishing the Freudian premise of purely subjective symbolism.

Some Christians misunderstand this last point. In fact, Darwinism can be traced back to certain conceptual deficiencies in the Christian theology of Europe. In their zeal to reject pagan idolatry, Christians have adopted the mistaken view that the form of the human body has nothing to do with the "image of God" in man.[13] This conventional theological notion seems intellectually sophisticated but has led directly to the conceptual triumph of Darwinism. The "image of God" is supposed to represent man's "invisible part," that is, the intangible faculties of conscience, reason, and the like. No one disputes that the "image of God" refers to conscience and reason; but the view that this image has nothing to do with the body is profoundly erroneous, even blasphemous, because it implies that God, in the Creation, failed to harmonize the form of the body with these faculties.

The enemies of Christianity can sense the futility of this theological flaw and have exploited it with profound effect. If the form of the human body derives from any other source except these divine faculties, then we might as well say that human form derives from purely casual causes, unrelated to the ideal mind of God. Darwinism is the logical result, namely, that God caused the animal and human forms to occur haphazardly and without regard to any dimensions of His own essence. The doctrine of special Creation loses all of its logical force once we assume that the animal and human forms fail to incarnate specific dimensions of God's creative mind. Every logically consistent Creationist is also a Christian idealist; and every man who doubts the divine meaning of the human body is in process of becoming a Darwinian. Under the influence of its doctrine of human form, the Christian Church could easily have invented the theory of evolution, on its own, except for the restraining influence of the Book of Genesis.

The organic nature of the secular apostasy has dictated an organic apologetic response, with implicit anti-Marxist, anti-Freudian, and anti-Darwinian dimensions. Living under the pressure of the apostasy, Christians have developed such a response whether or not they are fully aware of it. Some of the response is more or less superficial or indirect in logic. Christian conservatives oppose Marxism, not through strong anti-communist logic, but through the simple awareness that the Soviet Empire equates communism with atheism and is determined to persecute both the Church and Israel. The anti-Freudian position is a simple defense of Christian sexual morality; and the anti-Darwinian, a mere detail of the general case for biblical literalism. In other words, many Christians are not consciously aware of the inner logic of the apostasy until it begins to conflict visibly with the "letter of the law." The task of confronting apostate logic has fallen to Christian intellectuals such as the British "Inkling"

group of C. S. Lewis, J. R. R. Tolkien, and Charles Williams.
Despite their community of interests, Tolkien, Lewis, and Williams
expressed three fundamentally different and complementary types
of apologetic testimony. A Roman Catholic, Tolkien shared in the
same principle of conservative nostalgia for Catholic Christendom
which inspired the historical romances of Sir Walter Scott and,
through Scott, the conversion of John Henry Newman. Because Scott
never turned Catholic, the Christendom ideal is larger than the
Catholic Church and has determined the conservatism of many Protestants. For lack of a better term it can be labeled "amillennial sentiment" or "the High Church consensus." It is essentially a cultural,
even literary spirit of cooperative harmony among the best minds
of Christian Europe and, as such, influenced Lewis and Williams
almost as much as Tolkien.

The chief target of Tolkien's school is Marxism. At its worst, the
amillennial spirit degenerates into fascism, a tendency which Lewis
occasionally noted in Tolkien.[14] Fascism originated as an anti-
Marxist movement. The point of conflict is easily defined. Marxism
assumes that every man's god is his belly: that the purpose of humanity is to feed itself. From the time of Thomas Carlyle down to Tolkien,
the enemies of Utilitarianism or Marxism have objected that Medieval
chivalry and feudal loyalty had actually worked because man "does
not live by bread alone" but is a spiritual being activated by conscience, ancient symbolism, and ideals of self-sacrifice. Through his
concept of the Hobbit race, Tolkien acknowledges that most men
appear to be comfort-loving epicureans but respond, inevitably, to
the mystical appeal of chivalric high adventure.

C. S. Lewis exhibited the Protestant gift of iconoclastic criticism.
Like the eighteenth-century poet-critic Samuel Johnson, he was at
his best in condemning the illogical follies of fashionable error. He
targeted Freudianism, matching the clever anti-Christian iconoclasm
of the Freudians with a clever anti-Freudian strategy of his own. The
common ground was an interest in sexuality. Freud, basing his concept of practical Christianity on the behavior of "repressed" Victorian Germans, was fascinated by the blind, irrational power of sexual impulses and was convinced, with Friedrich Nietzche, that respectable, timid people are merely scandalized by powers which they
neither understand nor ultimately control. In other words, Freud
interpreted sexuality as a dark, quasi-religious mystery, deeper than

any religion and, thus, the key to all religions. Lewis despised this argument through the Christian perception that "resurrection power" is akin to sexuality and simply superior to it.

Lewis' apologetic approach, grounded in reason, is not well adapted to those parts of the world where apostasy has advanced so far that anarchy reigns and Freud's "dark power of the Id" vies for immediate social supremacy. Confrontation with such satanic power was the specialty of Charles Williams. The final form of apologetics is supernaturalistic, apocalyptic, and judgmental. It threatens the enemies of Christianity with the consequences of unrepentant death, requiring them to choose heaven or hell today and experience one or the other tomorrow. As an apologetic strategy, threats of judgment are worthless apart from metaphysical support, given evidences of supernaturalistic change within the human context of life. Although most apostates are infuriated by threats of judgment, the human conscience remains open to this very elemental sort of conviction.

This final branch of apologetics correlates with what is known as "gothic" fiction and, in fact, can be labeled the "gothic argument." Gothic stories differ in religious tone from the comparatively Christian *Dracula* of Bram Stoker to the surface secularism of most Poe stories. They also differ in their capacity to represent the preternatural as an empirical given. *Dracula* is boldly heroic in this respect. M. R. James' stories are especially clever in making us feel that the preternatural should be regarded as "gross and palpable." Nearly all works of this kind have the same tonic effect on the human conscience, intimating to secularists that their flight from the supernatural is a childish attempt to whistle in the dark.

To the Freudians, of course, these works merely "play on our fears"; but when we ask secularists where these fears originate, they discuss the circulatory, glandular, and nervous systems in the manner of Ebenezer Scrooge's psychomatic explanation of Marley's Ghost as an "underdone bit of potato." The Freudian arsenal of explanations features repressed childhood memories; but the logic remains the same and similarly limited. To demonstrate how fear is registered in the psyche has little bearing on whether beings and situations capable of inspiring fear actually exist. In this respect as in others, Freudianism functions as the domestic handmaiden of Darwinism, where the real strength of the anti-supernaturalistic position lies and where the ultimate confrontation with the "gothic argument" must take place.

It is no coincidence that M. R. James, cleverest of the gothic writers, based his stories on a formula taken from the field of archaeology. His *Ghost Stories of an Antiquary* appeared in 1903, twelve years after the discovery of the Gundestrup Caldron. The overriding theme of his stories is that antiquity implies a cosmos of powers which have only been sleeping, like the bodies of the Christian dead, "in the dust of the earth." In Christian apologetics, the greatest of all doctrines is the resurrection of the dead, an idea so powerful that it, rather than sex, holds the key to the mysteries of human existence. Wherever it is clearly conceived as a metaphysical reality, resurrection annihilates every premise and every conclusion of the Marxist, Freudian, and Darwinian schools of thought. It erases the premise of Marxism by positing a version of humanity independent of the natural food chain; it cancels the premise of Freudianism by furnishing a degree of vitality so absolute that temporary sexual euphoria loses all meaning; and it destroys the whole point of evolution by bringing mankind to absolute physical perfection in an instant of transformation.

James' stories do not, in fact, present resurrection motifs as such. Like the North American gothicists Algernon Blackwood and H. P. Lovecraft, James rivets his attention on the preternatural and, thus, confirms the secularistic attitude that supernaturalism of any kind is rather unsavory. But, like all art, his stories imply more than they state. The evil in his stories serves a dramatic, as opposed to a moral purpose. The effect is not indignation, but surprise. In classic gothic fiction, evil tends to be metaphor for apocalyptic power, just as Halloween imagery tends to stir the spirit of a child more deeply than the pallid imagery of Easter. Freudians explain the imaginative preference for Halloween as evidence for the irrational power of the Id; but there is a far more Christian explanation.

A great gulf separates resurrection as a perennial doctrine of the Church from resurrection as an accomplished metaphysical fact. Sooner or later the conscience must come to grips with this difference. Christians are fortunate to live in the twentieth century because Einsteinian physics has made it so much easier to conceptualize the glorified body of the resurrection. In the absence of such scientific insight, the Victorian Matthew Arnold supposed that the Apostle

Paul was dabbling aimlessly in metaphysics in his account of the resurrection body in I Corinthians 15. Arnold labored under the delusion that Christianity is a tissue of moral sentiments; and Victorian Christians had fed his delusion by treating the "blessed hope" of the resurrection as a wistful, consoling sentiment rather than a sincere belief about the future transformation of mankind. The gothic writers should be honored for the way their work scandalizes passive, materialistic notions of reality and strips away the cloak of sentimental palaver from the stunning metaphysical promises of the faith.

Of course, gothicism, like all art, has a dual potential of false and true. It is always possible to glorify the occult for its own sake and miss the tonic, apocalyptic message altogether. One gothic writer differs from another in this regard; and readers bring a host of presuppositional attitudes to such works. The distinction between Christian gothic and unwholesome occultism depends on nuance. Poe's Romantic goal was to make rationalists aware that they have souls poised between life and death. *Dracula* is based on the commendably Christian theme that Satan is very dangerous yet conquerable. M. R. James remains the most significant gothic writer for our purposes because of his steady commitment to associate antiquarian study with apocalyptic power. A brief exposition of "The Treasure of Abbot Thomas" should suffice to reveal his method. A Mr. Somerton has "undertaken" a personal "expedition," like a true archaeologist, to investigate "Lord D---'s private chapel."[15] The combined note of unsuspected adventure and deadpan empirical method symbolizes the first stirrings of supernatural awareness in the hearts of a skeptical generation. Somerton's empirical memory just happens to stir up an echo of the Apocalypse: " 'They have on their vestures a writing which no man knoweth,' " an evocative paraphrase of different passages from the Book of Revelation, plunging the reader's mind into a context all the more compelling for being somewhat irrelevant and half-digested, as based on archaeological data and free association.

Somerton manages to uncover and decipher a cryptogram promising buried treasure at the house and well of Abbot Thomas, once these can be located. He discovers that the well, like an inverted Tower of Babel, is about seventy feet deep and equipped with a circular staircase leading downward. At the descending thirty-eighth step, he finds a patch of cement disguised as stone, removes it, recognizes some prerequisite imagery, penetrates further, and sees, "some round light-coloured objects within which might be bags." He reaches for one of these and precipitates the climax of the story:

> I got the thing fairly in front of the mouth and began drawing it out. Just then Brown gave a sharp ejaculation and ran quickly up the steps with the lantern. He will tell you why in a moment. Startled as I was, I looked round after him, and saw him stand for a minute at the top and then walk away a few yards. Then I heard him call softly, "All right, sir," and went on pulling out the great bag, in complete darkness. It hung for an instant on the edge of the hole, then slipped forward on to my chest, and *put its arms round my neck.*[16]

Freudian logic is on the right track in interpreting such a fiction as a myth of parturition. The well, hole within the well, and "complete darkness" all suggest the womb. The "great bag" simulates a birth sac; and the act of "put[ting] its arms round my neck," typifies the behavior of a more mature infant, juxtaposing time frames in the classic manner of a dream. Freudianism, like all great non-Christian ideologies, begins with a truth, idolizes it, and "comes short of the glory of God." Because symbolism is a synthetic reality, parturition is only one dimension, though an important one, of James' story: a kind of "psychological local color" element.

According to the literal surface of the story, Somerton's animated bag is the furthest thing from a lovable infant: a loathsome preternatural being attached by a curse to the Abbot's treasure in the same way that mythical dragons guard treasures in folklore. Again, anthropologists will satisfy themselves that they exhaust the meaning of the story once we identify the dragon-guard motif. Why, then, does the story identify the dragon-guard with suggestions of a newborn infant? In the first place, the story adds a further suggestion, namely, that Abbot Thomas himself is the infant's "father." Somerton's assistant Brown explains what had startled him:

> So I looked up and I see someone's 'ead lookin' over at us. I s'pose I must ha' said somethink, and I 'eld the light up and run up the steps, and my light shone right on the face. That was a bad un, sir, if ever I see one! A holdish man, and the face very much fell in, and larfin', as I thought.[17]

Abbot Thomas' laughter is appropriate because the outcome of the story is both horrible and ludicrous yet horribly and ludicrously sublime in the same way as the miracle of childbirth or greater miracles yet. James concludes his story with a doubly ironic quotation of Latin Scripture, "Depositum custodi," "Keep that which is committed to thee."

The concluding words "Depositum custodi" can be read two ways. To the unimaginative, they are a blasphemous distortion of the Apostle's exhortation to preserve the Gospel for future ages. To the Christian who understands the gothic argument, they mean, "Keep the glorious hope of an actual resurrection (when the Gospel will take care of itself), under a cloak of darkness and horror until someone actually dares to believe it." The words, like the story, satirize the incapacity of soulish human beings to take the supernatural seriously until it literally reaches out and "puts its arms around their necks."

The gothic argument, therefore, represents the defiant, apocalyptic side of Christian testimony. This argument, like the milder forms of Tolkien and Lewis, has much to gain from the development of Noahic science.

Noahic Science and the Ideal of Christendom

A truism of Protestant belief is that the Edict of Constantine was a misfortune because it opened the door to worldly compromise in the Church and inspired the corruptions of Rome. This belief is a half-truth based on a failure to recognize the interplay between the Christian and Noahic dispensations. As "powers that be," the Roman emperors inherited a certain limited relationship to God from their Noahic ancestors; and for them to abandon the policy of persecuting the Christian Church was an inevitable step forward in the Christian plan of the ages. If the same event channeled worldly corruption into the Church, the result was a preordained testing experience for the Church, the temptation pattern established by the letter to Pergamos in Revelation 2.

The ideal of Christendom means the Edict of Constantine at its most fruitful through the overruling providence of God in the development of Christian Europe. At the root of the ideal lies the mystery of the Pauline Apostolic commission. Why did Paul turn his attention toward Europe; and why has Christianity taken such deep root in the cultures of that continent? A familiar answer has always been that Europe is the continent of Japheth, brother and spiritual ally of Shem in the Noahic prophecy of Genesis 9:27. Although this view is based partly on genetic over-simplification, there is much truth in it. We have seen that Japheth's original fief coincided with Syria, the fraction of Noah's primitive geography nearest Europe. The immediate key to European origins was the White Branch of the Akkadian Age, bringing the ancestors of Hellenes, Romans, Celts, and Teutons to Northern Europe. The formation of the White Branch was sealed in the blood of Japheth's sons at the nome of Metelis and, thus, triggered the esprit of the Gundestrup Mithraic cult, key to the peculiar militaristic culture of chivalric Christendom.

The equestrian panel of the Gutian attack on Agade is the archetype of the Christian Crusades, originating like them in Europe and aiming at what was to become the Islamic heartland of Mesopotamia and at the same Semitic linguistic stock common to Islamic Arabia and to the Akkadian Empire. The lunar cult of Ur linked the adversary Naram Sin to his grandson Abraham, whose son Ishmael is often regarded as the forerunner of Islam. Like Naram Sin at Metelis, Islam has sometimes "shed the blood of the saints"; and the vendetta against him easily translates into the Crusader vendetta against Islam.

Like the Edict of Constantine, the Crusades have often been a target of iconoclastic Protestant criticism; and it is certainly meaningful to question the spiritual value of a vendetta against Abraham's ancestral family. If the Crusades were the essence of Christianity, there would be little to choose between the faith of Jesus Christ and religion of Mithras. On the other hand, a strong case can be made that the Crusades were to the Edict of Constantine what the apocalyptic letter to Thyatira was to the preceding letter to Pergamos. The conflict with Islam is a given temptation. Europeans did not invite the Islamic armies of the eighth century to invade France; and the Medieval Christian burden of having to live with Islam was as valid a Christian temptation pattern as any other. The letter to Thyatira holds the key to this temptation and to the Crusader mystique because, for one thing, the symbolically chosen city of Thyatira originated as a military camp of Alexander the Great, who, like the Gutians two millennia earlier and Crusaders a millennium and a half later, invaded the heart of the Middle East from a base in Europe.

At the opening of the letter to Thyatira, Christ praises the

Thyatiran Christians for their great patience,[18] an apt prophetic characterization of Medieval Europe under the endless pressure of Islam. Christ goes on to warn the church at Thyatira against the spiritual infiltration of a malign cult symbolized by Jezebel, the Old Testament queen who antagonized the rugged separatist Elijah and worshipped the god Melqart, West Semitic version of Peleg's brother Joktan. As Enmerkar, Joktan had embodied the Mesopotamian cause against the Iranians, adding weight to the view that the "Harlot of Babylon" and cult of Jezebel are the same. The problem lies in the identity of this cult relative to the Noahic heritage, on the one hand, and Christian Europe on the other.

The Harlot of Babylon, whatever its prophetic meaning, was focused by Jezebel's cult of Melqart in its full Phoenician setting. The identity of Melqart with Joktan is certainly a strong clue. In the Hellenic Argonautic tradition where Melqart appears as Melicertes, the latter's mother Ino, a version of Inanna, plays a role much like Jezebel's in seeking the blood of her innocent stepson Phrixus,[19] the Messianic heir Peleg, head of the anti-Mesopotamian forces. The Ino-Phrixus conflict furnishes some of the clearest definition of the Harlot of Babylon in all of pagan tradition. But the conflict represents only an instant in the political history of the Noahic world; and, even if we can generalize successfully about the spiritual significance of that moment, we are still far from determining the relationship between the Harlot of Babylon and the various ethnic and religious factions of Medieval and modern history.

If we view Inanna as the tragic source of Jezebel's cult, that cult originated in wounded pride. Inanna failed to duplicate in her son Joktan what she had achieved through her earlier son Salah. Like Cain and Esau, Joktan ranked high as a rejected heir, having lost the Messianic birthright to his brother Peleg. The text of Genesis 10 testifies to just how high he ranked, assigning him thirteen vassals through the political outcome of Inanna's Erech-Aratta War. All that Peleg retained was the Messianic birthright; but that much was sufficient to infuriate Joktan's mother.

In view of Jezebel's devotion to Melqart, the core of the Harlot system was a Phoenician triad defined by Albright:

Melcarth *(Milqartu)* of Tyre, Eshmun *(Iasumunu)* of Sidon, and Ashtart *(Astartu)*. These three are called upon in the curse formula to punish any violator of the treaty

by sending storms against the ships, tearing up mooring-posts, causing the ships to be swamped by mighty seas.[20]
The human originals of these gods were Joktan, Canaan (Resheph-Eshmun), and Arphaxad's daughter Uzal; and, corporately who were these? The triumvirate of the world on the eve of the Erech-Aratta War: Enmerkar of Erech, Aka of Kish, and Inanna, goddess of Aratta and empress of the Medb zone of Iran. This political structure explains the meaning of Jezebel's cult as Canaan's rebel cause in the moment of its first political revival after the judgment on the Tower of Babel. Just what this rebel cause consisted of has not been defined except as political opposition to the leadership of Noah and Shem and, presumably, spiritual conflict with the "Yahweh Elohim of Shem."

And it is precisely the "Yahweh Elohim of Shem" who gives meaning to the Crusader mystique of Christian Europe. Naturally we conceive of Yahweh as the national God of Israel, remote from any Gentile cult. But Genesis 9:26 links the name Yahweh to Shem, who preexisted Israel by some 600 years. Some have attempted to identify Israel with the Semitic linguistic stock in general. That view is a half-truth, precisely a half-truth, based on one-half of the Hirschnatur panel, which displays Shem's prehistoric control of the two linguistic stocks represented by the languages of the Old and New Testaments, Semitic Hebrew and Indo-European Greek.

When the Semitic Apostle Paul turned to the Greeks, he reunited the two spiritual components of the Hirschnatur panel. The secret of Christendom is a prehistoric link between the Indo-European linguistic stock and the worship of Yahweh, a principle which barely survived to explain the heroic motifs of Heracles, Thor, and Mithras. Salvation is entirely of the Jews; but the God of Moses had been known, through the personal mediation of Shem, to the ancestors of the Greeks, Celts, and Teutons; and these ancestors were, in fact, the peculiar people of Yahweh in the original structure of the Noahic cosmos.

This prehistoric cult of Yahweh degenerated to little more than a peculiar European instinct to invade and punish the tyrannies of Mesopotamia. The Spanish bull-ring reenacts year after year this primordial Aryan commitment to strike and destroy the false leadership of the Mesopotamian world order, the corrupt spiritual regime of Jezebel and her gods. The irony of the situation becomes abundantly obvious when we consider that Joktan, the human Melqart of Jezebel, reappears as East Indian Vishnu, Teutonic Odin, and Celtic Esus. But, then, it is erroneous to identify Melqart with any of these gods outright, each god representing a distinct dimension of Joktan's Noahic image. There is no question that, at the outbreak of the Erech-Aratta War, Joktan embodied a version of the rebel cause; but he evidently ceased to play such a role in later generations.

The ancient Indo-Europeans became every bit as pagan as any other stock; but buried deep in their origin was a distinction adequate to explain the mystique of Christendom. The power of Christianity brought this distinction to light. God used it to suit His ends. The Nazis have plunged it back into pagan chaos. The spiritual ambivalence of the situation is captured beautifully in the Eddic myth of the "Twilight of the Gods," in the revived mythology of Wagner's "Ring" operas, and in the analogous fiction of Tolkien's "Lord of the Ring" trilogy, with its convincing blend of Christian humility, high vocation, and tragic ambiguity of destiny.

Wagner and Tolkien realized that the strands of good and evil, glory and shame, in Aryan Christendom can barely be disentangled, but that the Aryans, like all cultures, must "work out their salvation in fear and trembling," without abandoning their first principles of spiritual life, their "eldest loyalties." Tolkien expresses the ambiguous destiny of Christendom through his spokesman for the Western land of Gondor in its death-struggle with the Eastern land of Mordor:

> But this very year, in the days of June, sudden war came upon us out of Mordor, and we were swept away. We were outnumbered, for Mordor has allied itself with the Easterlings and the cruel Haradrim; but it was not by numbers that were defeated. A power was there which we have never felt before.[21]

When the full story of the Gundestrup Caldron is laid out in epic form, scholars will realize just how accurately Eddic mythology and the poetic fictions of Wagner and Tolkien mirror the universal moral intrigues of Noahic mankind. The embattled voice of Tolkien's Gondor originated with the hero Shem, dispossessed of his nuclear fief of Akkad, and with his ancient father Noah, who had seen millennial utopia slip through his hands and fall shattered to earth, eternally divided into warring factions, the European Gondor of Shem and Islamic[22] Mordor of Canaan.

Noahic Science and Protestant Logic

A distinctive belief of Protestants is that the Christian Church is corporately invisible because Christ, the head of the Church, has ascended to heaven without leaving behind any Vicar or supreme representative on earth. This principle of invisibility makes the existence of the Church and the reality of its authority a test of faith, the "substance of things not seen." Because of this reliance on faith, Protestantism has fostered the development of historical science, the realization of richly developed worlds in the invisible past, some with advantages denied to us. Protestant theologians, for example, have emphasized the distinction between the visible religious cultus of Mosaic Israel and the Christian's own sparsely elaborated cultus, based on a few ordinances. They see themselves as laboring under a stoical test to make do with limited religious resources, even to the extent of acknowledging that "miracles have ceased" since Apostolic times.

For this reason, the intellectual health of Protestantism depends on a reasonably complete, logically coherent Weltgeschichte or universal history, such as the one featured in the panorama of the seven dispensations. Any major gap in history implies a gap of faith, that is, a lapse of meaningful "substance" in "things not seen." Such gaps can be exploited with devastating effect by the enemies of Christianity. The failure of Bryant, Faber, and others to develop a satisfactory Noahic science around 1800 was one of the greatest disappointments of Protestant history and one of the first hints that Protestantism, like Catholicism, had "come short of the glory of God." Sir William Jones' remark on the authority of Genesis and the integrity of "our national religion" was prophetic. The collapse of many Protestant leaders into Liberal infidelity was inexcusable but followed logically from one of the greatest scientific failures of modern times. In his critique of Protestant orthodoxy, Matthew Arnold could easily claim that Protestant faith had "materialized itself in fact and the fact had failed it."

Arnold's criticism was unjust in many respects but was appropriate for a literary man because the failure of "fact" to which he referred was actually a failure of historical imagination, a lapse of the sort of synthetic power which poets represent. The Protestant attempts at Noahic science failed because Noah's world remained largely inconceivable. Neither Bryant, Faber, nor Hislop acted, imaginatively, on the high-longevity-low-chronology factor of Genesis 11 to visualize the uniqueness of early postdiluvian mankind.[23] Conservative logic is instinctively uniformitarian, slow to conceptualize the changes which punctuate the dispensational Weltgeschichte. The "fact" had failed Protestants because the "fact," as conceived by them, lacked imaginative substance.

In 1869, Mark Twain, in *Innocents Abroad,* dramatized the failures of Protestant conceptual power by contrasting his firsthand impressions of Palestine with the grandiose and incoherent conceptions which he had imbibed from pious travel literature. Since Twain's time, biblical archaeologists have pursued the sort of revision he recommended: the reduction of grandiose images of biblical kingdoms to the humble, domestic miniatures of Middle Eastern reality. This sort of revision has run its course. We are familiar enough with the concrete texture of Middle Eastern life and can distinguish between Queen Elizabeth in all her heavy finery and the compact barefoot loveliness of a Mediterranean and Jewish Virgin Mary. The real conceptual challenge in 1774, 1869, and now has been to invert the meaning of that domestic small scale of Middle Eastern life to realize that the "Czar of all the Russias" and the whole of world civilization originated with the eight "primitives" of the Ark. We need to recover Michelangelo's vision of a single anthropomorphic body as a cosmos and the organic measure of all things; otherwise we will never realize what happened in the third millennium or what Weltgeschichte consists of.

Twain's imagination was too impressed by mere size and too oblivious to the concept of power, that curiously inverse quantity measurable by brevity of duration. Christianity is a religion of divine power; Protestantism, the recovery of biblical power; and Noahic science, the recovery of a lost heritage of civilizing power. Does it surprise anyone, today, that the power of lightning resides in the electron, a particle so small that it lacks full definition as matter; or that the greatest destructive and constructive powers of the physical universe lie in processes which we term "nuclear" after the core of the atom? Why, then, should it be difficult to conceive of the origin of world civilization in a boatload of eight primitives, chosen by the Creator of the universe for that purpose? Noahic science is the "atomic physics" of world history.

Accordingly, polygenesis remains a kind of retrogression toward Newtonian physics, the philosophical heritage of the Protestant seventeenth century. In the Newtonian scheme, every star and planet operates its own gravitational powers like a small family business financed by limited supplies of energy and sliding in gloomy isolation through endless fields of "free enterprise," that is, through nothing at all, except for the possibility of encountering something as isolated as itself. In the monogenesis of Einsteinian physics, every star belongs to an organic cosmos, a space-time continuum in which matter and energy are modes of the same thing, and space itself a variation of substance subject to gravitational influence and organic curvature. The history of Noah's family will be clearly understood in the day that Einsteinian physics is taken to heart.

It was precisely the undercurrent of Newtonian or Lockean polygenesis—the failure to recognize an organic cosmos—that undermined the scientific enterprise of Bryant, Faber, and Hislop. The Newtonian bias is a conceptual spirit, measurable in literary terms. We can detect it in the very wording of Bryant's preface to his *New System:* "I shall lay before the reader what the Gentile writers have said upon this subject, collaterally with the accounts given by Moses."[24] Bryant might have written, "I shall recover the voice of Noah through his gentile sons"; but no such organic relationship existed in his mind. Instead, he must "lay before" us what the gentiles have written, stacking it "collaterally" next to the Bible, like frozen corpses. He goes on to explain, in effect, why every gentile tradition is a frozen corpse: "I shall proceed to shew what was subsequent to Moses' account after the migration of families, and the dispersion from the plains of Shinar." Like so many other readers of Genesis, Bryant assumes that the dispersion from Babel was the absolute beginning of gentile tradition, lacking any depth of relationship to the world Noah had created beforehand. This view derives from the common assumption that the Confusion of Tongues originated languages and that the Tower of Babel occurred too early in postdiluvian history to have allowed time for the development of a monogenetic world order.

Bryant's inorganic conception of Noahic mankind influenced all dimensions of his theory. Compelled, like us, to trace the gentile apostasy to a specific source, he proceeded in polygenetic fashion by claiming that the sons of Cush originated the apostasy and were joined, casually, by other Hamite families "in their expeditions,"[25] that is, through random "Newtonian" encounters. The worship of Ham, as the Egyptian Amon, had little to do with Ham himself, at least as a son of Noah caught up in specifically Noahic intrigues. Above all, Bryant's inorganic conception contradicted the demands of Noahic science for theoretical boldness:

> What may appear very presumptuous, I shall deduce from their own histories many truths, with which they were totally unacquainted, and give to them an original, which they certainly did not know.[26]

Bryant meant that he must de-mythologize the pagan traditions according to the historical test of Genesis 9-11. To do so meant to separate concrete pagan memory from abstract pagan logic by showing that the gentiles remembered Noahic events without comprehending their meaning. Bryant's Newtonian worldview could account for the dislocation of such traditions but not for their original formation. He was so obsessed by the dispersion of Babel and the image of casually migrating stocks that his efforts to attribute Noahic "originals" to gentile tradition seemed needlessly "presumptuous," even to himself. He could sense the doom of his scientific cause from the outset because he sensed the inadequacy of analytic mental habits to perform the primary synthetic task of envisioning past events as imagined wholes.

Protestants have always been troubled by the scribal misconception that they can take historical truth directly from the "sacred page" (or any page) without imaginative effort. Their own doctrine tells them that the Bible cannot be understood apart from the active influence of the Holy Spirit; but they have little idea of what the term "spirit" means relative to the formation of intellectual life. The conservative mind takes existing concepts for granted, failing to review the sorts of power and enthusiasm required for the birth of such concepts. Throughout his *New System,* Bryant tries to be objective by treating the various families of Genesis 10 like wandering Newtonian planets in a context of empty space, devoid of meaning.

The source of Bryant's difficulty is readily apparent. He suffers from the "humor of a scholar." He is less interested in the subject matter of Genesis 10 than in the text itself, together with other texts. The Protestant Reformation coincided with Renaissance Humanism, the cultivation of books and their languages largely for their own sakes. Renaissance scholars read books in order to read more books and left the final apocalypse of new worlds to explorers. Although the field of archaeology combines textual learning with exploration, the vital synthesis of learning and adventure remains incomplete. Creative energy pours into exploration and stops there. Too little energy goes into interpretation because scholars cannot make themselves believe in an organic and animated Noahic cosmos.

In many respects, Bryant's historical logic and ours run a parallel course. We agree, for example, that the political control of Mesopotamia was under dispute among Noah's family. Influenced by the logical tenor of the Tower of Babel account, together with Genesis 10:10-11, Bryant concludes that Shem and Japheth obeyed the command to disperse into their respective lands:

> But it appears that the sons of Chus, under the influence of their imperious leader Nimrod, stood their ground, and maintained themselves in opposition to the general partition. They usurped the lot of Ashur: and Nimrod, to secure what he had unjustly seized upon, immediately set about fortifying the country.[27]

The "lot of Ashur," based on Genesis 10:11, answers to our concept of the fief of Akkad as held by Shem in the era of the Hirschnatur panel previous to the Tower of Babel era. By interpreting Asshur's migration from Mesopotamia to Assyria as a forced expulsion, Bryant anticipates our concept of colonial dispersion in the Akkadian Age.

These analogies demonstrate the power of the biblical text to inspire a logical consensus; but the quality of the consensus, in this case, is not very impressive because Bryant and this writer have brought to the text different presuppositions based on different dimensions of the Protestant heritage. Although Bryant was obviously more interested in the story of Noah than the average Protestant, his motive remained to dispose of difficulties rather than to illumine a lost dimension of human history. He envisions the historical ellipses of Genesis 9-14, not as a challenging mystery, but as a momentary pause in the logical flow of Scripture, for example in his remarks on the mysterious political context of the Abrahamic war of Genesis 14:

> It is plain from the history of this war, as it is given us

by Moses, that some notable occurences had preceded: which, not relating to the grand scheme of Providence that was carrying on, are omitted by the divine historian.[28] For any reader concerned for third millennium history, Bryant grossly understates the problem of ellipsis (missing context) in a passage such as Genesis 14. But the "grand scheme of Providence" takes precedence; and these words characterize the eighteenth-century evangelical sense of Gospel priority, as ministered by a divine pragmatism, the Pauline commitment to "know nothing among you save Christ crucified."

Gospel pragmatism has influenced every dimension of evangelical thought and life. The goal of any pragmatic book is to teach or reveal something to a specific audience; and, for many evangelicals, this audience is invariably the great mass of simple folk who need primary exposure to the elements of the faith. Writers for such an audience make short work of historical mysteries in the Old Testament, even vast structural mysteries with a bearing on how we understand the Gospel itself. For example, in *Understanding the Bible,* John R. W. Stott assures his readers that the Bible is limited in purpose to the "moral" rather than "intellectual," thus confirming, in a general way, Matthew Arnold's concept of biblical "Hebraism." C. S. Lewis, in the same evangelical tradition as Stott, builds the apologetic system of *Mere Christianity* from the common ground of man's moral sense.

In effect, Stott disposes of the mysteries of Genesis 9-14 by assuring his readers that "the purpose of the Bible is not scientific."[29] Neither, he adds, is it literary or philosophical. If we conceive superficially of "science," "literature," and "philosophy" (and Stott intends no other), his position is quite understandable and realistic. But if, like Matthew Arnold, we demand to "know the thing in itself as it really is" Stott's terminology has a very different meaning. To say that the Bible has no scientific purpose is to say that it does nothing to reveal God to man; to call it non-literary is to claim that it was never inspired in words or written down by inspired authors; and to describe its message as non-philosophical is to concede that it is logically incoherent in itself and lacking in any sort of universal authority.

When we trace the pragmatic impulse to limit the purpose of the Bible back to the source, we encounter different explanations. According to Arnold the source lay with the Hebrews themselves, an ethically-minded race devoid of Greek intellectual curiosity. Stott argues, in the reverse, that his pragmatism, like the Apostle Paul's, derives from the need to teach Hebraic religious mysteries to ignorant gentiles: "With the spread of secularism in our day, an increasing number of people are being added to Christ and His Church who have no religious background whatever."[30]

Evangelical pragmatists should understand (and probably do) that, unless certain intellectual projects are undertaken "for the defense and confirmation of the gospel," the "religious background" to which Stott refers may disappear altogether. The Bible functions as a book of salvation precisely because it is a book of science, literature, and philosophy. True science is salvation from ignorance; historical literature is salvation from pagan amnesia; and true philosophy is the Logos Jesus Christ, the Truth and Savior. One reason that "secularism has spread in our day" is that persons of "religious background" have become spiritually and, therefore, intellectually lazy, unimaginative, and apathetic toward key issues of faith.

Protestant history began as an exercise in quickened historical enterprise. The first wave of Protestant historical research ended in a certain conception of Apostolic times, as a basis for reformed ecclesiology "pure and undefiled." One hundred-twenty years after Calvin's *Institutes,* the French Huguenot Bochart raised what appeared to be a second wave of such enterprise: the study of Noah's family. Through inadequate data, lack of vital imagination, secular opposition, and simple apathy, Bochart's cause had come to nothing by 1860; and most Protestants are probably unaware of its existence. For purely apocalyptic reasons, however, Bochart's cause must eventually succeed.

NOTES

[1]Charles Darwin, *The Voyage of the Beagle,* ed. Leonard Engel (Garden City, NJ: Doubleday, 1962), p. 501

[2]Frederick W. Farrar, "Aptitudes of Races," *Transactions of the Ethnological Society* 5 (March 27, 1866), 115-116.

[3]Ibid., 126.

[4]Clark writes, "Mass murder? Well, and why not? It was only a matter of the working of evolution. It went to prove that Europeans were the fittest to survive." Robert E. D. Clark, *Darwin: Before and After* (Chicago: Moody, 1967), p. 112.

[5]The genealogies of Matthew 1 and Luke 3 speak for themselves. Typical of Christ's candor in stating his purpose in life is John 6:38-39, where He defines this purpose as introducing others to the resurrection of the just: concrete eternal life.

[6]Passages from the Epic of Gilgamesh are from Pritchard, *The Ancient Near East,* First Princeton Paperback Edition, pp. 40-75.

[7]Hislop, *The Two Babylons,* p. 307.

[8]Typical of the idealistic side of the Inanna cult are the seven hymns to the goddess translated in Diane Wolkstein and Samuel Noah Kramer, *Inanna: Queen of Heaven and Earth* (New York: Harper and Row, 1983), pp. 93-110.

[9]Epic of Gilgamesh, VI, 1. 93.

[10]Samuel Noah Kramer, *The Sacred Marriage Rite* (Bloomington: Indiana University, 1969), pp. 56-57.

[11]Ibid., pp. 62-63.

[12]Ibid., p. 64.

[13]Calvin states the conventional position by attacking Osiander for "indiscriminately extending God's image both to the body and soul" and thus "mingling heaven and earth." The issue, overlooked by Calvin, is whether things on earth correspond to things in heaven or form a closed, secularistic, evolutionary system of their own. John Calvin, *Institutes of the Christian Religion,* ed. John T. McNeill (Philadelphia: Westminster, 1960), I, 187.

[14]Carpenter notes Tolkien's sympathy toward Franco's cause in Spain and his passing affinity for one Roy Campbell who represented

"a particular blend of Catholicism and Fascism." Humphrey Carpenter, *The Inklings* (New York: Ballantine, 1978), p. 212.

[15]M. R. James, *Ghost Stories of an Antiquary* (Baltimore: Penguin, 1975), p. 140.

[16]Ibid., p. 150.

[17]Ibid., pp. 151-152.

[18]Revelation 2:19.

[19]Zimmerman, *Dictionary of Classical Mythology*, p. 137.

[20]Albright, *Yahweh and the Gods of Canaan*, p. 227.

[21]J. R. R. Tolkien, *The Fellowship of the Ring* (New York: Ballantine, 1963), p. 322.

[22]For the apocalyptic significance of Islam, a student of antiquity can look again at Albright's Phoenician triad: Canaan of Kish, Joktan of Erech, and Inanna of Aratta. As Gunidu of Lagash and Dorus of the Hellenes, Canaan is the nominal patriarch of the Huns or Turks. The name Joktan is synonymous with Arabia; and Inanna, with the land of Iran. The ethnic heart of the Islamic world is threefold: Semitic Arabia, Ural-Altaic Turkey, and Aryan Iran. No stretch of imagination is required to identify militant Islam with the Erechite cause as focused by the West Semitic tradition of Melqart, Eshmun, and Ashtart. Islam is the Medieval and modern religious form of the ancient spiritual cause of Mesopotamia as defined by the Marduk Epic.

[23]For example, Hislop habitually ignores Noah's role in building the postdiluvian world. At one point, he reacts to a verse mentioning the plurality of Noah's generations: " 'Noah was a just man, and perfect in his *generations,* that is, in his life before the flood, and in his life after it.'" He thinks instinctively of the broad dualism of the antediluvian and postdiluvian worlds rather than the succession of thirty-year generations which were the chronological building blocks of Noah's postdiluvian world. *The Two Babylons,* p. 135.

[24]Jacob Bryant, *A New System or An Analysis of Antient Mythology,* 3rd ed. (London: J. Walker, 1807), I, xxvii.

[25]Ibid., I, xxx.

[26]Ibid., I, xxxiii.

[27]Ibid., VI, 190.

[28]Ibid., VI, 202-03.

[29] John R. W. Stott, *Understanding the Bible* (Grand Rapids, MI: Zondervan, 1979), p. 13.

[30] Ibid., p. 7.

Chapter 9

Noah and the Christian Apocalypse

Apocalyptic Christianity

The Book of Revelation differs, not only in style, but in thematic emphasis from the rest of the New Testament. Jesus Christ dominates the book as Judge, beyond the temptations of mortal life and armed with explicit and unlimited supernatural powers. Most of the text refers to events beyond the present age; and, under these circumstances, the Gospel of salvation has accomplished its work and is overshadowed by new priorities. Salvation has become a means to a further end; and the very word "gospel" has lost its connection with any explicit salvation motif. Angels, rather than mortals, dominate the practical ministries of the book; and an "everlasting gospel," preached by an angel to the inhabitants of the earth, replaces salvation with justice and worship.[1] In view of the pragmatic salvationism emphasized by Stott, it is a wonder that the Book of Revelation ever found a place in the Canon.

Yet the Book of Revelation belongs to the Canon and its doctrines to foundational Christian theology. In fact, it furnishes an authoritative context larger than the Gospel of salvation and larger than salvation itself. The term "salvation" simply means deliverance from trouble. As mortals, we remain in various kinds of trouble; and salvation strikes us as an all-consuming, universal concern. Yet the angels of heaven have never been saved; the demons cannot be saved; and the redeemed in heaven have nothing from which to be saved. If life in the resurrected state has a purpose, goals must exist beyond salvation. Because the Book of Revelation has been given to us in our present mortal condition, we are able to anticipate these goals despite our natural preoccupation with personal salvation. Theologians normally distinguish between soteriology and doxology, that is, between doctrines which pertain to salvation and those which pertain to the glory of God. The doxological focus of the Book of Revelation is so profound that, even where processes of salvation occur, the terminology of the text diverts attention toward the glory of God. Each of the seven letters in Revelation 2-3 features a process of temptation or trial of works, including demands to "repent" and, therefore, including processes of salvation.[2] Yet none of the letters exhorts the readers to "save" themselves. Instead, each ends with an exhortation to "overcome" temptation as though life were a conquest and the issue were not life and death but glory and shame: a question of achievement. The seven letters invite us to reinterpret our efforts to "work out our salvation in fear and trembling" as attempts to win immortal glory through works approved by the God of glory.

Instead of countering Apostolic Christianity with something new, the Book of Revelation interprets Apostolic Christianity as part of a larger intrigue. It represents Christianity as a faith larger than the Christian cultus of the present age, transforming the testimony of the Church into a message aimed, in a new way, at the general "inhabitants of the earth." In it, the doors of the third heaven have swung open exposing mankind to a new note of confrontation, defiance, and universal intrigue. To possess such a book now, under the limitations of the present age, is to distinguish between the Christian religion, as it must exist today, and the Christian faith, as it exists in all ages and in eternity.

Apocalyptic Christianity, therefore, is "Romantic" Christianity, an undercurrent of defiance against the limitations of the present age, as judged against other states of existence: the Adamic, Noahic, and Mosaic past or the Millennial future. Such defiance can take many forms, some just and others unjust. Twentieth-century conservatives have sometimes concluded that Romanticism is alien to Christianity. They have made a Romantic straw man of Rousseau, whose defiance took the form of self-pity, or Shelley, who set himself against orthodoxy. Others have acknowledged the undercurrent of evangelicalism in Wordsworth or the triumph of orthodox Trinitarianism in Coleridge. Both the critiques and appreciations are beside the point. All the leading Romantics sensed, from the shock of the French Revolution, that the Christian cultus of the present age and, indeed, the world system itself are mortal, doomed, in one way or another, to apocalyptic extinction. After the Rapture of the Church, valid services are no longer to be held at Bible Hall.

The cornerstone of apocalyptic Christianity is the doctrine of the general resurrection of the just and unjust. Cloaked in sentimental stock response, this doctrine is a limitless source of radical wisdom. The Apostle Paul teaches that the resurrection body incarnates the human spirit in the same way that the mortal body incarnates the human soul. Three of the greatest words of the Greek New Testament are the ones which conclude I Corinthians 15:44: *estin kai pneumatikon*, "there is also a spiritual body." To appreciate the practical significance of this verse, one should read Coleridge's "Dejection Ode" or other Romantic works which lament the evanescence of spiritual empowerment, the brevity of creative enthusiasm. Mortals have spirits; but mortality, in the spirit, is a flickering flame. The new nature of the resurrection body will consolidate and fix motives through an eternal stamina essential to explain both the worship of the redeemed and the condition of the lost in hell.

In order to develop a Noahic science, elegiac ideas of mortality and remnant survival must be countered by heroic ideas of creative world enterprise. This readjustment cannot occur until the universal implications of I Corinthians 15:44 are firmly grasped. Although the resurrection is a future event, it sheds eternal light on the heroic dimension of human existence. The connection between the grandeur of the Egyptian pyramids and Egyptian beliefs about resurrection is quite apparent. Men have always known, through the subjective power of creative spirit, that they are destined for one sort of immortality or another. Those who doubt the resurrection are to be pitied because they have allowed the elegiac spirit of mortality to take possession of their souls. Doubt of the resurrection is the intellectual correlative of simple depression; and modern materialistic skeptics have sunk below the level of the Noahic pagans, forfeiting, not only the Christian heritage, but its ancient antecedents. Their science has become a medium of bathos, a new and effective "art of sinking."

As Alexander Pope recognized, a "taste of the bathos" is implanted in man from the ground of his existence, the very "dust of the earth" named by Paul as the foundational principle of the "natural," soulish, or unresurrected human body:

> The first man was of the earth, made of dust; the second Man is the Lord from heaven. As was the man of dust, so also are those who are made of dust; and as is the heavenly Man, so also are those who are heavenly. And as we have borne the image of the man of dust, we shall also bear the image of the heavenly Man (I Corinthians 15:47-49).

There is no question that the "second Man, the Lord from heaven" is Jesus Christ, who has introduced the resurrection body to mankind by adopting it himself as "firstfruits from the dead." For Noahic science, however, it is essential to realize the revolutionary contrast between antediluvian and postdiluvian mankind and to recognize in the descent of the "Ka" a prototype of the "second man, lordship from heaven." We owe the origin of world civilization to such lordship, the flickering lamp of immortal charisma in mortal man. Like Raphael's "Poetry," the cities and temples of early postdiluvian mankind were *numine afflatur,* "breathed by divine command."

Apocalypse and the Gundestrup Imagery

The logical connection between future Apocalypse and high antiquity is a truism of Christian prophecy and has been strengthened by the American fundamentalist stress on the "seventieth week of Daniel," the concept that the entire Church Age is a hiatus in the ancient struggle between Jew and Gentile for the mastery of the earth. These prophetic concepts intensify interest in archaeology, giving each new find the immediacy of an international news report. Under their impact, the Victorian notion of world progress fades into secondary importance as a description of the "interstices" of progressive development at low intensity between the "inspired moments"[3] of dispensational revolution. The artifacts of high antiquity become pieces of the same puzzle which we are completing in modern times. The ancients are a peculiar variety of "moderns"; and we are a peculiar variety of "ancients."

The apocalyptically inclined "Romantic" shares a deep affinity to the charismatic world of Noah, the world of ancient art which acts as a magnet on Shelley's Romantic persona Alastor:

> His wandering step
> Obedient to high thoughts, has visited
> The awful ruins of the days of old:
> Athens and Tyre and Balbec, and the waste
> Where stood Jerusalem, the fallen towers
> Of Babylon, the eternal pyramids,
> Memphis and Thebes, and whatsoe'er of strange
> Sculptured on alabaster obelisk,
> Of jasper tomb, or mutilated sphinx,
> Dark Ethiopia in her desert hills
> Conceals.[4]

Instead of deriving casual inspiration from such objects, Alastor is drawn to them by "high thoughts" of his own, motives both modern and apocalyptic. They reinforce an existing sense of meaning and purpose which operates, like all poetic charisma, "above and beyond consciousness."[5]

Alastor's "thrilling secrets of the birth of time" have been vastly augmented by modern archaeology; but familiarity breeds contempt, especially if the familiarity takes the form of evolutionary condescension toward the limitations of "early man." The spiritual challenge of antiquarian study is to maintain a balance between learned discipline and numinous awe. The status quo, today, favors achieving this balance by letting the ancient artifacts speak for themselves. At the heart of this approach is Pritchard's *Ancient Near East Pictures*. The camera or transparent exposition can work wonders, but only where the "birth of time" still implies "thrilling secrets." Mature Darwinian thought, gradually but inevitably, banishes every hint of numinous power from all reasoning about the past.

Our capacity to receive "thrilling secrets" as such depends on the condition of the human spirit. Beauty is in the eye of the beholder because the "eye" is either healthy or sick. A modern spirit, thoroughly indoctrinated by Freud, Marx, or Darwin, cannot conceive of a "thrilling secret," no matter what the objective facts. Men imagine that they have been disillusioned by experience; whereas they have slandered experience with disillusioning beliefs of their own wilful adoption. For this reason, the actual key to science lies where Shelley found it, in the preconditioning power of imaginative art and literature. Apocalyptic awareness lives on through the underground mythology of popular art, especially the post-Romantic fictional and dramatic subgenres of historical romance, gothic fiction, science fiction, the murder mystery, and local color fiction. These modern forms, socially remote from the world of sober scientific reasoning, testify to what is lacking in modern attempts to interpret high antiquity: spiritual dimensions of legendary reverence, supernaturalism, cosmic amplitude, coherent intrigue, and personal memory.

Because the subgenres function socially as entertainment, they seem naive, in much the same way that the imageries of the Gundestrup Caldron or Mesopotamian seals seem naive. But what is entertainment? Enthusiasm all the more compelling and significant for being spontaneous and unforced. A man's taste in entertainment is a symbolic lie detector test of spirit, more revealing than opinion and more precisely discriminating than analysis. Entertainment art holds the key to what has become of the unforced enthusiasm of ancient religiosity in modern translation.

A striking analogy exists between the subgenres and the exterior panels of the Gundestrup Caldron. The Dragon panel is clearly "gothic," featuring a pair of monsters, and a hideous double-headed serpent in the act of dismembering a pair of human victims. The allied panel of the Braided Goddess reads like a puzzling murder mystery. The Trinity panel proclaims an apocalypse of cosmic power in the manner of invader science fiction; the Hirschnatur panel expresses legendary veneration for a sainted monarch in the vein of a Scott romance; and the Sphinx panel anticipates local color writing, in its Edenic idealization of a harmonious environment.

These analogies point directly into the heart of the Christian Apocalypse. The gothic principle corresponds to the apocalypse of Antichrist and the preternatural reign of terror introduced by him after the Rapture of the Church. The murder mystery anticipates the motif of judgment and incrimination which begins, even before Christ's Second Advent, by replacing the Raptured Church with a new body of believers, not only Jewish but Judaistic or judgmental in spiritual temperament. Invader science fiction captures the cosmic impact of the Second Advent, as a public event witnessed throughout the world. The Scott romance, in its excitement over the physical presence of monarchs,[6] anticipates the popular impact of Jesus Christ, the supreme sainted name, as visibly present on earth and accessible to its inhabitants. Finally, the Edenic idealism of local color fiction anticipates the Edenic qualities of Christ's Millennial Kingdom.

The exterior panels also celebrate specific members of Noah's family, opening up a new branch of apocalyptic typology. The "gothic" logic of the Dragon panel lays the cult of Antichrist squarely at the feet of Ham and the Hamite "Titan" faction. Despite all that can be said in defense of this family, the forces of Antichrist were unleashed by their rebellion against Noah. The complementary panel of the Braided Goddess tells a slightly different story. As Tiamat of the Babylonian epic, Ham's mother headed the loyalist faction of Peleg's Iran. We have seen that the panel echoes the orthodox logic of Genesis 9-11 in tracing the error of the Tower of Babel back to the sin of Ham. Its apocalyptic function is to incriminate the gentile world order by revealing the pathetic ruin at its foundation. The Dragon panel expresses what the gentile powers know themselves to be in their full flush of preternatural manifestation; the Braided Goddess panel picks up the pieces of a gentile criminality which has run its course.

The Hirschnatur panel treats Shem as a sternly venerable Noahic type of Christ. Despite the genetic blend of Shem and Ham in the Messianic line, Shem remains the exclusive moral type of Christ, among the eight survivors of the Flood, because the cult of Yahweh Elohim distinguishes Christ in His special relationship to Israel and His role as apocalyptic Judge. The two stags of the panel, in symbolizing the Semitic and Indo-European stocks, also suggest the elements of Jew and Gentile which make up the Church. Thus the era of the Hirschnatur panel bears the same relationship to the Church Age as the succeeding Tower of Babel era to the reign of the Antichrist in the succeeding Tribulation era. In claiming the Tower era, the curiously dislocated Braided Goddess panel interprets the Tribulation period as the beginning of a process of apocalyptic judgments.

For the benefit of skeptics, what are we saying about the prophetic implications of the Gundestrup Caldron? Are we saying that the Hirschnatur panel, for example, is a pagan prophecy of the Church Age as governed by Christ? No. The analytic orthodox must be granted the privilege to restrict the letter of prophecy as narrowly as they wish. The Hirschnatur panel is a pagan memorial to the ancestral relationship between Europeans and Shem. If we regard Shem as an implicit type of Christ, this opinion is our synthetic privilege and must stand the test of further biblical study of the significance of Shem to the Christian faith.

The Trinity panel identifies Shem's royal wife, the Yellow Matriarch, with the explosive, sensational power of Christ's Second Advent, the rising "sun of righteousness with healing in his wings." The Mongoloid race is synonymous with the choleric humor, the royal "element of fire." Christ pictured His Second Advent as a bolt of lightning shining from east to west.[7] The Egyptian mythology identified the image of a lightning bolt with the Yellow Matriarch's Hamite son Mizraim (Min). The choleric humor implies the compulsive power of volition, the privilege to decide and command. At the Second Advent, Christ initiates a new age of such commandment, an age of "ruling the nations with a rod of iron." The stark visual impact of the Second Advent will symbolize the new order of the Noahic outpouring of the despotic "Ka," technically featured as the special topic of the panel.

The Sphinx panel, in the same apocalyptic context, symbolizes the continuity of Caucasoid, European, or phlegmatic values from the Church Age to the Millennial Age. Once the thunder and lightning of the Apocalypse are over, mankind will experience, once again, the cultural benefits of peace, a revival of something like Austrian Catholicism. The resurrection of the Christian dead will have added a new dimension to this ideal. Aside from "ruling the nations with a rod of iron, " resurrected Christians, in selflessly perfect bodies, impervious to injury, will function as a uniquely effective servant race, analogous to the ministering spirits of Shakespeare's *Midsummer Night's Dream*. Tolkien's version of the same ideal rests on the same premise, European amillennialism, which simply means the irenic dimension of millennialism relocated in time. H. G. Wells, in his characteristically pejorative way, has given the same ideal a futuristic value in the fairylike upper crust of evolved human society in *The Time Machine*. All such authors deal with the same potentiality of the same Noahic world community faced with the same schedule of apocalyptic changes.

Noah and Israel

Outside the Book of Genesis, direct references to Noah occur only five times in the Old Testament and eight in the New, not an especially impressive record for the physical ancestor of all nations. The statistics are much the same for Adam. Stott is quite correct about the pragmatic nature of the Bible in its focus on the salvation history of Israel. In reality, the world of Adam belongs to physical science; and the world of Noah, to the field of secular political history. As long as we follow the pragmatic guidelines that limit the fields of science, history, and theology, Noah will remain just another name in the Messianic genealogy of Christ.

Noah takes on a higher structural importance, however, in abstract dispensational theology where he emerges as the second of an elite company of five dispensational founders including Adam, Abraham, Moses, and Christ. Adam participated in the formation of the first two dispensations; Noah, in the third; Abraham, in the fourth; Moses, in the fifth; and Christ, in the sixth and seventh. In reducing the seven dispensations to five personal lives, these men furnish another explanation for the apocalyptic pattern just described. Adam's Eden accounts for the ethos of the Sphinx panel; Noah's third millennium, for the gentile horror of the Dragon panel; the tradition of faithful Abraham, for the Messianic veneration motif of the Hirschnatur panel; the Law of Moses, for the judgmental ethos and blood sacrifice motif of the Braided Goddess panel; and Christ, ultimately, for the "Oriental despotism" of the Trinity panel.

Noah's comparative place in the scheme is tragic. The biblical narratives of Genesis 6, 9, and 11 establish an unmistakable note of tragedy: the destruction of mankind, the corruption of the new world order, and God's comprehensive judgment on high human enterprise. Nothing can change this tragic accent. Tragedy and even gothic terror, however, can inspire high hope through a potent reverse psychology.[8] Our consciences convict us of sin; and the apocalypse of gothic tragedy clears the air. Once we know the worst, we can anticipate the best, unless we are foolish enough to neglect atonement.

Once we grasp the spiritual importance of gothic horror, we have nothing to hide from ourselves in estimating Noah's worth or the value of gentile mankind. We recognize the importance of Mosaic sin-consciousness in preserving the Noahic heritage, in its plainest terms, in the Hebrew Old Testament. The logic of Genesis 6-11 reveals how glorious and magnificent Noah's privilege was; but we must take that logic with the bitter seasoning of the narrative text. From the hour that Canaan threw Noah's curse back in his face, the glory of the gentiles has become an unspeakable horror. Unless we accept the Jewish explanation of that horror, we have no right to recognize the glory; and the proof is that the same Hebrew text establishes both the one and the other.

Noah's true impact on Israel is not to be measured by direct allusion but by analogy, beginning with the striking parallel between Jacob's prophecies in Genesis 49 and the ethnic system of the Cernunnus panel. The strict analogy was between Cernunnus (Peleg the Divider) and Jacob himself. The geographic focus of Peleg's power was Camp 11, capital of a Martu claim extending westward to the sea and encompassing Jacob's Palestine. The prophetic Greater Israel,[9] in extending to the Euphrates, encompassed Martu in turn. If Jacob was the third from Abraham, branching heir of the lower Semite line, Peleg was the third from Salah, branching heir of the upper Semite line. Peleg divided the whole Noahic community, creating gentile ethnology. Jacob, in dividing his tribes, created the ethnology of the counter-world of Israel. The tribes of the Cernunnus panel number eleven; and the tribes of Israel, twelve, as determined by eleven sons of Jacob.

The holy war between Joshua and Canaan recapitulated the struggle between Peleg and Canaan over Camp 11 and over the political destiny of mankind during the seventy-five years following the judgment on the Tower of Babel. We have seen that the substance of Jezebel's apocalyptic cult—the triad of Ashtart, Melqart, and Resheph-Eshmun—celebrated the ruling order of the world at the Eanna epoch in 2308. Jezebel's triad was the rebel counterweight to Peleg's loyalist faction, which had come to power thirty years earlier. There is no question that the heroic prophet Elijah found Jezebel the spiritual epitome of all that was evil in the Canaanite race of Palestine and Phoenicia. Thus, the Israelites, after the Exodus, had resumed Peleg's struggle against Canaan. The loyalist faction of the First Kish dynasty was the moral equivalent of Israel, including, as it did, both Noah and Shem, as the fabulous Etana and his son Balih.

A careful study of the Exodus will reveal just how the nation Israel, in its birth hour, confirmed its privilege to represent the righteous cause of Shem and Noah without putting a stop to the "times of the gentiles" altogether. The sacred history of Israel is a study in overlapping privileges. Shem and Noah had given something of themselves to the gentile world; and, without canceling all effects of this heritage, the Israelites made good the imperial Messianic claims of Abraham in a manner peculiar to themselves. At the center of this mysterious process was God's act of judging the gods of Egypt by striking all the firstborn of the land. A superficial reading of Exodus 12:12 might suggest that, in the Exodus, God simply discredited the Egyptian religion in the same way that he might discredit any form of paganism. But the Egyptians were a unique part of the pagan world;[10] and the Exodus judgment on their gods was a unique, revolutionary act, essential to forming the Mosaic dispensation.

In the first place, the Egyptians differed radically from the Canaanites because of the shifting perspective of the two rebel eras before and after the First Kish era. The Tower of Babel era, beforehand, was as "Egyptian" as the Erech-Aratta era was "Canaanite," dominated by the house of Canaan and especially, by Canaan's grandson Salah, the Semitic hero Marduk. Egyptian paganism, rooted in the Hamitic linguistic stock and in the peculiar spiritual climate of the Tower of Babel era, differed so greatly from the Canaanite paganism of the Eshmun triad that Israel's entire relationship to Egypt belonged to a separate category of spiritual confrontation. Israel was never told to exterminate the Egyptians. On the contrary, Moses was reared on Egyptian soil, bore an Egyptian name, and was "learned in all the wisdom of the Egyptians."

The Israelites sought to exterminate the Canaanites precisely because the latter were linguistic and physical kinsmen, false representatives of a Semitic stock which was supposed to have belonged to the spiritual heirs of Shem. As Hamitic speakers, the Egyptians belonged to a separate branch of the Noahic theocracy and made no claim to the Semitic "Enlilship." The evil of Canaan, focused by the notorious populace of the Cities of the Plain, had taken root in the Semitic linguistic stock; and the Hebrew task, through their own populace, was to reclaim that stock and its proper territory for the God of Shem, not to dispute the Hamitic claim to the Nile. The Egyptian evil, the Tower of Babel, was subtler and less virulent than the Canaanite. It dated from an earlier era, when the opposing spiritual factions of Noah's family were less distinct.

The Egyptians were simply more civilized than the Canaanites, more disciplined in their expression of pagan values; and they owed this distinction to the most mysterious of all pagans, their god Ptah, creator of their system of gods, Enki of the Sed pole Seal 684, Canaan's Solomonic firstborn Sidon. God's disciplined slaying of the Egyptian firstborn, linked to Ptah's system of gods in Exodus 12:12, alluded to the firstborn Sidon, as architect of civilized world paganism.[11]

Sidon was the supreme compromiser and peacemaker of the rebel faction, responsible for all the synthesizing and reconciling powers of civilized world paganism. The Semitic tradition of Ugarit remembered him as the ally of Shem, Koshar, architect of Aliyan Bal's temple; and the Teutons remembered him as Loki, erstwhile ally of Thor. This testimony arose from the fact that Sidon voluntarily yielded power to Shem's loyalist faction at the First Kish epoch in 2338. Sidon lent his theocratic authority of the Enkiship of El Olam to the Messianic line, preserving the concept that Shem should remain its spiritual head, even allowing Shem to name the successive heirs of each generation below Salah.

Never before or since have good and evil been so closely intertwined as in Sidon. The key to his temperament was the Caucasoid phlegmatic humor, that low-energy approach to life which achieves prodigies of civilized neutrality. Sidon understood more clearly than any other postdiluvian the nature of Noah's privilege to build world civilization. When Canaan's rebellion gave him a chance to supplant Noah as architect of the gentile world, he proceeded with such care and discipline that the world system he organized has lasted to the present moment and will continue until Christ destroys it at His Second Advent.

In contrast with Caucasoid Sidon, Noah was a choleric Mongoloid, just compulsive enough to have cursed Canaan as he did and just bluntly honest enough to have been outwitted by Sidon. To gain insight into the struggle between Noah and Sidon one need only review the history of Mongoloid-Caucasoid relations: the shortlived Tatar Empire, with its even shorter-lived potential for becoming Christian; the explosive confrontation of Imperial Japan and the United States; or the alienation of Communist China from the Soviet Union. There is nothing inscrutable about the Orientals. The modern Caucasoids have shown themselves inscrutable and nothing more so than the infinite deviousness of the secular Enlightened, with their myriad philosophical adjustments to a religion which they are simply too dishonest to believe.

Yet God has chosen to work through the Caucasoid race, beginning with Noah's white son Shem, because of the peculiar tendency of the low-energy temperament to cooperate with processes of grace. If the white race of Europe has hesitated long enough to devise ways to reject Christianity, their ancestors also hesitated long enough to recognize its subtle power and to accept it. The same logic applies to Sidon, to the religious culture of Egypt, and to civilized world paganism generally. Apart from Christ, the choice is between the elegant idolatry of Egypt and the savagery of the Aztec ritual.

The ultimate question of Israel's conformity to Noah, therefore, is a question of how much of the Mongoloid Orient enters into the religious culture of Israel. To what extent does the Jewish quest for the Messiah anticipate the Mongoloid ethos of the Trinity panel, the interests of Shem's Mongoloid wife, or the values of his "only begotten son," the only Messianic heir of his male line, Arphaxad I? Conversely, what will become of Arphaxad's people, the Far Eastern Mongoloids, in Christ's Millennial Kingdom? The obvious answer is an extremely affirmative one, namely, that the Mongoloids will function in the Millennial Age as the Caucasoids have done in the present age. Noah's tragic loss of power over his sons translates into the temporary theocratic eclipse of the Mongoloid race; and the worldwide restoration of his principles of righteousness, in the Millennial Age, will assure the popular importance of the Chinese, Koreans, and Japanese. But what sort of Mongoloid undercurrent actually exists in the Bible or in the history of Israel?

We are faced with the striking fact that Abraham came from Arphaxad's lunar cult center of Ur and migrated to Arphaxad's birthplace of Harran, as though the Messianic hope were the cause of Arphaxad in particular. What sort of man was Arphaxad? Hindu mythology pictures him as the sternly judgmental Daksha, infuriated by his daughter Sati's engagement to the slovenly Shiva, much as Nanna might have been outraged at the notorious "harlotry" of his daughter Inanna. In fact, Arphaxad emerges as Noah's Mongoloid alter ego, duplicating in his wrath against his erring daughter Noah's wrath against his erring son Ham.

Most students of the Christian heritage understand this pivotal role of wrath in the tragedy of "carnal Christianity" or orthodox futility. On the face of it, Noah's anger against Ham accomplished little. The Apostle James assures us that, "The wrath of man worketh not the righteousness of God" (James 1:20). The phlegmatic sophisticates of Europe have taken this lesson to heart and turned back the tide of "graceless zeal" time and again. While separatists warn of the wrath to come, cool masters of the social arts protest that they have never seen it. An ethical challenge of Christianity is to balance the claims of a divine wrath which few have witnessed against a human wrath which many have seen and despised. In view of this challenge, the most important of all pagan myths was the one which pictured Shem's Messianic son as wrath personified.

The Wrath of Telepinu

The Hattian myth of Telepinu outranks most others in establishing the Noahic pagan correlatives to Judaeo-Christian orthodoxy. In it, both Taru and his son Telepinu, Shem and Arphaxad I, appear as storm gods because the central theocratic power of the myth is the Storm God, Noahic version of Yahweh. The myth attempts to cope with the wrath of Yahweh, as expressed in the Flood and in the judgment of the Tower of Babel, the myth's unstated premise. It acknowledges the characteristic effect of apostasy as the withdrawal of God's presence and favor. It identifies the wrath of Yahweh specifically as Arphaxad I's motive and claims that such wrath has been appeased through the good offices of Kamrusepas, the Red Matriarch, and her command of Abel's principle of ram sacrifice. In short, it furnishes a Noahic counterpart to the Christian doctrine of propitiation and atonement.

Because the prime movers of the myth are the angry Telepinu and solicitous Sun God, its historical focal point is the First Kish epoch of the Trinity panel, which features these two deities, Arphaxad I and his solar son Obal, at either side of the Yellow Matriarch, who appears in the myth as Hannahannas. Telepinu has gotten angry for reasons lost with the opening lines of text.[12] He has withdrawn from the other gods, causing universal famine and eventually a flood. We have seen that the Chinese Flood date of 2357 refers to the judgment on the Tower of Babel, nineteen years before the First Kish epoch to which the Sumerians referred the Flood. Clearly, Noahic thought perceived the judgment on the Tower of Babel as a duplication of Yahweh's wrath in the Flood. The Hittite myth associates both judgments with some separatistic policy adopted by Arphaxad I. The Sun God takes a series of measures to appease Telepinu's wrath. The Egyptian polarity of the Tower of Babel scheme meant, in effect, that the Sun God of the Hamitic tongue had sought to promote unity among the gods. Through the conceit of polytheism, the judgment on the Tower was held to have meant conflict between the solar and judgmental qualities of God Himself. Thus the myth treats the dualism of the Trinity panel as a conflict of values between separatism and imperial world union. More important, the myth interprets these two principles as synonymous with the two factions of Shem and Canaan. In the Trinity panel, the bearded Arphaxad I displays the "Ka" of the loyalist faction, and smooth-shaven Obal, the "Ka" of the rebel faction, hence Meskiaggasher's claim of descent from the Sun God at the outset of the rebel Eanna dynasty. The myth acknowledges, in its own amoral way, that the wrath of God, in the form of Arphaxad's loyalist faction, had determined to thwart the rebel hopes for world union.

The process of the myth is supernaturalistic, whimsical in imagery, and allegorical in meaning, more so than the Marduk Epic where the motif of warfare is a literal value. The council of the Sun God designates three divine agents to act in conjunction with three lesser agents to find and reconcile Telepinu: the Sun God sends out an eagle, Hannahannas sends out a bee, and Kamrusepas employs the same propitiatory magic which is assigned to a "mortal man." The eagle fails to find the angry god. The bee finds and stings him, provoking him to further anger and a destructive flood. Eventually, either Kamrusepas, working through "twelve rams," or the "mortal man" succeeds in appeasing the god's wrath.

Despite the whimsical surface, the myth reveals a systematic framework through its total of six agents who seek appeasement. These represent six qualities of the theocratic octad, excluding the Storm God and Air God, which were compounded into a unit by the "Yahweh Elohim" of Taru and Telepinu. The Sun God speaks for himself; and his eagle represents the motif of Etana's ascent to heaven, Noah's cult of the Heaven God, paired with the solar cult in the first two fiefs of the Taranis panel. The Yellow Matriarch Hannahannas, in dominating the Trinity panel, represents the cult of the Moon God; and Kamrusepas, the Red Matriarch's cult of the Shepherd God. Their secondary agents, the bee and "mortal man," are interpretive cruxes.

As Hannahannas' agent, the bee symbolizes the cult of the War God, which superceded her lunar cult in 2308. Nimrod, as chief priest of the War God, had anticipated the use of war in completing the Tower of Babel by forcing laborers into the "bee swarm" of the plain in Shinar. The Yellow Matriarch took responsibility for this swarm because of her larger responsibility for childbirth and the growth of population, a motif characteristic of her image as Hannahannas, Ninhursag, and Nekhebet. The bee's sting provokes Telepinu to cause a flood precisely because of the conceit of the Chinese Flood, dated at the judgment on the Tower of Babel rather than the Flood itself. At the judgment on the Tower of Babel, Yahweh was angry both at the concentration of populace at Camp 12 and at Nimrod's militaristic means of pursuing the Tower scheme.

The subtlest part of the myth is the "mortal man" who acts in parallel with Kamrusepas. We think at once of the fallen mortal, whom the Red Matriarch cradles beneath her arm in the Braided Goddess panel. Because that panel describes the Red Matriarch's ruined boar-holding structure, the mortal can only be her son Ham. In the context of the Hattian myth, Ham represents the eighth and last cult of the Water God, sacred to his royal wife, the White Matriarch, and to her Sumerian race. Thus the final appeasement of Telepinu rests with the two Havilahs of Genesis 10, Ham and his mother, descendants of the patriarch Abel. A further mutilation of the text obscures their cooperation; but their common descent from the first priest of blood atonement speaks for itself.

The final implications of the myth are as tragic as the textual themes of Genesis 6-11. Although the concluding appeasement motif can be read in the light of the Christian plan of salvation, its overall fabric yields the classic status quo of civilized paganism. Motivated by their version of the imperial Sun God, civilized pagans have always sought world union in their own way, as a presupposed amillennial reality, a gentleman's agreement about the eternal scope of their collective authority. They realize that separatistic dissent exists and alternately despise and fear it. In their higher moods, they pursue the idealism of the "ascending eagle," various efforts to storm heaven by lofty enterprise. As these efforts fail, they lapse into the bee-stings of warfare, transforming themselves from Greek philosophers into pragmatic Roman warriors. All the while, their consciences are perpetually troubled by their inability to control or influence the God of Telepinu, the "Yahweh Elohim of Shem," that separatistic God who threatens to judge them adversely. In their darkest moods, when idealism and pragmatic violence have failed, they emulate the darker side of Kamrusepas' cult and embrace occult religion.

Noah and Baptism

The only answer to this dilemma lies in separatism itself. The Yahweh Elohim of Shem must be approached and worshipped on His own terms by rejecting one system of values for another. The name Yahweh Elohim represents one quarter of the Noahic octad; and this quarter lies beyond the range of gentile mankind, whose practical worship of the other three quarters was already saturated with rebellion by 2357. Psalm 75 testifies to this state of affairs:

For promotion cometh neither from the east, nor from the west, nor from the south. But God is the judge; he putteth down one, and setteth up another (Psalm 75:6-7).

To the eastern realm of Chac belong the Sun God and his Eagle; to the southern realm of yellow Kan, the Moon God and War God; and the atoning alliance of the Shepherd God and Water God belongs to the white realm of Zac or Dwat, Egyptian realm of the dead. But the God of Judgment claims the black realm of Ed, the north, for Himself and lies beyond normal access, in the silence of Psalm 75:6, threatening to subvert the "powers that be" at any moment. He is the objective, separate, and separatistic God of Judgment; and all who abuse power dread Him with an agnostic and atheistic dread beyond consciousness.

The radical ethic of the separatist has always been simplicity itself: "I am in the right, my enemies are in power, they will lose power some day, and I will live to see it." Because of the specious egotism of his position, he persuades no one. His function is to antagonize unbaptized society as long as he lives, keeping the consciences of such men alive to the existence of something not themselves, something anthropomorphic, something refractory, and something beyond their spiritual control. His purpose is to hint to the consciences of men that they are keeping ill company among themselves.

The Christian ritual of separatism is baptism, one of several ordinances which program the "four quarters" of the Noahic octad in its Christian manifestation. The bread of the Eucharist, as bread, answers to the "lunar" principle of sustenance and to the "southern" alliance of the Moon God and War God.[13] In Christian terms, the Body of Christ, symbolized by the bread, represents Christ's capacity to embody El Shaddai, the God of Abraham, "father of many nations"; and the same term "Body of Christ" stands for the Church, as a popular assembly drawn from "many nations." The wine of the Eucharist symbolizes the sacred blood of the "western" Shepherd God, whose ally the Water God is manifest in the "water of the Word," the Holy Bible,[14] as authoritative explanation of the Shepherd's work of atonement. The "eastern" alliance of Heaven God and Sun God finds expression in the ordinance of communal prayer or local church fellowship, the authoritative means of storming heaven and achieving unity.

Baptism completes the picture and enacts the worship of Yahweh Elohim, separatistic God of the objective, "northern" throne of judgment. The true Church is inevitably separatistic because the New Testament word for "church," *ekklesia,* means that which is "called out." All sincerely baptized Christians understand that God has called them out of one social fellowship into another. The historical, interpretive problem has always been to define just what it is that Christians have been called from. Some content themselves to equate the "devil's crowd" with the poor souls at the local tavern; others recriminate against all forms of wealth and power; and others pit all of their separatistic zeal against the Roman Catholic Church. The plain New Testament fact is that the *ekklesia* stands opposed to a *kosmos* or designed system, whose existence and character is taken for granted. One of the chief goals of the present study has been to suggest how that *kosmos* originated and what it consists of.

In 2518, the *kosmos* originated as a holy *ekklesia* of Noah, a "church in the wilderness" analogous to Exodus Israel after the Red Sea crossing. The New Testament associates baptism both with the Red Sea crossing, in I Corinthians 10:2, and with Noah's Flood in I Peter 3:20-21, where the eight who survived the Flood form a baptized church in contrast with the lost souls of the antediluvian world:

> Who at one time were disobedient, when once the longsuffering of God waited in the days of Noah, while the ark was preparing, in which few, that is, eight souls, were saved by water; The like figure unto which even bap-

tism doth also now save us.

Because Noah's surviving family were the moral equivalent of a baptized church, a prodigious explanation is required to show how it lost its character as a church, if, in fact, it ever did.[15]

In estimating the spiritual worth of Noah's cosmos, we are faced with the striking fact that its gentile populace, if not the cosmos itself, will survive all subsequent judgments into the millennium and eternal state. The type of world annihilation featured in the Flood will never be repeated because of the intervention of the resurrection body as a means of preserving humanity through the "great conflagration." No matter what its corporate fate, the Noahic cosmos originated as a separatistic body and preserves this characacter, in some remote sense, to the end of time.[16] On the other hand, the prophecy of Daniel 2:44 reveals that this cosmos, as the seat of political authority, must be destroyed. Gentile political power must yield to the Messiah of Israel and, in doing so, will extinguish a peculiar regime dating back to Noah's postdiluvian lifetime.

The interpretive challenge is to distinguish this mortal regime from the eternal aspect of Noah's salvation history. When, precisely, did Noah's *ekklesia* become the *kosmos* of the gentiles? The answer lies with the Trinity panel of the Gundestrup Caldron. Despite the loyalist polarity of the First Kish order, the gentile world system came into existence at the epoch of First Kish in 2338 B.C., nineteen years after the judgment on the Tower of Babel. As an expression of the gentile status quo, the Sumerian Kinglist omits the first 180 years after the Flood because these constituted the inconceivable "wilderness" age of an inconceivable *ekklesia*. The dual "Ka" of the Trinity panel expresses the tragic "cold war" reality of irreconcilable conflict between two factions of Noahic mankind, ultimately Jew and Gentile. By 2338, the loyalist faction had exhausted whatever spiritual resources might have enabled them to effect the repentance of the rebels. In fact, the high rebel Sidon had displayed a more irenic spirit than the loyalist Arphaxad I. Above all, Yahweh Himself sought no compromise, having searched the consciences of the rebels and determined to make peace, in the future, through the sacred history of Israel in the Person of Jesus Christ.

Just as Christ left the Pharisees with the "sign of the prophet Jonah," Yahweh left the rebel faction with the "sign" of Noah's Flood, which they persistently post-dated to the time of the Tower of Babel judgment and epoch of First Kish. In context, the lesson of the Trinity panel is that gentile political power exists and will remain only so long as the separatistic "Flood" voice is clearly distinguishable from the apostate voice. In seeking to destroy the Jews as adversaries to his secularized version of Christendom, Adolf Hitler was undermining the dualistic foundation of the very gentile authority which he represented. Antichrist will undermine his own position and destroy the "times of the gentiles" precisely by threatening Israel's existence. Every enemy of Israel is his own worst enemy. To maintain power, Nebuchadnezzar must consult Daniel; Telepinu must be appeased; gentiles must remember the Flood which gave them their corporate origin; secularists must realize that baptism exists and that dissenters against their values must plague them until the end of their world.

The Sed Festival

Dispensational theologians have sometimes overlooked the fact that the apocalyptic millennium, as a fixed period of one thousand years, establishes an order of magnitude for all of the previous dispensational ages. By rejecting the third millennium Flood and suggesting that the event might have occurred thousands of years earlier, they have begun to tamper with the coherent logic of Weltgeschichte. The single millennium is an apocalyptic measuring-stick against which to judge the character of each earlier dispensation. According to the tight chronology of Genesis 11, the exclusively Noahic dispensation of human government was the briefest of the postdiluvian dispensations, just as the present age of the Church has been the longest, nearly twice the length of the future millennial age.

The extraordinary brevity of the dispensational interval between 2338 and Abraham's career, around 2100, reveals the virulence of the gentile apostasy together with the extraordinary creative powers of Noah's family. Able to build world civilization within Noah's lifetime, the Noahic princes were also capable of forfeiting their collective relationship to God within the same period. We have seen that Abraham's birth occurred shortly after Noah's death,[17] as though to suggest that Noah's species of righteousness died with him. This chronology accords far better with the moral logic of dispensational theology than do the high chronologies introduced by scholars who are rarely, if ever, dispensational in viewpoint.

Nevertheless, the formative principles of the dispensation of human government have lived on through every subsequent generation; and the fate of this dispensation is a study in transformation. Every discrete era of political history has modified the Noahic privileges and drawn the Second Advent of the Jewish Messiah a step closer. In fact, startling political changes had occurred during Noah's lifetime; and, despite Noah's death and the career of Abraham, a peculiar, "Egyptian" status quo existed until the Mosaic judgment of Exodus 12:12, forming a kind of gentile Millennial Age, from the Tower of Babel to the Exodus.

Niessen's chronology dates the Exodus to 1446 B.C.[18] If we extrapolate a millennium backward, the year 2446 occurred seventy-two years after the Flood, when Noah's family was on the Nile building the tradition of the nomes, specifically, at the twelfth nome from the north, in Lower Egypt. We have seen that the nome sequence, reckoned southward, duplicated the Syrian-Mesopotamian camp sequence, so that Camp 72, in Egypt, duplicated Camp 12, later site of the Tower of Babel in Akkad. Camp 72 duplicated Seba's Camp 12 in Seba-Osiris' Busiris, "House of Osiris Lord of the Sed,"[19] that mysterious cultic pole which reappears as the sign of Seba and Camp 12 in Mesopotamian Seal 684.

If the Exodus judgment of 1446 terminated a Noahic millennium, beginning 2446, nothing outranks the Sed pole of Busiris as a sign of the Noahic ideal, the dimension of gentile hope which outlived the three tragedies of Genesis 6-11. The Egyptian Sed festival was the sacred mystery of civilized paganism, a spiritual order which stood, in some sense, until the God of Moses "judged the gods of Egypt." Erman describes part of the festival as follows:

> So far, we can understand the festival; it represents the joyful moment when the dead Osiris awakes to life again, when his backbone, represented in later Egyptian theology by the Ded, stands again erect. The farther ceremonies of this festival however refer to mythological events unknown to us. Four priests, with their fists raised, rush upon four others, who appear to give way, two others strike each other, one standing by says of them, "I seize Horus shining in truth."[20]

The chief goal of pagan orthodoxy was to rationalize the eternal strife between the two Noahic factions and to come to grips with the pagan inability to win the favor of Yahweh Elohim. The pagans felt a desperate need to stabilize instability and transform disfavor into complacent hope. Enough elements existed in the Noahic heritage for the religious genius of Sidon to build a case for such stability and to celebrate the solution in an appropriate ceremony. The four priests who rush against four others symbolize the victory of half the Noahic octad over the other half, as though the two factions had divided the octad into equal shares. This conquest and subordination pattern explains certain imbalances of prestige in the Sumero-Akkadian pantheon where the Sun God of Sippar outranks the shrineless and ambiguous Heaven God; the Air God Enlil eclipses the Storm God Ishkur; the Water God Enki rules a land vacated by the slain Shepherd God; and the latter-day Sidon, as Gudea, contends for the War God of Lagash, rather than the Moon God of Ur. The same pattern appears throughout the Egyptian pantheon where the Sun God reigns supreme, the Storm God degenerates into the hated Seth, the nation "abominates a shepherd," and Ptah outranks both lunar deities, Zehuti and Khons.

Because resurrection is the central apocalyptic reality and the premise behind Christ's Millennial Kingdom, it is impossible to exaggerate the importance of the Sed festival. Frankfort acknowledges its synthetic power in holding together the quasi-millennial world order of the Pharaonic institution:

> In the five days of its duration multifarious connections between gods and king, land and king, people and king, were woven into that elaborate fabric which held society as well as the unaccountable forces of nature by strands which passed through the solitary figure on the throne of Horus.[21]

He adds that it was sometimes celebrated thirty years after the Pharaoh's accession, an evidence of the Noahic premise, with its formal thirty-year generation. When we understand the depth of this Noahic origin, we can appreciate the iconoclastic scope of Exodus 12:12. Noah's millennium lasted as long as it did because the resurrection motif of the Sed festival was neither polluted nor harmless nor "prescientific" but a theocratic reality, attuned somehow to the future millennium of Christ. If the orthodox underestimate the value of the Sed festival, they undervalue the revolutionary power of the Exodus itself.

The Sed festival included the familiar theme of unification of the two lands of Mizraim, linked to a foot-washing ritual preliminary to the main celebration. Frankfort describes a relief showing this ceremony at a Sed festival of the Pharaoh Neuserre:

> While the "Great Ones of Upper and Lower Egypt" kiss the ground before him, two courtiers of the rank of "Friend" wash his feet. They pour water from a vase shaped like the hieroglyph *sma,* meaning "Union" and used especially for that basic rite of the accession, the "Unification of the Two Lands."[22]

Yet these two lands originally belonged to the eternal antagonists Seth and Horus. Whether we identify the two gods as Obal and Arphaxad I (Ra and Khons) of the Trinity panel or Seth and Horus makes no difference. The "Unification of the Two Lands" supplied what all civilized paganism demanded: the impossible dream of millennial reconcilation between the two spiritual factions of Noah's family. Whoever created the Sed festival understood all aspects of the spiritual tragedy which had frustrated the Noahic hopes to achieve a perfect millennium.

Because the feet are the formal end of the body, the foot-washing motif symbolizes the phenomenon of *teleiotes,* or vocational "perfection," the completion of spiritual preparations to undertake some lofty task. In a sense, the "perfection" of New Testament logic means "complete preparation" rather than sinlessness; but the sinless perfection of the resurrection body is another premise behind Christ's Millennial Kingdom. The Pharaoh of Egypt, in his absolute despotism and sense of eternity, comprehended this demand for millennial perfection and, in his own way, achieved it. Foot-washing of the Pharaoh from a vase in the form of "union" was as precise a symbol as the Apocalypse demands. The eternal "Pharaoh" Jesus cannot enter His Kingdom until apocalyptic events such as the Battle of Armageddon have "United the Two Lands," terminating the struggle between Shem and Canaan forever. The Christian foot-washing ordinance of John 13, directed toward the Apostle Peter, signified the same principle of millennial perfection, as premise toward "building the Kingdom," under the limitations of the present age. It follows that the Christian "Union of the Two Lands" becomes the explicit reconciliation of Jew and Gentile in the Body of Christ.

At the same time that the Sed festival celebrated the millennial ideal, the Egyptians also found ways to acknowledge the pagan reality of irreconcilability between the two factions:

> In the hieroglyph of the Sed festival, the two thrones appear, empty, in two pavilions placed back to back. This may be merely a graphic way of combining the two royal seats, which in reality stood side by side.[23]

Frankfort conjectures that the back-to-back construction of the hieroglyph may have resulted from graphic convenience. We offer another explanation. The side-by-side construction of the ritual matched the design of the Trinity panel; but the back-to-back design of the hieroglyph suggested the mystery of irreconcilability.

The next detail of Frankfort's summary confirms that this ritual celebrated the epoch of the Trinity panel. The Pharaoh's climactic act, during the festival, was to dedicate a field by marching swiftly across it is a "fourfold course according to the points of the compass." He performed the first axis as King of Lower Egypt and the second as King of Upper Egypt. Aside from introducing the two gods Obal and Arphaxad I, the Trinity panel celebrates the epoch of Peleg's "division of the earth." Both the Noahic prototype and Egyptian ceremony symbolize Christ's inevitable act of dividing the Millennial earth into specific jurisdictions under the resurrected Saints or "gods" of the Millennial Age:

> The king, by crossing this "field," would dedicate it and, therewith, Egypt, to the gods and at the same time assert his legitimate power over the land. This is strongly suggested by a Ptolemaic text from Edfu which refers to the "will" as the "Secret of the Two Partners"—Horus and Seth. Since their "secret" is the division of Egypt—with Horus predominant, and yet with a reconciliation of the two—it is likely that the "will" concerns the land as a whole and kingship over it, not merely as a basis for some transaction such as the transfer of a field to some god or temple.[24]

In expanding the range of the ceremony from a concrete field to the whole land, Frankfort stops at the borders of Egypt. In the First Kish period, Mesopotamia was the world; the Egyptians regarded Egypt as the focal part of the earth; and the Millennial reign of Christ will cover the earth from the central "field" of Israel, that land which happens to intervene, geographically, between Mesopotamia and Egypt. Frankfort adds a further detail confirming the cosmic scope of the ceremony. At one point, he touches on a ritual with cosmic ethnographic value, another essential of Christ's Millennial Kingdom:

The king then shoots an arrow to each of the four points of the compass; and he is, moreover, enthroned four times—each time facing one of the four directions—upon a curious throne base, ornamented with twelve lion heads.[25]

The Egyptian ceremony of the four arrows matches the Amerindian ceremony of the red and black arrows. A synthesis of the two traditions implies the dispersion of the four variously colored races of Noah's family to the four quarters of the earth. Such dispersion did not begin to occur until sixty years after "Peleg's division," the tribal order of Cernunnus in and around Mesopotamia. By dividing the lion of Cernunnus, the Hamitic stock, into its basic red and white subdivisions, the Egyptians reckoned the tribes of Peleg's system twelve, rather than eleven, in keeping with "Emperor Shun's" division of the land into twelve provinces. Because the rebel faction had succeeded in compelling all these tribes to speak Hamitic, during the previous era, the base of Pharaoh's throne is marked with twelve lion heads, as the foundation of world ethnology.

Conclusion

It is a pathetic thing to witness fellow Christians who content themselves with earthly affairs and who adopt dull, skeptical, agnostic views of history. The Christian Rapture hope is ecstatic on the face of it; and, no matter what sorts of adjustments we make to mortal life in a hostile world, our minds should remain attuned to the sublime and extraordinary. What else can "heavenly things" mean except things pertaining to a sublime world beyond the limits of everyday life? And how can one "set one's affection on things above" without active, meditative conceptions of sublimity or "aboveness"? What an ironic thing for Christians to disavow the Romantic heritage, in general, when their beliefs make them the supreme Romantics of the world.

The challenge of the third millennium Flood lies passively and objectively in the text of Genesis 11. Without scientific scruples de-

rived from outside the text, no one would bother to question that
Abraham was born only four centuries after the Flood. Christian
scholars have yielded to such external scruples for cultural reasons
extending beyond the immediate issue. Equipped as we are with
historical consciousness, the third millennium Flood offers us a
strong dose of apocalyptic sublimity, a riot of extraordinary
phenomena: a Shem contemporary with Abraham, an international
community of Noahics princes, patterns of unique monogenetic incest and polygamy in the will of God, the wedding of paganism and
orthodoxy in the same place and time, the sudden origin of cultures
and civilizations through supernatural endowments of special power,
and a principle of human deification in the will of God.

Some of these phenomena contradict our sense of practical Christian ethics. Neither incest nor polygamy is lawful or profitable for
any Christian. The whole pattern of separatistic baptism warns us
to distinguish between things sacred and profane; and the historical
blending of such things, in the second half of the third millennium,
is morally troublesome. Some of the other points may seem concep-
tually ludicrous. Because the Book of Genesis does not state, in so
many words, that Shem encountered Abraham, their contemporaneity may strike us as theologically meaningless and bizarre. Above all,
the notion of charismatic endowment of Noah's family and of the
sudden origin of civilization violates some dogged principle of our
European culture revealed in the Progress cult and Darwinism of
the Victorian Age.

The missing dimension in such reactions to the Noahic world is
habitual apocalyptic thought. If we take the resurrection of the dead
seriously enough to reason from it instead of toward it, these objec-
tions disappear. Noahic marital irregularities arose from unique
genetic circumstances. Although these circumstances differ radically from the resurrection state, a serious understanding that redeemed
humanity can live and function without marriage (in the resurrection) enables us to conceptualize such revolutions in the past. The
Christian resurrection has the same sort of logical effect on Judaistic
fears of compromised separatism, the illicit mixture of things sacred
and profane. Because the resurrection of I Corinthians 15 is
organically total, it seals holiness into the physical processes of an
organically distinct "master race." Once we comprehend this sort
of transcendence, we perceive the separatistic struggle between Jew

and Gentile as a condition of mortality and a product rather than a premise of Noahic history. To suggest that separatism existed among the eight survivors of the Flood implies that Noah failed in his attempt to form an *ekklesia* and that the salvation experience of the Flood does not pertain to sacred history or to the ritual of baptism.

Above all, a serious meditative grasp of the resurrection enables us to appreciate the charismatic endowment and high privilege of Noah's family after the Flood. According to Revelation 5:10, resurrected believers have become "kings and priests to our God" destined to "reign on earth." The apocalyptic promise to the believers at Thyatira includes "power over the nations" (Revelation 2:26). Once we take these promises to heart and connect them with the unique status of the resurrection body, we can afford the luxury of an unbiased appreciation of Noahic privileges to form the same "nations" which resurrected saints are to rule "with a rod of iron." We begin to feel familiar and easy in the company of the Pharaohs of Egypt or the feudal aristocrats of Europe or the angels of heaven. Such powers may scorn us today but can hardly afford to despise us in the superhuman condition of the resurrection. Not only do we claim the mighty promises of the Christian faith; but, in claiming them, we adopt the "powers that be" and the very pagan gods as generic brethren of power, sharing, as all creatures must, in privileges which an uncreated God chooses to bestow on them. The very words and images of apocalyptic mythology pertain to us and belong to us, in a loosely cultural sense, through a Christ greater than all the Pharaohs, a Christ privileged to reign, like them, over the four quarters of a ritually subdivided earth.

NOTES

[1]Revelation 14:6-7.

[2]In Revelation 2-3, explicit repentance is a factor in five of the seven churches of Asia Minor.

[3]The definitive radical Shelley understood that theories of development, in art, refer to mere extrapolative "filler" between moments of empowerment. The same logic applies to theories of general progress. "A Defense of Poetry," Mahoney, p. 548.

[4]Shelley, "Alastor" (11. 106-16), Ibid., p. 456.

[5]Shelley, "A Defense of Poetry," p. 539.

[6]Scott features incognito monarchs (or the private lives of monarchs) in *Quentin Durward* (Louis XI), *Ivanhoe* (Richard I), *The Talisman* (Richard I), *The Fair Maid of Perth* (Robert III), *Kenilworth* (Elizabeth I), and various novels on the seventeenth century featuring the Stuarts. The possibility of a casual encounter with a monarch lay at the heart of Scott's creative enthusiasm.

[7]Matthew 24:27.

[8]Such is the theme of John Keats' candid "Ode on Melancholy."

[9]Deuteronomy 11:24.

[10]The numinous beauty of Egyptian civilization is a spiritual fact rooted in early postdiluvian charisma and reflected, for example, in Jeremiah 4:20: "Egypt is like a very fair heifer, but destruction cometh; it cometh out of the north."

[11]The Egyptian judgment on the firstborn obviously contrasted with the Canaanite judgment of extermination.

[12]Beyerlin, *Near Eastern Religious Texts,* p. 160.

[13]A Sumerian legend of the Erech-Aratta War features the Erechite ploy of withholding grain from Aratta, mingling the issues of war and sustenance in classic fashion. We have noted that the Moon God represents nationalism and destructive power, prerequisites of war.

[14]We have seen that the Water God stood for the world of authoritative literature or propaganda. The resemblance between certain parts of the Epic of Gilgamesh and the Bible is no coincidence.

[15]The English and German words for "church" derive from a Greek derivative of *kurios,* the familiar New Testament word for

"lord" applied to Christ as Lord. In this sense, a church is a kind of house of lordship; and any focus of the postdiluvian "ka" of human government is a kind of church. The separatistic aspect of Noah's church of eight yielded to a catholic or universal variation of itself in the spread of lordship after the First Kish epoch. It must be remembered that Jesus Christ, the Lord, is "head of all principality and power" (Colossians 2:10).

[16]Such is the implication of the foundational prophecy of Genesis 9:11: " 'Thus I establish My covenant with You: Never again shall all flesh be cut off by the waters of the Flood; never again shall there be a flood to destroy the earth.' "

[17]The standard date of 2166 for the birth of Abram fell 352 years after Niessen's Flood date of 2518; whereas Noah died 350 years after the Flood (Genesis 9:28).

[18]Niessen, "A Biblical Approach to Dating the Earth," 60.

[19]Moret, The Nile and Egyptian Civilization, p. 58.

[20]Erman, Life in Ancient Egypt, p. 279.

[21]Frankfort, Kingship and the Gods, p. 79.

[22]Ibid., p. 83.

[23]Ibid., p. 85.

[24]Ibid., p. 86.

[25]Ibid., p. 88.

Select Bibliography

A. THE MONOGENETIC EUHEMERIST TRADITION

1. Christian Euhemerism

Banier, Antoine. *La Mythologie et Les Fable Expliques Par L'Histoire.* 3 vols. Paris: Briasson, 1738-40.

Bochart, Samuel. *Opera Omnia. Hoc est Phaleg, Chanaan, et Hierozoicon.* 3rd ed. Amsterdam, 1692.

Bryant, Jacob, *A New System, or an analysis of ancient mythology.* 3rd ed., 6 vols. London: Printed for J. Walker et al., 1807.

Davies, Edward. *Celtic Researches.* London: Printed for the author, 1804.

Faber, George Stanley. *A Dissertation on the Mysteries of the Cabiri.* 2 vols. Oxford: University Press for the author, 1803.

Faber, George Stanley. *The Origin of Pagan Idolatry.* 3 vols. London: F. and C. Rivingtons, 1816.

Feldman, Burton and Robert D. Richardson. *The Rise of Modern Mythology 1680-1860.* Bloomington: Indiana University Press, 1972.

Hislop, Alexander. *The Two Babylons.* New York: Loizeaux Brothers, 1966.

Jones, Sir William. *Works.* 13 vols. London: Printed for John Stockdale and John Walker, 1807.

Pezron, Paul. *The Antiquities of Nations.* trans. D. Jones. London: Printed by R. Janeway for S. Balland, 1706.

Stukeley, William. *Stonehenge, a temple restor'd to the British Druids.* London: Printed for W. Innys and R. Manby, 1740.

Stukeley, William. *Abury, a temple of the British Druids.* London: Printed for the author, 1743.

Tooke, Andrew. *The Pantheon, representing the fabulous histories of the heathen gods.* New ed. London: C. Elliot, 1784.

Wise, Francis. *The History and Chronology of the Fabulous Ages.* Oxford, 1764.

2. Monogenism and Diffusionism

Badiny, Francisco Jos. *The Sumerian Wonder.* Buenos Aires: School for Oriental Studies of the University of Salvador, 1974.

Giraldis Cambrensis. *Historical Works* including *History of the Conquest of Ireland,* trans. Thomas Forester and Sir Richard Colt Hoare. ed. Thomas Wright. London, 1863; rpt. New York: AMS Press, 1968.

Gordon, Cyrus. *Before Columbus.* New York: Crown Publishers, 1971.

Keating, Geoffrey. *The History of Ireland,* ed. trans. David Comyns. 4 vols. London: David Nutt for the Irish Texts Society, 1902-1914.

Macalister, R. A. Stewart, ed. trans. *Lebor Gebala Erenn, the book of the taking of Ireland.* 2 vols. Dublin: Educational Company of Ireland for the Irish Texts Society, 1938-39.

Mertz, Henriette. *Pale Ink, two ancient records of Chinese exploration in America.* 2nd ed. Chicago: Swallow Press, 1972.

Miles, W. Augustus. "How did the Natives of Australia Become Acquainted with the Demigods and Daemonia, and with the Superstitions of the Ancient Races?" *Journal of the Ethnological Society of London,* 3 (1854), 4-50.

Prichard, James Cowles. *The Eastern Origin of the Celtic Nations.* Oxford, 1831.

Prichard, James Cowles. *An Analysis of the Egyptian Mythology, in which the philosophy and the superstitions of the ancient Egyptians are compared with those of the Indians and other nations of antiquity.* 2nd ed. London, 1838.

Vallancey, Charles. *An Essay on the Antiquity of the Irish Language.* 3rd ed. London: Printed for Thomas Thorpe, 1822.

Waddell, Laurence Austine. *The Makers of Civilization in Race and History.* London: Luzac and Co., 1929.

Wilford, Francis. "An Essay on the Sacred Isles in the West, with other Essays connected with that Work." *Asiatic Researches,* 8 (London, 1808), 245-375 and 9 (London, 1809), 32-243.

Wilford, Francis. "Of Swetam or the White Island, called also Sacam." *Asiatic Researches,* 11 (London, 1812), 11-109.

Wise, Francis. *Some Enquiries Concerning the First Inhabitants, Language, Religion, Learning, and Letters of Europe.* Oxford: J. Fletcher et al., 1758.

B. THE POLYGENETIC STATUS QUO

1. Criticism of the Euhemerists and Monogenists

Allen, Don Cameron, *The Legend of Noah.* Urbana: University of Illinois Press, 1949.

Cannon, Garland. *Oriental Jones, a biography of Sir William Jones (1746-1794).* London: Asia Publishing House for the Indian Council for Cultural Relations, 1964.

"Celtic Researches." *Edinburgh Review,* 4 (July, 1804), 386-99.

Crawfurd, John. "On the Early Migrations of Man." *Transactions of the Ethnological Society of London,* 3 (1865), 335-50.

Crawfurd, John. "On the Physical and Mental Characteristics of the European and Asiatic Races of Man." *Transactions of the Ethnological Society of London,* 5 (1867), 58-81.

Crawfurd, John. "On the Plurality of the Races of Man." *Transactions of the Ethnological Society of London,* 6 (1868), 49-58.

"Dissertation on the Mysteries of the Cabiri." *Edinburgh Review,* 3 (January, 1804), 313-20.

Farrar, Frederick W. "Traditions, real and fictitious." *Transactions of the Ethnological Society of London,* 3 (1865), 298-307.

Farrar, Frederick W. "Fixity of Type." *Transactions of the Ethnological Society of London,* 3 (1865), 394-99.

Farrar, Frederick W. "Aptitudes of Races." *Transactions of the Ethnological Society of London,* 5 (1867), 115-26.

Grimm, Jakob. *Teutonic Mythology,* ed. trans. James Steven Stallybrass. 4 vols. London: George Bell and Co., 1883.

Grote, George. *History of Greece.* 2nd ed. London, 1849; rpt. New York: Harper and Bros., 1870.

Heath, Dunbar I. "On the Primary Anthropoid and Secondary Mute Origin of the European Races, versus the Theory of Migration from an External Source." *Anthropological Review,* 4 (1866), xxxiii-xlviii.

Hungerford, Edward Buell. *Shores of Darkness.* New York: Columbia University Press, 1941.

Huxley, Thomas H. "On the Geographical Distribution of the Chief Modifications of Mankind." *Journal of the Ethnological Society of London,* N. S. 2 (1870), 404-12.

Milman, Henry Hart. "Egyptian Antiquities." *Quarterly Review,* 43 (May, 1830), 111-55.

MIlman, Henry Hart. "Sanskrit Poetry." *Quarterly Review,* 45 (April, 1831), 1-57.

"Mr. Bryant's Reply to the Dutch Reviews," *Gentlemen's Magazine,* 48 (May, 1778), 210-13.

Müller, Georgina Adelaide. *The Life and Letters of the Right Honourable Friedrich Max Müller.* 2 vols. London: Longmans, Green, and Co., 1902.

Müller, Friedrich Max. "Comparative Philology." *Edinburgh Review,* 94 (October, 1851), 297-339.

Müller, Friedrich Max. "On the Philosophy of Mythology." *Contemporary Review,* 19 (December, 1871), 97-119.

Müller, Friedrich Max. *Lectures on the Science of Language, delivered at the Royal Institution of Great Britain in February, March, April, and May 1863,* 2nd Series, 2 vols. New York: C. Scribner and Co., 1870-74.

Müller, Karl Otfried. *Prolegomena zu einer Wissenschaftlichen Mythologie.* Gottingen: Vanderhoeck and Ruprecht, 1825.

Neff, Emery Edward. *The Poetry of History.* New York: Columbia University Press, 1947.

Schlegel, Carl Friedrich Wilhelm von. *Sämmtliche Werke.* 2nd ed. 15 vols. Vienna: Ignaz Klang, 1846.

Westropp, Hodder M. "On the Analogies and Coincidences among Unconnected Nations." *Journal of the Anthropological Institute of Great Britain and Ireland,* 1 (1872), 221-25.

2. The Anthropological Consensus

Blumenbach, Johann Friedrich. *The Anthropological Treatises of Johann Blumenbach,* trans. Thomas Bendyshe. London: Longman, Green, Longman, Roberts, and Green, 1865.

Burrow, J. W. "Evolution and Anthropology in the 1860's: The Anthropological Society of London, 1863-71." *Victorian Studies,* 7 (1963), 135-54.

Cox, George W. *The Mythology of the Aryan Nations.* New ed., 2 vols. London: C. Kegan Paul and Co., 1878.

Darwin, Charles. *The Voyage of the Beagle,* ed. Leonard Engel. Garden City, NY: Doubleday and Co., 1962.

Dorson, Richard M.. *The British Folklorists, a history.* Chicago: University Press, 1968.

Frazer, James George. *The Golden Bough, a study in comparative religion.* 2 vols. London: Macmillan, 1890.

Huxley, Thomas H. *Man's Place in Nature and Other Anthropological Essays.* New York: D. Appleton and Co., 1909.

Lang, Andrew. *Modern Mythology.* London: Longmans, Green, and Co., 1897.

Lubbock, John. *Pre-historic Times, as illustrated by ancient remains, and the manners and customs of modern savages.* London: Williams and Norgate, 1865.

Tylor, Edward Burnett. *Anthropology, an introduction to the study of man and civilization.* New York: D. Appleton and Co., 1909.

Wallace, Alfred Russell. "On the Varieties of Man in the Malay Archipelago." *Transacations of the Ethnological Society of London,* 3 (1865), 196-215.

C. NEAR EASTERN STUDIES

1. Mesopotamia, Iran, and Anatolia

Beyerlin, Walter, ed. *Near Eastern Religious Texts Relating to the Old Testament.* Philadelphia: Westminster Press, 1978.

Falkenstein, A. "Die Anunna in Der Sumerischen Uberlieferung." *Studies in Honor of Benno Landsberger, on his seventy-fifth birthday, April 21, 1965.* Oriental Institute of the University of Chicago. Assyriological Studies No. 10. Chicago: University Press, 1965.

Gordon, Edmund I. *Sumerian Proverbs.* New York: Greenwood Press, 1968.

Hallo, William W. *Essays in Memory of E. A. Speiser.* New Haven: American Oriental Society, 1968.

Hallo, William W. and William Kelly Simpson. *The Ancient Near East.* New York: Harcourt Brace Jovanovich, 1971.

Hallo, William W. and J. J. A. Van Dijk. *The Exaltation of Inanna.* New Haven: Yale University Press, 1968.

Heidel, Alexander. *The Babylonian Genesis.* 2nd ed. Chicago: University Press, 1963.

Kramer, Samuel Noah. *The Sumerians.* Chicago: University Press, 1963.

Kramer, Samuel Noah. *The Sacred Marriage Rite.* Bloomington: Indiana University, 1969.

Lewis, Brian. *The Sargon Legend.* Cambridge, MA: American Schools of Oriental Research, 1980.

Pritchard, James B., ed. *The Ancient Near East in Pictures.* Princeton: University Press, 1954.

Pritchard, James B., ed. *Ancient Near Eastern Texts.* Princeton: University Press, 1955.

Pritchard, James B., ed. *The Ancient Near East, an anthology of texts and pictures.* Princeton: University Press, 1958.

Rogers, Alexander, trans. *The Shah-Namah of Fardusi.* Delhi, India: Heritage, 1973.

Schollmeyer, P. Anastasius. *Sumerish-babylonische Hymnen und Gebete an Shamash.* Paderborn: Druck und Verlag von Ferdinand Schoningh, 1912.

Strommenger, Eva. *Art of Mesopotamia.* New York: Harry N. Abrams, n.d.

Sumerological Studies in Honor of Thorkild Jacobsen, on his seventieth birthday June 7, 1974. Chicago: University Press, 1976.

Van Der Meer, P. *The Chronology of Ancient Western Asia and Egypt.* 2nd ed. Leiden: E. J. Brill, 1963.

Wolkstein, Diane and Samuel Noah Kramer. *Inanna Queen of Heaven and Earth, her stories and hymns from Sumer.* New York: Harper and Row, 1983.

2. Syria and Palestine

Albright, William Foxwell. *Yahweh and the Gods of Canaan.* Garden City, NY: Doubleday and Co., 1968.

Astour, Michael. *Hellenosemitica, an ethnic and cultural study in West Semitic impact on Mycenaean Greece.* Leiden: E. J. Brill, 1965.

Bermant, Chaim and Michael Weitzman. *Ebla, a revelation in archaeology.* New York: Times Books, 1979.

Brown, Stephen Glendon. "The Serpent Charms of Ugarit." Diss. Brandeis University, 1973.

Farbridge, Maurice H. *Studies in Biblical and Semitic Symbolism.* New York: KTAV Publishing House, 1970.

Kenyon, Kathleen M. *Archaeology in the Holy Land.* New York: Frederick A. Praeger, 1960.

Kitchen, K. A. *The Bible in Its World.* Downers Grove, IL: Inter-Varsity Press, 1977.

Matthiae, Paolo. "Ebla in the Late Early Syrian Period: the Royal Palace and the State Archives," *Biblical Archaeologist,* 39 (September, 1976), 94-113.

Pettinato, Giovanni. *The Archives of Ebla.* Garden City, NY: Doubleday, 1981.

Speiser, E. A. *Oriental and Biblical Studies.* ed. J. J. Finkelstein and Moshe Greenberg. Philadelphia: University of Pennsylvania Press, 1967.

Young, Gordon D. *Ugarit in Retrospect.* Winona Lake, IN: Eisenbrauns, 1981.

3. Egypt.

Erman, Adolf. *The Ancient Egyptians, a sourcebook of their writings.* trans. Aylward M. Blackman. New York: Harper and Row, 1966.

Erman, Adolf. *Life in Ancient Egypt.* trans. H. M. Tirard. New York: Dover, 1971.

Frankfort, Henri. *Kingship and the Gods.* Chicago: University Press, 1948.

Gardiner, Sir Alan. *Egypt of the Pharaohs.* New York: Oxford University Press, 1966.

Kantor, Helene J. "The Relative Chronology of Egypt and Its Foreign Correlations before the Late Bronze Age." *Chronologies in Old World Archaeology.* ed. Robert W. Ehrich. Chicago: University Press, 1965.

Kaster, Joseph, ed. trans. *Wings of the Falcon, life and thought of ancient Egypt.* New York: Holt, Rinehart, and Winston, 1968.

Lichtheim, Miriam. *The Old and Middle Kingdoms.* In *Ancient Egyptian Literature, a book of readings.* 2 vols. Berkeley: University of California Press, 1975.

Morenz, Siegfried. *Egyptian Religion.* trans. Ann E. Keep. Ithaca, NY: Cornell University Press, 1973.

Moret, Alexandre. *The Nile and Egyptian Civilization.* New York: Barnes and Noble, 1972.

Neugebauer, O. and Richard A. Parker, *Egyptian Astronomical Texts.* Providence, RI: Brown University Press, 1969.

Smith, William Stevenson. *Interconnections in the Ancient Near East, a study of the relationships between the arts of Egypt, the Aegean, and Western Asia.* New Haven: Yale University Press, 1965.

Wilson, John A. *The Culture of Ancient Egypt.* Chicago: University Press, 1951.

D. MYTHOLOGICAL STUDIES

1. Old World

Cox, George W. *The Mythology of the Aryan Nations.* 2 vols. Port Washington, NY: Kennikat Press, 1870.

Dixon, Roland B. *Oceanic Mythology.* In *The Mythology of All Races.* 13 vols. New York: Cooper Square, 1964.

Egyptian Mythology. London: Paul Hamlyn, 1965.

Holmberg, Uno. *Finno-Ugric and Siberian Mythology.* In *The Mythology of All Races.* New York: Cooper Square, 1964.

Ions, Veronica. *Indian Mythology.* London: Paul Hamlyn, 1967.

Jacobsen, Thorkild. *Toward the Image of Tammuz.* Cambridge, MA: Harvard University Press, 1970.

Jacobsen, Thorkild. "The Eridu Genesis." *Journal of Biblical Literature,* 100 (December 1981), 513-29.

Larousse Encyclopedia of Mythology. London: Paul Hamlyn, 1959.

MacCana, Proinsias. *Celtic Mythology.* London: Paul Hamlyn, 1970.

MacCulloch, John Arnott. *Eddic Mythology.* In *The Mythology of All Races.* New York: Cooper Square, 1964.

Olcott, William Tyler. *Field Book of the Skies.* ed. R. Newton Mayall and Margaret W. Mayall. 4th ed. New York: G. P. Putnam's Sons, 1954.

Radcliffe-Brown, A. R. *The Andaman Islanders.* Glencoe, IL: Free Press, 1948.

Roberts, J. J. M. *The Earliest Semitic Pantheon.* Baltimore: Johns Hopkins University Press, 1972.

Vermaseren, M. J. *Mithras, the Secret God.* New York: Barnes and Noble, 1963.

Wakeman, Mary K. *God's Battle with the Monster, a study in biblical imagery.* Leiden: E. J. Brill, 1973.

Zimmerman, J. E. *Dictionary of Classical Mythology.* New York: Harper and Row, 1964.

2. New World

Alexander, Hartley Burr. *Latin American Mythology.* In *The Mythology of All Races.* New York: Cooper Square, 1964.

Bierhorst, John. *Four Masterworks of the American Indian Literature.* New York: Farrar, Strauss, and Giraux, 1974.

Heizer, Robert F. and Martin A. Baumhoff. *Prehistoric Rock Art of Nevada and Eastern California.* Berkeley: University of California Press, 1962.

Marriott, Alice and Carol K. Rachlin. *American Indian Mythology.* New York: New American Library, 1968.

Nicholson, Irene. *Mexican and Central American Mythology.* London: Paul Hamlyn, 1967.

Osborne, Harold. *South American Mythology.* Feltham, Middlesex: Paul Hamlyn, 1968.

Waters, Frank. *Book of the Hopi.* New York: Ballantine Books, n.d.

3. Gundestrup Caldron

Dillon, Myles. *The Celtic Realms.* London: Weidenfeld and Nicolson, 1967.

Grosse, Rudolf. *Der Silberkessel von Gundestrup, ein Ratsel keltischer Kunst.* Dornach, Switzerland: Philosophisch-Anthroposophischer Verlag am Goetheanum, 1963.

Hubert, Henri. *The Rise of the Celts.* New York: Biblo and Tannen, 1966.

Klindt-Jensen, Ole. "The Gundestrup Bowl: A Reassessment." *Antiquity,* 33 (1959), 161-69.

Klindt-Jensen, Ole. *Gundestrupkedelen.* Copenhagen: Nationalmuseet, 1961.

Müller, Sophus. "Le Grand Vase de Gundestrup en Jutland." trans. E. Beauvois. *Nordiske Fortidsminder,* 1 (1890-1903), 35ff.

Norton-Taylor, Duncan. *The Celts.* New York: Time-Life Books, 1974.

Sandars, N. K. *Prehistoric Art in Europe.* Baltimore, MD: Penguin Books, 1968.

E. ETHNOGRAPHY AND GEOGRAPHY

Barraclough, Geoffrey, ed. *The Times Atlas of World History.* Maplewood, NJ: Hammond, 1978.

Bartholomew, John. *Physical World Atlas.* 5th ed. New York: American Map Co., 1964.

Beek, Martin A. *Atlas of Mesopotamia.* trans. D. R. Welsh. ed. H. H. Rowley. London: Nelson, 1962.

Cary, Henry, trans. *Herodotus, a new and literal version.* New York: Harper and Brothers, 1884.

"Indians of South America," Map. Washington, DC: National Geographic Society, 1982.

The International Standard Bible Encyclopedia. Grand Rapids, MI: Wm. B. Eerdmans, 1939.

May, Herbert G., ed. *Oxford Bible Atlas.* London: Oxford University Press, 1962.

The New Encyclopedia Britannica. 15th ed. Chicago: Encyclopedia Britannica, 1974.

Nordenskiold, A. E. *Facsimile-Atlas to the Early History of Cartography.* New York: Dover, 1973.

Palmer, R. R., ed. *Atlas of World History.* New York: Rand McNally, 1957.

"The Peoples of Africa," Map. *National Geographic,* 140 (December, 1971), Supplement.

"The Peoples of China," Map. Washington, DC: National Geographic Society, 1980.

"Peoples of the Soviet Union," Map. Washington, DC: National Geographic Society, 1976.

Smith, William, ed. *Dictionary of Greek and Roman Geography.* 2 vols. Boston: Little, Brown and Co., 1870.

F. BIBLE, THEOLOGY, AND CREATIONIST APOLOGETICS

Clark, Robert E. D. *Darwin: Before and After*. Chicago: Moody Press, 1966.

Custance, Arthur C. "Flood Traditions of the World." *Symposium on Creation IV*. ed. Donald W. Patten. Grand Rapids, MI: Baker Book House, 1972.

Custance, Arthur C. *Noah's Three Sons, human history in three dimensions*. Grand Rapids, MI: Zondervan, 1975.

Custance, Arthur C. *Genesis and Early Man*. Grand Rapids, MI: Zondervan, 1975.

Delitzsch, Franz. *A New Commentary on Genesis*. Edinburgh: T. & T. Clark, 1899.

Fraser, Gordon Holmes. "The Gentile Names of God." *Symposium on Creation V*. ed. Donald W. Patten. Grand Rapids, MI: Baker Book House, 1975.

Gish, Duane T. and Donald H. Rohrer, eds. *Up With Creation!* San Diego, CA: Creation-Life Publishers, 1978.

Morris, Henry M. *The Twilight of Evolution*. Grand Rapids, MI: Baker Book House, 1963.

Morris, Henry M. *Scientific Creationism*. San Diego, CA: Creation-Life Publishers, 1974.

Morris, Henry M. *The Genesis Record*. San Diego, CA: Creation-Life Publishers, 1976.

Niessen, Richard. "A Biblical Approach to Dating the Earth: A Case for the Use of Genesis 5 and 11 as an Exact Chronology," *Creation Research Society Quarterly*, 19 (June, 1982), 60-66.

Patten, Donald W. "The Pre-flood Greenhouse Effect." *Symposium on Creation II*, Grand Rapids, MI: Baker Book House, 1970.

Pentecost, J. Dwight. *Things to Come, a study in biblical eschatology*. Grand Rapids, MI: Dunham Publishing Company, 1958.

Ross, Allen P. "The Table of the Nations in Genesis 10—Its Contents." *Bibliotheca Sacra,* 138 (January-March, 1981), 22-34.

Ryrie, Charles Caldwell. *Dispensationalism Today.* Chicago: Moody Press, 1965.

Seaver, William L. "A Statistical Analysis of the Genesis Life-Spans." *Creation Research Society Quarterly,* 20 (September 1983), 80-87.

Seiss, Joseph A. *A Miracle in Stone.* Philadelphia: General Council, 1877.

Stott, John R. W. *Understanding the Bible.* Grand Rapids, MI: Zondervan, 1976.

Walvoord, John F. *The Revelation of Jesus Christ.* Chicago: Moody Press, 1966.

Whitcomb, John C. and Henry M. Morris. *The Genesis Flood, the biblical record and its scientific implications.* Philadelphia: Presbyterian and Reformed Publishing Company, 1964.

Wilder-Smith, A. E. *Man's Origin, Man's Destiny, a critical survey of the principles of evolution and Christianity.* Wheaton, IL: H. Shaw, 1968.

Wilder-Smith, A. E. *The Natural Sciences Know Nothing of Evolution.* trans. Petra Wilder-Smith. San Diego, CA: Master Books, 1981.

Zimmerman, Paul A. "Can We Accept Theistic Evolution?" *A Symposium on Creation.* Grand Rapids, MI: Baker Book House, 1968.

Index

A

Z

Biblical References